Acclaim for

JOHN KEEGAN's

FIELDS OF BATTLE

"A gracious book, artful and filled with surprises. . . . It reaffirms, in a moment of national self-doubt, the enduring strengths of American culture."
—*The New York Times Book Review*

"He has the knack of combining scholarly discipline with passion and assertive judgments. . . . Highly engaging."
—*Wall Street Journal*

"An extended love letter to the United States . . . enhanced by Keegan's sharp eye for terrain." —*Cleveland Plain Dealer*

"A warm and wise and witty volume that offers delight as well as instruction. . . . To say that the author writes well is to say that Robert E. Lee was a skilled commander."
—*Baltimore Sun*

"The dreams that fueled three centuries of contention over who was to rule the North American continent are outlined brilliantly. . . . Keegan reveals geography as destiny, the beautifully described coastlines, rivers, valleys, forests, mountain ranges and wide open spaces of the continent becoming every bit as important to the story as the generals and the armies who bled and died within it."
—*Washington Post*

JOHN KEEGAN

FIELDS OF BATTLE

John Keegan is one of the world's most distinguished
historians and the author of many acclaimed books,
including, most recently, *A History of Warfare* and
The Battle for History. He has been a Fellow at Princeton University, was for many years senior lecturer in
military history at the Royal Military Academy, Sandhurst, and is now defense correspondent for the *Daily
Telegraph* in London.

FIELDS
OF BATTLE

The Wars for North America

JOHN KEEGAN

VINTAGE BOOKS

A Division of Random House, Inc.

New York

To Brooks and Lucy

The perfect Anglo-American marriage

FIRST VINTAGE BOOKS EDITION, JUNE 1997

Copyright © 1995 by John Keegan

All rights reserved under International and Pan-American Copyright
Conventions. Published in the United States by Vintage Books,
a division of Random House, Inc., New York. Originally published
in Great Britain in hardcover in 1995 by Hodder and Stoughton,
London, as *Warpaths: Travels of a Military Historian in North
America*. Subsequently published in the United States in hardcover
by Alfred A. Knopf, Inc., New York, in 1996.

Portions of this work were originally published in *American Heritage,
MHQ: The Quarterly Journal of Military History,*
and *The Yale Review.*

Library of Congress Cataloging-in-Publication Data

Keegan, John, 1934–
[Warpaths]
Fields of battle : the wars for North America / John Keegan. —
1st Vintage Books ed.
p. cm.
Originally published: Warpaths. London : Hodder
and Stoughton, 1995.
Includes index.
ISBN 0-679-74664-1
1. North America—History, Military. 2. Battles—North America—
History. 3. Keegan, John, 1934– —Journeys—North America.
I. Title.
[E46.5.K44 1997]
970—dc21   96-46868
CIP

Random House Web address: http://www.randomhouse.com/

Printed in the United States of America
10 9 8 7 6 5 4 3 2 1

Contents

Maps

Illustrations

Acknowledgements

The United States and Canada are countries of warm hospitality and ready friendship, of which I have experienced so much over the decades that I risk giving offence in the list that follows through sheer forgetfulness. I beg forgiveness from all whose names are not there but should be.

In rough chronology I should like to remember first Major Robert E. Gray, U.S. Corps of Engineers, of Dayton, Ohio, my younger sister's godfather, now deceased, the first American of whom I have memory. He was one of those who came to Britain in 1943 to fight for the liberation of Europe, and I honour him as a representative of his brave comrades. Next my American Oxford friends, mostly Rhodes scholars, Frank Sieverts, Paul Sarbanes (now U.S. Senator for Maryland), Paul Sheats, Bob Collins, Tom Brown, David Chandler, John Sears, Keith Highet, Bill Carmichael, and Eliot Hawkins, and the Canadians, Roger Bull, John Lewis, and Ian Macdonald. I remember with deep gratitude Bill Coolidge, founder of the Balliol Pathfinder scheme, whose generosity made possible my first visit to the United States.

Among American and Canadian friends made over many years are Gwynne Dyer, Max and Allie Furlaud, Ormonde de Kay, Bill and Nancy Hochman, Nikolai and Shirley Stevenson, Stephen and Sally Smith, Conrad Black, Judith Jackson, Naomi Epel, peerless author escort, Sydney Mayer, godfather of one of my children, and Virginia Rutter, who cared for them all in infancy. As a fellow at Princeton in 1984 I enjoyed the friendship of Sean Wilentz, Ted and Tamar Rabb, James McPherson, the great historian of the American Civil War, Richard

Challener, Robert Darnton, and Gloria Emerson. Journalism introduced me to Bill Tuohy, a Pulitzer Prize winner, Malcolm McPherson of *Newsweek*, Leon Wieseltier of *The New Republic*, David Gergen of *U.S. News & World Report*, George Will of the *Washington Post*, Pat Rice of the *St. Louis Post-Dispatch*, and Robert Silvers of *The New York Review of Books*. I have American army friends without number, but hold in particular affection General John Foss, Colonel Joe Stringham, Colonel Keith Eiler, and Colonel Al Baker. My academic friends, also, are too numerous to enumerate, but include Professors Douglas Porch, Samuel Huntington, Victor Davis Hanson, Joe Guilmartin, Williamson Murray, Derek Leebaerts, John Shy, Richard Gabriel, and Elihu Rose. In the American and Canadian publishing worlds I would particularly like to remember and to thank Alan Williams, Elisabeth Sifton, Lucinda Vardey, and Lois Wallace.

Frances Banks typed part of this manuscript, and has my thanks as always. The rest was typed by Lindsey Wood, whom I thank for that, and for becoming an indispensable secretary. I would like to thank the librarians of the Royal Military Academy, Sandhurst, Bristol University, and the London Library, Anne-Marie Ehrlich for again doing the picture research, Martin Lubikowski for making the maps, Jane Birkett for her meticulous copy-editing, Angela Herlihy for her help at Hodder, and Matthew Bates for his at Sheil Land Associates. To Anthony Sheil, my literary agent, are due more thanks than I can easily express. I thank also Roland Philipps, my English publisher, and Ashbel Green, my American publisher, both wise counsellors. Finally my thanks to all my friends at the *Daily Telegraph*, in my home village of Kilmington and roundabout, and, above all, to my darling wife, Susanne.

Kilmington Manor,
10 February 1995

FIELDS OF BATTLE

ONE

....

One Englishman's America

I LOVE AMERICA. I wonder how many Englishmen can say that? Most of us know it too little to feel strong emotion one way or the other. New York, Washington, San Francisco, Los Angeles, the Florida holiday resorts—that is the America of most English people. My America is larger altogether. I have visited, for reasons that will emerge, thirty-two of the fifty states and most of Canada as well, and I have been making those visits for nearly forty years. In an idle moment I counted up not long ago the number of U.S. Immigration Service entry stamps in my passports and found nearly fifty. "Boston," the first one says, in a passport from which a schoolboy face stares back at me; underneath, in the space for "occupation," I see that I have struck out "schoolboy" and written "undergraduate," perhaps in preparation for my first transatlantic crossing.

Then there is a gap of exactly twenty years, 1957 to 1977. After that the stamps come thick and fast. The face gets older, the travels spread wider—Chicago, St. Louis, Dallas–Fort Worth, Atlanta, San Francisco, Los Angeles, Newark, Boston again several times, Denver, Seattle, Honolulu. There are Canadian stamps, too: Montreal, Toronto, Vancouver. Had my passport been stamped every time I touched down at an America airport, what a kaleidoscope there would be: Charlotte, North Carolina; Charleston, South Carolina; Montgomery, Alabama; Colorado Springs; New Orleans; Manchester, New Hampshire; Columbus, Ohio; Kansas City, Missouri; as well as Quebec; Kingston, Ontario; Calgary, Alberta; Victoria, British Columbia; and a host of small places I can scarcely decipher from the pages of my

3

travel diaries. Some places linger in the mind because of the extreme precariousness of the flights I made to them. I remember a seaplane in Canada where the co-pilot's role seemed to be that of helping the pilot hold the engine at full power as we headed down-harbour, their hands clasped white-knuckled one over another on the throttles; I remember a night take-off somewhere on the Great Plains where a James Cagney lookalike simultaneously worked the joystick, carried on a conversation with the passenger next to him, and wiped the inside of the windscreen with a handful of cotton waste. Most of those small places have blurred into one: the strip of concrete surrounded by a prairie of brown grass, the concrete terminal, sometimes unconvincingly advertising itself, after the placename, as an "International Airport," the porterless luggage collection point, the photographs of local scenic attractions, the advertisements for local commerce, the Avis and Hertz car rental representatives staring speechlessly into space, the welcome sign from the Lions or Kiwanis or Rotary, the breathless hush of the encompassing car park, the hint of habitation somewhere beyond the horizon.

No matter; I *like* American airports. Their sameness is reassuring. It is a guarantee that just a car-drive away there will be small white single-storey houses, neat streets, chainlink fences, signs at corners signalling Sunday service, white plastic letters behind glass for Church of Christ, gold-leaf Gothic for Episcopalian, and then, as the town centre nears, grass verges, spaced elms, Victorian villas in gardened lots, verandas, parked cars, lonely bus stops, doctors' signboards, funeral chapels, and the first outcrops of shopping and eating. "Liquor" in neon lighting, sometimes with an arrow that flashes on and off, is familiar; so, too, is the Chinese Garden with parking space for diners, the hamburger place, White Castle if we are in the Midwest, the cocktail lounge with smoked-glass windows, the gun shop, the sports-goods store, the magazine and book outlet, insurance and travel and savings and loan offices, City Hall. Small American airports, like small French railway stations, are the prelude to something fixed and unchanging. English visitors look forward, when they detrain from a branch line in the French provinces, to finding white tablecloths and iron chairs at the edge of the town square, the scent of limes as they take their aperitifs, tomato salads, and white Burgundy with their omelettes *fines herbes*. I look forward, when I deplane in Tennessee or Montana or Ohio, to something quite immaterial: a sense of timelessness, an absolute similarity of architecture and street plan, a pervading calm, a curious slow-ness—Europe, not America, is the continent of fast driving and pe-destrian bustle—the certainty of identical food and service and accom-modation and friendliness and uncuriosity.

I like that. Uncuriosity is one of the reasons I love America. In France, though I speak French well, my accent brands me as an Eng-lishman. In England my accent brands me as—what? Other English-men would tell: accent is the first characteristic by which English people make judgements about each other. In America my accent means nothing at all. When I first visited the country in the 1950s and foreigners were exotic, my voice excited interest. Now, when America is almost as cosmopolitan as anywhere else, it passes without com-ment. Nothing about me causes comment. I am one of the crowd, sim-ply another atom in a great, shifting, restless, busy, amiable, almost undifferentiated multitude that is the American people. There are other large countries on earth, Russia, China, India. Only the Americans have succeeded in creating a society of complete cultural uniformity, in which one can travel for a thousand, two thousand miles in the sure-ness that at the end of the journey one will emerge from aeroplane or bus or motor car to hear a common language being spoken in an iden-tical form, to find people living in identical houses, to see the crowd dressed in identical clothes, to walk streets built in identical style, to find towns served by identical schools, businesses, public utilities. To an outsider the uniformity of America is profoundly relaxing. America makes no demands on one, imposes no expectations, asks no ques-tions. It accepts the foreigner as it accepts the native traveller, someone without origins or fixed abode or past or future, a being of the here-and-now, just passing through. I love passing through. A curious, de-lectable, weightless, free-floating trance possesses me when I stop for a moment in places like Hardin, Montana, or Half Moon Bay, Califor-nia, or Springfield, Ohio, born of the knowledge that no one will ask me who I am or what I do or whence I come or whither I am going.

Where am I going? Usually to the next small airport, to park my rented car amid the acres of shimmering metal, to check my bags with Ozark or Comair or Skywest or Precision, to thank the dentured desk clerk for the return of my ticket, to emplane through Gate 1, to take seat 22F, to listen to the Walter Matthau voice of the pilot confide in-telligence about height and speed, to hear the door close, to watch the brown grass accelerate past the porthole, to see the water tower and

high-school football field and insurance skyscraper and freight yards
and highway interchanges of Harrisburg or Madison or Tallahassee or
Buffalo or Wilmington dropping away behind me, to detect the aircraft
reaching cruising height in the great, continental, horizonless, cloud-
flecked blue, and then to sink into the dream of American domestic
aerial travel. Dreamlike it is. For hour after hour, the hypnotising, unchanging note of the engines, space passes below one, space that seems
to move no faster than the ocean on a transatlantic flight, space that
seems to stretch for ever, space before, behind, to right, to left, space in
the abstract, space without beginning or end. Sunlight—it is always
sunny on American domestic flights—illuminates contours and rivers
and lakes and roads and geometrical field divisions and forest and
patches of woodland and tiny towns and larger cities and yellow and
brown and green and sometimes the grey of passing cloud shadows
and sometimes the glint of water but there is no sense of place in the
slowly approaching, slowly receding kaleidoscope of landscape. Two
hundred and sixty million people have their habitations somewhere below but for me, as I gaze mesmerized out of the window, through the
angle that the glittering silver wing makes with the fuselage, it is as if I
am a cosmonaut circuiting an orbit through the atmosphere of a fertile,
watered, welcoming but uninhabited and unexplored planet.

Then the Walter Matthau voice announces that we are approaching
Denver or Atlanta or Cincinnati or Dallas–Fort Worth, with connections to Shreveport and Little Rock and Oklahoma City and Austin
and Lubbock and Amarillo, and that the agent at the desk will confirm
reservations and that we are to fasten seat belts, and the undercarriage
clunks down and the patches of green become little copses and spin-
neys and the grey-painted water tower appears at the airport edge and
the brown grass flashes past the window and the aircraft brakes at the
end of the concrete strip and the speechless businessman in 22E collects
his sample case from the overhead locker and the aircraft sits decom-
pressing with sharp metallic clicks outside the concrete terminal. Soon
we are off again through the high clouds and continental blue to the al-
titudes where the great American forest or the great American desert or
the great American farm that American agricultural fingers have won
from the wilderness these two hundred years, takes on again its almost
imperceptible motion below the wing, unwinding like the image of a
dream landscape in the sleep of childhood. Sometimes a sensation in-
terrupts the trance, the outline of the Rocky Mountains or the great

cluster of man-made pinnacles at Chicago, visible two hundred miles away across the prairie, but these to me, for all their beauty, for all their differences from what surrounds them, are unwelcome interruptions. I like, I positively crave, the undeviating sameness of America from the air. It is what America is about, it is the story of America. I hear the historian in me, as I watch cornfield and pasture hacking away mile after mile into the remnant of forest, forest waiting forever its chance to creep back, as I watch irrigation stretching its fingers into the desert, desert biding its time, as I watch Canadian wheat rolling to the horizons, horizons beyond which the north wind stirs, saying, "Remember, all this was wilderness but a twinkling ago."

For the American landscape that creates the flight of dream across its endlessly unfolding, neat, and productive geometry is the most rapidly constructed large artefact in the world. It is not, at close hand, beautiful as the English landscape that surrounds the village in which I live is beautiful. There every field has a name, every patch of woodland surviving from the primeval forest that was disappearing before the Romans came is pruned and coppiced, every farm is primped and cosseted and mown and gardened. England really is a garden, whose beauty never ceases to entrance me, and I find nothing like it in the United States or Canada. There the seasons are too harsh, the hands of man too few to give the landscape that temperate, trimmed, frost-free, succulent look and feel that pluck at English heartstrings. American hedges are rough, field boundaries straggle, woodland is choked with the debris of years of fall and rot, grasses are slow to green and lie long sere and yellow; under the microscope the American countryside is coarse and unkempt. It is from a distance, above all from an altitude, that the beauty of the landscape asserts itself, comes into focus, demands a response from the onlooker. The response I make is simultaneously aesthetic and historical and mystical. Mystical because, like the aerial photographers who have discovered the Mexican dust drawings too large to have been executed by any earthbound eye, I wonder how the haphazard work of farmer and forester can have combined to construct the work of art that the American landscape is; aesthetic because that landscape is a great work of art, drawn with a limner's hand, painted by a master of the palette, in a perfectly modulated pointillism of sepia and umber and ultramarine and viridian and ochre and auburn and sable and cobalt and Payne's Gray, that alters with the play of sunlight and varies with the change of season but never, even under snow-

fall, loses its form and subtlety; historical because I know that every
straight line, mathematical curve, sharp edge, softened gradient, flat-
tened contour, raised hollow, rectilinear river-course tells of the effort
of man's labour on the face of the continent. It is a labour without parallel in my own small country, where age has worked with nature to
soften the work of man into something that appears natural and time-
less in itself. It is impossible to recreate in the imagination what England must have looked like before the forest went four thousand years
ago; it is impossible in America not to feel the power of the forest or
the desert or the rivers lurking at the edge of what man has wrought in
two hundred years, watching for a moment of inattention or a relax-
ation of effort, waiting to return.

Over the years the drama of the American landscape has ceased to
be simply a spectacle. It has awoken in me a powerful and continuing
curiosity in what it means for what I do. I am a military historian.
Rivers, mountains, forest, swamp and plain, desert and plough, valley
and plateau: these are the primary raw materials with which the military historian works. In constructing a narrative, in charting the movements of armies, the facts of geography stand first. What sense is there
in setting out to describe the campaigns of Napoleon, which wander
across the face of Europe from Portugal to Poland, from Naples to the
Netherlands, unless one understands, and causes the reader to understand also, how the Alps and the Pyrenees, the Rhine and the Vistula,
bore upon the campaign plans he made? The necessity is greater still
for the conquests of Hitler, whose tank columns captured first what
was easiest, the North European plain, were then slowed by the forests
and marshes of western Russia, and finally petered out of energy on the
great rivers of the steppe and the mountain barrier of the Caucasus.

America, too, is a continent of conquest, by the Spanish, the
French, and the English, but the military problems with which it confronted the Europeans were different from those the great conquerors
of the Old World had to overcome. Because it was indeed an old
world, old before imperialism began, its geography was already known
to travellers, its natural obstacles and barriers understood, and many
were penetrated by long-distance trade routes. The venturers to America knew nothing and the native Americans they encountered could tell
them little but rumour of what lay beyond their tribal lands. Conquerors had therefore to be explorers also and geographers before they
could be traders and settlers. For their own security they had to build

forts but forts built in the wilderness were useless unless they commanded a natural line of communication or penetration into the interior. When the venturers came to fight each other, as they did as soon
as their legal claims to territory and material spheres of interest
clashed, they needed topographical knowledge, above all maps, all the
more. It is not accidental that Champlain, the founder of French
Canada, was a skilled mapmaker or that George Washington, the victor of the War of American Independence, was by profession a surveyor who had recorded the topography of wide areas of the back
country over which he was later to campaign.

So when I look now at the American panorama from 35,000 feet,
it is not just the mosaic of field and forest that passes before my eyes.
Before my conscious mind unrolls also a running list of speculations
and questions. They are, I know, the same sort of questions soldiers always ask in unfamiliar country. I continue to seek answers on the
ground. Looking out of my hotel window not long ago, I struggled to
identify the river flowing between the twin cities of Minneapolis and
St. Paul. The Mississippi, I was told; but surely it was already too wide,
so far from Memphis and Natchez and its delta in the Gulf of Mexico;
and it seemed to be in the wrong place, too far to the west. How, I
asked an interviewer as we sat in the offices of the Toronto *Globe and
Mail*, with Lake Ontario under our gaze, did it connect for navigation
with Lake Erie, since the Niagara Falls was the natural waterway between the two? The Welland Canal is the answer, but he did not know
and neither then did I. Where is the South Pass through the Rockies,
the gateway to Oregon and the Northwest, whose discovery opened
settlement in the early nineteenth century? I thought I identified it from
an aeroplane on a flight to Seattle, only to be told that it is so incon-
spicuous wagonmasters often missed it on the ground on their way
west.

All these conundrums of intercommunication, still so difficult for
the individual to solve from hazy memory of exact and available information, were total and almost impenetrable mysteries to the pioneers.
They were solved only by dangerous and half-blind ventures into the
great American forest, by laborious boat journeys up uncharted rivers,
running rapids, portaging past shallows, by unguided voyages across
lakes as big as seas, by packtrailing over mountain passes higher than
most European peaks, by pony trekking into the featureless and apparent infinity of the Great Plains. Finally and miraculously, when the

pieces of the jigsaw had been cut out one by one, they had been assembled into the man-made wonder of settled America. It is the most stupendous achievement of military as well as human history.

I love America because of the miracle of its landscape and I love it,
too, because of the excitement I feel in flying to it, in the knowledge
that after the ocean there will be those sculptured woods and con-
toured ploughlands and Cloudy Ways of city lights and distant, diminished mountain ridges, and infinities of forest reaching beyond the
horizon. Going to America, even in an era of air travel, recreates in the
voyager something of the sense of danger and discovery that the first
voyagers must have felt when they took ship on the stormy Atlantic to
pick their way below the ice and fogs to landfall on the far shore. The
aircraft door closes, shutting one off from those cosy English voices,
tea, taxis, Tube, Terminal 4. The transatlantic jet hurtles down the runway. Windsor Castle flashes for an instant under the wing, the Thames
becomes a silver ribbon, tiny, familiar places appear and disappear
through holes in the cloud, Ireland, even more patchworked, passes for
a moment through the field of vision, and then the Atlantic begins its
hours of journey under one's gaze. Sometimes I read, sometimes I
think, sometimes I talk to the passenger next to me, for people do talk
on transatlantic flights, often intimately, telling me what they do, even
confiding the story of their lives. The most confident air traveller is
touched by the unreality of suspense between ocean and infinity, between continent and continent, on the Atlantic great circle and I have
heard secrets in that empty passage between the cloud-stacks, told secrets myself. Yet I never quite give my full attention, for I am waiting,
with growing excitement, for what I know the crawling hands of my
watch will show me two hours, one hour hence: the awful, icebound
interior of Greenland, sterilised by glaciers two miles thick, perhaps a
glimpse of the coastal footholds on the Canadian side where the great
cold of the Middle Ages killed the Viking settlers to the last man in the
fifteenth century; then the tundra of the Canadian north, numberless
lakes, mouthless rivers, nameless mountains, numbing desolation.

Optical illusion begins: can that be a road? No, shadow at the foot
of a long barren ridge. Then there is indeed a road, and a building by a
lake, and a man-made swathe in the scrappy tree-cover and then a settlement, a solitary vehicle in motion, a village, a little town. The
wilderness, the wilderness of the ocean and the Arctic, is receding,
civilisation promises. Soon I see harbours and the white strands of a

softer shore and the wake of ships ploughing to a known place and forest cut back from the sea and the landscape squared for cereal and pasture. The sun casts slanting shadows across a countryside cleared and
shaped and networked and canalised and bridged and more and more
densely settled. Suburbs appear among surviving woodland and then
the outskirts of a city and then, if we are approaching over water, the
star shapes of the fortresses built by the Federalists to guard America
from the great outside two hundred years ago, and then the boundary
fence of the gateway airport, the familiar brown grass beside the runway, the blur of airport buildings, the huge painted sails of other
transatlantic aircraft parked at their piers, the sudden twilight as our
own aircraft comes to rest.

A new excitement begins. First there is the excitement of encounter
with American bureaucracy, uniformed, brisk and purposeful, suddenly
and disconcertingly friendly. "What is the purpose of your visit? What
sort of lecture? History? I'm interested in history. I read a lot of history.
Military history? Are you interested in the Second World War?" Next
there is the excitement of America on the move, a travelling nation
which travels with energy, despatch, and a multiplicity of ways—taxis,
hire cars, hotel shuttles, car-park service vehicles, cars, limousines to
out-of-town, downtown buses, subway, Greyhound, Trailways, inter-
terminal courtesy coaches, connections to regional airports by USAir,
Air America, Delta, Northwest, to Harrisburg, Rochester, Syracuse, Albany, Hartford/Springfield, Wilkes-Barre/Scranton. At the sidewalk beyond the terminal door a bewildering variety of vehicles circulate,
appearing, disappearing, reappearing in stately rondo. Ramada Inn,
Long-term Parking, Westchester County Limousines, La Guardia
Transfer, AAA Taxi, Checker Cab, Midtown Manhattan—Buy Ticket
from Driver. The university or the publisher or the literary agency have
said they will send to meet me. In what—cab or car or stretch limou-
sine? Something separates itself from the procession. I have been
found. I am collected. The purr of the motor guides me away through
Premier Air Freight and Federal Express and Budget and Precision
Flight Maintenance and Flying Kitchen to the brown concrete under-
pass that leads to the chain of yellow lights that glare on the four lanes
of traffic corralled between the brown concrete walls of the freeway as
it flows at exactly measured interval, at exactly regulated speed, city-
wards. Bridges of Cylopean granite blocks—what bridges America
builds, as massive and permanent as the bedrock from which they are

hewn—cast their shadows on the traffic stream, tunnels swallow it, tolls arrest it—"Exact Change, No Pennies"—towering steel suspension spans drag it upwards over half-glimpsed bodies of water, brown concrete exit ramps deposit it in city streets. I have arrived.

The excitement of American greetings follow, the excitement of American friendship. The English greet their friends with warmth but not with demonstration. What is there to demonstrate? Not surprise that we have been brought together, not concern for the travails of the journey. England is a tiny country in which anyone of my age and background does, in that loose but not untruthful phrase, know everyone else. America is different. It is a single culture but it is many societies. Americans do not know each other. English people move house infrequently, and then perhaps only a mile down the road. The dense network of English social connections—school, university, regiment, club, aunts, seaside holidays, friends of friends—reknots itself a fraction and relations are re-established. Americans do not move house, they relocate, go to another state, another coast, lose touch, make new friends, perhaps no friends at all, just acquaintances, people passing through. That free-floating weightlessness that entrances the European traveller in North America bears heavily on its inhabitants. Who do they know, where do they stand, what are the foundations, where do they begin? The extraordinary slowness of American conversation is a clue to their uncertainties. On introduction, the English fall instantly into rapid chatter, transmitting, as in the high-speed encipherments of a John le Carré novel, a compact code of social and geographical allusions, incomprehensible to a stranger, deeply reassuring to sender and receiver. Americans sound each other out, wondering if they will be understood, ending their sentences with question marks. English speech is emphatic, American interrogative. There are twenty-four cities called Springfield in the United States—the largest of them in Colorado, Georgia, Idaho, Illinois, Kentucky, Minnesota, Missouri, Oregon, South Carolina, South Dakota, Tennessee, and Vermont, two of them two thousand miles apart—and so twenty-four necessities for clarification, twenty-four occasions for ending a statement of whence one comes on that distinctive, upward, American lilt.

No wonder that American social reconnaissance proceeds so slowly. No wonder that any reunion of friends is so instant and intense. A traveller from another state receives, merits exclamations, endearment, solicitude. A traveller from another continent enjoys endearment tenfold. Those filigrees of friendship which alleviate the loneliness of Americans inside their vast homeland bind even more closely people from different worlds. How long has it been? How good to see you! How was the journey? How did you travel? Where did you stop over? Have you eaten, rested, slept? What do you need? How long can you stay? It is so good to see you, to see you, to see you.

I love America for its friendship. Instant friendship, they say, the dawn friendship, is the distinctive American gift to human kinship. I have made instant friendships in America, and many have lasted. Some, too brief to last, remain with me still. I recall the friendship of a young sailor, proud of his new uniform, utterly innocent of the world, who sat beside me on the train from Boston to New York forty years ago, told me of the country place he came from in the Midwest, trembled with the adventure of his new life, solemnly lettered out my transatlantic address, assured me we should meet again. I recall the friendship of a fragile Italian-American girl, become suddenly conscious of her ethnic roots as third-generation immigrants do, a college graduate hoping to teach high school, who heard my English voice buying a ticket across the bus, produced an Italian newspaper from her purse, asked me about Europe, told me of her efforts to learn Italian, of her yearning to discover whence her grandparents came, of her tentative dissatisfaction with the Anglo-Saxonism which their decision to emigrate had imposed on her, and asked me if she would be happier in the old country. I recall the friendship of a young Texan lawyer, marooned beside me at 35,000 feet somewhere between Denver and Chicago, who revealed when I told him I had been at Oxford that his chief interest in life was the work of C. S. Lewis—this was a decade before *Shadowlands*—interrogated me about The Inklings, asked if I had ever drunk beer in the Eagle and Child, walked me into corners of the university I had never visited, and urged we should explore it together when a break in his practice gave him the chance to travel.

There are other instant friendships in my recollection of America; but old friendships are best, and I have a host of old American friends, to whose friendship I look forward as one of the keenest of pleasures awaiting me at the end of the great transatlantic passage. University friends, first met forty years ago in England, academic friends, encountered on campuses across America, military friends, some chanced on as far away as Lebanon or Saudi Arabia, publishing friends from Boston and New York, newspaper friends from St. Louis and San Francisco, literary friends from almost everywhere, and family friends—for as a father I have acquired an American son-in-law and so American relatives by marriage—in Manhattan and Long Island and Cambridge, Massachusetts.

American friendship is intense, far more intense than friendship in England. English friends hold each other at a distance, only hinting at what they feel and believe. In a sense we know each other too well, in our tight little island, to reveal anything more about our inner selves than code and ellipsis will. Americans, at least to this Englishman, bare their souls. I know the life story certainly of three Americans in more detail than I know that of any fellow countryman or countrywoman. I know the life story of an American woman from her upbringing in trust-fund ease, through her Seven Sisters college education, her early excursions to Europe in search of wearables from Schiaparelli and Worth, her two marriages to foreigners, one brief and unhappy, one of deep mutual love abbreviated by fatal illness, her discovery of literary talent, her rise to fame as a foreign correspondent, her encounters with the great of the international literary world, her disenchantment with it, her withdrawal to quietude on the fringe of campus life. I know the life story of a modest American hero, the graduate of a great Ivy League university, who decided on the day he got his degree that America would enter the Second World War, went down the street to the recruiting office, joined the Marines, and spent the next four years leading a company of infantry up island beaches in the Pacific until death and wounds brought him command of his battalion; the war over, he married a childhood sweetheart, raised a large family, made a modest fortune, devoted his retirement years to travelling the United States, encouraging other sufferers from a progressive illness to which he had fallen victim to look on the bright side, see the best in life. I know the life story of another American who spent a similar war, returned to teach college, espoused pacifism, became a towering exemplar of the principles he held to two generations of students, worked tirelessly for tolerance and civil liberty and yet cherished above all his wartime comradeships and the life friendship he had made with the British captain who rescued his ship's company from a minefield off the D-day beaches in June 1944.

It is friendships with people like these that await me at the end of the great transatlantic passage, and renewing them is one of the things that makes the journey worth while. Another is the knowledge that there will be new encounters, new acquaintances, new friends—and new discoveries among the natural and man-made geography of the continent. Discovering Canada has come late to me, and I still know it only patchily, far less well than I want. Something of what I feel for it I hope I have transmitted in the pages on the English and French wars in North America that follow. My discovery of the United States continues. I take a growing pleasure in adding to my acquaintance with an American dimension which Americans ignore and are constantly surprised to find of interest to Europeans, which is the oldness, the growing and surprisingly extensive oldness, of their civilisation. "I live in an old house," and then, hastily, "not old, of course, by your standards." How often that has been said to me. It was said by a young, vaguely Marxist, and highly Europeanised professor at Princeton. I pointed out to him that, as he lived in colonial Nassau Street, his house was certainly older than mine, built in 1810, and just to emphasise the point, that the dean's building, Nassau Hall, was older by forty years than that in which I taught at the Royal Military Academy, Sandhurst. Princeton is not unusual in its oldness. The length of the Atlantic coast and parts of the interior are dense with clusters of eighteenth-century building, not just in such famous beauty spots as Charleston and Savannah but in hundreds of other settlements as well, where, contrarily, it is often neglected and decaying. I have found a disfavoured eighteenth-century waterfront quarter in Manchester, New Hampshire; much of Alexandria, Virginia, is Georgian in a raggle-taggle state; the Federalist river-front in St. Louis, Missouri, is being pillaged for its bricks; Benefit Street in Providence, Rhode Island, one of the most magnificent Georgian townscapes either side of the Atlantic, is only slowly being brought back from decrepitude. History drags Americans across the sea, to Canterbury and Bath and Aix-en-Provence, when it might drag at their heels to stay at home, to discover the beauties and charm of all those small places that enchant me whenever I stumble upon them. A month or two ago, in Stonington, Connecticut, I chanced on one of the most beautiful small town centres I have ever seen, colonnaded shops, pillared churches, green-shuttered colonial houses on brick-paved sidewalks, order, proportion, dignity. Who would ever want to leave Stonington?

To linger in old America, however, or to look for it where it no longer exists, is to misunderstand the continent. Americans have ruined their cities. Places like Hartford and Newark and Providence and Atlanta once had city centres built on a human, European scale, as early photographs show; Atlanta has lost its in my lifetime. Yet to regret what is gone is to wish that America is other than it is. Space, not time, I once heard George Steiner reflect in a lecture, is the American dimension. The old cities have lost their hearts because they were built by people who thought at a foot's pace, journeyed by horse. The vastness of America, for all the heroism of early journeys made by foot or horse into its unexplored interior, demanded other means of motion, the locomotive, the motor car, the aeroplane, means of devouring space, not of submitting to it. It is the space that surrounds American cities, the interminable distances between them, that have done for small streets and town squares, felled the shade trees, left the porticoed churches standing amid desolation, driven freight yards and interchanges and airport expressways into the order that once was. It could not have been otherwise. Once Americans decided to command their continent from coast to coast, all three thousand miles of it, to have no internal frontiers, to spend a common currency, to obey, often not to obey, a uniform code of law, to recognise a single government, to be one people, the life of the small city, the shape of the pedestrian neighbourhood, was doomed. Travelling America confronted settled America and travelling America triumphed.

I am a traveller in America, and I travel further and faster there than I ever do at home. Here I alert my wife if I am going down the village street to the post office, decide the day before on a journey to our market town eight miles away. Our annual migration to Scotland takes weeks of preparation and entails an overnight stay with friends to break a drive of four hundred miles. In America, at a publisher's behest or a personal whim—"I must walk the Malvern Hill battlefield again"—I whirl about the continent, sometimes recrossing my track between the Great Lakes and the Chesapeake in a single week. I always travel with elation, looking forward to arrival in new places, old places, looking forward again to moving on. The litany of placenames set out on the travel agent's itinerary, like the litany chanted by the announcer at Grand Central Station, can intoxicate. I see I am going to Austin and Minneapolis and Seattle and Sacramento and Montgomery and Tucson and my spirit lifts. I am travelling in America, I am freefloating over the United States.

And yet: there is something terrifying about a country, a society, a people which lives, in George Steiner's phrase, not in the dimension of time but space. Time is space for Americans; here we say "five miles" or "fifty miles" and time our departure accordingly. Nowhere is more than an hour or two from anywhere else. "Nine hours," Americans say, when they discuss a car journey, or "a day" or even "two days." American space devours time, dominates lives, can consume whole swathes of years on earth. "I travel a lot," Americans say, or "I used to travel a lot." Decades of a lifetime have been paid out on interstates, over small airport check-ins, at car rental returns, in Ramadas and Holiday Inns. Space has greyed hair, lined faces, made a history of itself in personal memory, a history of coming and going, stopping over, moving on. It has made a history in the collective life of America, a country always moving on inside itself, never stopping over for very long. The history of America is the history of its vastness, of man's wandering over its face, his probing for passageways through its towering natural barriers, his tinkering with the power of its stupendous rivers, his ventures into its dark forest, his tentative, always dangerous, never completed efforts to take and dominate land and climate.

A people who live in space, not time, are different from others, certainly different from the peoples of Europe whose wilderness, never large or very fierce, disappeared four thousand years ago. Different most of all from the English, seagirt in their tiny gardened island, on whom space scarcely intrudes at all but history circumscribes everything they think and do. Their transmission of a common language and law to the Americans creates a resemblance entirely delusive. No two peoples on earth capable of intercommunication can be less alike than they. I love America; but I am not at home there. I love the mystery of America; but mystery it remains to me. I love Americans; but even American friends are strangers. America has changed my life. America has saved my world, the European world threatened by two pitiless dictatorships which overshadowed my childhood and growing up. Yet, though I think of America always with admiration and heartfelt gratitude, I go there in a mood of exploration and wonder. I meet Americans who come to me in a similar mood of anticipation and discovery. Who are they, these people from the great spaces of their continent? What do they think, what do they feel, what do they know that I do not know? They have a secret, the secret of a way of life different from any other lived on earth. What it is, I am still trying to find out.

America at a Distance

When did I first see an American? On celluloid, I suppose, for the cinema of my childhood was an American possession. It was American films we queued to see in wartime Britain, not their tepid domestic imitations, and American stars we took as our heroes and heroines. Not that I had the slightest interest in heroines at the age of eight or so, when I first penetrated the magic darkness of a cinema. It was heroes I sought, and Hollywood supplied the real thing. Gary Cooper was a particular favourite, perhaps because he resembled my father, then the centre of my universe, but almost anyone tall, lanky, and slow-spoken would do. I was entranced by the way the men in *Destry Rides Again*, say, or *Stagecoach* walked, with that loose, let-me-at-the-horizon lope, and even more so by the way they spoke, as if one word were almost too much for them and a second would choke in their throats. It was not only the cowboy films that cast a spell: *Mr. Deeds Goes to Town*, that sleepy epic of plain folk, caught me up in what I suppose I would now call the American dream, and I was riveted by an Anglo–North American film, *The Forty-ninth Parallel*—blatant propaganda it would seem today—in which an escaped U-boat crew, at loose in Canada, try but fail to bring down the Four Freedoms.

All these misty experiences must have come to me in Britain's glory-time, between Dunkirk and Pearl Harbor, when Hitler's army stood on the French coast and only a filigree of Spitfires hung between my unthinking self and invasion. No inkling of that impending danger touched my childish happiness, in what I remember as an eternal summer, no shadow fell over the hay meadows where we played, not a single tremor of anxiety disturbed the serenity of our family life. I suppose my parents must have discussed between themselves what hope Britain had of extricating itself from its perilous isolation as Hitler's only enemy. I suppose, too, that they must have pondered—as Winston Churchill, we now know, did day and night—whether the United States would come to our rescue and, if so, how and when. I am sure that what hopes they had were pinned on the United States alone, for I clearly remember that the peremptory alliance with the Soviet Union which followed Hitler's surprise attack of 22 June 1941 pleased my father absolutely not at all. He was not only fervently anti-Bolshevik but held unwaveringly to the view that we had entered the war to defend Poland, of which country he rightly identified the Soviet Union to be as deadly an enemy as Nazi Germany.

Yet, if we were waiting for the Americans, by not a single word do I remember my parents reproaching them for the delay. In so far as I recall any mention of the United States at all during those eighteen months of danger and privation—distant air raids, daily shortages of everyday necessities—it was as the source of a fairy-tale gift called "food parcels," heard about if not actually received, and as a doughty co-belligerent in the First World War. My father had met and made friends with Americans on the Western Front and never spoke but with a chuckle of their open manner and easy ways. He mentioned names, now lost to me, and may even, I think, have kept in touch for a time with a doughboy against whom he had boxed—he had been a lightning middleweight in his youth—in the Rhineland championships after the Armistice.

There was more, however, to my parents' feelings for America than suppliant hope or old acquaintance. Neither of them had been to the United States—no Briton had in those days unless very rich or very poor—but they were nevertheless what today we could call Americanophiles. This was not a common attitude in the Britain of my childhood, when affection for any country except one's own was thought—except again by the rich or the poor—to be vaguely unpatriotic. Most of the British were chauvinistic, and if my parents were not, it was, I surmise, because of their sense of belonging to a minority. They were Irish by ancestry and Catholic by religion. Their Catholicism supplied a sort of cosmopolitanism to our family life, since an interest in the Catholic social movement had taken my father abroad and made him friends in France, Germany, and the Low Countries, while a family tradition had sent my mother to school in Belgium where she had learnt excellent French. Curiously, however, it was not the culture of France or Germany that I remember being discussed in the family circle. Perhaps it was taken for granted; I cannot, at this distance in time, reconstruct the atmosphere. What I do very strongly remember, by contrast, is their shared admiration for American literature. The American cinema was admired too, of course, but some concession was made to the charm of French films. In the field of the novel no concessions were admitted. The American novelists were held to be the modern masters. It is unlikely, I now realise, that the exigently Catholic

outlook of my parents would have allowed them to recognise virtue in
D. H. Lawrence or Joyce or hedonistic Bloomsbury. Nevertheless, my
unbelieving grandfather, who lived with us, was as adamant as they
that the "real" novelists were all American: Hemingway, Steinbeck, Eu-
dora Welty, Willa Cather. The craft of the novel was believed to have
migrated across the Atlantic and to have found its highest modern
form in—if I recall family conversations correctly—*Death Comes to
the Archbishop.*

If it was important in forming my first view of America and Americans that my parents admired their literature, it was even more important that they saw and spoke of that other world as a place with a
reality beyond that of print. They also recognised, and in some way
communicated to me, the idea of America as a separate civilisation
from our own. There was, I seem to hear them saying, a world across
the Atlantic where the permanencies which set us apart—established
religion, monarchy, empire, fixed division between one class and another, unequal opportunity in education—did not apply, and that the
absence of these permanencies made perfect sense in a society that was
both autonomous and admirable. The United States, I was led to understand, was a real country, to be thought about and appreciated on
its own terms. That was not how most of their British contemporaries
saw the United States; but, it must be said, nor did Hemingway or Hollywood—the main influences then on British perceptions of the other
English-speaking culture—help them to do so. Hemingway's subver-
sion of convention was taken to be distinctively American; yet his real
gift, of course, was to have turned the freshness of an American eye on
Europe itself, which was largely what he wrote about. Hollywood's
achievement, by contrast, had been to mythologise America's exotica—
the Wild West, the super-rich, organised crime, Broadway, and the
kitsch of immigrant and small-town life. The result was that the English of the 1940s had an *Arabian Nights* picture of the civilisation
across the Atlantic, peopled by crooners, funny Irish priests—in *The
Bells of St. Mary's,* Bing Crosby and Barry Fitzgerald gave them both—
monosyllabic sheriffs, high-stepping showgirls, egomaniac millionaires,
scar-faced gangsters, and puritanical private eyes. It was not a world
with which the English could identify at all, since their own decorous,
deferential, and law-abiding society yielded no equivalents to any of
those figures. Real Americans, had they met any, could have told them
that real America was quite different from Hollywood and, in the

everyday essentials of food on the table, clean clothes for school, and getting to work on time, not so dissimilar from real England; but there were no real Americans on hand to make the point. Like listeners, therefore, to the tales of a traveller to an unimaginably distant land, a Marco Polo, a Mungo Park, a Richard Burton, they took Hollywood as truth, truth perhaps to be savoured with a pinch of salt, but real enough to satisfy their need to know how life was lived on the other side of the Atlantic; and very strange they thought it.

There were, it is true, some English people, neither rich nor poor, who grasped that there was another America beside the Hollywood version. They were, for the most part, academics and intellectuals who had read, or knew of, James Bryce's *The American Commonwealth*, an explanation of the workings of its government and constitution by a Victorian admirer, and had begun to follow that remarkable Scot, Denis Brogan, in his exploration of the politics of Roosevelt and the New Deal. Soon they would be listening to Brogan as a participant on the static-troubled airwaves of *Transatlantic Quiz* and, even more enthusiastically, to the expatriate Alistair Cooke's *Letter from America* (it is evidence of the imaginative distance separating the New from the Old World in the 1940s that a broadcast should have been represented as a communication by post). Brogan's immensely erudite—and entertaining—political science could, however, do little to counter the more widespread impressions left by those stories and books by British authors about America known to all English people (I contrast "British" with "English" here because the Scots and Irish had, through their continuing tradition of emigration to the United States and Canada, their own direct access to first-hand news of those countries). Such stories were few, but the list certainly included Conan Doyle's *A Study in Scarlet*—the book in which he first brought Sherlock Holmes to the world—and Kipling's *Captains Courageous*, the fruit of his—unsuccessful—attempt to settle in his American wife's homeland. I cannot remember when either first came my way, but read them I certainly had by the age of ten or thereabouts, thus joining a majority for whom Sherlock Holmes and Kipling were winter-evening standbys. I certainly cannot now reconstruct how influential those tales of desperate adventure on the Great Plains and of derring-do on the Grand Banks were in forming my first impressions of American life, so overlaid are they by a lifetime's reading and by scores of transatlantic journeys, but some frisson of the excitement they aroused remains. Distance, space, danger, sudden riches, extravagant character, grandeur of scenery, unpredictability of action, unexpectedness of outcome—those were the ingredients. If they cast their spell still, how much more strongly then. The spell did not touch me alone, of course; it was a common part of the English perception of the transatlantic world and a positive reinforcement of the newer and more immediate impression left by Hollywood. For it, too, dealt in tales of danger and sudden riches, filled the screen with images of space and distance, peopled its plots with extravagant characters, and drew them to unexpected conclusions; no wonder if the English doubted whether such a world, so unlike their own circumscribed little universe, could be a real world at all.

Americans at First Hand

Then, suddenly, in 1942, they found real Americans among them. Soon after Pearl Harbor, American servicemen—GIs, as they came instantly to be called—started to arrive by ship and aeroplane to begin building the great military base from which the bomber offensive against Hitler's Germany and then the seaborne assault on his Fortress Europe were to be launched. Americans turned out to be flesh and blood, not celluloid, after all. Moreover, they were friendly, indeed positively eager to make friends, and fluent in what unmistakably was a common language. This was a relief after the natives' efforts to grapple with the tongues of the only allies they had seen heretofore—Poles, Czechs, Free Frenchmen. Official propaganda about a great alliance of English-speaking peoples turned out to be true. These young men in a slightly different shade of khaki had no difficulty at all in making themselves understood, indeed were not much different in appearance or needs or military manners from the British soldiers training, like them, in their millions to set off on the liberation of Europe from Nazi occupation.

Yet they were entrancingly different. They spoke, as the girls they were all too keen to sweet-talk delightedly discovered, just like film stars. Some of them actually looked like film stars, GIs being generally taller than British soldiers—the superabundance of the American diet made for bigger frames—and bearing the handsomeness brought by a mixture of immigrant genes. Handsome or not, their voices often made them seem so to women whose hearts had fluttered to Clark Gable's drawl on dozens of Saturday evenings at the cinema. It was not only the way they spoke, moreover, but what they said which gave pleasure; men as much as women were charmed by American circumlocutions, formalities, courtesies, and exotic slang, by an intriguingly combined slower cadence and sudden urgency of delivery, but above all by a directness of speech that the British avoided. The American voice, I now know, is not classless, but it seemed so in 1942 in England and thus was hearteningly refreshing to a people whose accents constantly set them at social sixes-and-sevens, who spoke too boldly if they felt sure of themselves, mumbled or kept silent if they did not. The idea of equality between Americans was perhaps the one reasonably accurate belief that had taken root this side of the Atlantic, and the British inability to distinguish between Bronx and Boston Brahmin, any more than between midtown Manhattan and Manhattan, Kansas, by ear alone strongly confirmed it. Because the Americans did not lower or raise their voices but maintained an even tone to whomsoever they were speaking, because they seemed to communicate by plain talk, they were taken for plain folk—making their arrival a threat to the natives with a stake in the social order but, to the majority who felt excluded by it, an excitingly subversive solvent of old rigidities.

There was a practical as well as social dynamism to the Americans. They got things done. Here, too, they brought a breath of fresh air from the New World. Britain's miraculous age of industry—which had made her the richest country in the world while the Americans were fighting over slavery—was long gone by 1942. The railways had been built, the factory towns were in decay, the enormous wealth of the Victorian age was draining away in a desperate and unwanted war; so, too, was the manhood already decimated in the war of the trenches a generation earlier. Britain's second war effort was halting and makeshift; it was inspired by flashes of the old inventive genius—in the development of radar, in high-grade aeronautical engineering—but it was geared to handicraft industries, was under-capitalised, and lacked the consistency of a mass-production economy. Not so America's: the GIs descended on the English countryside like the pioneers of a new industrial revolution, tearing up the soil to build runways for the strategic bombing campaign, covering farmland with townscapes of hutted camps and hospitals, piling up enormous dumps of ordnance and equipment, and filling an antique road network with endless convoys of trucks and transporters. They brought equipment never seen in England before—bulldozers and graders and scrapers and dumpers, which, wherever they worked, altered the landscape as dramatically as the navvies had done in the nineteenth century.

This was a wonder-time in English life, one I remember vividly to this day. In my corner of the West Country the population thrilled to the incursion of the Americans, talked, indeed, of little else. Sheer numbers was in part the reason for that: the strangers actually outnumbered the natives over wide areas, choked the roads, filled the pubs, monopolised the girls. Every family seemed to have a quota of American friends, of suitors if there were single daughters and of semi-chaperoned attendants if husbands were away at the war. American largesse was a second cause. Wartime rations were small and peacetime luxuries absent altogether. The GIs, supplied from home, were fed on scales the British had forgotten. Steak and butter—my mother's anxiety over the shortage of butter has left me with a neurosis about saving scraps—leaked out of American camps on to local tables, and so did strange foodstuffs spoken of as if shipped from the Spice Islands: tinned ham, Spam, sweet corn, maple syrup, soup cubes, frankfurters, powdered coffee, and—almost useless to the British, among whom only the rich owned refrigerators—enormous quantities of ice-cream. The Americans, however, also provided priceless durables: camera film, dry cell batteries, and, famously if mysteriously, nylon stockings.

The American incursion also brought direct wealth. The U.S. forces bought goods and services, paid cash, and were excellent employers. Small fortunes were made by local businessmen who could meet American deadlines, and ordinary people drew better than average wages on the proceeds. The economic relationship, however, was not exceptional; Britain was generally prosperous during the war, as the capital accumulated in a century of empire and industry was recirculated through the economy by extortionate war taxation. It was the cultural exchange that made the real impact. Had the incomers been wholly foreign, they might have been regarded as a transient source of material benefits and little more. Precisely because they spoke the native language, if in an intriguingly different style, they presented the inhabitants with glimpses, if erratically and refracted by distance, of another way altogether of living life.

The Americans did not defer; that was the first and strongest of the impressions they made. European travellers to the United States had made that observation even in the eighteenth century, and it was made wholesale by British observers of the GIs. In a society which worked by deference, there were many who were shocked by the upstandingness of the individual American soldier. Enlisted men did not know their place, and their officers seemed unconcerned by the free-and-easy ways of their men. Many of the British, who had been taught their place too well, found they liked the Americans for their casualness and admired a system of discipline which worked by getting things done. American energy: that was the second impression. The British were seeing the Americans at a good time. They did not realise how deep the Depression had bitten—there had been a mild boom in Britain in the 1930s—and they knew scarcely anything of the bank collapses, the industrial crisis, the depopulation of the farm belt, the hopelessness that had afflicted America even into Roosevelt's second administration. They were catching Americans on the rebound. The war had kindled in the British a national spirit of unity and defiance that the Americans, like all wartime visitors, found attractive. Americans on the rebound from the Depression years were filled with a still more attractive spirit, a rekindling of optimism in their own ability to overcome almost any obstacle that life put in their path. America was on the move again in the 1940s. Twelve million Americans joined the armed forces, and twenty million Americans left home to take up war work, causing thirty-five of the forty-eight states to lose population in an internal migration not known since the settlement of the Great Plains. No such movement of people was possible or even thinkable in the overcrowded British Isles, making the effects of its spillover all the more dramatic. The British were tempted to think that the Hollywood illusion bore some relation to reality after all.

How did the cultural exchange work in the other direction? The oldness of Britain had its effect. I often get letters from veterans, writing to me about their experience of the Second World War, who recall visiting castles and cathedrals in the months while they were waiting for D-Day. I am sure they did; but old men forget. I suspect that they were more interested then in what was young and lively about an unfamiliar country. Young English people were certainly most of all interested by the new and modish in imported American life. They learned to jitterbug, they bought zoot suits, they had Frank Sinatra haircuts, they patronised some fairly shaky imitations of milk bars, they chewed gum, they cadged Lucky Strikes, they crooned the tunes and parroted the words of incomprehensible popular songs; "Mares eat oats and

does eat oats and little lambs eat ivy" is a jingle that repeats itself infuriatingly in my ears whenever I recall the hay-scented invasion summer
of 1944. "Don't Fence Me In" was another hit—ironically for the
Americans, who, as D-Day approached, were confined behind barbed
wire as a final security measure.

That meant a poignant separation for many of them, for the most
important cultural exchange in their direction was emotional: they had
fallen in love in their tens of thousands. Warriors abroad always, of
course, go on a spree—and sensible parents lock up their daughters.
The Americans, however, were serious. They pledged eternal fidelity.
Why was that? Sexual chemistry between nations is a mysterious thing.
De Tocqueville had noted in Federal America a striking submissiveness
of the female to the male; in that we may identify the roots of the femi-
nist rebellion which transfixes late-twentieth-century America. I suspect
that its first stirrings were afoot in the 1940s and that American
women had already begun to display some of that reactive masculinity
which, to European men today, is their most striking characteristic.
English girls, more certain in their European way of the value of their
femininity, must have been deeply attractive to American men in the
war years; and then, too, they had physical attributes which American
women generally lack—creamy complexions, fine hair, soft voices.
Americans fell for them in a collective swoon—a war-years word—and
they responded. All those Saturday nights in the cinema with Clark
Gable had aroused anticipations akin to those felt in Jane Austen's
households of unmarried maidens at news of the arrival of eligible
bachelors in the neighbourhood.

The lightning struck in unpredictable ways. My schoolmistress, a
reserved girl of good family, whose enormous bosom impressed me
even at the age of seven, fell blushingly in love with an equally smitten
American airman and, I believe, lived happily ever after. A widowed
friend of my parents went the same way. Our Welsh nursemaid managed to be simultaneously in love with several GIs at the same time for
much of 1943 and eventually departed heaven knows where. These
were but three in a host of British women who lost their hearts to the
incomers, often very quickly and with almost total incomprehension on
both sides of what transatlantic marriage might mean. Yet, in an astonishingly large number of cases, romance did mean marriage. "We'll
Meet Again," the great British hit of the war, turned out to imply
"Yours Till the End of Life's Story," the other great popular song, for

over sixty thousand couples. The Americans who departed into the blue for Normandy and Germany with a promise on their lips came back, or sent a ring, or married by proxy or tied the knot in some other way, causing an army of GI brides to follow them homeward in the year the war ended. They remain one of the most cohesive groups of immigrants ever to reach America's shores, linked by a network of GI bride clubs, keeping in close touch with the homeland and still casting a curiously expatriate spell of Englishness over their offspring. The barman of the Museum Café near Central Park West in New York, a graduate of what he told me was the best drama school in southwest Texas, assured me in 1984 that he was English too, his mother having been a GI bride from Liverpool.

American Friendships

The Americans left as swiftly as they had come. By 1947 only a remnant of GIs remained to man the huge complex of airfields left over from the strategic bombing offensive in the fenland of East Anglia and on the downs above Oxford. The homegoers returned to the continuation of the most sustained economic boom ever known in any country in history. Paul Edwards, one of Studs Terkel's oral historians, went off to the war from Roosevelt's National Youth Administration. When he got home, "Farmers in South Dakota that I had administered relief to, and gave 'em bully beef and four dollars a week to feed their families . . . were worth a quarter-million dollars, right? What was true there was true all over America." It was not true in Britain. There life became even more pinched in the first years of peace than it had been during the worst of the war years. Bread, freely available while the U-boats were sinking the grain ships from North America, was rationed from 1947; I clearly remember, on the first occasion my father took me to dinner in a London hotel, the head waiter asking us at the door of the restaurant to choose between bread and potatoes and issuing the appropriate coupons. Coal almost disappeared that winter, the harshest of the century, a real affliction in a country where an open fire was still for most people the only form of heating. Were there electrical power cuts? I certainly remember the family huddling in an upstairs bedroom over the only gas fire in the house. I remember, too, my mother's constant anxiety about food; in the country, where the family had spent the war years, there had been an unofficial overflow of eggs and poultry from the local farms; in London, to which we returned in 1945, we were limited to what our ration books allowed. That made American food parcels all the more important, and these we had now intermittently started to receive from a civil engineer in Dayton, Ohio, who, as a result of a wartime friendship, had become my younger sister's godfather. The contents—Sunblest raisins, Fray Bentos corned beef, Puritan Maid lard—were picked over with a sort of wonder; they contrasted surrealistically with the lumpy carrots and clodded parsnips which were the only foodstuffs in unrestricted supply.

My father's car disappeared in 1946; in London he lost the petrol coupons to which he had been entitled in the country. The city worked almost exclusively by public transport, red buses crammed with shabbily dressed people, cold from long waits in queues. Our clothes were wearing out collectively, for clothing was rationed as strictly as food; men wore their military overcoats to work and women re-machined items of uniform into civilian shapes; a fashionable item was a floppy peaked cap, modelled on a hat worn by Princess Elizabeth, our future queen, at the first post-war Birthday Parade for her father. He was presumably not short of cigarettes, since he died of lung cancer in 1952; his subjects, by contrast, were obsessed by the shortage of tobacco, which had to be paid for from Britain's shrinking dollar credits, and some were even driven to growing it in their back gardens, a futile experiment in Britain's fitful summers. Officialdom, in any case, took a severe view of such efforts to circumvent the excise on luxuries: American food parcels omitting to declare on the manifest that they contained Virginia cigarets—we noted the different spelling—were, if opened for inspection, impounded by the Customs. The post-war years were high times for bureaucrats. Their powers were pervasive, expressed in a stream of regulations that perpetuated the regimentation of wartime in a climate from which the mood of national self-sacrifice had departed. Londoners had become surly, as ungracious as the battered streets and unpainted houses in which they carried on their lives. Something of the atmosphere informs George Orwell's *Nineteen Eighty-four*, which he was writing at the time; I recognised it instantly, amid the residue of war-damaged buildings, when I visited Warsaw in the last year of Communist government forty years later.

I fell ill in 1947 with tuberculosis, the result, I suspect, of dietary deficiency, and spent most of the next four years confined to bed in an open-air hospital. That made for an odd education—Greek and Latin from the hospital chaplain, French from the schoolmistress, much miscellaneous reading—but somehow I assembled the entrance requirements for Oxford, and there I went in 1953. It was a euphoric liberation, both from immobility and the pessimism that long spells of illness induce; at times I had doubted whether I would pass any exams at all, let alone those for university admission. Yet even the Oxford of the early 1950s, though its beauty was untouched, its academic routine as measured as ever, was pinched by the national poverty; at breakfast in my first term we sat in hall, under the portraits of prime ministers and viceroys, at tables littered with the jam jars of butter and sugar that were our individual rations. We remained no better dressed than the rest of the population—undergraduates who had been conscript officers brought with them any bits of uniform that would serve civilian purposes—and, though Oxford life still required frequent appearance in dark suits, dinner jackets, even tail coats, most of our finery was hand-me-downs from fathers.

Of course, we were as high-spirited as undergraduates have ever been, and with good reason. The Oxford intake was a tiny national élite, in a country which then had only twenty universities, and we could afford to skylark in the certainty that we had a future. Yet it was not the future of our collegiate ancestors. My college, Balliol, had been for three generations the country's most famous training ground for rulers of empire; it had produced Indian civil servants and colonial proconsuls by the hundred and its network of influence had once extended from Delhi to Johannesburg; Balliol men filled British cabinets, ambassadorships, high commisions, university chairs wherever English was spoken; Asquith, the last Prime Minister in a majority Liberal government, had been a Balliol man, and so too had Curzon, the greatest Viceroy of India of the century, Edward Grey, Foreign Secretary at the outbreak of the First World War, Alfred Milner, Governor of British South Africa after the Boer War, and Herbert Samuel, High Commissioner in Palestine during the institution of the Balfour Declaration, which made it a Jewish National Home. We liked to tell each other that the loudest sound in the world was that of Balliol fingernails scratching Balliol backs; but we ought to have wondered who beside ourselves was listening. The outbreak of the First World War had been a disaster for Britain, its effects all too evident in our country's diminishing circumstances; among them had been the extinction of the Liberal Party in British politics and its supersession by Labour, which was bent on the dissolution of the Empire Balliol had served so devotedly. It had already conceded independence to India, an unavoidable step but the single greatest diminution of British power in the world in our lifetime then or later; it had also acquiesced in Palestine's dismemberment between its Jewish and Arab inhabitants, the cause of many of the world's troubles at that time and since; while South Africa, on which Milner had tried to impose an enlightened colonial administration, was already relapsing into the racialist darkness of Boer apartheid rule.

I had gorged myself on the literature of empire—Kipling, Conrad, Buchan—in my hospital isolation, so I took particularly hard the dawning realisation that those days were past. Realise it I did none the less, perhaps because my parents, despairing of my passing any exams, had sent me after my illness to school in France, where I found myself—as most of my Balliol contemporaries had not in those days before foreign travel was the norm—among people only too keen to point out that Britain had come down in the world. They seemed more impressed by the United States. I could see why, even though they intermixed their deprecation of British self-regard with some stringent anti-Americanism, then *de rigueur* at almost every level of French society. The landowners whose property had suffered in the battle for Normandy complained constantly about the damage; but I noticed that it was the Americans they blamed, not the British, and not out of any concern for my feelings; the liberation was, in their eyes, an American achievement. A landed family with whom I stayed in the Indre in 1952 had let half the château to American officers building a NATO air base nearby; they took it for granted, and helped to persuade me, that the defence of Europe was now in American hands. The Americans, in any case, were evidence of this; they were bursting with energy and brought to that sleepy corner of France—Jacques Tati had shot the first of his classical denunciations of modernity, *Jour de Fête*, in a neighbouring village the year before—a gust of the same Americanism I remembered stirring the cobwebs in the English countryside on the eve of D-Day.

So it was with a half-formed appreciation of what America meant that I first began to make friendships with the American undergraduates I found at Oxford. They formed the largest of the foreign groups and were particularly numerous at Balliol, to which an outpost of old members at Harvard sent Rhodes scholars in a steady stream; others came to us from Yale, Princeton, the great Midwestern campuses of Michigan and Illinois and the leading liberal arts colleges, like Swarthmore. What impression did they make? Visual impressions were the most immediate. The Americans looked American, just as in those days the French looked French; the bland, indeterminate, international style had not yet been invented. Their hair was crew-cut and they wore large, heavy, highly polished shoes, waistless tweed jackets, and, whether they had been in the service or not, khaki cotton trousers winter and summer. Many had been in the service, which, after four years of college, made them older than British undergraduates; yet there was nothing elderly about their enthusiasm for university life. They threw themselves into rowing—the domination of the University Eight by Americans dates from those days—into hockey and lacrosse, even into rugby, which they played as a substitute for their own football; the transplantation of rugby as a collegiate sport to American universities owes almost everything to Rhodes scholars. They had an equal enthusiasm for the life of college clubs, particularly the political societies. Americans had a passion for debate and took their political differences with a seriousness British undergraduates did not feel in theirs. There were, as it happened, real differences between the programmes of the British Conservative and Labour parties not matched by the conflict between Republicans and Democrats; but few of us were committed one way or the other. There were exceptions—two of my contemporaries became Conservative cabinet ministers—but they formed a tiny minority. The hedonism of Oxford life was an escape from the dreary politics of a once great imperial country in decline and we scoffed at the preoccupations of undergraduate Tories and Socialists, openly laughed at the intensities of the handful of Stalinists.

Americans, on the other hand, clearly believed in the power of politics to alter the future. Their convictions foreshadowed the future which their own achievements had already preordained for them. They were a national élite—the elevation of the Rhodes scholarship to the status of undisputed prize for "most likely to succeed" in institutions as dissimilar as Harvard and the U.S. Military Academy is the subtlest of many cultural holds Britain still exerts over the United States—and knew it. All were of outstanding ability and a few of exceptional intellect; one of my Balliol contemporaries was to become a Nobel prizewinner. The majority of the Americans were not, however, pure academics. Those with whom I became friends included a future sena-

tor, a head of the Exxon Corporation, a leading Wall Street lawyer, an
ambassador, a writer of distinction. I was slow to get to know them.
My pre-university years had been unconventional, and on arrival I inclined to friendship with my college's less conventional members: a Roman Catholic baronet in flight from both his mother and his faith, a
Canadian of devastating good looks who had come to England in pursuit of free love, not then the norm, an Indian whose parents had married across caste, a would-be poet who thought life was a Keatsian
dream. After my years of confinement in hospital, I thought Oxford
was a Keatsian dream, until a recurrence of tuberculosis took me away
for another year. On my return I recognised that time was not on my
side, began to pick up the threads of work and to make friends with
people who had a purpose in life.

No group had a stronger purpose than the Americans. Americans
in the Eisenhower years must have felt there was nothing their country
could not do. That was certainly the spirit exuded by the Balliol Americans; it touched those British undergraduates with any imagination; it
touched me. I made friends with every American in college; I remember
each one of them vividly; many remain my friends to this day. The
making of friendships between America's and Britain's best had been
the chief purpose for which Cecil Rhodes had left his money. I would
certainly not count myself among the British élite, but a surprising
number of my Balliol contemporaries were destined to join it. My Balliol years formed a talented group, and the friendships which the foremost of them made with the Americans have lasted, to the very great
benefit of my country and with some, I hope, to theirs. Through such
friendships Britain succeeded in sustaining the mutuality which the victory of 1945 had bequeathed. The 1950s were the Eisenhower years.
The United States bestrode the world, militarily, diplomatically, scien-
tifically, industrially, financially. It had, through the Marshall Plan, just
put Europe back on its feet after its orgy of self-destruction in the Second World War. It was girding its loins to face down Stalinist Russia in
an ideological struggle for the minds of half the world. It was building
a nuclear arsenal to lend its ideology force. It was pouring out money
to fund the developing economies of poor countries and pouring
money into science that would better the lives of poor and rich alike
the world over. It was in the midst of its own economic boom which
guaranteed the dollar, through the Bretton Woods programme, as the
world's unit of exchange. It was bursting with intellectual, literary, and

artistic vitality. The petulance of French anti-Americanism in the 1950s was in large measure a reaction against the creativity of contemporary American writers, painters, dramatists, and scientists, to say nothing of the country's economists, historians, philosophers, and political scientists.

It was not surprising that I was drawn to the friendship of citizens of such a country. The Oxford Americans of my youth were fitting representatives of the United States at one of its high moments. They were public-spirited, they were able, they were attractive in looks and character, they were brimming with self-confidence, about their own futures and that of the world we shared. Little wonder that I found in them confirmation of my parents' assertions that the United States was neither a pale imitation of England nor a land of Hollywood fairy-tale but a civilisation in its own right. There was, of course, no hope of seeing it for myself. Britain in the 1950s was semi-bankrupt and in the grip of a dollar famine. Even had I had the money to finance a transatlantic visit, I would not have been allowed to exchange it. That was not a deprivation. None of my English counterparts had any thought of travelling to the United States either, and for the same reason.

Then, in 1956, a strange rumour began to circulate Balliol. An American who had been at the college before the war had conceived the idea of founding a sort of Rhodes scholarship in reverse, confined to Balliol undergraduates, so that young Britons could get to know the United States as Rhodes scholars knew the United Kingdom. He was rich, he was serious, and he did not want those selected to attend university but simply to travel through the United States in pursuit of some interest in the country that they could justify to the selecting committee. The first group of six departed that year. In 1957 I submitted a proposal to make a tour of the battlefields of the American Civil War. As I had chosen military history as my special subject in the Oxford final exams my proposal was taken seriously. There were some months of anticipation. Then, just before graduation, I was told I had been successful. Tickets and money would be sent on. I was going to go to America.

An American Journey

So began my first American journey, a greater journey than I had ever made before, a journey that remains the most memorable of my life. I

had never flown, and committed myself to a transatlantic crossing in a
tiny propeller-driven airliner with perfect insouciance. The incidents of
the flight included an engine failure in mid-Atlantic which changed
that, to wholly beneficial effect. Immediately affected by fear of flying
which lasted almost into middle age, I avoided aircraft whenever I
could for many years, thus bringing myself to make enormous transits
around North America by train and bus and so see at eye-level places
and things I would have missed altogether had that particular PanAm
DC-6—called, I remember, *Ponce de León*, after an early explorer of
the Americas—undergone a more stringent bout of maintenance at
Heathrow.

A flight of twenty-eight hours would not today leave me in any
condition to receive lasting impressions of an unknown country on arrival. I remember deplaning at Boston with almost physical recall. Heat
of a sort I had never experienced struck as we descended the steps to
the runway and was to oppress me throughout the remaining months
of an American East Coast summer. Air conditioning, also a new and
for a moment gratefully experienced sensation, had an equally oppressive effect. It upset my allergic balance, causing me to suffer violent
bouts of hay fever whenever I went through a temperature barrier. So
was formed my first impression of the New World. It has—I have not
changed this view and I do not apologise if it causes offence—one of
the world's worst climates.

I melted, drooped, and sneezed for the next three months. There
were compensations. The first was an expedition to buy new clothes.
The English of my youth wore the same clothes winter and summer,
grey flannel trousers and tweed jackets. The day after arrival I descended, with the first instalment of dollars my scholarship provided,
to the Coop in Harvard Square and outfitted myself with chinos and a
seersucker suit. This was an intense excitement. New clothes were still
a new experience for my wartime generation. New clothes that gave
one a different identity were fancy dress. I did not quite dare the seersucker suit for several weeks and wore it first when I took the train for
Washington from Pennsylvania Station in New York. Late and flus-
tered, I threw my bags into a coach at the feet of two very large and
black sleeping-car porters who saluted my appearance with a cry,
"Here comes a Princeton man." I have cherished it ever afterwards as a
compliment.

I do not suppose that today a Princeton man would stand out; the

Princeton undergraduates I knew when I was a Fellow there in 1984 were no better- or worse-dressed than any other young Americans. America had changed in thirty years. The America, and particularly the New York, I encountered in 1957 was a more stratified country than it is today—safer, too. I have never encountered anything but kindness in the United States. Statistics seem to show, nevertheless, and Americans clearly feel, that they live now in a violent and dangerous society. Before my seersucker sortie I had spent a solitary fortnight of perfect serenity in New York, in an apartment lent by briefly encountered friends of Oxford American friends. The apartment was on Union Square in lower Manhattan; its owners were an experimental film-maker and his artistic wife. He had been at Harvard, she at Wellesley, and the contents reflected their interests—books, paintings, a large, leafless tree that touched the ceiling of the double-storey drawing room. Across the way was a diner where I ate lunch. In the square in the evenings clusters of passers-by listened to soapbox orators denouncing the supporters of causes they held repugnant, a mixed bag of revivalists and civil libertarians. During the noon hours I retired from the tropical heat. In the cooler evenings I wandered the streets, sometimes as far as Central Park forty blocks northwards, sometimes just round the corner to Gramercy Park, Stuyvesant Town, and the sidewalk tavern called McSorley's Wonderful Saloon, not yet a tourist attraction, which I knew about from Joseph Mitchell's marvellous collection of ethnic *New Yorker* pieces of the same name. I loved New York on first acquaintance. It was an exotic city, rich with instant friendship, but easy and slow moving. I wish I could say the same about it today.

I would have lingered longer in New York, but an arrangement made with a fellow travelling scholar, now by chance my brother-in-law, required me to be in Washington by a certain date; it was that which put me at Penn Station in my seersucker suit. He had the car in which we were to set off to the South. He also had an identical seersucker suit, bought at the Harvard Coop on the same day. So outfitted, we set off together in a Ford station wagon one morning in July 1957 to discover the United States.

Sonnenreise, the young Goethe called his expedition to the lands of lemon blossom. He set a fashion among young Northern Europeans for expeditions southward that lasts to this day. Neither Maurice nor I was a young Goethe, but we were little travelled, over-educated, abrim with reading about the Civil War, and filled with expectation of what we would find in the old Confederacy. Our journey, I see now, was to be a sort of *Sonnenreise*. I have not consulted Maurice about his memories. A *Sonnenreise*, however, it remains to me, a passage of new and strange and wholly un-European experience, steamy, tropical, alien, alluring, cast through a landscape and among peoples which had no equivalents in the green, chilly, and formal little island from which we had begun.

Today long-distance travellers by road in the United States make their way along the great interstate highways. There were no interstates in 1957, only the old numbered Federal highways which wandered the stagecoach routes between city and city. U.S. 1 was the route we chose southward out of Washington on an itinerary only partly planned, and it took us first to Richmond, Virginia, then—Americans still laugh when I tell them—to Goldsboro, North Carolina, thence to Charleston, South Carolina, and so to Atlanta, Georgia. Gentle memories of Goldsboro, hick town though Americans may think it, remain with me still. I liked it because, in the middle of unfettered space, its citizens had chosen to build what then passed for a skyscraper in the South, a touching symbol of civic pride. I liked it because it was the first town in which I stayed in a motel, that brilliantly creative American contribution to the conveniences of travel, the American caravanserai, without vermin, camel smells, importunate hangers-on, or unspeakable sanitation. I liked it because, in the growing cool of a Southern evening, I could sit outside above the dust of an unpaved sidewalk and watch the beautiful legs of girls otherwise unseen in the dying twilight walking—where? I longed to know. I longed to follow. The English girls with whom I had grown up wore skirts below their knees. Southern girls, even in 1957, wore abbreviated shorts above golden, athletic thighs.

Then Charleston. Charleston, though perhaps not then, is twinned with Bath, the miraculous Georgian, golden-stone city of the West of England, founded by the Romans around the warm-water springs that bubble up from its bedrock, formalised and terraced by eighteenth-century classicists. Charleston—wood, paint, and plaster—is as perfectly classical as Bath, but softened by palmettos, bougainvillaea, and flowery, trailing tendrils. I was enchanted by Charleston at first sight, decided then that it was the most beautiful city I had ever seen, a decision from which visits to Venice and Aix-en-Provence have scarcely deflected me, and settled down to enjoy it. Introductions brought us meetings with eccentric Charlestonians; explorations down side streets and along waterfronts introduced us to oysters in hot tomato sauce drunk with Arctically cold beer; pressing on doorbells took us into colonial interiors which seemed scarcely changed since Barbadian sugar merchants had unshipped their English furniture and silver into them two hundred years earlier.

Charleston tempts one to linger and calls one back. I have been there since, more often than to any other small city in the United States. In 1957 I had to leave, sooner than I wanted, for Georgia and the deeper South. In Atlanta, then still recognisably the *Gone with the Wind* city it has ceased to be, we met the governor, brother of a notorious gerrymanderer. Further on, in a soda fountain in a tiny backwoods place, we were mistaken for travelling revivalists—"You-all preachers?"; seersucker suits had a different semiology south of New York— and made our first encounter with red earth roads, verandaed, ramshackle cabins, and the water-melon culture; however cold the interiors of the pensioned-off Coca-Cola chests from which they were sold by the roadside I never acquired the taste.

Deep, deep in Georgia, drawn by Maurice's inexplicable urge to visit something called the Okefenokee Swamp, we spent one of the most memorable of our dozens of nights on the road. In Lumber City—"Population 69," said the signboard at the city limits—there was only one place to eat, we were the only diners, and the dinner hour was already over before our arrival. The proprietress nevertheless relented, covered a wooden table with what she had to offer, and left us with her father and infant son to pick through dishes of okra, grits, black-eyed peas, pork, and potatoes. Grandfather remembered Lumber City as a thriving place, full of immigrants who had come to cut timber from the virgin pine stands. He had difficulty placing us. "England? New England?" When we said no he mused while the little grandson surveyed us with wide eyes in a silent face. Grandfather tried again. "How long you-all been over?" Six weeks, we said. He mused some more. "You sure have learned the language fast." In memory I see planked walls, planked floor—can I have imagined oil lamps? The heavy insect sounds of a Southern night filled the gaps in conversation. Second-growth timber stood close about the shanty. It might have been a sinister setting. I remember kindness, gentle hospitality, the utterly innocent curiosity that travellers among remote peoples report.

I suppose we were among descendants of our own stock who

might have been settled since the eighteenth century. Next day, when we ventured in a shallow metal boat among alligators and water snakes in the still, steamy interior of the swamp, our guide was a lean, masculine young waterman. He had left the Okefenokee only once, to do his military service, and had no desire to do so again. Sometimes to our alarm he leapt on to floating islands of reed and grass to stir an alligator into activity or shake an egret into flight from a shallow-rooted tree; sometimes he stopped in a backwater to smoke a hand-rolled cigarette. We might have been with the Marsh Arabs.

Just over the border in Florida we turned west to begin our circuit of the Gulf Coast. Jacksonville I remember for the night-time glimpses it gave into the sort of sprawl of cabin life I was not to see again until I visited Africa; St. Augustine for its tiny, bastioned fort, first outpost of Spanish power in the Americas north of Panama. St. Augustine had charm—gone now, I am told—a Caribbean charm compounded of rum punch and shrimp dinners served in lopsided, wooden tourist places that mass tourism had not yet found. One evening a restaurant pianist welcomed "our English guests" by hammering out "Maybe It's Because I'm a Londoner" on his old upright, to our embarrassment; neither of us knew the words.

Beyond St. Augustine, on a morning of pearl-like stillness, we crossed the St. Johns River, filled with mothballed destroyers surviving from the Battle of the Atlantic, and then on by day-long hops to Tallahassee and Pensacola and Mobile and Biloxi towards the mouth of the Mississippi. We had a date with friends of friends at, I forget now, either Bay St. Louis or Pass Christian. I remember our arrival and the blissful days that followed. The friends of friends were either rich or had found that way of living without money that seems rich. It had no equivalent on any of the shivery, shingled English strands where we had spent our childhood summers. Their beach houses had sandy surroundings which merged with each other and with the shore, about which they padded in permanently bare feet, unfussed by work, timetables, or set hours for lunch or dinner. Fires were lit, fish suppers cooked in the light of the flames, strong cocktails passed from hand to hand. Sunburnt boys and girls emerged out of the twilight in scraps of ragged clothing that might once have been sold over the counter at the Harvard Coop, beautiful, different, utterly uninterested in Europe or England or anywhere a dozen miles distant from Bay St. Louis. Occasionally a worried, responsible, barefoot adult padded through the throng, trying to organise entrants for tomorrow's regatta.

Sonnenreise. I would, at twenty-three, willingly have settled for life in that corner of the Gulf Coast; but we were bidden onwards to New Orleans and then up the Mississippi Valley. In the delta back country, in compensation for Maurice's insistence that we visit the Okefenokee Swamp, I took him for a day into the parishes of the Cajuns, the descendants of French settlers who had taken land there in the eighteenth century or come down the river from the north after the fall of French Canada. I wanted to practise my French. There was plenty of Frenchness about: severe, whitewashed burial chambers in graveyards surrounding Breton-looking churches, French names—Laforge, Labranche—on the mailboxes at entrances to roadside cabins. My French was a success—"*Vous venez de Paris, Monsieur?*"; perhaps it was not. They understood me. I did not understand them. French America was a long time ago.

The Mississippi Valley: oily meanders a mile wide between levees, long, ditched tracts of cultivation leading to the flat horizon, causeways over standing water. I remember the interminable passage across Lake Pontchartrain, where land disappears from sight in the centre. Somewhere hereabouts, where Afro-Americans were then a majority, we had our first encounters with black America. We gave a lift to two young black men who dropped the rocks they had been nerving themselves to throw at a car whose driver had rudely refused them a ride, eavesdropped in a country store on a courteous conversation about cotton between a white farmer and his grave, elderly black tenant, conspired with a respectable black salesman at a gas station over use of the lavatory—"I'll wait until you white folks have gone on." Unimaginable today the apartheid of American life only forty years ago. A little further on we encountered the issue of apartheid in tangible form. The Governor of Arkansas had refused admission to the Central High School in the state capital, Little Rock, to a black girl. There had been riots; he had called out the National Guard; there was the threat of more trouble. On an impulse we decided on a diversion, crossed the Mississippi and the vast rice fields that lay beyond, and drew up outside the school, an unpleasing concrete monolith. There was not a bayonet in sight, not even a state trooper. We ventured into Little Rock's black quarter. I would like to record that we were hissed in the streets. On the contrary: I recall sensing a certain surprise on the part of the inhabitants at the sight of two young white men in seersucker suits tramping about between shop signs advertising palm-reading and hair-straightening but otherwise only friendliness, greeting, and concern that we had lost our way. There was trouble again later, which would eventually prompt the Supreme Court judgement ruling school segregation unlawful, but not a hint of it in the Little Rock we saw. What a quiet revolution America's revolution in race relations was to prove; when I next visited the country in 1977, twenty years after Little Rock, it was as if to an India that had abolished caste.

Somewhere beyond Little Rock, Maurice and I parted. He was shortly due back in England. We had done much else that I have not recorded. We had visited the Tennessee Valley Authority, that Rooseveltian experiment in the public ownership of natural resources which liberal America then foresaw—visitors from England watching the mismanagement of the national economy by civil servants could have warned otherwise—as the way of the future. We had taken a long hike in the wilderness of the Great Smoky Mountains, encountered rattlesnakes, met firefighters whose days were spent perched in their towers watching for fire, conceived some sense of the vastness of the American forest, without parallel in Europe—west of the Russian border—a brooding presence at the verge of settled land, not to be forgotten, never forgotten by me. We had visited black public housing, a black college—I cringe still at the memory of our white host joking that the students learnt Greek—grand, white-fenced horse farms where owners and trainers made pets of their lithe, black stable lads. We had stayed with an urbane academic family at the University of Virginia, savoured the serenity of Thomas Jefferson's Monticello outside Charlottesville, tiptoed the fringes of Virginian country-house life: pillared porticoes, broad acres, not much concern about bank balances, a distinct neurotic frisson over who would be coming to drinks.

We had seen a great deal of the Old South, the elegant summer retreats of Natchez, the New Orleans French Quarter, preserved plantations approached through hanging avenues of Spanish moss, sanitised slave cabins, most of the battlefields—the ostensible purpose of our great journey—of the Civil War: Bull Run, the Peninsula, Petersburg, Fort Sumter, Atlanta, Stone Mountain, Vicksburg. Scraps of memory of the Vicksburg bluff and the Petersburg crater were to help me, two or three years later, teach my class on the Civil War to British officer cadets at Sandhurst in sleepy afternoon halls of study.

We had also seen much of the new South—smoking oil refineries at the Mississippi mouth, a vast new automated glass factory somewhere in Arkansas where the handful of workers wore Hawaiian shirts and seemed possessed by holiday mood, courts of justice, city halls, public hospitals, the beginnings of what I suspect must have been one of the first interstates. New it may have been by contrast with the antebellum world of Gray and Blue; it struck me then, as the memory still does strike by comparison with the South I know today, as an unchanging and almost empty land, short of people, settlement, and traffic. I remember hours of scrub pine landscape, on roads untravelled by another car, advertisements for Burma Shave or pecan pie in towns miles ahead through which we had passed before realising they were intended stopping places, poor little farms, houses with porches bigger than living space, pretentious placenames, tired soil, weary people, dull hot skies, interminable, featureless distance. Oddly I came to like the South and still like it more than any other part of the United States. It retains for Europeans a trace of cultural familiarity, as the rest of the country does not. *Sonnenreise*: I have often tried to analyse why I should have a sense, however slight, of being at home in Dixie. Class system, yes; history, yes; but more important, I suspect, the lingering aftermath of defeat. Europe is a continent of defeated nations; even Britain, the offshore survivor, has had occasion to lick its wounds. Victorious America has never known the tread of occupation, the return of beaten men. The South is the exception. Its warrior spirit, which supplies the armed forces with a disproportionate flow of recruits, is a denial of the decision of 1865. The famous femininity of its women—not a myth, not to European men at least, who find them feminine as other American women are not—is a quality that comes from grandmothers who found a strength their men had lost, learnt to comfort, helped to forget, never, never said the unsayable thing. Pain is a dimension of old civilisations. The South has it. The rest of the United States does not.

I left the South with regret. I was to spend several months longer in the United States and learn much more about it, particularly about American family life, for, as a lone traveller, I was handed on from household to household through the Midwest and back to New England. I was to make long, solitary journeys by bus and train, stay in cheap hotels, fend off homosexual pestering—Maurice and I had already found that our English complexions, floppy haircuts, and, I suppose, air of innocence abroad made us a target—hope but fail to meet girls, fall into odd experiences. On a train somewhere in Ohio a kindly,

armed army sergeant indicated a young black man whom he explained
he was escorting to a military prison to serve time for a drugs conviction. In Tennessee, at the state fair, my host casually pointed out
William Faulkner leaning on a piece of farm machinery. In New York
my Union Square hosts, re-encountered, showed a surprising interest in
trekking off to Bear Mountain to visit the sister of an English family
friend; she was married to the film producer John Houseman, and it
was only afterwards that I realised why an experimental scriptwriter
would have wanted to meet him. I stayed with doctors, lawyers, an in-
dustrialist in Indiana who owned the town. In Washington I went to
smart Georgetown cocktail parties full of clever young State Department people who were friends of my Rhodes scholar friends. In Boston
I copy-edited manuscripts for a friend of a friend beginning in publishing at Little, Brown. At Cambridge I walked Harvard Yard with friends
of other friends, stayed in Eliot House, from which so many of my Oxford American friends had come, at last talked into a lunchtime date an
American girl, intelligent, Jewish, darkly beautiful, not the least interested in me.

My months alone in the United States were a succession of invitations, friendships, allurements, sudden elations, a proper culmination
to any young man's *Sonnenreise*. The odd English contemporary who
had decided to chance his luck in the New World urged me to stay. I
felt the temptation. After the mystery of the South, however, the spell
had somehow gone. I felt my future life was in England, with parents,
sisters, brother, contemporaries, known places and things. I was not
brave enough for the great adventure of emigration. Perhaps, for all the
uncertainty anyone of twenty-three must feel about the years ahead, I
sensed that I enjoyed too many advantages in the old country to need
to make a new life in the land of opportunity. As the American winter
of 1957 began to cast the leaves from the trees, I took ship aboard the
old *Queen Elizabeth* and sailed homeward.

America After Twenty Years

I thought I should never see America again. For twenty years I did not.
I had conceived the odd aim of becoming a military historian and
quickly identified on my return that the only place where I might be

paid for pursuing my private interest was the Royal Military Academy, Sandhurst, Britain's West Point. I did not get an appointment there at once. I was told that one might be available, but not for two years, and I filled the interim by working as something called a political analyst in, by happenstance, the American Embassy in London. This prolonged my exposure to American life—and brought me the slightly colonial experience of deferring to Americans as employers in my own country—but was otherwise without significance. At twenty-five I joined the Sandhurst staff, settled down to learn my trade, began an exploration of the anthropology of the British Army, which remains a lifelong interest, married, raised children, and experimented with writing. My literary impulsion was entirely practical. On an academic salary I could not support the family of four children who surprised my wife and myself by their frequent arrival, and thought writing might bridge the gap. Articles and paperbacks did so for a decade, during which I lived a sort of married monastic life, isolated inside the grounds of Sandhurst, serenely beautiful, quite cut off from the England, or anywhere else, outside. Then I conceived an idea for a serious work of history, about the changing experience of the individual on the battlefield over the centuries. I had listened to soldiers discussing what really happened on battlefields for a dozen Sandhurst years. They included survivors of the Second World War. They also included the West Point liaison officers who, after 1965, were invariably Vietnam veterans. In 1972 I settled down to write a book eventually entitled *The Face of Battle*. In 1976 it was published, and shortly afterwards I found myself a celebrated author, curiously more celebrated in America than at home. *The Face of Battle* was chosen as Book-of-the-Month in June 1977, so bringing me enough money to pay for my elder son's fees at the expensive boarding school at which I had imprudently entered him. Its publication also brought me an invitation to lecture at the National War College in Washington, D.C. Other invitations shortly followed, to the University of Chicago, to West Point, to Harvard. I was to see America again after all.

America after twenty years made an impression as indelible as America in 1957, but different. I was different, less light-hearted but more self-assured. America was different, less itself, more like anywhere else. I regretted both changes. There could be no *Sonnenreise* for me again, no pearl-like mornings crossing the St. Johns River towards Bay St. Louis, barefooted evenings on the beach, hopeless gazings at blonde girl-children whose heroes were the teenage victors of yester-day's regatta. Equally, there could be no old America again, the Amer-ica of Lumber City whose inhabitants thought only Americans spoke English. Americans had ceased to look American. The faces were the same, the gait, the gestures, but the American haircut—the coir mat crew cut, the iron perm—had gone, and so had distinctively American clothes, the waistless suit, the universal shirtwaister dress, bobby socks, enormous shoes. Americans dressed like Europeans, just as we all dressed rather like them. There had been another assimilation: in the intervening twenty years growing prosperity at home had brought us all the accoutrements of American domestic life—washing machines, refrigerators, dishwashers, television sets—that had been such a cause of wonder in the 1950s. That made for a lowering of barriers; we were less the poor relations we had been. Other barriers had lowered also. The great age of international air travel had begun. In my twenties I had been almost unique among my English contemporaries in having travelled widely in the United States, in having been there at all. In the 1970s an American summer tour was becoming an ingredient of stu-dent life; in the 1980s all my children would cross the Atlantic quite as casually as they would cross the English Channel. Americans were making the journey in the opposite direction in large numbers and Eu-rope was becoming demystified for them in the process. The extraordi-nary inwardness of America, which was part of the spell it had cast upon me, was dissolving. Casements, not so magic when opened, were letting in light from both directions.

America was changing, too, because its people were changing. In the 1950s there had mainly been white Americans and black Ameri-cans. By the 1970s a new tide of immigration was beginning—as immigration also was in Europe, until 1950 a completely white conti-nent—to blur the division; there were Chinese, Indian, and Hispanic faces on the streets in increasing numbers. The most important racial change, however, had been in relations between black and white. Dur-ing my great tour I had scarcely spoken to a black person and the sta-tus of blacks had been completely menial. Twenty years later I met African-Americans at every level of society. Returning on a book pro-motion tour to Atlanta, a city where in 1957 the only black person with whom I had passed the time of day was the barman in the Atlanta Athletic Club, I found that all the interviewers who gave me time on their television or radio programmes were black. Well-educated, professional, they gave no hint of having passed through a revolution; such was their self-assurance that all the questions I longed to ask about the transformaion of their expectations, in less than half my lifetime, died in my throat.

But then for me the time of questioning, of the night-long conversation, of heartfelt revelation and enquiry, was over. I was older. I was also a transient, coming and going, living on impressions rather than deep experience. From 1977 onwards I began to visit the United States—and Canada—two or three or sometimes five times a year, at first to lecture, then also to promote books or to write for the London newspaper which, after a long academic career, I joined in 1986. I gathered impressions in sheaves, first and most plentifully about American university and college life. Its richness has never ceased to surprise or to delight me. In the England of my youth there had only been twenty universities; at the beginning of the nineteenth century, when college-founding was almost as American as town-building, there had been only two. On the great circuit of the college lecture tour into which literary success cast me I encountered the results of the American passion for higher education in wonderful variety.

Some of the places to which invitations brought me were rich, world-famous, and intellectually intimidating. Harvard I knew, but only as the Alma Mater of old friends who had treated it with easy familiarity. As an academic society, briefly giving a visitor its attention, it proved formidable and demanding. Nowhere, not even at Oxford, had I encountered a professoriat which exuded such a sense of academic aristocracy. Scholarly eminence, security of tenure, wealth, knowledge of the world: these were the marks of the Harvard historians and political scientists before whom I tried to show my paces. Once, in a light-hearted mood, I scored a success; on a second occasion, trying harder, I flopped. I know the signs: polite questions, the intimation that the audience's time has been wasted. I have flopped, too, at Princeton, at Yale, at the University of Chicago, that outpost of Vienna Circle intellectuality in the Midwest; America's grand academe imposes pitiless standards.

I felt more at home in that uniquely American institution the liberal arts college, the reason being, I surmise, that it is the equivalent of the English public school. Strictly it is the American prep school—Groton, Hotchkiss, Lawrenceville—which is the equivalent, but, while the public school is dominant in English life, the prep school in America is an exotic outgrowth. Liberal arts colleges, by contrast, are a point of aspiration for the educated parents of many American children. They offer a first degree but, more important, the friendship of professors, usually remote figures on the great campuses, social grooming, an all-round education, and, in many cases, an emphasis on moral purpose in life. A high proportion of the students at one liberal arts college were, a professor told me, "PK—preachers' kids"; the same would have been true of many English public schools in the nineteenth century, when clergymen of the Church of England were still paid a gentleman's wage. I came to know liberal arts colleges in their many forms, from Swarthmore, the most celebrated of them all, a virtual forcing house for Rhodes scholars, to the small religious foundations, Lutheran or Methodist, which cluster so thickly in Ohio and the rest of the Mid-west first settled by god-fearing, hard-working German immigrants in the nineteenth century. I grew very fond of St. Anselm's, a small Catholic college in New Hampshire, centred on its magnificent chapel, where jolly young Franciscans mingled in their brown habits at lunchtime with boys and girls in sneakers and T-shirts. I got to know even better Colorado College in Colorado Springs; a "rich kids' place," a state university professor once described it, but I found it governed by teachers of awesome fidelity to the ideals of truth and learning. "You," my closest friend there said to me, "are an Oxford humanist." You, I felt like replying, are an Abraham Lincolnian populist, believing in the equality of all before the book as well as the law.

I also came to know the great public universities, where a clever in-state student can acquire, given desperately hard work and a willing-ness to wait at table or wash dishes, an Ivy League education at a fraction of the price. Athletic prowess also sees a student through. At Ohio State, where the footballers had signed up en masse for the elec-tive in military history, I spent a social evening once craning to catch questions dropped down chests that looked like the lower slopes of Mount Everest. These amiable, almost wordless man-mountains were invariably in the charge of minute, demure girlfriends, who shepherded them about as if they were docile prize bulls at a state fair in the South-west. The large private universities came my way, too, New York Uni-versity, the University of Southern California; between them and their state equivalents I could detect no difference at all. The students, it seemed to me, enjoyed no better facilities, no greater intimacy with professors. They were merely exercising a choice the poorer students did not have, even if it were only the choice to waste their parents' money. But choice is the essence of American higher education, and so is wastefulness. The dropout was unknown in my Oxford years; if you were admitted, you graduated; there were no credits, to be taken on perhaps later to another place, and that kept noses to grindstones; equally, there were degrees even for the laziest, including the legendary fourth-class degree, whose handful of recipients were admired almost as much as those who got firsts. There was no studying for a year or two, taking time out, going on to another place, graduating eventually in a discipline entirely different from that in which you had started out. English university education was ruthlessly élitist. The tiny group who secured entrance were destined to be a national élite, theoretically guaranteed a secure career for life ever after.

Between the English system of my youth and the American system already coming to prevail when I first visited the United States I see no middle way. The first makes for a society of haves and have-nots, well organised, well governed but unequal, and destined, in a post–Industrial Revolution world, for economic inertia. The second, though it may lay the seeds of discontent with prevailing government and organisation, fertilises creativity. Education ought to be wasteful, as American education is. It ought to offer chances to the greatest possible number, and ought to offer them in manifold variety and over and over again. No social scientist ever born has been able to predict who will benefit from education or when. Some of the cleverest of my Oxford contemporaries, who took firsts and swept the board of university prizes, have golden futures behind them; some have disappeared without trace; a tragic few, overburdened by intellect and neurosis, have taken their own lives. I think of the successful Americans I have known with interest. Paul Sarbanes, the son of an immigrant Greek waiter, is a United States senator; Barry Blumberg, Nobel prizewinner and head of my Oxford college, took his first degree somewhere I cannot place; Moses Finley, the greatest classical scholar of his age and eventually Regius (Royal) Professor at Cambridge, began life as an economist in some obscure university and taught himself Latin and Greek. There is no telling.

There is, of course, élitism in American education, and in 1984 I savoured it at first hand. Elected to a fellowship at Princeton, which kindly granted me the title of professor, I spent the first semester of the year on that limpid campus. I spent it alone; my wife was supervising

the school-leaving exams of our two younger children. That made for
loneliness. To my surprise, I found the faculty club empty in the
evenings. Oxford and Cambridge dons dine together at high table;
American, certainly Princeton, professors go home to their wives.
Moreover, they do not gossip, nor do they waste time. Gossip and
time-wasting fill the spaces of English university life, to the great pleasure of inhabitants and interlopers alike. American, certainly Princeton,
professors work. They work at teaching, at seminars, at books. I began
a book at Princeton but really wanted an opportunity for the sort of
casual conversation with clever people which is, I find, the key to creativity and the eventual completion of books in hand. I did not get it.
There were clever people aplenty; but they were always between
classes, between lectures, breaking off to see a student or get in an hour
at the Firestone Library. I would suggest a lunchtime drink. I might
have been suggesting fire and brimstone. My only co-consumer of
twelve o'clock gin and tonic in the faculty club—what is this American
passion for early lunchtimes?—was the curator of the art collection,
heavily Europeanised—and even he did not speak. Descending to the
restaurant floor, I would spend an hour mesmerised by the sight of distinguished academics transfixed by their lonely reading, raising their
heads only to take savage canine bites at enormous, indigestible sandwiches clutched in a free hand. Strange, zoo-like feelings possessed me,
as if I were present at the feeding-time of a species of superintelligent
primates hitherto unknown to science.

Yet there was wonderful talk at Princeton—in the Friday-morning
seminar. The only obligation attached to my fellowship was that I
should attend that seminar, where papers were read, and once present a
paper myself. The obligation was no burden. English academics treat
faculty seminars as an occasion for languid speculation or for settling
private scores. American seminars are dedicated to the pursuit of truth.
Historical discussion of a quality I have never encountered before or
since was carried on at Princeton on those Fridays. Elaborate, lifelong
learning was condensed into a few minutes of exposition. Arcane con-
cepts, batted about between believers and doubters, yielded their significance in a flurry of question-and-answer. Words of which I scarcely
knew the meaning—"topos," "stochastic"—took on sense. Authors I
had never heard of were cited with familiarity, obscure languages
quoted with facility, hidden ideas brought to the surface, fallacies of

which I was ignorant trampled to death. After one or two Princeton Fridays, I was left in no doubt that I was in the presence of very clever people indeed.

Some of them, despite their preoccupations, were to become my friends. I was meanwhile making friends in other institutions round which Princeton would have raised its skirts, the American service academies and colleges and the American armed forces. Oddly, the closest friend I made in that world was a Princeton graduate, John Guilmartin, who had not been happy there while he completed his doctorate, though I continue to think him one of the most creative military historians in the world; equally he had not been happy, though he was a combat helicopter pilot, at the U.S. Air Force Academy. Military history is a betwixt-and-between subject. I, as an outsider, enjoyed my forays into American military academe very much. It was, nevertheless, eyebrow-raising. Sandhurst, not exactly a university, not exactly a public school, partakes of the qualities of both, the intellectual liberalism of the former, the head prefect disciplines of the latter. The mixture does not seem available in the United States. There it is either Prussia or Parnassus. West Point prides itself on Prussianism—short haircuts, instant obedience. It provides the politest audiences in the world, but the lecturer feels his listeners' minds are on other things. Colorado Springs, the U.S. Air Force Academy, exudes, in a *Star Trek* setting, much the same atmosphere; I did not beam up many Scotties in the classes I taught there. At the war colleges, by contrast, the ambience is cerebral, quite as much so as at Harvard or Princeton. The Naval War College, at Newport, Rhode Island, is populated by visiting scholars of great eminence; the physical facts of warfare seem as remote as they certainly were from the nearby mansions, the famous fifty-room cottages, of America's late-Victorian leisure class. The staff colleges at Fort Leavenworth and Maxwell Air Force Base have become homes to schools of advanced military thinking, where the cleverest young officers of their class are left free for a year to read and to speculate; Prussia, perhaps, but Kant's Königsberg rather than the Kriegsakademie. Only at Annapolis, the naval cadet academy, cramped in its sylvan Ivy League setting on the banks of the Chesapeake, have the American armed forces managed to combine the liberal arts ideal with the rigours of training for the service life.

Rigorous American service life is. When I first joined the staff at

Sandhurst in 1960 the ethic of the officer as a gentleman occasionally in uniform prevailed. At lunchtime instructors and cadets alike changed into civilian clothes; a pupil who appeared at afternoon class in khaki would be asked to explain the reason. Hours were short, vacations long, the weeks of the summer term largely given over to cricket and sailing. I often spent days at a time in the magnificent library, browsing in its collections of history or biography, untroubled by either superiors or students. A Princeton friend who came to visit in the 1980s, when a more exacting regime had come into force, was still able to remark that I was leading the life of a country gentleman. I could not disagree. Squirearchy is not the American military way. Our West Point exchange officers were flabbergasted by our easy habits. "Goodbye Alice in Wonderland," said one of them to me on getting his return orders, "back to reality." Reality for American officers meant seven-o'clock starts, grabbed sandwiches, hours in the maintenance hangars swinging engines out of tanks, days "down range," and an all-pervading deference to higher rank. British officers did—still do—call each other by their Christian names; only commanding officers are accorded "sir." Colonels in America, I discovered when I first began to visit units, are "sirred" by majors, while generals' ears reverberate with sirrings, the susurrations of salutes, the sibilation, it sometimes seemed to me, of sycophancy. Authority in America is a strange thing; absent where it is so often present in English life, its human instruments, its legitimate exercise commands conformities and obeisances alien to us. English subordinates go through rituals of obeying without appearing to do so, superiors of exacting obedience without seeming to require it. Americans, so much less fettered than we in social and everyday life, obey ostentatiously, order obtrusively. Subordinates and superiors alike seem bound to the wheel, as if sensing that, in their enormous society and vast land, systems can be sustained in motion only by the most exaggerated utterance of yea and nay, I and thou, who whom.

The American services were having difficulty with "who whom?" when I first began to visit them. The Vietnam War was not long over. Indiscipline had ceased to plague, but the groundswell of doubt over why the war had been fought still swirled. Indeed, I ascribe the success of *The Face of Battle*, an enquiry into the origins of human failings before danger as well as of triumph over it, to the troubled self-enquiry of America in the post-Vietnam years. I had asked questions not usually put, not easy to answer in a country at odds with itself for the first time since the Civil War over a great national military purpose. My friend John Erickson, the master historian of Russia's resistance to Hitler, had found himself in the Cold War years invited by Soviet generals to pronounce on their problems, impartially they thought because his was an external voice. Lesser historian though I am, Americans accorded me a similar status. My opinion over "combat motivation" was sought, my responses accorded quite undeserved respect. Nevertheless, I could detect in the 1970s that all was not well. At Fort Carson, visiting a tank battalion, I noted that the commanding officer's clerk, seated in one chair, feet in another, did not rise when the colonel and I entered his office. He was delighted to see us and full of news; I could only think that in a British regiment he would have been quivering to attention at the sound of the colonel's footfall.

Over the next decade things changed. The dress and turnout of private soldiers recovered style and glitter, non-commissioned officers began again to stand apart, officers resumed the expectation of instant obedience. When in the mid-1980s I visited the 1st Infantry Division at Fort Riley, Kansas, I found an organisation of exact hierarchy, manifest purpose, pride in work. Every member, from staff officer to enlisted man, bristled with pleasure at the appearance of the commanding general, who had made himself my escort. They overflowed with eagerness to tell him what they were doing, emphasise commitment, listen for his word of approval. This was an army responding to the decision, taken by stalwarts like Norman Schwarzkopf after Vietnam, to persist with the institution and return it to its old traditions; when I came to interview him, then a civilian, after the Gulf War, he told me that his life's fulfillment had been to see the dispirited formations of the 1970s transformed into the relentlessly battle-winning elements of the expeditionary force that had secured victory in Kuwait.

The army was not the only institution of state I came to know over this period. The Marine Corps, unaffected by the Vietnam trauma, was another; struck as any Englishman would be by its Brigade of Guards ethos—lofty distance between ranks, complicity of sergeants and officers in the maintenance of unthinking discipline, easy-borne burden of countless battle honours—I fell into instant admiration. The uniforms helped; the Marines' dark khaki and black buttons combine the distinctions of our Guards and Rifle regiments respectively, with the difference that the Corps is larger than the whole British Army. It was an un-uniformed service, however, that I came to know best and to admire very greatly, the Central Intelligence Agency. Casually remarking one day to an American met at an academic conference that I thought "order of battle analysis"—the reconstruction from scraps of evidence of the organisation of armies—the most intriguing of all problems in military history, I received some months later an invitation to lecture at a CIA training course on the appropriate techniques. The lecture was a success and the invitation was repeated. When I next turned up at Langley it was to a more elaborate reception. The escorting officer who collected me at the airport told me that we would be going to the main building, not the training block; after I had completed some elaborate paperwork—the Agency seemed to know much about me already—I was let into the secret that the Director of Central Intelligence, then William Casey, had expressed a desire to meet me.

My escort set off confidently up a series of elevators and down anonymous corridors. After a while he was, I could see, flagging. We were on the wrong floor, then another wrong floor. There was embarrassed whispering with bypassers. Eventually, behind an anonymous door in another anonymous corridor, the director's office was run to earth. Some very large and fit-looking young men occupied the floor space of the antechamber. Much of the floor space of the room within, a modestly-sized, book-lined study, was occupied by the director himself. William Casey was—fatal disease already had him in its grip—a large man. He had an anomalously small voice and a habit of swallowing his words. Placed at the corner of his desk, I found myself edging forward to catch what he was saying. As a newspaperman, which I had then become, rather than as a writer of history, I had jumped to the conclusion that a scoop was in the offing—some confidence about the Russian campaign in Afghanistan, perhaps, or the progress of nuclear disarmament talks. In fact, when a senior subordinate joined us, there was a revelation—that America was supplying Stinger missiles to the Mujahidin—on which I should have jumped. By then, however, I was disoriented. The Director of Central Intelligence, I had at last identified, was talking to me as one historian to another. The purpose of our meeting was to discuss our common craft. What was my working technique? Did I write longhand or on to a word processor? Did I make a point of visiting the battlefields about which I wrote? I stumbled out answers as best I could. After a long passage of almost mutual incomprehension, the director rose to his feet, plucked a book from the shelves—it was to prove of the greatest value in composing some of the pages that follow—inscribed it ("with esteem and admiration for your writing"), and said, I presume, goodbye. In the corridor outside my escort had been joined by others I already knew. "What did he have to say?" they asked. "I'm not altogether sure," I answered, "I couldn't really understand." There was suppressed, insider laughter. I was looking at the book I had been given. It was entitled *Where and How the War Was Fought: An Armchair Tour of the American Revolution*, by William J. Casey. "We call him Mumbles," a member of the group commented, "the only man in Washington who doesn't need a secure telephone."

Casey's cover was clearly very deep indeed; a second identity as a historian is a le Carré-esque disguise of great sophistication. Oddly, when a year or two later I was met at the entrance to the Pentagon by an escort who told me that the Secretary of Defense had also expressed a desire to meet me, I found on entering Caspar Weinberger's office (what a contrast with Langley—vast space, colonial antiques, portraits of American military paladins at the door, cinquecento paintings lining the walls within) that he, too, wanted to talk about our common craft, writing history, the literary analysis of the trade of diplomacy; but by then I was attuned—and, anyhow, Caspar Weinberger enunciated our common language with exquisite clarity. I like the American Foreign Service very much and take great pleasure in the perpetuation by so many of its members of the Dean Acheson look and manner—neat moustaches, the slightly pained expression, an accent more Canadian than American. I continue to find, however, its sister intelligence service more interesting.

"Vietnam was our Raj," one of its old field hands once said to me. The CIA does indeed carry on the traditions of the Indian Political Service, the ethos of *Kim* and the Great Game. Whatever suspicions American libertarians maintain about the Agency, its officers are people of suavity, subtle understanding of remote but important parts of the world, urbane realism about the exercise of state power, high but underplayed patriotism. I have met the same set of qualities in American military men on detached duty, notably in a lean, brown colonel encountered in Lebanon at the height of the civil war, who spoke T. E. Lawrence Arabic and continued to brief me over a lunch of shish kebab and unleavened bread wholly unperturbed—as I was not—by a government battery firing howitzer shells over our heads into the mountains beyond Beirut. I met similar qualities in the local represen-

tative of the United States Information Service in Peshawar, on the
North-West Frontier, real *Kim* country; suffused by local culture, he
had arranged an evening of Pushtu folk-singing to entertain us and had
chosen as principal performer the English wife of an Oxford ethnomu-
sicologist whose high break notes reduced his Pakistani guests to exha-
lations of appreciation. Old Raj, new Raj; I sat beside a cavalry officer
who was delighted I remembered that his regiment had once been
Fane's Horse. The significance of the evening was that an American
mediated between empire and independence.

Mediation between the old power of the Anglo-Saxon world and
the new is the CIA's calling. It has assumed the mantle once worn by
Kim's masters as if it were a seamless garment. American politicians
may waffle and Washington civil servants choke on their worries about
reconfirmation by an incoming administration. The tenured ranks of
the republic's professional intelligence officers continue to learn difficult languages, deal in the history of minority peoples, delve into fac-
tion, sect, and subculture, dissect the dangerous foreign policies of
dissident states, discuss the way the world works in a spirit of detached
realism some dying echo of which I had caught in youth among the
dwindling servants of the British world system on which the sun was
then setting. Theirs is an urbane and sophisticated service, closer in
spirit to the higher bureaucracies of the old European powers than
any other body I know in the United States. It is not surprising that
it attracts the suspicions of populists, anti-Washington politicians,
and, above all, investigative journalists. The ethos of American journalism—disrespectful, hypercritical, self-confident—is one of the most
potent gifts the republic has transmitted to the European world. The
spirit in which its pioneers—Martha Gellhorn, John Hershey, Theodore
White, the *ciné-vérité* photographer Robert Capa—set out in the 1930s
to unmask the wickedness of dictators and demagogues in the un-
Rooseveltian outside, the deviousness of its diplomatists and secret services, has taken root, particularly in the United Kingdom, a country
still distinguished by the uncorruptness of its public life. Imputation of
corruption, of executive excess, has become a reflex action here. It has
bled back into the reporting of government activity in the land of irrev-
erent journalism's origins, threatening to render the execution of national policy so difficult as to make the effort scarcely worth an elected
politician's while.

What is admirable about the CIA, as it is about the State Department and the armed services, is that it persists in its task and holds to its standards, despite the dirt thrown at it. Foremost among those standards is an intellectual and academic approach to the eternal problem faced by a dominant civilisation of exercising power in the world. Power tends to corrupt individuals; civilisations are prone to corruption also. American civilisation by its essence finds the exercise of power profoundly antipathetic and is consequently drawn to a blundering, clumsy, and over-violent response when its vital interests are threatened. Unchecked, unguided, America has always risked being a Cyclops in world affairs, a blinded giant striking wildly at cunning outsiders. High-minded public servants—George Marshall and Dean Acheson are exemplars—have succeeded in the era of American world power in constraining and directing such impulses; but they could not have succeeded had they acted alone. American public service—that of its regular officers, career diplomatists, professional intelligence analysts—has supplied an essential underpinning. America undervalues their patriotism and dedication, wisdom, and intellectuality. I have learnt not to do so.

An Evening with the President

Becoming a newspaperman after a lifetime as an academic historian, I found my American acquaintanceship widened. My newspaper encouraged me to seek interviews with high officials of state, and their familiarity with my books facilitated, to my surprise, the arrangement of personal meetings. In this way I met William Casey's successor as Director of Central Intelligence, two Supreme Allied Commanders Europe, several Ambassadors to the Court of St. James's, two Secretaries of Defense, a Chairman of the Joint Chiefs of Staff, an Army and an Air Force Chief of Staff—and Henry Kissinger. "Like meeting Metternich," I remember saying to a colleague who asked me about the encounter. It was an off-the-cuff answer but accurate none the less. So many notables are uninteresting in the flesh, uncommunicative or preoccupied or patronising. Henry Kissinger was none of those things. Committed though he was to take an aeroplane in an hour or two's time, he devoted breakfast in a grand London hotel to witty characterisations of other world statesmen, reflection on the problems of war and peace, courteous dissection of my own views on the subject. Acolytes hovered, room servants announced taxis at the door. Kissinger withdrew to a sofa, installed me in another, introduced the Congress of Vienna, embarked on an analysis of the Reagan–Gorbachev summit in Reykjavik. "What a wonderful man," the concierge breathed as we finally slippered him into a car for Heathrow. I was too breathless to assent.

I suppose, had it not been for this gradual initiation, that I might have timorously declined the invitation to meet the greatest of America's public officials when it eventually came my way. Most of us are modest enough to recognise that we have little to say of interest or importance in the wider world; I, except as a military historian, have never thought my opinion on anything worth tuppence. Military history, moreover, is an antiquarian calling; however its practitioners flatter themselves to the contrary, it impinges little on the real world. It helped me to predict, accurately, the outcome of the Gulf War; I did not think that my familiarity with battles long ago would prove of contemporary applicability again. In the spring of 1994, however, military historians suddenly found themselves courted by the media and governments. The great public event of the year was to be the commemoration of the invasion of Europe fifty years earlier. Anyone who had written about the subject—as fortuitously I had—was in demand. I signed up for a raft of articles in British and American journals. Late in May a former editor of an American magazine on whose masthead I appear telephoned to enquire whether I planned shortly to be in Washington. I suppose I could be, I answered; why? The President, he explained, was convening a conference of Second World War historians in the White House to acquaint him with the outlines of the campaign and also to suggest to him appropriate messages to transmit to the participant countries. I would, I said rapidly, be there. He could count on me.

I had been inside the White House once before, as a tourist in 1957, when Washington was an empty city and queues short. A vague memory of stuffy rooms and clumsy furniture lingered. I remembered better crossing the Mall and climbing by the internal staircase to the top of the Washington Memorial, a feat of Alpinism which would be quite beyond me today. I did not know what to expect. We would, I was told, each speak to the President for five minutes, answer questions, and then dine with him. The arrival at journey's end had a familiar routine, a student escort, a chauffeur-driven car; but the student was a White House intern, bubbling with excitement at learning his political science on the hoof, the chauffeur a Transportation Corps sergeant in sober plain clothes. He dropped me at my hotel and said he would be back. At the dinner hour he reappeared: "We shall be going to the Diplomatic Entrance." The White House is an island of tranquillity inside Washington's bustle. Beyond the railings and the power-operated gates one might be in the gardens of a great Southern plantation house, cut off by rose arbours and ornamental groves from the world outside. Once admitted, moreover, one is made to feel a guest, not a visitor. At 10 Downing Street, on party evenings, the throng passes one by one through an electronic scanner and pockets are emptied for policemen. At the White House a charming girl told me that I would find the others at the end of the hall; "you'll hear voices." I wandered away through a succession of corridors, past the open doorways to rooms of perfectly arranged and exquisite furniture—Jackie Kennedy's hand, I thought to myself—all dusted and polished a moment before, and found some grave, greying, black, tail-coated footmen offering iced tea outside the theatre in which the President would hear us.

Inside were some familiar faces: Paul Fussell, the great cultural historian of the Anglo-American war experience; Carlo d'Este, master of the documentation of the Normandy campaign; Stephen Ambrose, biographer of Eisenhower; Forrest Pogue, the official historian who interviewed wounded survivors of Omaha Beach offshore on hospital ships in the evening of D-Day; General Hal Nelson, U.S. Army Chief of Military History. They and I were the briefing team. Among the other guests I knew was General Andrew Goodpaster, a former Supreme Allied Commander, an incarnation to me of the George Marshall world of high-minded public service; as a young colonel, convalescing from wounds suffered in Italy, he had served both Marshall and Stimson, the Secretary of War, as confidential secretary. General John Eisenhower, Ike's son, a distinguished military historian himself, was there; we had met a few months earlier in Washington. There were other faces I recognised without knowing their owners: Warren Christopher, the Secretary of State, Lloyd Bentsen, the Secretary of the Treasury. I felt in a slight blur. It was suddenly borne in on me that I was the only non-American present in a gathering of the great republic's establishment; and we were waiting for the President.

There was a delay. The President was detained at a meeting, dis-

cussing most-favoured nation status for China. Conversation buzzed
on; I was surprised by the absence of unease. British subjects in Buck-
ingham Palace are on stiff best behaviour; these American citizens in
the Executive Mansion were courteously relaxed. There was no stir
when the President entered; hands were shaken; "Thank you for
making the long trip," he said to me; we settled down to work. The
historians sat on a row of fragile, gold chairs facing the President; he
balanced a notebook on the arm of his seat and took notes relentlessly.
Abstractedly I observed that he is left-handed. Maps were arranged on
an easel, sequences of events described. I had been told I would be the
last to speak. I wondered what to say. Gradually it dawned on me that
my American colleagues were not simply making presentations. They
were also telling the President what he should say in the speeches he
would have to make when he visited Europe ten days hence. He must
remember to emphasise the contribution of the French Resistance. He
must allude to Italy's co-belligerency. He must pave the way—even
though the Germans had not been invited—for the reconciliation
which would be the theme of the 1995 commemorations of the end of
the war. "The Germans suffered, too," repeated several speakers. You
weren't bombed by the Luftwaffe, I thought, and bit my tongue; but
when my turn came I found the words I wanted. "Remember the
Canadian contribution," I said—I know how overlooked Canadians
feel, when the capture of one of the five D-Day beaches was wholly
their achievement; "Remember the Poles"—it was they who plugged
the Falaise Gap; most heartfelt of all, recalling my childhood, "Remember that the British date the making of the great alliance to the
coming of the GIs." My generation does not forget. You do not need
to remind us of what America did. We know and we shall be grateful
to our graves.

"I've kept you too long," said the President. He led us upstairs to
dinner. China so beautiful I scarcely dared put knife to plate, presenta-
tional cuisine, almost invisible service; not long before I had been a
guest at a similar evening in a British royal palace and reflected on the
differences. There is a certain knockabout quality to palace life, old re-
tainers grown saucily familiar, odd bits of obsolete serving equipment
parked in corners, polished silver boxes full of spent matches, beautiful
liveries but shabby shoes. The Prince Consort noted the deficiencies
when he married the young Victoria. The White House is like the
grandest of grand hotels, in which the major domo pounces unforgiv-

ingly on the slightest failing by kitchen or waiters. The President is co-
cooned by perfection. He is not, however, allowed to think for one moment that he is royal. Head of State he may be, but his fellow citizens
speak their minds directly and unaffectedly. At my palace evening the
guests spoke hesitantly and into the middle distance. In the White
House the President's guests addressed him over dinner face-to-face,
and made polemical points. A senior congressman who had fought for
his country warned him that America's place in the world rested on its
possession of preponderant military force. A former commanding general emphasised that the armed services require recruitment from the
country's best. An old Washington power-broker dismissed the idea of
interdependence as an American alliance policy and declared that there
is no substitute for leadership.

I was, I realised, present at an occasion when the American voice
makes the American mind unequivocally clear to the chief of the nation. I could imagine no similar occasion in England. We defer, not
only to our hereditary but also to our elected leaders; collectively, we
are as independent and as difficult to govern as any people on earth; individually, we shuffle and stumble our words and bob our heads and
hope we have not broken any of the rules. There are no rules between
Americans, except those of the common politeness that ought to govern free people. I love America. I have long wondered and tried to explain why, most of all to myself. After my evening with the President, I
grasped a little more of the answer. The Americans are truly free and
equal people. It was I who had "sirred" and "Mr. Presidented" in a reflex of the manner I would have used at home. The Americans had
"Mr. Presidented" also, but as the preliminary to statements of what he
ought to say, what he ought to think. I had been listening to a process
of the making of policy, not much different, perhaps, from the process
that had made the Constitution at Philadelphia in 1787. The stakes, of
course, were of an altogether lower order. The temper of the meeting
cannot have been much dissimilar. I had seen the President as a first
among equals, a relationship which is the essence of the American political system. I went back to England—followed by a signed letter of
thanks so charming that I framed it to hang on my study wall—pondering even deeper on the differences between monarchy and republic.

War is at the root of the differences between American republic
and British monarchy. The British state, for centuries the most centralised in the world, was made by conquest. The Roman conquerors

made Britannia, the Anglo-Saxons first broke, then rebuilt it, the Normans inherited it by force of arms. Their England, which nature had placed athwart the sea entrances to Northern Europe, never ceased to be at war with its neighbours thereafter and the dynasties that succeeded them sustained the struggle, forever seeking to exploit the maritime advantages that fine harbours and strategic position bequeathed them. The English, in a warlike continent, became an exceedingly bellicose people, who would not rest until they had incorporated the rest of their archipelago—Wales, Scotland, Ireland—into their polity. Meanwhile they were extending the tentacles of their maritime power into the surrounding seas, the Channel, the North Sea, sometimes the Baltic, eventually the Mediterranean, and then the great oceans. Fortified footholds of British power began to appear on coasts far from home. While the interior of the home islands was decastellated—English kings were the most ruthless in Europe in slighting the strongholds of over-mighty subjects, so that by the sixteenth century the only castles that counted were royal castles—British forts were springing up in the islands of the West Indies, on the coasts of the New World, in Africa and India and the Mediterranean. Fortifications bristled along British coasts also; a people who had chosen to take the world as its empire could not afford to leave their best harbours unguarded when the fleet was sent to roam great waters.

A people numerically weak who challenge the world bind themselves with heavy chains, oppressive taxation, protectionist and costly tariffs, the cruelties of the press gang, fierce treason laws. They bind themselves thereby to relentless political continuities. A war-making people cannot afford revolution. The English may have killed a king and founded a parliamentary democracy; but the warlord who sent the King to the scaffold became a sort of king himself and the parliament he used as an instrument of his power arrogated executive power to itself when he was gone. English monarchy survived and became British monarchy because it served British purposes, as a focus of popular loyalties but also as a vessel of the national will. The British may bob their heads and bite their tongues; but through the symbolism of crown and sceptre they ground away century after century at carrying the ethic of conquest that had constructed their state to half the world: India, Arabia, the East Indies, the South Seas, Africa from Cairo to the Cape— even in my boyhood that was where the flag flew. The pincers of the trading forts the British had bult at Calcutta and Madras had closed on the Mogul Empire; from the citadels of Malta and Gibraltar they had made the Mediterranean a British *mare nostrum*; the fortified coaling stations of the Gulf and the Red Sea had subdued the dhow kingdoms to their power; slave castles on the fever coast had made them masters of the African west and then the east also; captured Dutch forts had given them the Cape; bastions and redoubts had assured anchorages for the White Ensign from Singapore to Hong Kong. British ships, British cannon, British castellation commanded half the globe. The British crown was the symbol of all these outposts; British power was the substance.

America was the exception in the pattern, the blank space on the map where British forts did not stand. We all know why. The Americans had escaped from the engirdlement of British power. They had no desire, moreover, to engirdle others. Jefferson, at his inauguration as President in 1801, had set out the national ethic, utterly at odds with that which had made Britain a power to be reckoned with wherever ships could carry cannon: "Peace, commerce and honest friendship with all nations; entangling alliances with none"; he might have added, "No fort-building either." The young United States not only eschewed all idea of overseas involvement. Its first act of major public expenditure, already undertaken before Jefferson's election, was to wall itself in against the outside world. The Monroe Doctrine—which, paradoxically, would draw on British naval power to define its separation from the bad Old World—lay in the future. Meanwhile Washington was raising the money to build huge coastal fortresses, at the mouths of the Chesapeake and the Hudson and off the Gulf Coast, whose purpose was to proclaim that the United States was a land apart. Jefferson's successors were to ram the message home, through the extension of a chain of fortifications around the whole periphery of the United States, from the Great Lakes to the Mississippi to the Bay of San Francisco; Alcatraz, before becoming home to America's most dangerous Federal criminals, was a link in the republic's Third System of coastal defences. Within the enceinte, the United States was intended to go its untroubled way, taking its laws from elected representatives, submitting their interpretation to an independent judiciary, and accepting leadership from a Head of State whose least responsibility was to declare or conduct foreign wars. A greater difference between its national philosophy and that of the belligerent transatlantic monarchy with which it had severed the umbilical cord in 1783 cannot be imagined. Britain, retiring to lick the wound of the loss of its first empire, would shortly embark on the conquest of a second; within a century it would add the Emperorship of India to the titles of its crown. The United States, kingless, lawful, peace-loving, would retire inside its continental frontiers to construct a new sort of civilisation.

So no forts abroad, no forts in the interior for those dissenting from the Declaration of Independence and the Constitution. Yet America is full of forts, Fort Worth, Fort Lauderdale, Fort Myers, Fort Smith, Fort Wayne—these are outposts that have grown into international or regional airports. Then there are the great military posts of the interior, Fort Sill, Fort Dix, Fort Knox, Fort Riley, Fort Carson, Fort Bragg. There are forts that have faded away altogether or been lost beneath city streets—who could find Fort Duquesne under the Pittsburgh Triangle? There are forts once important which have become backwaters, suburbs, or townships—Forts Adams, Clark, Cobb, Collins, Davis, Dodge, Fisher, Gaines, Garland, Thomas, Towson, scattered between North Dakota and Oklahoma. There are forts which are now but names in history books, Fort Carillon, Fort Necessity. What were they for, why do some still exist, why have some—perhaps the vast majority—gone back to forest or grass?

The answer is that, though the Founding Fathers may have wanted to wall off their American world from the rest of the globe, Americans could only begin to make the interior of the continent their own by repeating within it exactly the same process of step-by-step fortification of key points through which Britain had made an empire around the oceans of the world. The interior of America might, in one sense, be seen as an ocean in its own right, an ocean of forest, of grass, of desert, through which navigable ways had to be found and, once found, secured and fortified. Many of those ways had been found before the Declaration of Independence and many forts built. Indeed, almost the first thing done by Jacques Cartier in 1536, when he found the estuary of the St. Lawrence, the "great highway into the continent," was to build a fort under the headland on which his successors would construct the citadel of Quebec. The Dutch, the Swedes, and the English would pepper the coasts, inlets, and estuaries of the Hudson and Chesapeake with forts during the century of their struggle to win dominance over the Northeast, and their settlers would fortify, against the French, the Indians, and each other, further inland. The French fortified on a continental scale, down the St. Lawrence, around the Great Lakes, into the Northwest, up to Hudson Bay—where the English fortified also—in the Ohio and Illinois country, and down the Mississippi. By the end of the French and Indian Wars of 1756–63, North America was one of the most fortified regions of the world, and the number of forts was added to by the British and Americans in the revolutionary war that followed. Such forts as were useful—they guarded portages, landing places, isthmuses, narrows, mountain passes, harbours—and remained from earlier stages of conquest, discovery, and exploitation were incorporated by the United States into its military infrastructure; those at West Point, for example, which had denied the narrows of the Hudson to the British, became the site of the military academy; others were abandoned or survived only because they became—as Fort Pitt (Pittsburgh) did at the Forks of the Ohio—a focus for town-building.

Even with the incorporation of the most important forts, however, the United States still had much fort-building to accomplish if the interior were to be secured—against British Canada, Spanish America, and, above all, the native Americans. The young United States built forts in the "Old Northwest"—the country between the Appalachians, the Mississippi, and the Tennessee; it built forts along the Mississippi and up the Missouri; by mid-century it was building forts along the Platte and the Kansas rivers in the Rocky Mountains, in the desert, and on the Pacific coast. Some were government forts, some those of trappers and traders; the difference between the two was not always sustainable: Fort Laramie, for example, which began as a trading post, eventually became one of the most important centres of government power in Indian territory during the era of settlement beyond the Mississippi.

Over forty years my travels in the United States and Canada have taken me to many of these places. The network they form within the geography of North America—overlaid though it now largely is by the network of modern roads and airline routes—is an essential key to the understanding of its natural barriers and highways and so to the military and thus the human geography of the continent. Chance was to make the continent home to mankind's most elaborate and sustained effort to found a revolutionary civilisation, based on philosophical principle, freed by distance and inaccessibility from external interference with its process of development. No one interested in mankind's history can ignore that of America. To me, a military historian, the pattern of fortification that human settlement has left since Europeans first began to venture inland from North America's coasts four hundred and fifty years ago is a cipher to the American mystery. Forts mark the footsteps of the human venture into the interior—French forts the endeavour by a European kingdom to win an empire in the New World without settling it with people, English forts the strategy of another European kingdom to create an alternative empire by sea power, American forts the piecemeal and often conscience-stricken attempt to accord native Americans their rights to historic territory while making room for the millions of non-native Americans who sought space for a new life far from the Old World.

For me nothing better epitomises the conflict between the ideals of the United States and the history of North America than the constructions that crown Liberty Island in New York harbour. Topmost stands the Statue of Liberty, given by France, the losing power in the struggle for the continent, to its sister republic at the moment when the United States was about to overtake Britain, the victor, as the dominant state in the world's economic system. On the base of the statue the visitor can read Emma Lazarus's words—"Give me your tired, your poor, / Your huddled masses yearning to breathe free, / The wretched refuse of your teeming shore. / Send these, the homeless, tempest-tost to me"— which have become an unofficial poetic expression of the American dream. Beneath the base of the statue the visitor may also notice the distinctive star-shaped bastions of a fort. These are the traces of Fort Wood, built under the United States' Second System of coastal fortification of 1807–12, on what was then known as Bedloe's Island, to defend the harbour against the Royal Navy. The fort was adapted to be the foundations of the Statue of Liberty when it was erected in 1885, but remained a military station until 1937. Throughout the period when nearby Ellis Island, also fortified as part of the Second System, was receiving up to a million immigrants a year, therefore, the symbol which had drawn them, tempest-tost, from the teeming shore of the Old World was still a link in the fortification chain designed to hold the Old World at arm's length. Here is a paradox between the idea of openness and the practice of seclusion, between free settlement and state power. North America is a land for everyone; it is also a land where the strongest do best. That, I suppose, is the theme of this book.

T W O

....

The Forts
of New France

I CAME TO THE OLD CITY of Quebec for the first time on a bitter
December day, and I am glad that I did; for who can understand
Canada who has not flinched from the searing cold of its winter?
No one from temperate Europe experiences at home the ache of that
frigidity, the pain that penetrates the inner ear, the burden of fatigue
that loss of heat lays so quickly on the body, the longing for shelter
that comes after only a few minutes in the open. I had felt winter extremes before—in northern Norway, on the Great Plains—but never
had I known a cold which the flesh tells the mind will kill if it gets the
chance, a message the mind believes with total conviction, for it can
think of nothing else.

This was not the Canada I had known on earlier journeys, to the
Great Lakes and the Pacific Coast, in spring or summer or fall. It was
other things which had left an impression then—space, first of all. I remember a flight across the whole width of the country, from Vancouver
to Calgary and then to the Atlantic Coast in brilliant sunshine on a
homeward journey in 1983. Our route took us across the Rockies, but
it is not the peaks but the plains beyond that stay in the memory: the
geometric division of the prairies, the isolation of the scattered settlements, the Calgary skyscrapers rising from the infinity like seastacks in
an ocean of grass, the relentless, undifferentiated, eastward progress
terminated in the senses only by the fall of night as we flew from the
setting sun. Water, too; its scintillation among the pattern of islands in
the Strait of Georgia on seaplane flights from Vancouver to Victoria in
British Columbia, its leaden heaviness at the shores of the Great Lakes,

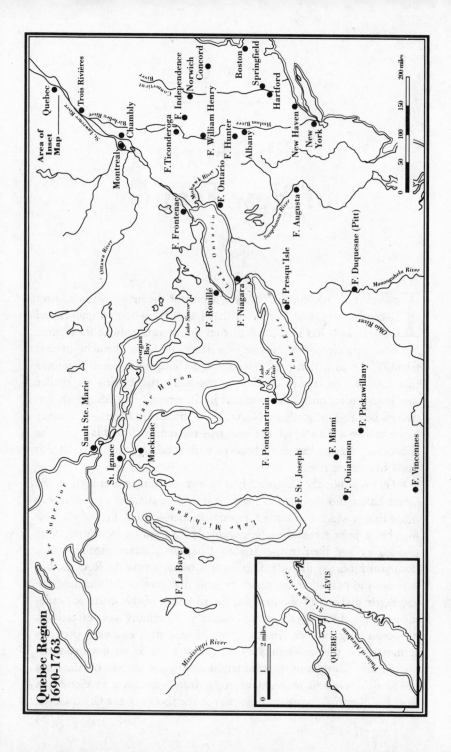

Quebec Region
1690–1763

Area of Inset Map

Trois Rivières

St. Lawrence River

Montreal

Chambly

Richelieu River

Ottawa River

F. Ticonderoga

F. Frontenac

F. Rouillé

Lake Simcoe

F. Niagara

Lake Ontario

Mohawk River

F. Ontario

F. Hunter

Albany

F. William Henry

F. Independence
Norwich
Concord

Connecticut River

Boston
Springfield
Hartford

Hudson River

New Haven

New York

Susquehanna River

F. Augusta

F. Presqu'Isle

Ohio River

F. Duquesne (Pitt)

Monongahela River

Lake Erie

Lake St. Clair

F. Pontchartrain

Georgian Bay

Lake Huron

Sault Ste. Marie

St. Ignace

Mackinac

F. St. Joseph

F. Miami

F. Ouiatanon

F. Pickawillany

F. Vincennes

Lake Superior

Lake Michigan

F. La Baye

Mississippi River

200 miles
150
100
50
0

QUEBEC

LÉVIS

St. Lawrence

Plains of Abraham

2 miles

1

0

its mindless spendthrift outpouring over Niagara, its universal permeation of the topsoil as the return of spring brings the snowmelt and the thaw to the inhabited regions. The plenitude of timber also strikes a European traveller. Wood, in Europe, is a scarce commodity and forest zones protected areas; trees in Canada grow like weeds and seem as little cared for, gathered lumber waiting in heaps for disintegration in the pulp mills, while the trunks of forest giants which have escaped from log rafts litter the shorelines of lakes, rivers, and islands.

This is a rich land; it is also an engaging one. The Canadian voice strikes the untuned English ear as so distinctively "American" that the British take little care to distinguish their Commonwealth fellow citizens from those of the Great Republic to the south; the easy consonants and slow cadences incorporate Canadians with Americans through an aural blur. Acquaintance sharpens the difference. The United States is a tough country, where the individual must shift for himself; I have discovered that in a series of painful lessons. Canada— British Canada at least—is gentler altogether, gentler in speech, in manners, in bureaucracy, in personal relationships. It is, underneath the North American accent and stripped of the superficialities of American cars, architecture, and clothes, a very English country, as English as Australia, without Australian irreverence, or sharpness of tongue, or readiness to take offence, a sort of Atlantic New Zealand in its concern for social welfare, legal propriety, electoral equality, and women's rights; the charm and self-confidence of Canadian women is the best of all advertisements for the decency of their country. With a little exposure, the British can feel quite at home in Canada, and those who make the transition find themselves quick—as I am—to rebut the lazy judgement that it is dull or provincial or imitative or characterless.

There is no lazy judgement to be made about French Canada, that vibrant, prickly, and separatist enclave of French civilisation in an Anglo-Saxon world, any more than there is about Dutch South Africa, a society to which it bears in certain fundamentals a striking resemblance. True, the French Canadians are not a minority isolated among peoples of a different race. They are of the same ethnic origin as the white majority in the rest of the North American continent and of the same European culture. Like the Afrikaners, however, they speak a minority language, brought from Europe but now spoken in a distinctively local form; like them, they are separated politically from the kingdom which planted their ancestors in what is now their homeland three centuries ago; like them, too, they have developed a distinctive way of life which is felt to lie under threat of extinction by pressure of preponderant and surrounding numbers. The most nationalistic Afrikaners currently agitate for their own *Volkstaat* in the heartland of their zone of historic settlement. French Canada is already such a national state, whose extreme nationalists seek to erect it as a sovereign polity, even at the expense of destroying the federal system which gives the whole of Canada its economic coherence. Whatever may be said—fairly or unfairly—about the rest, French Canada is almost too full of character for comfort.

How full may be grasped in a few minutes' walking within the walls of the old city of Quebec. There are other nuclear cities in the world into which are packed the whole record and chosen symbolism of their history: Vienna inside the Ring, Istanbul between the Blue Mosque and St. Sophia and the Topkapi. Quebec preserves the legend and the institutions of the settlement, and its development, and its tragic fall, in an almost unique intensity. Cheek by jowl stand the statues of Samuel de Champlain, French Canada's heroic founder, Montmorency, its dynamic military champion against English America, and Bishop François de Laval, architect of the dominance of the Roman Church over New France; nearly wall-to-wall rise the buildings which defined the mission of France in the New World from the outset, the basilica of Notre-Dame, the Convent of the Ursulines and the Seminary of Quebec. Rebuilt in later or modern form are the hospital of the Hôtel-Dieu and the Citadel, the whole surrounded by the ramparts and bastions of the city walls, much nineteenth-century British work but parts still surviving from the years when the outpost of Quebec challenged the power of Britain with that of France for control of the American heartland. Also within the walls, beside the extraordinary fantasy of the Château Frontenac, rises the monument to Wolfe and Montcalm, while immediately outside the city gates extends the battlefield of the Plains of Abraham, where, on 13 September 1759, each general received his fatal wound, the first to die the victor of the decisive American conflict between the two empires, the second to achieve apotheosis as the martyr of the French defeat.

Defeat did not rob Quebec of its Frenchness; despite the intrusion of some modern buildings and the architectural reminders of the British conquest—extraordinarily akin in style to the monuments of British rule found as far away as Sydney or Calcutta or Corfu—Quebec remains a distinctively French place. Its narrow streets and shuttered, agoraphobic housefronts are those of a provincial town in any of the provinces from which Quebec's settlers originated—Aunis, Normandy, Perche, Poitou—familiar to me from my boyhood explorations of the country immediately across the English Channel. As a schoolboy I walked streets exactly like these in the Vexin and the Ile-de-France, trod the same uneven cobbles, sniffed the same unfamiliar street smells, paused to decipher the same baffling street signs—rue St.-Angélo, des Grison, Dauphine, Côte de la Citadelle, de la Fabrique, de la Montagne, Avenue Ste.-Geneviève, Avenue St.-Denis—stopped to peer into the same puzzlingly foreign shopfronts or to perceive nothing at all through the same impenetrably curtained parlour windows. There is, to an un-French European, a comforting foreignness about old Quebec, an architecture and atmosphere which bring a sense of being away from home in the Old World, not in the infinitely more alien New World of the English-speaking states and provinces. New France, old France: to an Englishman, but also, I am sure, to a German or a Spaniard or an Italian, the distance which separates the two seems insignificant. Quebec within the walls is a place in which he instantly picks up his European bearings.

It is not only the material surroundings which impart a distinct Frenchness. So, too, do the people and the way they live their city life. The Librairie Garneau is, with its jumble of tawdry paperbacks and obscure scholarly works, exactly the sort of bookshop to be found in the shopping streets of any French provincial centre, while the interior of the Café de Paris, tucked away in a corner off the rue St.-Louis, uncannily resembles that of my favourite Parisian restaurant, Chez Paul, in the Place Dauphine on the Ile de la Cité; there is the same grained woodwork under a low ceiling, the same back-to-backness at table, the same choice of dishes—*tête de boeuf, rognons à l'estragon*—the same cheery ease between regular customers and patron, the same sense of devotion to food, as one of the good things of life, by all parties to its arrival on the plate. I had taken refuge in the Café de Paris from the blizzard threatening outside; in an instant I found myself transported thirty years back in time to the Place Dauphine, where my wife and I had dined at Chez Paul on one of our honeymoon nights.

Most strikingly, the inhabitants of New France look and sound as French as their fellow Francophones of the modern Fifth Republic. The American face is not European; something has happened in the United

States to alter its contours and colouring. The French Canadian face, by contrast, is as French as that of the boy in the next desk to me at the Ecole St.-Martin at Pontoise in 1951, of my elder son's godfather, once a *capitaine de chasseurs à pied*, now a *général de brigade*, of our infant children's *jeune fille au pair*, of the matriarch in whose house I first underwent the English—and French—summer ritual of the holiday exchange. The voices I recognise instantly also; not the accent, for that is even more reverberating than the regional dialect of the Indre, where I strained as hard to understand as to be understood throughout a long summer in 1952; it is the rhythm and turn of phrase to which I reflexively respond. *"C'est terminé?"* asks the waitress at the end of breakfast; *"Monsieur désire quelque chose d'autre?"* enquires the motherly proprietress of the café-bar in the shadow of the Château Frontenac; this is the patois of the eating place from Calais to Cannes. In the United States I comprehend automatically what is said to me by waiters, taxi-drivers, sales ladies, airline agents, but there is a momentary desynchronisation as I translate the form of words into its British equivalent. In French Canada, once I have reaccustomed myself to speak its language, reception and transmission fall into well-travelled grooves. My over-grammatical diction may disconcert the listener, but in return is a reassuring reminder of dozens of visits to the France of my youth.

Of course, it is a help that the France I remember is not the new— the France of advanced industry or international business or European Community politics—but the old, the France of the remote countryside, the Church, and the army. It was at a Catholic boarding school, on manorial estates, and at the Ecole Spéciale Militaire de St.-Cyr that my early acquaintance with France was made. Such an acquaintance is the best of all introductions to French Canada, a land settled from exactly those rural areas I know well—Normandy in particular, but also Aunis at the mouth of the Charente—and dominated, for as long as it was a French possession, by priests and soldiers. The romance of the French penetration of the American continent may belong with the *coureurs de bois* and *voyageurs*, the gatherers of furs whose canoes took them as far as the waterways of the Great Plains by the middle of the seventeenth century, but the structure rested on the missionary labours of the men in black robes—Jesuits and Récollets—and the services of the military officers, particularly those of the Régiment de la Marine, specifically raised for duty in France beyond the seas. My first

months in France were spent in the care of men in black robes, priests
of the Oratory, while I continue to know officers of the Troupes de
Marine to this day. The anchor badge of the *marsouins* and *bigors*, as
the French army's slang denotes its amphibious infantrymen and can-
noneers, recalls a succession of great conquests and tiny wars fought
the length of the coasts of Africa, Asia, and America from the seventeenth century up to the present.

So I feel, if not exactly at home in French Canada, then at least
that I know where I am; and it brings back memories, most of them
warm and all compelling, since France was the first foreign country I
came to know and any first experience of otherness—the otherness of
people who are not the family, surroundings which are not home,
speech which is not the mother tongue, habits which are not native—
leaves an indelible impression. Indelible to me are the memories of my
first venture by packet steamer across the English Channel to join a
very un-English steam train that took me to the wholly un-English
Gare St.-Lazare, where, amid a throng of fussily homeward-bound
commuters, none resembling any social type I could identify from
home, I sought out the friend of a friend who was to put me on to the
suburban train from Paris to school. He was a nice young man who
bought me a glass of beer I suspected he could not afford and then
steered me through a platoon of dazed-looking Algerian riflemen with
the star and crescent on their collars to find the platform for Conflans
St.-Honoré and Pontoise and a seat in a compartment filled with ladies
in black, shopgirls in startling make-up, aloof schoolboys in knicker-
bockers, and a babble of urgent conversation I could not understand
at all.

These were the first of many train journeys in France, one most notably—for it was taking me to a region not much changed since the
days when the settlement of Canada had begun—that carried me in
midsummer of the following year across the enormous wheatfields of
the Beauce, the sweep of the Loire, and the lake-studded woodlands of
the Sologne to a tiny halt in the very heart of France. I arrived in the
warm dusk to be put into a rattletrap car and driven to a decaying little
château on the outskirts of something that was not quite a town but
rather more than a village and unmistakably akin to the setting of
Jacques Tati's *Jour de Fête*, that poignant little comedy of rustic revel
which had entranced English foreign cinemagoers the previous season.

Jour de Fête had been made only four years earlier in a village no distance from La Boutinière, but I am glad that I did not know this then, for I might have spoilt my pleasure in it by reproaching Tati with what he had left out. There was even more to the life of a village in the Indre in the early 1950s than he had conjured up, a moreness derived from an antiquity of habit and routine and relationship perhaps taken too much for granted by a Frenchman, as Tati was, to be perceived by him, but perceived by an English schoolboy abroad for the first time—I could not really count a French boarding school run on English public-school lines as abroad—with intense fascination. Tati's device in the film is to use the depiction of American dynamism in a documentary shown at the fair's travelling cinema as a counterpoint to the villagers' grumpy mistrust of anything that threatened the skinflint, wine-bibbing, old-shoe lethargy of their accustomed ways. They accept the documentary as a form of reality, but it is a reality they do not want, and, as the travelling fair packs up to take its sensations to a neigh-bouring, identical backwater, they relapse untouched into an ancient timetable of activity—and inactivity—fixed by the harvest, the *ven-dange,* and the next annual *jour de fête.*

The routines of La Boutinière and its nearby village were, by chance, interrupted during the summer I spent there by just the sort of American intrusion that Tati had contrived in his film. The château was too big for its occupants—a widow and her spinster daughter—and, moreover, the income of the estate was too small to support its expense, which was why they had taken in an English schoolboy as a paying guest. As I paid little and occupied only a remote attic, the chatelaine had also decided to take in two American officers posted to build a NATO base nearby, their wives, and their impediments, which included two cars bigger than any ever driven in the district, refrigerators—heard of but never seen—and a washing machine, which was a wonder not even imagined. The installation of the Americans entailed upsets unknown in the history of the château: puzzled plumbers and electricians were summoned to run pipes or wires into rooms where nature denied they were needed; offence was taken at the implication that a single bathroom would no longer suffice; the improvisation of a second, but not a third, kitchen provoked an outbreak of domestic warfare between the American ladies. Reluctantly they conceded that servants might be a solution, and a succession of blushing, stumble-tongued, pinafored farmers' daughters were engaged. Their and their employers' ideas of how a house should be run proved so wholly at

variance that none lasted; one departed the evening she arrived, overcome by a dry martini she had been offered in welcome.

On the other side of the house, life unrolled day by day as un-
changingly as it had done since the family had enlarged the château—
the cause of all the trouble—in ampler times two centuries before. The
property was almost as completely self-sufficient as it had been then,
or as a plantation or *seigneurie* in the New World might have been.
The wine we drank at dinner—La Boutinière stood on the ecological
boundary between northern grain and southern grape—came from a
vineyard a hundred yards from the house and was brought to table in
an earthenware pitcher; that it was barely drinkable was disregarded,
for one did not buy what one could produce oneself. The sour and
crumbly cheese was also made on the property, and so, too, were the
pots of *rillettes*, coarse pork pâté, with which dinner unalterably began; eggs were collected from the chickens which clucked outside the
kitchen door, milk drawn from a house cow, and butter churned in an
outhouse. Electricity—the château was the only electrified building on
the property—came from a petrol generator brought falteringly to life
in another outhouse each evening, but bathwater was heated with
wood carted from an enormous *fagottière* in the fields. The same *fagottière* supplied the logs over which once a month the travelling washer-
woman boiled the dry linen; stirring her cauldrons in the courtyard,
flushed, soot-flecked, and muttering, she unfailingly brought to mind
the witch scene at the opening of *Macbeth*.

There were other travelling functionaries. A licensed distiller
brought his wheeled still to turn the surplus of the vintage into brandy,
an operation demanding the attendance of the village gendarme to
record the final quantity, while the completion of the harvest was followed by the arrival of the threshing team and their travelling steam
traction engine. For the week that threshing lasted, the chatelaine's gar-
dener, husband of the cook and an ex-spahi who had soldiered in
North Africa, stood all day to count the sacks of grain as they were
filled. The home farm was let on the ancient *métayage* system, a form
of share-cropping by which the tenant paid his rent through division of
the harvest with the landlord. La Boutinière's was the widowed chatelaine. Grey, distant, and disapproving—was she Anglophobe or did she
just dislike me?—she appeared occasionally at the threshing to register
her presence. There were respectful murmurs and nods as she advanced
across the stubble.

It was all very much as life on a *seigneurie*, in Old or New France, must have been lived for centuries; La Boutinière, largely untouched by revolution or republic, remained a little lordship. The chatelaine's word was something like law to her servants and tenants, and even to her children, who, though mostly married, spoke respectfully at table if they came to dine and retired to the nursery wing if they stayed the night. Madame had a single intimate, La Maréchale, a famous French officer's widow, with whom she exchanged disapproval of the goings-on at neighbouring properties by telephone. During the summer I spent there it was the marital difficulties of a younger chatelaine that engaged them; her husband's tendency to violence required her to spend the day at La Boutinière, but she departed each evening to sleep at home. Dark, leggy, alluring, she came and went in a pre-war touring car that might have been a prop from Jean Renoir's château drama *La règle du jeu*; the lines of the car greatly impressed me, and so did hers. The only half-innocent questions I asked about the reasons for her nightly de- parture were I suspect exactly those on which the two older ladies brooded telephonically together at such frequent intervals. In the end the violent husband resolved matters by shooting himself. I was sur- prised by the lack of stir the suicide caused; but guns and even sudden death were familiar ingredients of manorial life thereabouts. La Maréchale's only son had recently been killed in action in Indo-China, while the heir to La Boutinière had a youthful history of playing Rus- sian roulette. It was his marriage to an unsuitable girl that exercised his mother, not his irresponsibilities; she was quite unconcerned by his wild crashing-about with a shotgun in the surrounding woodland and would not have been much moved, I felt, had he caused an accident, not at all by one which disposed of his socially regrettable bride.

Am I wrong to imagine that my memories of La Boutinière assist an understanding of the life of New France before the British conquest? On the contrary, I am sure that they do, just as I am sure that my schooling by the priests of the Oratory and the time I spent teaching on exchange at St.-Cyr assist also. Church, army, *seigneurie*—these were the pillars of French Canada, and what I learnt of them even two hun- dred years later retained its value for a budding historian, all the more so because the conservatism of French institutions—La Maréchale, a citizen of the Fourth Republic, was widowed from a husband whose office originated at the court of the Valois kings—ensures that they change very slowly. French Canada has, indeed, changed very much more since the *ancien régime* had planted it in the seventeenth century than had the France I knew in the mid-twentieth—hence the disorientation of the Americans who came to lodge at La Boutinière, though they would have been quite at home in contemporary Montreal. Much of the *ancien régime* still persisted in my France, above all in the social distance which La Maréchale and her associates insisted should separate them from their tenants, work people, suppliers, and servants, from the minor officials of the bureaucracy, from their professional attendants—the local attorney was *un jeune homme très bien* but not quite to be entertained to dinner—and even from younger blood relations; and as it is *ancien régime* Canada that concerns me, I am persuaded that my summer in the Indre forty years ago brings me, in images however refracted by time and distance, some true reflection of the land which the settlers from Normandy and Aunis voyaged across the Atlantic to colonise under the lilies of Louis XIV.

That is why, under the steep housefronts and on the cobbles of Old Quebec, I found myself so strongly reminded of the old France I already knew so well. I risk overlabouring the point; it is equally important to emphasise the differences that exposure to Canada brings home, differences of climate, landscape, ecology, physical dimensions, density of population. France is a large country, over twice the size of Britain, though bearing the same population, but it is tiny beside Canada, and overpeopled by comparison. France has its wildernesses and its lakes and its forests, in the Camargue, the Landes, the Vosges, but they are small and tame in the Canadian scale of things. There are physical splendours in France, oceanic estuaries and alpine peaks which make Britain's little rivers and green hills look almost comically miniature, yet nothing in France approaches in magnitude the St. Lawrence or the Rockies. France is the most productive farming country in Europe, but its output of grain and livestock is a fraction of Canada's. The French climate shows wide winter and summer variations, particularly in the centre, at the eastern border and as between north and south, but the differences would seem trivial to a dweller on the prairies or the Great Lakes; Provence is never as hot as the southern prairies and Grenoble, on the flank of the Alps, never so cold as Montreal, where the winter temperature may dip to thirty below zero Fahrenheit. Distances, above all, are the great variant. France, from the mouth of the Seine on the English Channel to the delta of the Rhône on the Mediterranean, measures five hundred miles. In Canada, five hundred miles takes a voyager from Anticosti Island, at the mouth of the St. Lawrence, only to Montreal, and the next five hundred miles only to Detroit (once French) at the western end of Lake Erie. Those thousand miles were, it is true, the extent of settled French Canada in the eighteenth century; but the tentacles of French penetration had already reached five hundred miles further west to touch the upper Mississippi, while the most adventurous of the French were venturing hundreds of miles beyond that to the edge of the Great Plains.

It was not only the distances which were un-French, un-European; so, too, was the terrain, the endless tracts of forest, so much of it unfamiliarly coniferous, the plenitude of waterways draining the enormous snow-melt into the basins of the heartland, the inordinate extent of that system's lakes, the shapeless, unquantifiable spread of the continental surface itself, bereft of those intimate reassuring delineations that the small and cultivated slopes and hills and valleys bring to the European landscape. There was, in truth, no landscape in forested North America before settlement began to impose one, only its opposite, the wilderness, which had disappeared from Europe six thousand years earlier, and in the wilderness not only were there no roads, an absence forcing all travellers to become boatmen or trailblazers, but there was a presence, that of warlike, tribal, and preliterate native people, whose like no European voyagers to any part of the world may yet have encountered. Aztec, Inca, or Maya, the victims of the Spanish conquest of the south, were subjects of organised states; the penetration neither of black Africa nor of nomad Central Asia was yet under way; Arabs, Indians, Ottoman Turks, and Chinese belonged to advanced civilisations; it was only in the forests of North America that European seafarers and the settlers, traders, missionaries, soldiers, and officials who followed in their wake were brought face-to-face in their venture to the interior with men—and women—for whom conflict was a condition of existence and war-making a paramount skill.

Who were they, then, these French men and women—nuns, wives, marriageable spinsters, spitfires like La Bombardière, Madame Courserac de Drucourt, heroine of the siege of Louisbourg in 1758, in whom even La Maréchale might have met her match—who carried the lilies up the St. Lawrence? That they were largely people of the Channel or Atlantic coasts we know, as we also know that they were very few in number: in 1645, twenty years after settlement began, there were only 300 French people in Canada, when there were 5,000 English in Virginia, and the discrepancy widened apace thereafter; in 1756, at the outbreak of the war which was to settle the issue of control of North America between Britain and France, the French in all their settlements, from Louisbourg on the Atlantic to New Orleans in the Gulf of Mexico, numbered only 55,000, when the British population of the American colonies stood at over a million, or twenty times as many. The French were exclusively Catholic (Huguenots were forbidden to settle) and, apart from some intermixture of Indian blood, wholly French by national origin, while the British colonists already included, besides tens of thousands of enslaved West Africans, sizeable contingents of emigrant Germans, incorporated Dutch, and transplanted Irish and Scots, many of whom had brought with them homegrown varieties of the Protestant religion not favoured by George III's Church of England.

British America was booming; its inhabitants were already among the richest people in the world, continually opening up new land to cultivation, trading in both the export and import of luxury goods and experimenting with manufacture; their seaboard cities—Charleston, Savannah, Philadelphia—were models of Georgian elegance while, at Harvard, Yale, William and Mary, and half a dozen other colleges, the colonists had created a network of degree-granting institutions already larger than that existing in the United Kingdom. Representative assemblies existed in each colony, if elected by very limited franchise, as did local militias officered by the native-born, while in the major cities there was a lively cultural and literary life. New France, by contrast, was a pinched and backward society, an overseas administration of the Ministry of Marine dominated by royal officials, bishops, soldiers, the lords of the *seigneuries*, and the profit-takers of trading companies. There was no elected assembly or university, and local military forces were subordinate to royal officers. The inhabitants generally lived well and their exports of furs and skins made a fine entry in the colonial balance sheet; but there were years when the settlements along the St. Lawrence survived only by the import of grain from France, while the administration was under constant pressures to achieve economies and staunch a net outflow of funds from the royal treasury.

And yet: while the million British were, at the outbreak of the Seven Years War, only just beginning to press their line of settlement to the crests of the Appalachians, and their most intrepid traders and hunters to move downslope into the Ohio country, the French already dominated an axis of communication which ran for 2,000 miles from the Atlantic to the Gulf along the waterways that drain the American heartland, and from that axis had pushed along the tributaries to reach Lake Winnipeg, the Saskatchewan River, and the eastern outcrops of the Rocky Mountains, 2,500 miles from Montreal. They had established a well-used canoe route between Lake Superior and Lake Winnipeg and built fortified trading posts west of Lake Manitoba and south of Lake of the Woods. The whole of an enormous region beyond the Great Lakes known to them as "the Sea of the West" was visited annually by several hundred *voyageurs*, who were merely the most venturesome of this hardy and warlike imperial people. Few in numbers the French Canadians may have been; they nevertheless had a good opinion and could give a good account of themselves, and had already weathered the storms of three great colonial wars with the British, to say nothing of much unofficial raiding and skirmishing, and frequent hostilities with the Indians. The outcome of the gathering war of seven years, in the American theatre, was by no means prejudged, as the British would have been the first to concede. How and why had this remarkable outpost of the French nation come to occupy its empire in the West?

French America

Brittany and the Bay of Biscay were the starting places for the French voyagers who began from the sixteenth century to follow the news of a new world to the west. They came from a chain of ports which begins at La Rochelle on the Charente and ends at Dieppe in Normandy. I know their home coastline well from the land—this is the tamed French seaside of *Monsieur Hulot's Holiday* and of several of my own holidays at Trouville, Deauville, and La Baule and on the Ile de Ré— but also from the sea. There is nothing tamed about western French waters. I remember struggling with them from a forty-foot cruising yacht in the Alderney Race—the fierce current west of Cherbourg, not a competition—with every stitch set in a fine breeze on a sunny day and having to start the motor to make the harbour of St. Anne in Alderney island. Due south, beyond the notorious shores of the Minkies, lies St.-Malo, a place of forty-foot tides, and home port of

Jacques Cartier, the discoverer of the St. Lawrence River; it was home also to "las Malvinas," the buccaneering men of St.-Malo, who were the first to stake a claim to the Falkland Islands. Round the corner of the great Breton peninsula stretches the long southward sweep of the Biscay coast, indented by the harbours and estuaries from which French sea power was exercised in the Atlantic during the centuries of naval conflict with Britain. La Rochelle, Les Sables d'Olonne, St.-Nazaire, Lorient, Brest: these are names that reverberate in French maritime history with the same resonance as Devonport, Portsmouth, and Bristol do in Britain's.

In a memorable yachting summer I sailed a traverse of this coast, from La Rochelle to Lorient, beating out from the south of the Charente past the fortifications of the Ile de Ré to tie up for the night in Les Sables d'Olonne, from which in the sixteenth century fishermen sailed each year to bring salt cod back from the Grand Banks on the other side of the Atlantic. On another night we anchored on the seaward side of the tiny Ile d'Yeu, another place of grim fortification which housed Marshal Pétain in solitary confinement after the Second World War. We fell asleep to the rocking of the Atlantic swells and rose by moonlight to catch a breeze on a rising sea that led towards Quiberon Bay and Belle Isle. In November 1759, the year of the fall of Quebec and the death of French Canada, a British fleet caught the French Brest squadron between the ocean and the land in a howling gale in Quiberon Bay and brought it to action; some French ships which kept their gunports open were sailed under in the storm, others dashed on to the rocks, in what still stands as the rashest of all the Royal Navy's victories, a defiance of nature as much as of the enemy.

The bay looked unthreatening enough on the bright morning we left it to starboard. Not so the fortifications of Belle Isle; every military and naval historian should see just once the seaward aspect of a great system of fortification, preferably from the deck of a sailing vessel, for only thus can he grasp the logic of its geometry, angle covering angle, rampart dominating rampart with a mathematical ingenuity that leaves no patch of beach or tidewater uncovered to the menace of artillery. We had the luck to pass Belle Isle on an afternoon of brilliant sunshine that threw into sharp shadow each deadly corner of its fortress's construction, our slow progression unfolding its secrets at no better pace than the captain of a man o' war could have managed on an offensive sally inside the range of its guns, waiting to watch for the splash of solid shot skipping towards him across the wavelets and knowing that he could count only on a fickle wind to carry him to safety if the enemy's fire told. The sight of Belle Isle's gleaming walls brought home to me the force of those eighteenth-century descriptions, "a strong place," "a very strong place"; they spoke not just of military difficulty but of danger and of power. No wonder that an agreement to destroy fortifications was one of the weightiest concessions an eighteenth-century state could make in a treaty to end a war. It literally altered geography to its disadvantage. Belle Isle, though captured by Admiral Keppel in 1761, was left intact by the treaty that ended the Seven Years War and stands today much as he must have seen it in that year. Our peaceful promenade under its sparkling walls left me filled with astonishment that it could ever have fallen to an amphibious assault, and all the more intrigued to know how its counterparts at Louisbourg and Quebec on the other side of the Atlantic were overcome in 1758 and 1759.

Louisbourg had not been planned, Quebec was not yet even a name known to Europeans when Cartier set off from St.-Malo, leaving Brest and Belle Isle on his left hand, to sail for America in 1534. He made an amazingly fast passage, of twenty days, arriving off eastern Newfoundland in late May. It was a good landfall but not a chance one; Portuguese fishermen had been working the chilly fogs of the Grand Banks, the richest grounds in the world, since the end of the fifteenth century and Bretons since 1504. John Cabot, a Genoan sponsored by the merchant-venturers of Bristol, had reached southern Newfoundland in 1497, making a landfall near L'Anse Aux Meadows, where, if one is prepared to take sides in the famous dispute over whether or not the Vikings discovered America, Leif Ericson is believed to have established base in the eleventh century. Cabot, unlike Leif, was not in search of room for settlement, but, like every other transatlantic voyager of those early days, seeking a short route to the riches of Asia, its teeming cities, jewelled palaces, and spice ports. He found nothing of value on Newfoundland's rock-bound coast, returned home, and was lost on a second voyage. This disappearance did not deter Cartier.

The French court had already had confirmation that a long barrier lay between Europe and Asia from the voyage made by Verrazano along North America's eastern seaboard in 1523, which had taken him into the mouth of what today is the port of New York. The Breton fishermen's reports on the lie of the land south of Newfoundland implied that it connected with the coastline he had surveyed, an implication that dashed hopes of guiding a passage to the Indies anywhere south of the Grand Banks, but they had also given a name, the Bay of Castles, to a long inlet that separated Labrador from Newfoundland—called today the Strait of Belle Isle (no connection with the island in the Bay of Biscay)—and that seemed to offer the prospect of a northwest passage to Asia. Cartier, as bold a mariner as ever sailed out of St.-Malo, was commissioned by King Francis I to penetrate the Bay of Castles and to "discover certain islands and lands where it is said he should find great quantities of gold and other such things."

He found the Bay of Castles soon after his landfall in Newfoundland, spent the summer exploring its coastline, made contact with the local Indians, two of whom he kidnapped, and determined that out of it a broad waterway led westward. He did not have time to enter it that year but in 1535, bringing back his two kidnaps, who by then spoke French, he returned to continue his exploration. Encouraged by his Indians—as so often elsewhere, the European discovery of Canada was in large measure a guided tour, courtesy of the locals—he pressed into the channel he had identified in 1534 and sailed up it, naming places and charting islands as he went, until he cast anchor under a high place where the shorelines drew together. The Indians called it Stadcuna. They were Iroquois, the powerful people of the region, which they told Cartier was called Canada. Stadcuna would later be known as Quebec—an Indian word for "narrowing"—and the waterway he had navigated to reach it was the St. Lawrence River.

That was not the end of Cartier's adventure. Still eager for gold and other rich things, in compensation for the northwest passage which the St. Lawrence clearly was not, he pushed on upriver to a large Indian town called Hochelaga. He called it Mount Royal, the first form given to the place that would become Montreal, but did not try to go further, for he saw from the top of Mount Royal that the upper reaches were impeded by cataracts, the Lachine Rapids, while the Indians told him that there were three more sets of rapids before the river became navigable again. He therefore turned back, reached Quebec three weeks later, found that his main party had built a fort at St. Croix on the northern shore, near the mouth of what is now called the St. Charles River, and settled down to winter there. He was to have a bad time. The Iroquois, with whom he had fallen out, warned that their god had predicted a winter of such ice and snow that all would perish.

Cartier was contemptuous, strengthened his fort—the first military structure to be erected in Canada, protected by a ditch and armed by artillery—and waited them out. Almost everything the Iroquois threatened proved true: his three ships were frozen in from November to April, snow four feet deep stood round his palisades all winter, and scurvy so severe attacked the garrison that twenty-five of his sixty men died. The rest were saved only when an Indian intermediary unwittingly revealed the secret of boiling cedar bark to retrieve a concentration of vitamin C.

Cartier showed little gratitude for the transmission of this life-saving secret when spring came. As he prepared to sail for home, he tricked the Indian chief from whom it came into boarding his ship, made him prisoner, and then kidnapped nine of his Iroquois followers to take back to France also. They were told that the French King would send support to aid the tribe in its quarrel with other Iroquois; but the truth was that Cartier wanted them as proof of what he had achieved. None would ever see Canada again.

Cartier would; he was back again in 1541 at the head of a sizeable party despatched to found a colony. International law, by strict interpretation and papal decree, reserved settlement in the Americas to Spain and Portugal; but a Spanish-Portuguese agreement of 1494 divided their sphere of interest at the longitude touching the mouth of the Amazon and so had given Newfoundland and its hinterland, east of the same longitude, to Portugal. Because Portugal was a power in decline, France could ignore its rights—as the English, Dutch, and Swedes were later to ignore Spain's—and make claims of its own. That was the purpose of Cartier's voyage, strongly reinforced by the proclamation that France was taking the Christian religion to the Indians.

Both colony and mission failed, as did a succession of subsequent attempts to settle Newfoundland and Acadia, the region known today as Nova Scotia. When Cartier died—in a plague epidemic at home in St.-Malo in 1557—the French impulse to colonise North America seemed to have died with him. He was buried, nevertheless, with great honour, and he deserved every shred of it, for not only was he as bold a venturer as ever followed in Columbus's wake but he had made the most important discovery in America after that establishing its existence: he had found the St. Lawrence, "a great highway into the continent," explored its length for a thousand miles, established that it extended far deeper, identified the key nodal points, Quebec and

Montreal, along its course, and opened relations—however ambiguous—with the indigenous peoples who populated its shores.

The man who was to capitalise on Cartier's endeavours, Samuel de Champlain, was of the same bold breed. As a voyager he exceeded Cartier in fortitude, since he made the Atlantic crossing no fewer than twenty-one times between 1603 and 1633—has any modern yachtsman risked those stormy waters as often?—while as an explorer he nearly equalled Cartier's achievements. He made the first ascent by a European of the water route between the St. Lawrence and the Hudson—via the Richelieu River and the lake that bears his name—and the first traverse of the Ottawa River to the head of Lake Huron and thence, roughly along the line of the modern Trans-Canada Highway, to Lake Ontario. In 1615 he got close to the future site of Fort Oswego, at the Canadian end of what would be the Anglo-French axis of campaign between the Great Lakes and Virginia, via the Forks of the Ohio River. As, in 1609, he had actually fought a little battle with the Iroquois in the St. Lawrence–Hudson corridor, he may well be regarded as the originator of military operations on those two bloodstained warpaths connecting the French and English Americas. He was also, in anticipation of Montcalm, to defend Quebec against an English fleet in 1629, and to lose it.

Champlain was not, however, a loser; he got Quebec, of which he was the founder, back again and survived to be buried within its walls at the Church of Notre-Dame de la Recouvrance. No wonder that he remains the chief hero of French Canada and no wonder either that they have erected a heroically defiant statue of him in the Old City. There he stands, sword in hand, chin cocked, moustaches abristle, and an Anglo-Saxon visitor can scarce forbear to cheer. Of all conquistadores he is the most attractive figure. He believed in Canadian America as a place worthy of settlement in its own right, not as a stepping stone along a route which might or might not lead to Asia, nor as a mere source of exportable wealth. He sought, despite his battles with the Iroquois, to establish harmonious and profitable relations with the Indians; deeply religious, he hoped to bring them the consolations of the Christian religion; industrious also, he sought to found a colony of farmers and craftsmen who would be a credit in New France to their homeland. To the world he bequeathed a wealth of topographical and cartographic information about the land he had explored, for he was a prolific author and skilled mapmaker who recorded meticulously every step of his journeys by canoe and on foot within the uncharted interior. His was an extraordinary life. A native of La Rochelle, a place as close to perfection of climate and surroundings as Europe offers, he devoted his amazing energies not to winning position or riches at home, for which he might realistically have hoped in the troubled times of the Wars of Religion, but to translating French civilisation to one of the harshest and most unwelcoming sectors of the American wilderness. I share the French Canadians' admiration for their Founding Father; beating out of La Rochelle a year or two ago in a sailing boat not much smaller than that in which he so often made the Atlantic crossing, I was brought to reflect on his courage and on how lucky I was to be setting course for Les Sables d'Olonne, a day's sailing up the coast, and not for the mouth of the St. Lawrence, three thousand storm-tossed miles away.

Cartier and Champlain between them gave France her start in North America; without their gifts of navigational divination and their breathtaking courage to press on down the openings into the continent their guesswork disclosed to them, the French might have been no more successful than the Dutch or the Swedes, in their Hudson and Delaware dead ends, in founding a transatlantic empire. Neither, however, possessed the organisational skills or acquired the political patronage necessary to translate the discoveries they made into a colonial enterprise. Champlain fared better than Cartier. By the time of his death in 1635 the French foothold had the makings of a settlement. What it lacked was government, finance, production, economy, and people.

Government was slow to arrive. The kingdom of France, like that of England, first chose to administer its overseas enclaves by devolving royal authority on to a monopoly trading company. Champlain had such a monopoly, attached to the fur trade. It was transferred in 1627 by the reformist Cardinal Richelieu to a company of New France, the Hundred Associates, mostly Norman and Breton traders and voyagers. The Associates, however, failed to sustain a necessary flow of capital into Canada and in turn they devolved their rights in 1646 into a local enterprise, the Compagnie des Habitants. Though under the authority of a royal governor and, from 1647, of a council also comprising the lieutenant governor of Montreal and the Jesuit Superior, its traders and land-holders were the effective administrators of business and agriculture. Yet in their turn they too were overcome by difficulty, though of a

strategic rather than financial sort. Indian wars between the Iroquois
and Hurons for control of the supply of furs to the exporters inflicted
such severe collateral damage on the French—particularly the heroic
Jesuits who had opted to take their chance in the villages of the interior
for the sake of winning converts—that the habitants were driven to
seek military help from home. It was eventually forthcoming, in the
shape of the Régiment de Carignan, but the price was the supersession
of local by royal authority. In 1663 Louis XIV dissolved the monopoly
companies and established government in Canada on the lines of a
French domestic *pays d'élection*, with an intendant as executive officer
under the governor; with him the Bishop of Quebec was associated as
head of society. The Council was retained, but progressively only as a
superior court of law, while the local militia, originating as a home
guard, was put under central control. From 1683 it was supplemented
by detachments of the Troupes de la Marine, regular soldiers recruited
by the French admiralty for colonial service. At a local level, along the
banks of the St. Lawrence, the *seigneuries* tended to become feudal, as
they were at home in France; the magistrates, officers, churchmen, and
merchants who held them grew more authoritarian in holding their
habitants to the duty of cultivating the land.

Under royal government there was a marked increase in the number of habitants, some discharged soldiers of the Carignan Regiment
who were induced to remain in Canada by the offer of several years'
half-pay, some indentured labourers, some *"filles du roi,"* poor girls
shipped out to furnish wives in a womanless land, some convicts, but
many willing emigrants who had learnt of the chance to lead a freer
and more prosperous life in Canada than was open to them in France.
Numbers grew accordingly; during the mid-seventeenth century, the
Crown sent some 6,000 men and women; thereafter natural increase
raised the numbers to 16,000 in 1706 and 25,000 by 1719; Canadians,
both boys and girls, married young and families were large. In the first
half of the eighteenth century the population almost doubled; there
were 42,000 in 1739. Moreover the habitants had by then acquired a
distinct personality; as described by W. L. Morton, the French Canadian had "a sense of freedom, a quickness to resist authority, a blithe
and cocky headstrongness. Frank, and quick to give his trust, the
Canadian could be persuaded to attempt almost anything by those he
loved but could not be compelled to do anything by those he disliked.
This independence of spirit was encouraged both by the subsistence

economy in which he was cradled—no one need go hungry in the parishes of the St. Lawrence—and by the high wages his labour commanded in industry, trade, or the canoe flotillas. The Canadian was an Americanized Frenchman . . . a man assertively independent and 'naturally undocile.' "

Of none was that more true than the adventurers of the fur trade, the early *coureurs de bois* of the northern forests, the later *voyageurs* of the lakes and southern rivers, who brought back to Montreal the skins from which the wealth of New France derived. They were a headstrong band in more senses than one: headstrong in taking physical risks, headstrong in defiance of the government when it sought to limit or curtail their voyaging. The court in France and the government at Quebec constantly sought to control the trade by lease or later by licences, granted to a fixed number for a specified period. The intention was to prevent private trading, ensure the return of all furs to the emporium at Montreal, and preclude the growth of a frontier population unfettered by colonial authority. Leasing failed in the seventeenth century because no royal officer could stop individuals from slipping away into the vastness of the interior to trade on their own account; licensing failed in 1696 because so few licences had been granted. The court wanted settlers of New France to devote themselves to husbandry and to building an economy which would rival that of the English on the Atlantic coast, trusting to Indian middlemen to bring down the fur wealth to controlled markets on the St. Lawrence. The bolder habitants, who had not emigrated in order to labour as they had done at home, continued to disobey the licensing system as they had that of leasing. In 1680 the royal intendant reported that "I have been unable to ascertain the exact number [of *coureurs de bois*] because everyone associated with them covers up for them" but thought that there were about eight hundred. By 1704, when the court was obliged for a second time to issue an amnesty to independent traders, the numbers may have been even larger. Many free fur traders had given up returning to civilisation altogether. Not only were they often in debt to merchants at Montreal, who had staked them their expenses against the promise of furs they had subsequently sold for better prices to English or Dutch factors; many of them had also set up with Indian women, bred families, and adapted to the life of the woods. A growing number, indeed, were Métis, French-speaking half-breeds who felt more at home on the fur frontier than they did on the St. Lawrence.

Whether half-breed or not, the fur traders were in any case too tough a lot to suffer recall to the farms of Quebec once they had learnt the life of the canoe and the forest trail. It was not one for "weaklings or the fainthearted," as W. J. Eccles describes. "Squatting on a narrow thwart, legs cramped by bales of goods or furs, [the *coureurs*] paddled hour after hour from dawn to dusk, pausing occasionally for a pipe while the professional raconteur spun a tale from his inexhaustible supply, singing folk songs to the dip of a paddle, forty-five to forty-eight strokes to the minute. For over a thousand miles the paddles thrust the canoes through the water. At rapids they were either roped upstream, the men wading up to the waist in the swift icy river, or the canoes and their cargoes were carried on a tump-line, sometimes for miles around the turbulent waters. Going downstream the temptation was strong to run the rapids, and at every portage crosses marked where men had paid with their lives. Time could not be spared to hunt, the only food was two meals a day of corn meal mush flavoured with salt pork, dried fish or jerked venison, washed down with water and a nip of brandy to aid the digestion. The casualty rate was high, and rheumatism too frequently made men old before their time, but the Canadians gloried in this life. Wherever a canoe could go, these men went, seeking Indians with furs, bringing them within the orbit and control of this trading empire. A few hundred such men held the west in fee for France."

The value of this empire to France was to be reckoned in the price of beaver skin, which yielded fibres pre-eminently suitable to felting fur hats. The European beaver had been almost exterminated by overtrapping at the beginning of the seventeenth century. On the rivers and lakes of Canada—and there are more lakes in Canada than in the rest of the world put together—the beaver remained abundant. In France a beaver hat, the mark of a gentleman, sold for thirty livres (about one pound sterling, an artisan's weekly wage); in Canada an Indian would sell a robe of beaver skins for one livre's worth of beads or brandy. Robes, known as "greasy beaver," fetched more than "dry" skins because the fibres were more easily felted; in either case the eventual profit approached 20,000 per cent. Inevitably there were fluctuations caused by glut, changes in fashion, competition, or withholding of exchange (the French administration attempted to outlaw the supply of brandy until defeated by free traders), but the lure of big returns never waned. They were the basis of wealth in New France, from which exports regularly amounted to several hundred thousand livres a year

during the seventeenth century; in 1687 the French Crown sold the fur
lease for half a million livres and still left the buyers with a handsome
margin.

Yet Crown policy inconsistently remained that of creating in
Canada an economy to rival England's in New York, Pennsylvania, and
Virginia. There the settlers hacked fields from the forest, planted, harvested, grew export crops, and lived in well-ordered communities
which replicated those of the Old World; that they were generally on
worse terms than the French with the Indians was discounted. France,
the most centralised state in Europe, was supported by *labourage et
paturage, les deux mamelles,* and it wished the overseas empire also to
live by ploughing and grazing. Along the banks of the St. Lawrence
there was such an economy, based on the narrow-fronted strip holdings
of the *seigneuries,* whose habitants did dutifully plant and till, to such
effect that in the first decade of the eighteenth century they were able in
some years to export grain and flour to the fisheries of the coast and
even to the sugar islands of the West Indies. Their churches and many
of their neat, single-storey houses survive to this day, as distinctively
Breton in appearance as those of similar date in New England, with
their steep roofs and massive chimney stacks, are distinctively East Anglian. The Ile d'Orléans, under the heights of Quebec, remains, like
Durham, Connecticut, a place into which the early settlers might step
back today with little sense of displacement in time.

Yet Versailles' desire for neatness, order, domesticity, Frenchness in
the regulation and economy of New France in fact misserved the homeland's real transatlantic interests. Failing the desire of native French
people to emigrate, and the readiness of the government to permit settlement by non-French, non-Catholic immigrants—to say nothing of its
disinclination to transport its dissidents and criminals with the will
shown by the British—the basis for any growth of population equivalent to that achieved in the English colonies was altogether lacking.
Like it though old France did not, the real energy of New France was
expended at its frontier with the wilderness, in the relations established
by its most adventurous traders, missionaries, and soldiers with the Indians and through the enterprise they showed in exploration. France
enjoyed enormous advantages in North America over the British, confined as they were by the Appalachian chain to the narrow littoral
along the Atlantic. By their possession of the St. Lawrence, the French
did indeed hold the key to the continent; from it ran, by way of lake,

river, or natural portage, a continental network of communication northward to Hudson Bay, westward to the Rockies, and southward to the Gulf of Mexico. There is a strategic logic to the geography of North America on which Cartier had stumbled the moment he found the opening of the St. Lawrence estuary; it forms a unity that Champlain, a geographer of genius, perceived by his divination of the existence of the continent's inland seas and the water system of which they are the heart. Champlain almost ensured that France would dominate the system unchallengeably, for as early as 1607 "he sensed the relation of the Hudson River, seen by Verrazano, but yet unexplored, to the St. Lawrence." It was only, as Morton explains, "short supplies and Indian skirmishers [which] drove him back from Long Island Sound," so denying to France the chance to make the site of New York "a new Rouen or a new La Rochelle." That was a mischance soon to be regretted by the champions of French imperialism, the loss of a link in their chain of ports, posts, and portages that would concede a crucial advantage to their English competitors. Yet the loss was not decisive. The great game of American empire had still a century and a half to run at the moment Champlain turned back from the endeavour of making the Hudson French. For most of these 150 years it was the French, not the English, who took and held the lead to penetrate the interior, comprehend its geography, and stake the claims to keep it as sovereign territory. The story of the French exploration of the American continent is the beginning of its strategic history.

Europe, Native America, and the Fur Trade

The geography of America, physical and historical, is today an open book. Not all of it was hidden from Champlain, that extraordinary clairvoyant, who had mapped Lake Ontario and guessed at the existence of Lakes Michigan and Superior. His vision of the interior, nevertheless, was patchy and shallow. He had no inkling of the existence of the Rockies, no knowledge of Canada's frozen north or of the rivers which ran through it to Hudson Bay, no conception that the mouth of the Mississippi, already entered by the Spanish, led northwards to headwaters in his own zone of exploration, and certainly no apprehension of the existence or extent of the Great Plains. He knew, of course,

of the Pacific, into which the Portuguese and Spanish had already voyaged, but was as confused as most explorers of North America from
the Atlantic coast were long to remain over the configuration of its
eastern shores; he presumed a *mer douce* in the American heartland
which gave on to the fabled realms of the Orient.

We can now arrange his scraps of objective discovery, and the outlines of the more distant topography gleaned from Indian descriptions,
quite exactly. New France, as it was to become, is, we understand,
what geographers have called "an empire of the spillways." In the
great ages of glaciation, ending twelve thousand years ago, an enormous sheet of ice had spread southwards from the Arctic to cover the
whole of Canada and the Great Lakes region, its southernmost edge
coming to rest in the crescent where today the Missouri and Ohio
rivers join the Mississippi. The advance of the ice had the effect of
blocking the northern outlets of the Canadian rivers into Hudson Bay,
thus forming enormous lakes which eventually overflowed their shores
and drained away southwards into the Caribbean and Atlantic. The
"spillways" gouged channels through the high ground interlying the
original river valleys, which, on the retreat of the ice, left a complex
network of natural portages—"carrying places" between waterways,
where goods and boats could be manhandled overland—making for
easy intercommunication over a vast area for canoeists and forest travellers. Such travellers, who became the *coureurs de bois* and *voyageurs*,
following the tracks left by and usually shown to them by the indigenous Indian inhabitants, were thus spared the long exhausting journeys
on foot which faced the Spanish and English in their explorations of
the interior mountainous and arid zones.

This is not to say that the task of the French explorers was simple.
As anyone knows who lives where streams and rivers run, the logic of
a waterway system is infuriatingly difficult to dissect. An eastward flow
may be no more than the bend in a brook whose eventual direction is
westward; the apparent connection between one stream and another
may be interrupted by a watershed which sends each in divergent directions; a clear and fast-flowing rivulet may waste itself in a swamp; the
feeder to a lake may have no outlet on the other side. I live at a high
point from which I can descend to cross four rivers, the Frome, the
Stour, the Wylye, and the Brue, with their many tiny tributaries; all rise
within a mile of my house. Though it stands only seven hundred feet
above sea level, each of these rivers nevertheless follows a declivity

which puts its mouth at least fifty miles away from any other; two of the rivers eventually drain into the Bristol Channel, opposite Wales, two into the English Channel opposite France.

All this can be seen at a glance from the Ordnance Survey map. There were no maps at all, however, of any part of North America when Champlain began his survey, for the Indians were not mapmakers; they carried the pattern of the rivers and lakes in their heads and marked their trails and portages by "blazes" on the trees. They in their turn had learnt something of the lie of the land from the tracks beaten out by the larger game which had roamed the wilderness before they arrived in America at the end of the last ice age. None of this amounted to a key to the continent; there were no song lines by which an aborigine could chant himself, as in Australia, from sea to sea. Walkabout, in any case, was not an American Indian habit. Tribal neighbours were more often enemies than friends, inclined to take and torture an interloper rather than help him on his way. The Indians, therefore, did not know the shape of the world they inhabited, and it would take the Europeans four hundred years to fix its features correctly into place on a single sheet of mapmaker's paper.

Yet the pattern of North American geography since the retreat of the ice may, by a reader of modern maps, be quite simply grasped. It consists of two mountain chains and two intermediate river systems. The mountains, Appalachian and Rocky respectively, the latter enormously exceeding the former in scale, march parallel to the Atlantic and Pacific borders of the continent, and from them comparatively short rivers drain east and west through the littorals to the oceans; an exception is the Rio Grande system, which flows southward from the Rockies to the Gulf of Mexico. The inland basin contained between the mountain chains is watered by their runoff, which feeds one of the two great intermediate river systems, the Mississippi, by way of the Missouri, the Arkansas, and the Red rivers through the Great Plains and by way of the Ohio and the Tennessee, the principal waterways of the Midwest and the South. The other great intermediate system is that of the St. Lawrence, deriving from the Great Lakes, where the source of supply is internal: the lakes form the largest freshwater complex in the world, which is a climatic zone in itself, attracting rainfall from its feeder rivers but also creating its own rainfall, by which the St. Lawrence and its tributaries are fed. Thus America's inland basin contains one outlet in the Gulf of Mexico and one to the Atlantic, with the

Great Lakes lying between them to form a strategic centre of intercommunication southwards and westwards for any power swift enough to make the lakes its own.

There is, of course, a third hydrographic system, that lying above the "Height of Land" which separates habitable Canada from the coniferous wilderness and tundra of the north. It contains the largest number of lakes in the world, lakes so numerous, indeed, that the modern Northwest Territories is almost as much water as land, as well as its own major rivers such as the Mackenzie, which flow either directly to the Arctic Ocean or else, indirectly, through the great inlet of Hudson Bay. Frozen in winter, swamped and insect-ridden in summer, the country above the Height of Land is scarcely fit for human life. In pre-Columbian times it was the most sparsely populated American region, occupied by scattered migrational bands of Athapascans and Algonquians, who followed the caribou, and of Eskimo fishermen. It was also home, however, to the world's richest population of fur-bearing animals outside the Russian taiga, fox, wolf, bear, and beaver, whose coats grew in the subarctic temperatures to luxuriant thickness. Thus one of the poorer regions on the globe's surface offered the allure of sudden riches to trappers, hunters, and middlemen adventurous enough to risk the hazards and hardships for profit.

They could not be the Spanish or the English, let alone the Dutch. Their *patroons* (landholders), *swanneken* (traders), and *boschlopers* (men of the woods) never succeeded in breaking far enough out of their Hudson foothold to find the primal sources of furs in the interior. The Spanish began the quest from too far away, while the English were frustrated by the barriers of the Appalachians, the gaps through which long hid themselves from discovery. It was the French, therefore, who started with the advantage, conferred by Cartier's discovery of the St. Lawrence's mouth and by Champlain's journeys up the Ottawa and Saguenay rivers into the territory above the great river, down the Richelieu towards the Hudson Valley and westward to Lakes Ontario and Huron. Champlain, however, did not succeed in uncovering the inner connections between the St. Lawrence and the further Great Lakes. Those were to come later, and to be opened to the Europeans by the local knowledge of Indian collaborators.

The pattern of the key portages is now well known to us, though their usefulness has been altogether obliterated by the building of the modern road system, which so often overlays them. They may be divided into three: (a) those along the main axis of the St. Lawrence and the Great Lakes, which allowed men to use that complex as a single east–west water highway; (b) those giving southward off that axis on to the Mississippi but also to its great tributary, the Ohio, and on to the short rivers draining into the Atlantic, in particular the Hudson; and (c) those leading northward to Hudson Bay.

On the St. Lawrence the most important of the portages was that in the narrows between Montreal and Lake Ontario, by which the traveller could reach Lake Erie through the portage round Niagara Falls, and thence both Lake Huron by the St. Clair portage above Detroit and Lake Superior by the portage at Sault Ste. Marie, on the route of the modern Soo Canal; Huron has an open connection with Lake Michigan at Michilimackinac (modern Mackinaw City) and, as a crucial junction, was fortified by the French as early as 1676.

The second set of portages included the Temiscouata, from the St. Lawrence estuary to the St. John River (in modern New Brunswick); that between Lake Oneida and the Mohawk River ("the Great Carrying Place"), giving a connection from Lake Ontario to the Hudson; that overland from Lake Erie to the headwaters of the Allegheny River, one of the forks of the Ohio; the Maumee, which connected to the Wabash River and so down to the Ohio near its confluence with the Mississippi; and the Chicago, on which the modern metropolis stands, which joined Lake Michigan to the Illinois River and, together with the Green Bay portage to the Wisconsin River, thus directly to the Mississippi again. The most important of all, however, was that in the Hudson Valley by which that river could be reached from Lake Champlain and so, via the Richelieu River, from the St. Lawrence. This Hudson–Richelieu corridor was to become the most heavily fortified and contested strategic route in American military history.

The third set of portages included the Matlawa, connecting the upper Ottawa River to the Georgian Bay of Lake Huron via Lake Nipissing; the Grand Portage, which led from the north shore of Lake Superior to Rainy Lake and so on to the Lake of the Woods and Lakes Winnipeg and Manitoba and along the Saskatchewan River to the prairies and the Canadian Northwest; and the Lake Nipigon portage, which, via the Ogoki and Albany rivers, took the traveller to James Bay of Hudson Bay. The Michipicoten portage to the Missinaibi and Moose rivers reached the same destination on a parallel route.

All this looks simple to the student of a modern atlas, and much of it was natural to the indigenous Indians. Indeed, in New Brunswick, to take one of many examples, the road system today does little more than replicate in blacktop the routes paddled and walked by the native inhabitants for millennia before the French arrived. The Trans-Canada Highway between Fredericton and Edmunston follows their canoe route along the St. John River; its branch from Bristol to Newcastle, Provincial Highways 107 and 8, replicates the Indian river route down the Miramichi, which involved two portages, while that from St. Leonard to Campbellton parallels another which portaged at the Restigouche River. Nothing, however, was simple or natural to the French, who either had to work things out for themselves or, if they were fortunate, submit to teaching by the Indians. In a strategic sense, they must be given the credit—very great credit—for working out the connection between the mouths of the St. Lawrence and the Mississippi, since no Indian's knowledge was extensive enough to encompass such a span of geography. Short-range connections were, by contrast, almost always divulged by the locals. Thus, for example, it was Iroquois who told Champlain of the Saguenay–Mistassini traverse from the St. Lawrence to Hudson Bay and of the key portage from Lake George, below Lake Champlain, to the Hudson River. In 1653 the Jesuit Father Poncet, then a captive of the Iroquois, was taken under escort from the Mohawk River to Montreal by the route normal to his captors: instead of descending to the Hudson, portaging and ascending the Richelieu, they took the short cut up Lake Oneida and the Oswego River, so into Lake Ontario and thence down the St. Lawrence; this inadvertent disclosure then became part of the French-Canadian route map.

The stages by which the pattern of key interconnections was established add up to a roll call of famous names. Cartier found the St. Lawrence in the sixteenth century. Champlain explored its source in Lake Ontario and discovered its connections with the Hudson and Lake Huron, via the Ottawa River, in the early seventeenth. A remarkable series of journeys was meanwhile undertaken by a young subordinate of Champlain's, Etienne Brulé, who was left by him to overwinter with the Hurons in 1615. These *hivernants*, as the French would call them, were to become the essential interpreters of Indian ways and language of the French and vice versa, but Brulé, a boy of wonderful self-confidence and high spirits, proved himself a great explorer in his own right. He lacked Champlain's cartographic training and so could give no exact record of his travels, but he undoubtedly made his way from the Great Lakes to the Susquehanna River and thence to its mouth in Chesapeake Bay.

French power would never suffice for an expansion in that direction, however; their course of empire lay westward, and the next men to make an imaginative leap forward were the trader Louis Jolliet and the Jesuit father Jacques Marquette. Missionaries and traders had done much land exploration around the Great Lakes from 1650 to 1670, and Jolliet in 1668 had been shown by an Iroquois the short route, via the St. Clair River, between Lakes Huron and Erie, on which Detroit now stands. In 1672 he and Marquette were commissioned by the royal intendant, Jean Talon, to authenticate reports of a route down the Mississippi—of which the missionaries Dablon and Allouez had heard but not had sight—to the ocean; whether that ocean was the Atlantic or Pacific was to be the subject of their investigation. Leaving Green Bay on Lake Michigan in the summer of 1673, they were shown by the Miami Indians how to portage to the Wisconsin River and thus entered the Mississippi on 17 June. Shortly afterwards, they passed the mouth of a "second Mississippi," the Missouri, but pressed on to see the confluence with the Ohio and did not finally halt until they met Indians with guns who frightened them by their warlike manner, just short of the mouth of the Arkansas. They were then told by friendlier locals that they were only ten days from the sea but judged it unsafe to go farther.

They had already voyaged over a thousand miles from their starting place and on the way back made the additional discovery of the portage from the Illinois to Lake Michigan on which Chicago now stands; astonishingly, an interim report in Latin of their adventures, given to an Indian encountered on the Ohio, was passed by him to a Virginia trader, who gave it to William Byrd, who gave it to William Penn, who sent it home to Robert Harley in England, where it turned up at Welbeck Abbey in Nottinghamshire in the 1890s. News of the Jolliet–Marquette discoveries, of course, reached New France somewhat earlier than that. The royal government, nevertheless, was slow to act. It was not until 1680 that the mysterious adventurer Robert de La Salle secured permission to trade with a monopoly in the Mississippi Valley and to discover its connections with Mexico. He had already traded and travelled widely in the Great Lakes region, and made an arduous journey on foot at the time of the snow-melt from the Illinois to the east, making new moccasins every night for sixty nights, that year. In 1682 he set off from the Chicago portage with a sizeable party, dragged canoes to the Illinois, and thence paddled down to the junction with the Mississippi, whose whole length to the mouth at what is now New Orleans he traversed in three months.

The inland circuit between the entries to North America's two greatest rivers, the St. Lawrence and the Mississippi, was now complete. All that remained to do by way of enumerating their tributary lakeland and portage connections with the interior west of the Rockies was accomplished within the next sixty years. Not all who made significant discoveries were French. Henry Kelsey, the first European to see the Great Plains, was an English employee of the Hudson's Bay Company, while some of the boldest rangers of the country between the Appalachians and the Ohio were unnamed Dutch *boschlopers.* Pierre-Esprit Radisson, who had done so much to establish the overland routes from the Great Lakes to Hudson Bay, was French but a turncoat who ended in the pay of the English; Lederer, who got from the coast to the Blue Ridge Mountains, was of German descent. A set of French names nevertheless stands out, that of Pierre de la Vérendrye and his sons, who together in the years 1727–43 opened up the routes westward from Lake Superior to Lakes Winnipeg and Manitoba and to the Saskatchewan River foremost. Vérendrye was a genuine Canadian—though he spent enough time in France to be badly wounded fighting against Marlborough at Malplaquet in 1709—whose father had been governor of Trois Rivières on the St. Lawrence. He and his sons secured a monopoly to trade around Lake Winnipeg in 1730, conditional on a promise to search for that old chimera, a route to the Pacific, and in fulfilment of it over the next thirteen years explored widely on the Missouri and the Saskatchewan, built chains of forts, established relations with many Indian tribes, including the Sioux, and pushed their ventures so far to the west that they are credited with having seen the Rockies. It is more probable that the mountains the Vérendryes saw were the Black Hills of Dakota, but they were certainly in the Badlands and penetrated to the Cheyenne River. There, almost touching the borders of the Spanish-Indian culture zone of the Southwest and in anticipation of the days of the Wild West, they planted the farthest outpost of New France in the Americas.

Yet little of all this adventure can be called exploration for its own sake; pure exploration, indeed, was a concept alien to Europeans before the onset of the Romantic movement of the nineteenth century. Pious Europeans explored for souls; the rest explored for riches. Riches in North America meant fur, and it was in order to dominate the fur frontier that the French drove so relentlessly north and westward from their lodgement on the St. Lawrence, always in pursuit of compliant trading partners whom rumour alleged to have access to an inexhaustible source of thicker and glossier pelts. No such source existed. Fur is one of the most rapidly depleted commodities in the natural world, as are ivory, horn, plumage, or any other animal product acquired by killing its bearer. The native Americans had, in the first millennium after their arrival in the continent from Siberia, exterminated as game the mammoth, the horse, and dozens of other species; fox, wolf, and beaver had survived only because they were not edible. The Indians of the fur zone, of course, killed as many beaver as they needed to clothe themselves, but the number was easily replaced by reproduction. Indian population density was low. Though some scholars claim that there were as many as ten million natives in pre-Columbian America north of Mexico, a figure of 750,000 in the modern United States and 250,000 in Canada is more generally agreed; even the "great" tribes, such as the Iroquois, could field against the French no more than 2,000 warriors from a total population of about 20,000. Once, however, the European appetite for furs impinged, animal numbers declined precipitately. Millions across the Atlantic wanted pelts; a few thousand trappers and hunters could easily supply the need. The gentle, domesticated beaver's pattern of life, centred on his conspicuous lodge and dams, made him easy meat; even the sly fox was trapped with regularity in the winter months when the snowfall betrayed his tracks and lairs.

By the mid-seventeenth century the immediate neighbourhood of the St. Lawrence was trapped out, as the New England rivers already had been. The fur frontier then moved to the eastern Great Lakes, where the Hurons of "Huronia"—the triangle of land between Lakes Ontario, Huron, and Erie—thrived as middlemen, exchanging their agricultural produce with the hunting and trapping Indians of the colder interior for furs and selling them on to the French for trade goods. War with the Iroquois, who coveted the middleman role but preferred English to French trade goods, destroyed Huronia in 1649 and temporarily interrupted supply. It was resumed when other Indians, notably the Ottawa, saw the opportunity to use their routes north of the lakes in an outflanking move and thus brought the produce of the Assiniboines and other trapping tribes directly down to Montreal. Individual Frenchmen were quick to see that what the Ottawa could do they might try for themselves, and it was these early *coureurs de bois* who set off to the upper Great Lakes, encouraged by the local administration and often accompanied by missionaries seeking new converts in the wilderness. By 1670 the fur frontier stood at Lake Superior but then took a southward direction when, through the discoveries of Jolliet, Marquette, and La Salle, the fur-bearing region of the Ohio was opened up to French trade. It was one in which they were shortly to find themselves in competition with the English, as also in Hudson Bay far to the north. The imperative to open up new, wholly French-dominated trading zones therefore persisted, and in the eighteenth century it was towards the Northwest that the effort shifted. The Indian response adapted accordingly; just as the Iroquois had sought to impose an exchange barrier on the Great Lakes, first it was the Illinois and then the Fox who attempted to create a monopoly west of Lakes Michigan and Superior, ironically often in conflict with would-be French monopolists of the export trade such as La Salle. The Vérendryes, last of the great French explorers, were in effect attempting to bypass the Fox and trade with such fur-trapping tribes as the Cree when they made their epic journeys along the Saskatchewan and into the Dakotas in the 1730s.

The French empire of the fur frontier was therefore an odd one, since it had no fixed boundaries; the value of land fluctuated with its fur-bearing properties. The empire has, indeed, been called unique, since, as W. J. Eccles puts it, the French "were no more interested in occupying territory than were New England seamen who voyaged to Africa for cargoes of slaves." Yet they had to claim occupation, none the less, as a means both of subjugating those Indians who contested trade rights with them and of excluding other Europeans who wanted trade rights for themselves. They were, in consequence, often at war, though the wars they fought varied greatly in intensity, duration, and legality. Some were extensions of great wars in Europe, some local, some quite unofficial. Almost every sort of war in the inventory, indeed, was waged in North America between the founding of New France and its overthrow 150 years later.

Champlain, friend to the Iroquois though he eventually sought to make himself, opened hostilities in 1609 when he accompanied a party of their Huron and Algonquin enemies on the warpath down the

Richelieu River. On 29 July, at what would become the site of Fort Ticonderoga on Lake Champlain, the Champlain party encountered a band of two hundred Mohawks. The two sides built barricades and exchanged insults, the preliminaries to "primitive" warfare almost worldwide, and next day advanced to contact. Champlain fired his quadruple-shotted arquebus and killed two Mohawk chiefs; a third was killed by another Frenchman. Their armour of wooden slats offered no protection against gunpowder weapons. Some fifty Mohawks were killed altogether, and the Hurons and Algonquins returned home rejoicing at the victory over their traditional enemies.

One skirmish could not, however, end a war in which the material interests of the two sides were so fundamentally involved. The European appetite for furs had overturned the Indians' subsistence economies, arousing in them a lust for trade goods and so a determination to intercept and control the flow of pelts from the Indians of the interior by denying them direct contact with the Europeans. Had the French themselves been able to deny all the would-be middlemen—Hurons and Iroquois alike—contact with other Europeans, conflict might have been moderated or even averted. They could perhaps have imposed a peace or lent decisive support to one side. As it was, the Iroquois succeeded in acquiring guns and support first from the Dutch, who established a forward base at Fort Orange (Albany) in the 1620s, and later, when the New Netherlands became New York, with the English. It was this accretion of power which allowed the Iroquois, whose Five Nations association rapidly transformed itself from a cultural to a political confederacy, to fall on the Hurons with such destructive ferocity in 1648–49 and thereafter to sustain endemic guerrilla warfare against the French mission and trading outposts until the end of the seventeenth century.

France responded to Iroquois hostility by a variety of means, diplomatic, military, active, and passive. One was fort-building. Fortification was not unknown to the native Americans, and the Iroquois in particular had numbers of stockaded settlements, against which Champlain showed the Hurons how to use a European-style siege tower. It was the Europeans, however, who understood "scientific" fortification, the style of walling and entrenchment designed to foil musketry and later to resist artillery bombardment, and by the end of the seventeenth century they were doing as the Dutch had done and the English were doing, busily building small but stout forts at whatever sites they had identified as commercially or strategically significant. The design tended to be standard, some variation of the star or more properly "bastion trace" plan already appearing along the coastlines, lakeshores, and rivers of the world wherever Europeans were planting empire; in North America, where timber was so plentiful, the material used was wood, supplemented by sod. Where musketry alone had to be feared, a timber palisade, with a trench in front, sufficed; forts threatened by field guns were built of earth or sod, revetted by timber; a few coastal, lake, or river forts, against which the enemy could bring waterborne cannon, were, at enormous expense, constructed of stone.

The extension of the French fortification can be dated with accuracy. Quebec was fortified by Champlain in 1612, and thereafter the works were frequently improved, and Cartier had built an overwintering fort at the mouth of the St. Charles River in 1535 and another at Cap Diamant in 1541, but both had returned to nature by the time of Champlain's settlement. During the 1620s a scattering of small coastal forts were built in Acadia (Nova Scotia) to protect the infant communities against the English, and this fortification was extended in the years 1630–40. In 1721 was begun what would become the strongest fortress in North America, Louisbourg on Cape Breton Island, intended to be a Gibraltar at the mouth of the St. Lawrence.

Along the St. Lawrence itself the French built forts for local protection against Indians: at Tadoussac, at the mouth of the Saguenay River, perhaps as early as 1600; at Trois Rivières at the mouth of the St. Maurice in 1634; and on the island of Montreal in 1642. The chain was extended down to and then within the Great Lakes by the building of Frontenac (modern Kingston) in 1673 and Detroit, guarding the St. Clair River connection between Lakes Erie and Huron, in 1704.

These outposts were links leading to a new fur trade fort built in 1676 at Michilimackinac, which stands strategically at the junction of Lakes Superior, Michigan, and Huron. From it, following the expeditions of Jolliet, Marquette, and La Salle into the Illinois country and down to the Mississippi, extra forts were emplaced on the upper Mississippi: Le Soeur, at its junction with the Des Moines River, and St.-Louis-des-Miamis and Crèvecoeur, both on the Illinois; all were built in 1680–81. Prud'homme, near modern Memphis, and Toulouse, on the lower Mississippi, were built in 1681 and 1699 respectively to connect with the recently founded Biloxi and New Orleans.

Northward from the system stretched the chain protecting the fur trade frontier opened up by La Vérendrye and his sons in the eighteenth century. Its starting points were at Green Bay, Lake Michigan, a post founded by the Jesuits in 1670, and at Cedar Lake (Fort Bourbon), founded in 1680. Kaministikwia was built at Grand Portage on the north shore of Lake Superior in 1718. It protected the route which led via Pigeon River to Rainy Lake (Fort St. Pierre, 1731), Lake of the Woods (Fort St. Charles, 1732), Lake Winnipeg (Fort Maurepas, 1734), the Assiniboine River giving on to the Red River (Fort La Reine, 1731), Lake Winnipegosis (Fort Dauphin, 1740), and finally the Saskatchewan River (Fort Paskoyak, 1750). This was the farthest northwest the French penetrated.

The shore of Hudson Bay, and its great inlet at James Bay, was also fortified at the points where the rivers of the Canadian shield—Churchill, Nelson, Hayes, Severn, Albany, Rupert—flow into the Arctic. Six forts had been established by 1701, but the approach was from the sea, not the land, and the duality of their nomenclature—Fort Albany and Ste. Anne, Moose Factory and Fort St. Louis, York Factory and Fort Bourbon—is a reminder of the shifting fortunes of the French and the Hudson's Bay Company in those northern latitudes. The history of the Hudson Bay forts does not connect with the larger military history of North America.

That was eventually to focus on two other river systems: the Richelieu–Hudson line, with its offshoot up the Mohawk River by which eastern Lake Ontario was approached from the south, and the Forks of the Ohio, a strategic complex of waterways leading northward to Lake Ontario and southward through Pennsylvania to Virginia, Maryland, and the waters of Chesapeake Bay. The French began to construct forts at the St. Lawrence end of the Richelieu River corridor as early as 1665, when men of the Carignan-Salières Regiment built Chambly and St. Jean; the smaller forts of St. Louis, Ste. Thérèse, and Ste. Anne were built the following year. Major engineering, however, did not begin until the eighteenth century, with the intensification of the Anglo-French struggle for empire, when St. Frédéric (Crown Point) was built on the bottom of Lake Champlain in 1731 and Carillon (Ticonderoga) in 1755. The British responded with the construction of Fort William Henry (1755) at the bottom of Lake St.-Sacrement, an arm of Lake Champlain, and Fort Edward on the upper Hudson. They had inherited control of the Mohawk corridor from the Dutch, whose fortification of Albany (Fort Orange, 1624) protected the connection with the Hudson. At the upper end of the Mohawk, where the portage of the Great Carrying Place led to Lake Oneida and so to Lake Ontario, control was exerted through Fort William and Fort Bull and Fort Oswego (1726), against which the French fortified Niagara the following year.

In the Ohio country the means of movement provided by two waterways is bafflingly intricate to the modern eye. The Ohio River itself, key to the geography, connects directly to the Mississippi, where Cairo, Illinois, now stands, but its northern tributaries, the Miami, the Scioto, and the Allegheny, lead towards Lake Erie, while those rising to the south, particularly the Monongahela, drop down from the Appalachian watershed. Just over that crest begin the short but important streams—Juniata and Susquehanna and Potomac—which furnish the way inland from Chesapeake Bay. For the French, therefore, to control the Ohio was essential. The watershed was British territory, unsettled but, from the 1720s, increasingly penetrated by English-speaking traders with attractive trade goods to offer to the Indians. The New Yorkers were already threatening the French position on the southern shores of Lake Ontario. Were the Pennsylvanians and Virginians to break out in numbers across the mountains, the Ohio country might be lost and then the St. Lawrence–Great Lakes–Mississippi axis, the backbone of French America, itself put under threat. From their coastal bases, outposts of their Atlantic power with its roots in the British Isles, but connected also to their spreading network of possessions in the Mediterranean, Africa, and the Indies, the British might, once they found and made passable the gaps in the Appalachian chain (the Cumberland Gap, later to be exploited by Daniel Boone, had been discovered by the Virginian Thomas Walker in 1750), overwhelm the scattered French with an army of land-hungry settlers. In anxious anticipation of such a development, the new governor of Canada, Marquis Duquesne des Menneville, had two new forts built on the southern shore of Lake Erie, Presqu'ile (modern Erie) and Le Boeuf, just inland, in 1753; when in 1754 the Virginians nevertheless voted funds to fortify the Forks of the Ohio, Duquesne pre-empted them by capturing the site (modern Pittsburgh) and creating a fort of his own bearing his name.

By the beginning of what we know, though the contestants did not, was to become the Seven Years War, North America was perhaps as extensively fortified a zone as any in the world, certainly more so than the interior of Britain or France, and bearing comparison—if allowance is made for differences of scale—with the densely defended waterway zones of the Low Countries and northern Italy. North America, moreover, already had its own bitter military history. Intertribal warfare was a fact of American Indian life long before the coming of the Europeans, as in so many "hard primitive" societies; Indians fought for honour, revenge, excitement, and in order to replace the casualties of war by seizing and "adopting" captives from the enemy. Later they fought against themselves over fur as well, particularly in the period 1649–84 when the Iroquois destroyed Huronia, raided the Susquehannocks, Nipissings, Potawatomi, and Delawares, and tried but failed to defeat the Illinois. There had been a series of Indian–settler wars by the Powhatan Confederacy against the Virginians during the years 1622–46, by the Pequot in Connecticut in 1636–37, by several tribes in the New Netherlands against the Dutch in 1643–44, and by the Algonquins in Massachusetts and Rhode Island (King Philip's War) in 1675–66. Indians also joined the imperial wars of the colonists on their own account, as the Abenakis of Maine did against the English in 1688, or at the side of European allies. The raids staged by the Comte de Frontenac, Governor of New France, 1689–98, into New York and New England in the years 1690–92 were mounted with Indian assistance, as were those by the French during the War of the Spanish Succession of 1702–13— Queen Anne's War—when Deerfield, the northernmost settlement on the Connecticut River (today home to one of the most famous American prep schools), was raided for the third time, to the usual accompaniment of massacre, scalping, kidnap, and other cruelties.

The menace of Indian raids was an endemic colonial anxiety; but every colony had its share of roughs who could wreak reprisal, or get their reprisal in first, and the Indians never, in any case, threatened to upset the balance of power in the New World. The settlers themselves, who had cannon, regular soldiers, and, above all, ships in which to shift their means of power about, fought war on a different scale altogether. In 1629, David Kirke from Boston turned Champlain out of Quebec, which was restored to France only at the peace of 1630; this was the first of many subsequent episodes in which the locals undertook hostilities against each other, often without approval from home. In 1654, Robert Sedgwick, a Cromwellian admiral commissioned to attack the New Netherlands in prosecution of England's first Dutch War, chose to attack French Acadia instead, and, though there was then no war with France, it remained in English hands until 1670. The Hudson Bay forts and factories were swapped about like counters in the late seventeenth century, Radisson, a figure of Conradian romance, selling his services between the trading companies as the bidding shifted. In 1689 another adventurer, William Phips, seized Port Royal in Acadia for the New Englanders, and, spurred on by the rewards of a knighthood, sailed with two thousand Boston men for Quebec the following year. They felt they had much to avenge, for Frontenac's raids into their northern farmland and townships had left many dead; they were also inflamed by the promise of loot from Quebec's churches and rich merchant houses. Frontenac was confronted with an ultimatum. It was backed with impressive force, for a fleet of thirty-four ships filled the St. Lawrence estuary around the Ile d'Orléans, and Phips's emissary, who had been blindfolded to make the steep ascent to the Governor's residence, demanded the city's surrender within the hour. The fortress was far stronger, however, than when Kirke had come in 1629. Frontenac curtly dismissed him with the words that he would answer "from the mouths of my cannon," and so the second siege of Quebec began. The Boston men at once began to discover how well its geography frustrated attack.

With winter approaching, which would freeze their ships in, they could not prepare a deliberate offensive. The height of the Quebec cliffs protected the city walls from effective cannonade from the river, and the steepness of the cliffs appeared to rule out a landing in the Plains of Abraham. Phips therefore landed troops on the lower ground of Beauport. Between those flats and Quebec, however, the St. Charles River discharges into the St. Lawrence, and across it the attackers could not get. The forts were defended by cannon and the Quebec shore of the St. Charles by French skirmishers. Smallpox, the ever-ready companion of unvaccinated armies, had also broken out among the attackers, who, after two days' floundering in the wetlands under galling fire, made a rush for the boats and got back to the fleet just in time for it to turn tail before ice began to spread from the shoreline to the navigable channel.

The New Englanders' failure at Quebec was the culminating event of what Americans call King William's War. Queen Anne's War was much slower to ignite than its predecessor had been, perhaps because the fiery Frontenac had left Canada, perhaps because the "policy of posts," advocated by Governor Denonville as early as 1686, was at last beginning to work. The French now really did control the St. Lawrence–Great Lakes–Mississippi line, had as a result brought the Iroquois to accept lasting peace, and were succeeding in turning the undisciplined *coureurs de bois* into wage-earning *voyageurs* who could be counted on to bring the harvest of furs back to the warehouses of Montreal. The French at last found themselves in a stronger position than the New Englanders and New Yorkers whose attempts to revive the war against Acadia, Quebec, and, for the first time, Montreal all failed in the years 1707–10. Port Royal, the Acadian capital and base of vexatious privateers, was eventually taken at the third attempt in 1710, but a maritime expedition to Quebec failed in 1711—the Church of Notre-Dame which stands in the Lower Town accordingly became "des Victoires"—and the British had no success in Hudson Bay either.

Yet at the Peace of Utrecht in 1713, France was forced to cede much territory in North America, the penalty for failure not abroad but at home. The defeats of Blenheim, Ramillies, Malplaquet, and Oudenaarde had to be paid for with American soil, which included all the French ports in Hudson Bay, such bits of Newfoundland as were French, and "peninsular" Acadia, which became Nova Scotia. All that was left to France of importance on the Atlantic was Ile St. Jean, the future Prince Edward Island, and Cape Breton Island (Ile Royal), guarding the mouth of the St. Lawrence.

In these circumstances, France decided on the necessity of fortifying even more stoutly the strategic entry points to her American dominions. Sieur d'Iberville, one of Canada's swashbucklers, had already founded Biloxi to protect the approaches to the Louisiana delta (1699), while Chambly at the St. Lawrence end of the Richelieu–Champlain corridor was now rebuilt in stone. The great work to be undertaken, at the urging of Philippe de Vandreuil, appointed Governor of New France in 1705, was the engineering of Louisbourg, on Cape Breton Island, to the highest European standard. Its walls, bastions, citadel, redoubts, demi-bastions, and ravelins, constructed of stone and in places wet-ditched, were to provide barracks for six companies of infantry, protection to and anchorage for a major fleet, and the assurance that no maritime expedition mounted by an enemy might enter the St. Lawrence estuary as long as France had men and ships to defend it. The work, begun in 1721, was continued, at enormous expense, for years afterwards.

Fortifying the entry points was a defence against enemies without;

the threat to New France, as the eighteenth century drew on, came increasingly from enemies within. The merchants and frontiersmen of the British colonies, whatever the policy of the government at home, had a policy of their own, which was to carry their goods—better and cheaper than the French could offer—into the interior and to bring back via Albany the wealth the Indians exchanged in furs. The British colonists, moreover, were prepared to fight for trade advantage, even when Britain was at peace with France in Europe. On the lower Mississippi they encouraged the Indians—Natchez and Chickasaws—to fight the French of Louisiana. Along the borders of Canada they were ready to fight themselves. The challenge was thrown down in 1726 when Governor William Burnet of New York sanctioned the building of Fort Oswego at the head of the Mohawk River axis to Lake Ontario. Though this was a violation of the Treaty of Utrecht, the French Canadians recognised that they were not strong enough to insist on its removal and it remained. Their riposte was to strengthen the Champlain–Richelieu corridor by constructing Fort St. Frédéric at Crown Point in 1731.

When international conflict returned to North America through the medium of the War of the Austrian Succession (1742–48) in 1744, it was also as a result of local enterprise. Again, a colonial governor, William Shirley of Massachusetts, saw the commercial opportunity and seized it. His militia, covered by a Royal Navy squadron, transhipped itself to Acadia, besieged the formidable fort of Louisbourg, and took it after a forty-seven-day siege. The American Gibraltar had proved to be worth little of the fortune spent in its building. This was but the major event in a campaign of inter-colonial raiding and atrocity, whose events included the French destruction of Saratoga, New York, in November 1746, a British raid as far as Montreal, and the French devastation of Northfield, Massachusetts. Along the Acadian coast, which the British saw as a nest of privateers, there was much naval activity. A French fleet failed to recapture both Louisbourg and Port Royal, while the British did succeed in taking the fort of Grande Pré.

The official peace of 1748 was, for the first time, to influence the strategic policy of the two great imperial powers in Europe. Hitherto France and Britain had fought in America because they were at war in Spain or Germany. In the next decade they were to find themselves at war in Europe because their colonists had precipitated a war in America. It was a messy multilateral conflict, which reached as far north as the shores of Hudson Bay and as far east as Acadia. Its focus, however, lay in the Ohio country, to which New France, the British colonists, and the Indians had also made claim. The French insisted on their rights through the alleged discovery of the Ohio by La Salle in 1669. The Iroquois claimed right of conquest over other tribes but had ceded it to the British by treaty in 1744. A Pennsylvanian, George Croghan, claimed it for the British Crown through a treaty signed with the Shawnees, Wyandots, and Delawares in 1748. The truth of the matter was that the Ohio country was a grey area, vital to both empires because of its fur wealth, which the Indians were willing to sell to the stronger party, but dominated by neither for lack of a military presence in the region.

In 1753, Governor Duquesne set out to supply this. In May 1753 he despatched a force of militia and marine infantry to construct a line of forts, linked by a new road through the wilderness, from Presqu'ile on Lake Erie through modern Waterford, Pennsylvania (Fort Le Boeuf), to the Indian settlement of Venango, thus establishing a military axis from the Great Lakes to the headwaters of the Ohio. The Virginians, whose Ohio Company (1749) was active in the region, were determined not to acquiesce. They could feel the Indians bending their way, knew that they respected force above all, and accordingly sent to London for permission to build a fort of their own in the disputed region. The trouble was that it was indeed disputed; in treaties made in Europe—that applying was the Peace of Aix-la-Chapelle ending the Austrian Succession War in 1748—boundaries in unmapped forest could not be delineated, and while diplomats might not be prepared to press the matter, the locals were. When, accordingly, Governor Robert Dinwiddie received permission from home to attack the French found "within the undoubted limits of His Majesty's dominions," he commissioned one of his young officers to journey to Fort Le Boeuf and warn the French off, in the certain knowledge that no one in London, or anywhere else, could say whether the French were trespassing or not.

The man he chose was George Washington, a provincial militia officer, an already experienced surveyor—it is striking how many of young America's great men, from Champlain to Ulysses S. Grant, were mapmakers or geographers—and acknowledged to be, as Dinwiddie would later hail him, "a braw laddie." Washington's mission was unsuccessful. At Le Boeuf he met a French officer whose manner impressed him—young George, a stickler for his own military dignity, recognised the authentic article—and, under the menace of the fort's nine cannon, was obliged to carry back a dusty answer. His version of the Frenchman's words was that "it was their absolute Design to take possession of the Ohio, and by G—— they would do so." This was a challenge to local, if not international, war. Dinwiddie's response was to pre-empt the French by building a Virginian fort at the point identified by Washington as strategic, the Forks of the Ohio itself, where the Allegheny and Monongahela joined the stripling stream on its course to the Mississippi. The spot today is overbuilt by modern Pittsburgh. In 1754, when Dinwiddie's men began their work, it was raw forest, a wilderness so dense that it disoriented even Washington the mapmaker. He had been sent back by Dinwiddie to reinforce the party at the Forks. When he returned in May he found that the Virginian party had been ousted by a French force, despatched by Governor Duquesne, which was building a fort of their own to be named after him.

Fort Duquesne, Fort Pitt, Pittsburgh: who could have guessed in the middle of the eighteenth century that a clearing in North America's ocean of trees was to become, in the nineteenth, a powerhouse of its industrial revolution? To both sides in May 1754 it seemed a nothingness, important only because the confluence of the rivers at that point gave access to markets in one direction and fur regions in another. It was certainly not worth a fight, and the French were under strict orders not to provoke one. When word reached them, therefore, of Washington's approach, they decided to send a *parlementaire*, whose commander would counsel him to withdraw. Washington, unfortunately, misapprehended the intentions of the French. They were adept at wilderness warfare, the sort of Indian raid which ended in scalping and torture. When he, in turn, learnt that the *parlementaire* had camped nearby, he decided to beat the French to the draw and, in a ghastly dawn descent, surprised them at breakfast and wrought what he feared to suffer. The French officer in command was instantly scalped by an Indian ally of Washington's, known as the Half King, and ten of his party of fifty were killed in a few minutes. Washington then legged it, in the certain knowledge that the French would seek to avenge the massacre. He had constructed a makeshift refuge called Fort Necessity to his rear, and there a strong French force found him five weeks later. Badly outnumbered, he was shortly brought to give his surrender, offered on surprisingly generous terms in view of what the French had against him. In return for a signed admission that he had assassinated his French opposite number, he was allowed to march out under arms and make his way home.

The French were meanwhile transforming Fort Duquesne into a strong place. With six bastions and a covered way to the Monongahela to assure a water supply, another front was covered by the Ohio River. News of the fortification of the Forks did not please the British government, increasingly harried by William Pitt (the Elder) to regard the cold war in the American wilderness as a violation of the treaties both of Utrecht and Aix-la-Chapelle. In January 1755 an expeditionary force was assembled in Ireland and shipped to America, where, after sailing up the Potomac, they debarked at Alexandria, Virginia, then already beginning to grow into what is today a major urban neighbour of the United States capital. It was commanded by Major General Edward Braddock, an officer of the Coldstream Guards, a duellist, a veteran of the Austrian Succession War, and, to his contemporary Horace Walpole, "a very Iroquois in disposition." On arrival he conferred with the governors of Virginia, Pennsylvania, Massachusetts, and Maryland and agreed on a strategy so aggressive as to make the official peace between the kingdoms of Britain and France appear a fiction.

There were to be attacks from Nova Scotia into Acadia, from New York on Fort Niagara, and from the Hudson on Fort St. Frédéric, while Braddock himself was to lead the regulars he had brought from Ireland through the wilderness to the Forks of the Ohio and there storm Fort Duquesne.

That last enterprise required cannon, which were too heavy to be boated and portaged via the Potomac and Monongahela. A road would have to be cut for wagons, longer and wider than the track Washington had hacked the previous year. Benjamin Franklin helped to procure enough wagons from his fellow Pennsylvanians, and on 21 June 1755, Braddock, his two regiments (today battalions of the Royal Anglians), and a force of provisional militia, including Washington himself—gravely compromised in French eyes—set out for Fort Cumberland, the extreme western point of Maryland. The distance between them was only about a hundred miles—the route paralleled that taken today by U.S. 40 from Cumberland via Frostburg to Smithfield and then U.S. 19 to Mount Pleasant—but the journey, which might last two hours by motor car, took nineteen days; Braddock complained of "an uninhabited wilderness of steep rocky mountains and almost impassable morasses."

His slow progress ensured that the French learnt of his approach, informed by Indians who hung about the British flanks. Shawnees and Delawares, they were encouraged by the French commander, Contrecoeur, to remember that the British had always been told not to cross the line of the Appalachian Mountains. Contrecoeur's force, even including his Indians and always supposing they could be motivated to fight, was smaller than Braddock's, eight hundred to his thirteen hundred; nevertheless, he had the initiative and, more important, knowledge of the skills of wilderness warfare. Braddock's 44th and 48th Foot were new regiments, full of raw East Anglian farm boys trained in close-order musketry drill. The French and Indians were raiders, ambushers, and skirmishers, and it was a forest skirmish that developed when the advance parties of the two little armies met just short of Fort Duquesne on the morning of 9 July.

The British managed to unlimber one of the cannon they had dragged so far, got off one round, and killed a French officer. Then, as their scarlet-coated regulars tried to form a front, their flanks were enveloped by the French and Indians working through the woods. The British front ranks fell back, jamming up against those on the narrow road behind. "Such was the confusion," wrote a survivor, "that the men were sometimes twenty or thirty deep, and he thought himself securest who was in the center."

From such disarray, no organised fire could be returned, and by midday the British were in panic-stricken retreat. French fatal casualties were twenty-three, which included fifteen Indians. The British suffered nearly five hundred, including Braddock himself. Washington got away unwounded, and other survivors included an extraordinarily large number of those later to be notable in the War of Independence and the life of the young United States: the most famous were Thomas Gage, who was to command the British troops at Lexington, Concord, and Bunker Hill, Horatio Gates, the American victor of Saratoga, and Daniel Boone, pioneer of the wilderness trail through the Appalachians and founder of Kentucky. It is an exhibition of both the vastness and smallness of eighteenth-century North America that this varied cast of characters should all have found themselves together in an unsurveyed patch of woodland several hundred miles from civilisation at the same time and for the same purpose.

The purpose of the powers was now for war. While Braddock was going down to defeat on the Monongahela, the New Yorker William

Johnson was winning a battle for control of the south of Lake Champlain and the Nova Scotians for dominance in Acadia. France and Britain had been locked in negotiation over their respective rights in North America since January 1755, which Louis XV's government, conscious of Britain's naval superiority and of the demographic imbalance in its disfavour in America, was willing to conclude on conciliatory terms. Their proposal was for the neutralisation of the Ohio country and a return to the *status quo* before the Austrian Succession War. The British, knowing their advantage, wanted nothing less than the destruction of the line of French forts built in Acadia, Canada, and Louisiana since the end of the Spanish Succession War in 1713, including St. Frédéric in the Hudson–Richelieu corridor, Niagara, Duquesne at the Forks of the Ohio, and Toulouse on the lower Mississippi. When the French demurred, the British pressed their demands harder. Both countries were readying fleets to sail for American waters, and when news came that Admiral Boscawen, then off Newfoundland, had intercepted a convoy carrying French troops and bullion to Canada, the French ambassador abandoned the talks and left London. Months of undeclared naval warfare ensued, culminating in a French expedition against Britain's Mediterranean base at Minorca. In June 1756, what was to be the Seven Years War was formally declared.

The Fall of New France

It is a crudity to say that Britain intended to win the war against France in America, while France intended to defend Canada by victories in Europe. Other interests were involved. France had recently made itself an ally of its old enemy Austria, while Britain had taken up with Austria's upstart foe, Prussia. The Austrians and Prussians cared not a whit about America, which meant equally little to the strategic and diplomatic traditionalists in France and Britain. Some Frenchmen, nevertheless, grasped the importance of keeping a strong position in the New World, and one party in Britain saw victory in the overseas empires as the key to future greatness. That party was led by William Pitt, who in December 1756 became effective Prime Minister and was to mastermind Britain's prosecution of the Seven Years War until its triumphant conclusion in 1763.

Under Pitt one thing concerning war in America was certain: it would not be about fur—fur, in any case, was becoming old hat—but about territory. Throughout the 130 years of the American quarrel between France and England, which had started when David Kirke shanghaied Champlain from Quebec in 1629, there had been little determined effort to strike at the heartlands. Champlain had wanted Louis XIII to buy the mouth of the Hudson; the New Englanders had twice tried but failed to take Quebec by amphibious assault. Otherwise their wars had been those of outposts, skirmishing, raids, extemporised sieges, the bloody charge for scalps and loot in the gloom of the great forests. It was a type of war, *la petite guerre*, known to Europeans only in their border campaigns against the Turks in the mountains of the Balkans. In that form of warfare the assistance of indigenous warriors had been a prerequisite for success, as the savagery of the Indians was a further replication of the bitterness of struggle between Christian and Muslim borderers on the Ottoman frontier.

From the outbreak of war in 1756, the conflict in North America was to be war European style, fought by large regular armies and directed towards the end of decisive close-order battles. In 1756 itself there was to be a brief continuation of wilderness warfare south of Lake Ontario, when French and Indians raided outposts on the Mohawk River portages to Lake Ontario and then in a more deliberate operation took and destroyed Fort Oswego, the termination of the Mohawk route to Lake Ontario, in a brutal assault. These successes did not alter the strategic balance, which now depended on the question of who could most quickly amass a preponderant conventional force at the decisive point.

France sent a strong reinforcement in the spring of 1756, comprising the whitecoat regular regiments of La Salle, Berry, and Roussillon, under the command of a competent general, Louis Joseph, Marquis de Montcalm. His opposite number, John Campbell Loudon, who would be succeeded by James Wolfe, also brought reinforcements: the 35th and 42nd Foot (the Black Watch of kilted Highlanders), the 50th and 51st, and a contingent of Royal Artillery. He had orders to raise a regular regiment in the colonies, to be numbered the 60th (Royal Americans), and to strengthen the provincial corps of militia. With the 44th and 48th, which were recruiting new men to replace those lost in the horror of the Monongahela, he would have ten battalions (the 60th was to be a large regiment of four battalions) and a powerful field and

ABOVE: Samuel de Champlain in battle with the Iroquois

French Canadian *habitant* on snowshoes, 1722

Samuel de Champlain, founder of New France

BELOW: Montcalm, Wolfe's opponent at the Plains of Abraham

LOUIS Joseph M¹⁵ de MONTCALM GOZON.
29 février 1712 + 14 Septembre 1759.

Montcalm and his troops celebrating victory
at Ticonderoga, 8 July 1758

Wolfe and his troops scaling
the cliffs to the Plains
of Abraham, 1759

The Plains of Abraham
today, with Quebec City in
the background

Quebec in 1730, with the Plains of Abraham to the left

TOP: Wolfe's landing, 13 September 1759

BOTTOM: *The Death of Wolfe* by Edward Penny, 1763

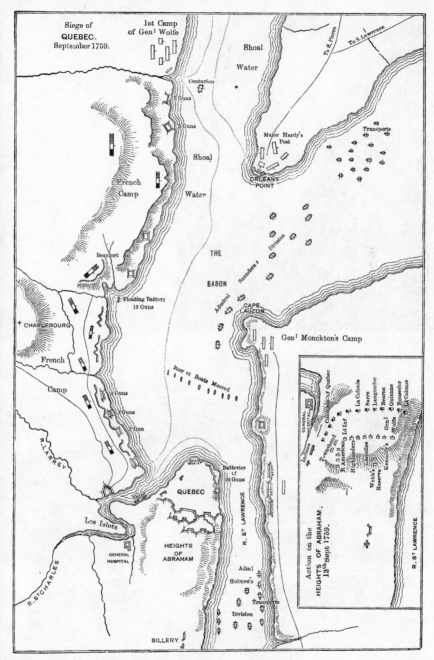

The Quebec theatre of operations
and plan of battle

YORKTOWN

George Washington
in later life

West Point on the
Hudson; the modern
academy stands on
the site of Fort Arnold.

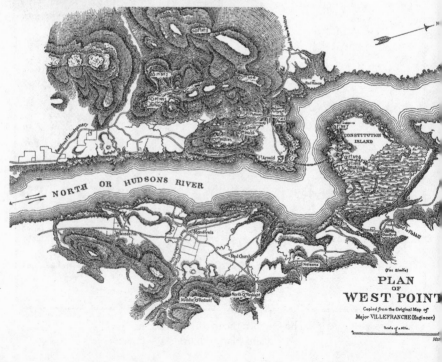

NORTH OR HUDSONS RIVER

PLAN
OF
WEST POINT

Copied from the Original Map of
Major VILLEFRANCHE (Engineer)

Scale of a Mile.

ABOVE: Cornwallis

Bougainville, who was
present at Quebec, 1759,
and Yorktown, 1781

The surrender of Yorktown
by Cornwallis to Washington, 1781

siege artillery supported offshore by a fleet of fifteen ships of the line and twenty-three smaller vessels. Such a naval force threatened to deny Montcalm further reinforcement once fighting started in earnest.

Loudon, moreover, had a plan. "Quebec is the Point we should push for, by the River St. Lawrence," he urged in a letter home. "I need not explain to you the consequences which would arise from our success there." Loudon had correctly simplified the strategic geography of North America; the plans of the previous year, which had embraced a four-pronged assault on Niagara and Acadia as well as Duquesne, had been a dispersal of effort, of which Braddock's defeat was a consequence and for which the capture of Fort Beauséjour in Acadia was no compensation. Unfortunately Pitt, now effective warlord in London, saw Loudon as a client of his political enemies and perversely took against his single-minded scheme. He chose to perceive the danger that Louisbourg, the American Gibraltar, presented to any expeditionary force bypassing it to run up the St. Lawrence. That the creation of such a psychological menace was precisely among the reasons for which Louisbourg had been built, Loudon did not dare to point out to him; nor did he argue that his strategy of forcing Montcalm to concentrate his troops at Quebec would prevent his using them to raid, in the feared "Indian style," the New York and New England frontiers. When in February 1757 Loudon received orders from Pitt that the offensive against Quebec would be preceded by the capture of Louisbourg, he acquiesced.

Had Loudon's whole naval force arrived from Britain at the same time as Pitt's order it might have been possible to mount the double campaign against Louisbourg and Quebec in 1757. It did not, however, being delayed by bad weather. As a result, the British and Americans spent the year in the pursuit of miscarried plans or plain idleness. By its end, Loudon had dispersed the regiments which had been concentrated to attack Louisbourg, keeping some in Nova Scotia and sending the rest to New York to join the garrison of Fort Edward at the bottom of the Hudson–Richelieu corridor.

The British were, unwittingly, playing the French game. Vaudreuil, the French governor, who was hoping for more reinforcements from Europe, saw that they had given him the chance to use Montcalm's troops in a frontier campaign and, after assuring himself that Forts Duquesne and Louisbourg were as strong as he could make them— thus blocking moves against the St. Lawrence from east to west—he despatched a force to raid down the southern approach and take by surprise Loudon's garrison below Lake Champlain.

Fort William Henry was new, a strengthened version of the camp which William Johnson of New York had pitched at the bottom of Lake St. Sacrement (now Lake George), the southern arm of Lake Champlain, in 1745. Its new opposite number was Fort Carillon, which Duquesne had planned at the tinkling falls where the two lakes joined, known to the Americans as Ticonderoga. Montcalm led his army out of Carillon on 30 July and embarked it in a fleet of boats and canoes. He had 3,600 regulars and militiamen, 1,500 Indians, and a dozen cannon. He was also soon in possession of a letter to the commander of Fort William Henry from nearby Fort Edward on the Hudson warning that no help could be expected. Montcalm proceeded to make a proper show of force, setting up batteries and digging saps forward in best European siege style. The effect was so impressive that it took only two days of bombardment for the British commander to speak under a flag of truce and one more for him to accept defeat. He and his garrison marched out to captivity, in a display of courtesy marred suddenly by an Indian massacre of many of the prisoners. They were New Yorkers, against whom Montcalm's Abenaki had a historic grudge. Though he managed to restore order, his sense of honour was outraged; it was the form of misconduct of which the French had accused Washington at Fort Duquesne.

The loss of William Henry, a small setback but humiliating none the less, was to be succeeded shortly by a genuine defeat. During the winter of 1757–58 the French, possessing the strategic initiative, operated along the southern shore of Lake Ontario, assuring themselves that the abandoned British forts had not been reoccupied, and raided down the Mohawk River into northern New York with the usual cruelties of "Indian warfare." Montcalm's intentions for 1758, however, were to capitalise on the success he had won on the Champlain route. There General James Abercromby, whom Pitt had sent to replace Loudon, had assembled a major force and showed every sign of attempting to break into the Richelieu route by seizing Fort Carillon. Montcalm decided to forestall him. Judging that Carillon had been badly sited, he set his men to improvising an earthwork on higher ground nearby and meanwhile sent out patrols to observe Abercromby's progress and harry his advance. Since he was bringing his fifteen thousand men—the largest army yet assembled in America—

northward by boat up Lake St. Sacrement, the orders to the patrols were to stop a landing at all costs.

In that they failed. On 6 July, Abercromby found a landing place at the head of Lake St. Sacrement, just short of the rapids linking it to Lake Champlain, and got his men ashore. While his vast fleet of boats was being moored, an advance party under the energetic Brigadier Lord Howe pushed forward and collided unwittingly with a French patrol. In the exchange of fire following, Howe was killed. The British halted in confusion, and word was got back to Montcalm that action was at hand. Throughout 7 July he harried his men to complete the earth-and-timber position on which he counted to stop the British offensive. By the morning of 8 July it was as complete as it could be made, and he arrayed his men in line of battle.

They consisted of seven regular regiments, La Reine, Béarn, Guienne, Royal Roussillon, Berry, La Sarre, and Languedoc, with which were intermingled marines and Canadian militia; the number of units was large but the strength only a fifth of the British. Abercromby counted on his preponderance to win without difficulty; but an attack on field entrenchments was always a risky thing in gunpowder warfare, all the more so in America, where the forest enclosed the flanks and supplied an abundance of timber for forward entanglements. Entangled the British became; "the ground was . . . clogged up with Logs and trees Intermixed with Brush which greatly interrupted the speedy and Regular march of our troops," a soldier wrote. Abercromby had decided, on advice, not to use his artillery against the entanglements; nor did he use his light infantry, the Americans of Rogers' Rangers, to work round the flanks. Instead his eight battalions of redcoats—Royal Scots, Inniskillings, Black Watch, and 34th, 44th, 46th, and 1st and 4th Battalions of the Royal Americans—marched straight into the French musketry and, throughout the afternoon, formed and re-formed to renew the attack. Eventually, with sixteen hundred dead and wounded on the forest floor, he accepted defeat, a pointless and terrible defeat, and withdrew. Montcalm, whose casualties were 377, had secured the St. Lawrence from attack by the southern route.

This, however, was to be the high point of French success in the campaign of 1758 and, indeed, in what was evidently swelling into a climactic war for empire. Abercromby, though bloodied at Carillon, retained an offensive preponderance, while Montcalm's forces were too small for anything but reacting to British initiatives. Though Montcalm was "operating on interior lines," in the technical language of strategy, Abercromby had the freedom to move around the perimeter of French Canada and strike at weak spots. That was what, in the aftermath of Carillon, he determined to do. Consigning a strong force of American provincial troops to his quartermaster, Colonel John Bradstreet, he ordered him to advance up the Mohawk corridor for the Hudson, cross Lake Ontario, and besiege and take Fort Frontenac (Kingston), which guarded its outlet into the St. Lawrence.

Bradstreet reached the Great Carrying Place between the Mohawk and Wood Creek in early August (the route today is U.S. 90 from Schenectady to Utica), portaged, followed the water route up the creek to Lake Oneida and the Oswego River, and arrived on the shore of Lake Ontario on 21 August. By 25 August, having crossed the head of the lake by boat, he was outside Fort Frontenac, whose garrison he outnumbered twenty to one. He opened his bombardment next day and the day following, 22 August, brought the French to surrender. They were allowed to march out and return to Montreal, in return for a similar number of British prisoners, while Bradstreet's men pillaged the place, destroyed part of the fortification, and burnt the fleet of little war vessels which harboured there. That "navy," Montcalm dejectedly and accurately reported to Paris, "assured us the superiority in Lake Ontario which we now lose."

The pincers were closing about French Canada, the inevitable outcome, once the British had chosen to make a major strategic effort in North America, of the failure of Paris to sponsor large-scale emigration to its dominions. Numbers tell, both in colonisation and warfare, and the advantage in this imperial war was now passing to the more populous English-speaking regions. In November the Forks of the Ohio passed definitively under British control, when Fort Duquesne was abandoned by its French garrison in the face of overwhelming numbers. What made this defeat significant was that the resumption of the effort to gain possession of the Ohio country had come from the Americans themselves, particularly the governors of Pennsylvania and Virginia, and it was those colonies which had supplied the troops, George Washington once again among them. French Canada had been in no position to oppose them with a like number of settlers; the best force assembled against the Americans by the French consisted of thirty Canadians and 140 Shawnees, Delaware, and Iroquois. Indians and militiamen could not hope to oppose English-speaking America on the march.

The worst of all French setbacks suffered by New France in 1758 came not in the interior but at the most important of the maritime entry points, the mouth of the St. Lawrence. The capture of Louisbourg had been high on Pitt's list of priorities the previous year, and might have been achieved had contrary winds not delayed the sailing of the expeditionary force from England. In 1758 Admiral Boscawen got away early. He commanded an enormous force, twenty ships of the line, eighteen frigates, and a hundred transports carrying twelve thousand soldiers. Joining forces with the smaller fleet already at Halifax, Nova Scotia, Boscawen arrived off Louisbourg two hundred miles to the northeastward on 2 June and anchored in Gabarus Bay just west of the fortress. The shore was hostile to a landing, rocky and beaten by the Atlantic surf, and it was not until 8 June that an attempt was made. Three points had been selected: all were defended by the French. As so often happens in amphibious assaults—Gallipoli and D-Day provide later examples—the successful foothold was found at a spot which the defenders had neglected to guard. A party under the young Brigadier James Wolfe got ashore, hidden from view by the smoke of the French guns elsewhere, and soon the defenders had to abandon the attempt to deny the shoreline to the British and retreat to the fortress.

The Gibraltar of America was, it had long been known, badly built and badly sited. It could be overlooked from higher ground, which was the main reason it had fallen in 1745. What had happened then was to be repeated now. Guns were emplaced by the British in the overlooking heights, fire was opened on 19 July, and the French defences and the dwellings within the walls were systematically battered to pieces. So were the warships in the harbour. The governor's wife, Madame Courserac de Drucourt, "La Bombardière," set an example to weaker men by manning the ramparts each day to fire cannon at the enemy; the gesture was splendid but empty. Boscawen's fleet had brought nearly 100,000 roundshot and explosive shells; the result, as a diarist within Louisbourg recorded of a typical day, was that "between yesterday morning and seven o'clock tonight from a thousand to twelve hundred shells have fallen inside the town." By 25 July the governor accepted that he could not sustain the defence. The fleet was destroyed, the town devastated, and the besiegers, who outnumbered his force four to one, prevented his breaking out. On 17 July he surrendered on honourable terms and his men marched out to captivity. It was by no means a disgraceful defeat. As at the future siege of Port Arthur during the Russo-Japanese War of 1904–5, which that of Louisbourg anticipated closely in character, the defence had bought time. In this case it had bought a whole year, for the postponement of the surrender until late summer precluded an assault in Quebec that year.

No British officer resented the delay more than the rising star of Pitt's American war, James Wolfe. He was sent off, after the fall of Louisbourg, to complete the depopulation of French Acadia, burning houses and ships and taking prisoners. Others who joined in the work recorded the slaughter of livestock and the scalping of humans. The war in Canada was not nice. Wolfe, however, believed it might be brought swiftly to an end if sufficient pressure were applied at the right place. New France had now been shrunk to a fraction of its cartographic extent. The destruction of Fort Frontenac had weakened the link between the St. Lawrence settlements and the Great Lakes, and also with the *pays d'en haut* which embraced Lake Winnipeg and the Saskatchewan River; a continued French presence at Niagara, between Lakes Ontario and Erie, was insignificant. The destruction of Fort Duquesne and its rebuilding as Fort Pitt had unfastened the French grip on the Ohio country. The seizure of Fort Carillon had positioned the British to advance up the Champlain–Richelieu corridor, a direct threat to Montreal. The only strong places left to France were the upper forts of that corridor and Quebec itself.

Vaudreuil, the French governor, and Montcalm, his military executive, pondered the dangers during the winter of 1758; they could not decide whether these were greater in the St. Lawrence or the Richelieu waterways. At home in England, Pitt had no doubts. He was now obsessed by his war in America—though he was waging others in Europe, India, and the West Indies and was determined to have a conclusive victory in 1759. During December he wrote sharp instructions to his generals. There was to be a southern offensive, up the Richelieu and against Lake Ontario or both, by a force of regulars and provincials under General Jeffrey Amherst, who had commanded at Louisbourg. There was also to be a Lakes campaign, to extinguish the last French outposts there, particularly at Niagara. The chief enterprise, however, was to be an amphibious offensive up the St. Lawrence, commanded by Wolfe at the head of twelve thousand embarked troops, to take Quebec.

Wolfe spent the winter months of 1758 in England, where he was directly commissioned by the commander-in-chief, Lord Ligonier, to take charge of the embarked force at Louisbourg in the coming spring. He promised in a letter to Amherst that he would "spare no pains, and should be happy if the sacrifice of my own health and constitution, or even my life, could anyhow contribute to bring this bloody war to an honourable and speedy conclusion." It was a prophetic statement of intention. Ill health had brought him back to London and was to plague him throughout the coming campaign. Death awaited him under the walls of Quebec. He sailed from Spithead on 17 February 1759, in company with Vice-Admiral Sir Charles Saunders, who was to command the St. Lawrence fleet, found Louisbourg too icebound to enter, harboured temporarily at Halifax on 30 April, and finally reached Louisbourg to complete preparations on 15 May. In the meantime, despite the ice, a fleet from France had slipped into the St. Lawrence to bring Montcalm essential supplies.

The final battle for empire in North America has often been represented as a personal conflict between Wolfe and Montcalm. There is just enough contrast between their ancestries and personalities to make the device arresting. Montcalm belonged to the old aristocracy of France. Born in the family château at Candiac, in what is now the department of the Gard on the Mediterranean, he was forty-seven in 1759, the husband of another aristocrat, and the father of ten children. He had gone to war first at the age of fifteen, had fought throughout the War of the Austrian Succession, been several times wounded, and been taken prisoner. He was a man of honour and intelligence, but a difficult subordinate; he and Vaudreuil, a less able man, were frequently at odds. Wolfe, who was fifteen years younger than Montcalm, is often called "middle class." It is true that he did not come from a titled family and that his house at Westerham in Kent is far less than a château. His father, nevertheless, was a regular officer, who had risen to the rank of lieutenant general. Wolfe, in short, belonged to the professional officer class. He, like Montcalm, had gone to war young, been present at the Battle of Dettingen at the age of sixteen, and fought in the defeat of Bonnie Prince Charlie's Highland army at Culloden in 1746. He had become a lieutenant colonel in 1750 and, for Quebec, had been promoted major general, a very senior rank for a man of only thirty-two. Wolfe, moreover, was both clever and a passionate student of his profession. His superiors, Pitt most of all, recognised him to be of outstanding ability and, though he could be a trying superior himself and an infuriating subordinate—his immensely tall and skeletal frame, gangling gait, upturned nose, and red hair seemed to set teeth on edge—his fitness to command the expedition was not doubted.

Wolfe had an excellent army. It consisted of ten regular battalions, the 15th, 28th, 35th, 43rd, 47th, 48th, 58th, the 2nd and 3rd Battalions of the Royal Americans, recruited respectively in New York and Nova Scotia, and the 78th Highlanders; their grenadier companies, comprising the tallest men, had been formed into a shock battalion called the Louisbourg Grenadiers; there was also a battering train of Royal Artillery, some light infantry, and the American Rogers' Rangers. Nevertheless, he was badly outnumbered, a factor that was to prey on him throughout the campaign and help to determine its character. Though Montcalm had only five regular regiments, La Sarre, Languedoc, Béarn, Guienne, and Royal Roussillon—white-coated Frenchmen from the southern seacoasts and eastern frontier of the homeland— Vaudreuil's decision to concentrate the bulk of his bluecoat Troupes de la Marine and Canadian militia at Quebec, leaving the rest of New France to be protected by a mixed force of 3,000 regulars, marines, and militia, gave him a superiority. Montcalm probably had nearly 15,000 men with whom to oppose Wolfe; he had, in his own words, "9,000 men, in England it is still called 12,000." All, however, were trained regulars, and he also possessed the inestimable advantage of a fleet with which to manoeuvre them against the long line of Montcalm's defences. Saunders, Wolfe's excellent naval colleague, commanded forty-nine warships, manned by 13,500 sailors, and 119 transports. Among his officers was Captain James Cook, the future Pacific navigator; among Montcalm's was Louis-Antoine de Bougainville, at twenty-eight already a Fellow of the Royal Society of London, whose Pacific voyages would match Cook's in boldness and extent.

Wolfe's problem was threefold: where and how to land his inferior force in such a way as to make its superior quality tell over Montcalm's superior numbers. The St. Lawrence at Quebec is tidal and treacherous, and the navigable channels were not then charted by the British; Cook was to spend much time in small boats taking soundings during the coming weeks. The shore itself presented as many difficulties to a landing force as it had on the two previous occasions the British had attempted to capture Quebec; more, for the north foreshore below the Quebec headland was impeded by earthworks and barricades, strongly garrisoned by militiamen. Direct assault on the city was out of the question. The cape on which it stood was too precipitous to be climbed by troops under fire, while the landward side was walled off by the line of the ramparts running between the St. Lawrence and St. Charles rivers. So high is the city that it was not easily to be bombarded from the water, and so broad is the St. Lawrence that a battery established across the water on the southern shore—as it was to be at Pointe Lévis—could hit it only at extreme range. The lower town, at water level, provided a platform, but was heavily defended and joined to the city proper by a single steep road known, significantly, as the Côte de la Montagne. The northern shore of the river, though low-lying, was not only fortified but, as the British had found in 1690, swampy; more important, through it two rivers discharged into the St. Lawrence, the Montmorency and, almost under the city walls, the St. Charles, both of which formed serious military obstacles. If Louisbourg had not proved an American Gibraltar, Quebec threatened to supply the deficiency.

Quebec's powerful batteries of guns, moreover, menaced all British movement upstream, both denying Wolfe the opportunity to create a strong base on the landward side of the fortress from which a methodical siege of the city walls might be mounted and at the same time assuring Montcalm a regular reprovisioning of the fortress from the two French strongholds at Montreal and Trois Rivières. The net was closing in that direction. In June the French failed in an attempt to repossess Fort Oswego at the head of the Mohawk corridor, while on 26 July a force sent by Amherst captured Fort Niagara. The lake end of the St. Lawrence was thereby placed under severe threat. As long, however, as its main course between Montreal and Quebec could be kept open, Quebec might be resupplied and Montcalm could hope to hold Wolfe off until the approach of the cold season forced him to up-anchor and retreat to Nova Scotia for the winter.

Wolfe had established his main base on the Ile d'Orléans, the beautiful island in the St. Lawrence just downstream from the city, on 26 June. An attempt by the French to burn his fleet with fireships failed the following night. On that day, 27 June, Wolfe also got gunners ashore at Pointe Lévis, opposite Quebec, to build a battery, which opened fire on 12 July, with six 32-pounders and five 13-inch mortars, and would sustain the bombardment for the next seven weeks, slowly battering the fine buildings of the city into charred ruins. On 9 July a third landing was made below Beauport on the north shore of the St. Lawrence at Beaupré. It was undefended, but a second river, the Montmorency, flowing parallel to the St. Charles, barred the approaches even to the Beauport defences.

Wolfe was now in a quandary. Time pressed. A Quebec that could supply itself could not be taken by siege before winter. Attempts to isolate it by working round the northern shore were foundering on geography and the defensive improvements to it the French had made. What he wanted was a battle, but Montcalm would certainly not lead his men out from behind Quebec's strong walls unless British cannon could be positioned to breach them by direct fire; ruination of the town by bombardment from over the water, though it meant misery for the inhabitants, would not crack its carapace. On 31 July, Wolfe tried a direct assault on the Beauport defences by landing a force of grenadiers on the French side of the Montmorency River, just beyond the spectacular waterfall by which it discharges into the St. Lawrence, to capture the eastern end of the earthworks. It miscarried, the grenadiers suffered 450 casualties, and the landing party withdrew in frustration.

No one was more frustrated than Wolfe, who was also suffering from the ills that chronically affected him: kidney stones, rheumatism, and, one suspects, neurotic hypochondria. Throughout August, often abed, he wrestled with his strategic problems, desperate for a battle but unable to perceive a means of bringing one about. Inspiration eventually came from his admiral, Sir Charles Saunders, who was a remarkable man. More remarkable still, in view of the long history of quarrels that joint army-navy operations seem to provoke, he and Wolfe got on. In Wolfe's favour it must be said that their good relations reflect well on him; but Saunders had the qualities of the best sort of naval officer. No narrow pettifogger, martinet, or nervous apprehender of the Board of Admiralty's displeasure, he was on the contrary liked by his sailors, for whose welfare he cared, and was a bold risk-taker. Someone more timid, more bound by regulations, might have insisted that he had done his duty by delivering the army to the appointed place. Sailors hate operations in confined waters, commonly stand on their right not to hazard their ships by grounding on shoal or reef, and resist suggestions that they should penetrate any further into hostile waters than the point at which they have debarked soldiers. Saunders seemed to relish the amphibious challenge. As early as 18 July he had run two of his frigates past the Quebec peninsula and rousted about in French territory. On 5 August he slipped five more ships up the river, and four days later another five. Montcalm, who was distracted by the campaign of burning and pillage that Wolfe's light troops were waging against the farms and villages of the St. Lawrence shore, now had to detail Bougainville to patrol the Quebec cliffs in an exhausting vigil against the British commando raids.

Saunders's enterprise became Wolfe's plan. "It will be necessary," he wrote to Saunders in early September, "to run as many small craft as possible by the town. . . . The small vessels can take us in occasionally . . . and run us back again in a tide. . . . perhaps we may find an opportunity to strike a blow." What blow exactly he could not still decide, however; he had asked his brigadiers for their advice on 25 August and they had concisely stated the realities: "We are . . . of the opinion that the most probable method of striking an effectual blow is by . . . directing our operations above the town. When we have established ourselves on the north shore . . . M. de Montcalm must fight us upon our terms. We are betwixt him and his provisions." That solved the "where" of the strategic dilemma in which Wolfe had begun his campaign. It did not solve the "how." Even with British ships above the Quebec batteries, the cliffs beyond the town and the troops on their edge formed a formidable obstacle. Wolfe had failed under the much less steep obstacle at the Montmorency River. How much more likely was he to fail at the Quebec escarpment itself?

Only reconnaissance and experiment would show the way. Boldly, Wolfe decided to abandon his established base in the Ile d'Orléans on 3 September, tranship his force to the south shore, and march it upriver beyond Quebec, leaving skeleton companies to maintain the appearance of a full camp behind. That served for deception. Even when he had repositioned his force to take advantage of the presence of Saunders's ships (commanded by Admiral Holmes) above the Quebec guns, however, he was still far from getting them ashore. The Quebec peninsula from the city as far as Cap Rouge, a distance of nine miles, is steep and rocky and the crest stands several hundred feet above the river. The whole length was patrolled by Bougainville's 3,000 men, ready to fall on any assault column which attempted to escalade the cliffs from boats at their foot. He had his orders. "The most important point," Montcalm had written, "is to follow every movement of the corps which you have on the water in front of you. You will thus always be on the spot to deal with their disembarkation." Batteries at Samos and Sillery were to cannonade the British fleet whenever it came within range. A foothold at the foot of the cliffs, called L'Anse du Foulon, was to be guarded by a special detachment under Louis du Chambon de Vergor. It was overlooked that he had been court-martialled four years earlier for surrendering Fort Beauséjour in Acadia without a fight.

Wolfe began his experiment with the French on 7 September, when Admiral Holmes took twenty-two ships, with 3,600 soldiers embarked, upriver as far as Pointe-aux-Trembles and drifted back with the tide; Wolfe watched Bougainville's troops following the fleet on the cliffs above and mounted a feint assault to test their reactions. On 8 and 9 September, in driving rain which drenched his troops on the transports' decks, Wolfe remained on the alert. He now knew that he could wear Bougainville's watchers out by forcing them to march and counter-march in rhythm with his movements but he could still not decide where, if anywhere, he might risk a landing. So miserable did the autumn rains make his soldiers that he disembarked many to dry their clothes; his own volatile spirits were fragile, as he wrestled with the difficulty of turning a plan he knew to be correct in conception into concrete reality. Time pressed heavier than ever. The rains presaged autumn, autumn the winter freeze, ice the failure of his enterprise.

Then on 10 September his mental cloud lifted. Deserters from the fortifications at Beauport below the city had come in with the news that Wolfe's manoeuvres upriver were interpreted as a move to intercept vital supplies coming down from Montreal—Quebec was close to starvation—and that Montcalm did not expect a landing to be made close to the city. This intelligence gave Wolfe the glimmering of a break in the apparent impermeability of Montcalm's wall of natural and artificial fortification, what he called in a letter to Loudon "the strongest country, perhaps in the world, to rest the defences of the town and colony upon." Disguising himself as a common soldier, he spent the whole day in a small boat examining the cliffs by telescope and decided that L'Anse du Foulon was the spot he wanted. Its closeness to the city, less than two miles away, seemed to qualify it as a place Montcalm discounted as a point of danger; the number of tents pitched above it revealed that the guard was small. The height of the cliff, 180 feet, and its steepness would make both the climb and surprise difficult; but it offered the only, if not the best hope. Wolfe made up his mind. His troops would land on 13 September at four in the morning.

He kept his plan largely to himself, meanwhile ordering Holmes to persist with the drifting up and down with the tide, twice in each twenty-four hours for the next two days. He was right to be secretive, even with his brigadiers. On 12 September a sergeant of the Royal Americans deserted to the French but could tell them nothing. Desertion before battle is usually a self-protective act. Those motives brought Wolfe two French deserters the same day who had news of crucial importance: Montcalm was expecting riverborne supplies from Montreal on the night of 12–13 September and the sentries had been warned to expect it. Fortuitously, Wolfe had been handed a perfect cover scheme.

He reinforced it by ordering Saunders to mount a cannonade and a feint attack opposite Beauport below Quebec. Meanwhile, in the darkness of the last hours of 12 September, Wolfe, his embarked landing force of 4,800 men, and the ships they were in, drifted up with the tide well above L'Anse du Foulon, hung there with the slack water, and then drifted down with the ebb. Bougainville and his exhausted watchers made little effort to keep pace with a now familiar manoeuvre. Precisely at two o'clock the oared craft carrying the army cast off and rowed across the river from the south shore, and at four o'clock it grounded in L'Anse du Foulon. The French sentries had been misled by answers to their challenges made in French, and there was no one to oppose Wolfe, the first man ashore, when he landed. Soon the Highlanders and light infantry had followed him, scrambled their way up by clutching at bushes and branches on the cliff face, and rushed de Vergor's encampment at the top of the cliff path. By six o'clock the whole of Wolfe's force was deployed in line of battle on the Plains of Abraham—the biblical allusion is indirect, the ground taking its name from Abraham Martin, a sea pilot who had farmed that land in Champlain's time—where it awaited action.

When news of their arrival reached Montcalm, which it did at about half past five, neither he nor Vaudreuil could credit it. They suspected another feint. Montcalm was soon disabused. Wolfe's position was hidden from the city walls by a swell of ground called the Buttes à Neveu; breasting it ahorse, he was horrified to see a scarlet line of battle occupying the whole width of the Quebec headland. "I see them where they have no business to be," he said to his aide-de-camp, the Chevalier Johnstone, a Scottish Jacobite who had escaped to France from the defeat of Culloden in 1746. "This is a serious state of affairs." He instantly decided to bring out the garrison and fight.

Vaudreuil dissented, fearing a second landing at Beauport below the city. He therefore refused to allow marines and militia to be brought up on to the Plains of Abraham. The decision was calamitous for Montcalm, for it meant that he would have only his regulars with whom to oppose Wolfe and would therefore be outnumbered. That makes his decision to give battle all the more difficult to understand. True, Quebec was short of supplies. True, Wolfe would now be able to haul cannon up the cliff and open a deliberate siege against the landward face of the city's wall and bastions. True, all military engineers agreed that the design of the fortress was defective, since the run of the ground downwards from the St. Lawrence to the St. Charles River meant that cannon outside the walls could dominate the lower bastions from the citadel end. Nevertheless, fortress garrisons have survived under siege on rats' tails and boot straps when there was sense in playing for time, and the approach of a Canadian winter supplied that sense. There was, moreover, no guarantee that Wolfe could starve Quebec before the snows, which might have come in October, nor that he could have battered a breach. Sieges can go awry.

Perhaps Wolfe's relentless probing had so shredded Montcalm's nerves that he could no longer find the fibre to protract the duel of wits. He may simply have wanted a battle to resolve the uncertainty one way or another; "I wished that the fight was fought," was the recorded thought of one of Wellington's soldiers before Waterloo. It is a very human sentiment and very common among warriors before action. It seems to have possessed Montcalm on the morning of 12 September 1759, and to have warped his judgement. He made no attempt to form a junction with Bougainville and his three thousand, who remained in Wolfe's rear, nor any to outgun the British. Wolfe had only two light field guns with him. The French may have had as many as twenty-five in the city but Montcalm gave battle with only three.

Quebec was therefore to be that rare thing in the gunpowder age, a firefight pure and simple between two lines of opposed infantry. There was no cavalry on either side and few light troops. Montcalm had some fifteen hundred Canadian militiamen and infantrymen, mainly on his right flank. Wolfe, though attended by an Indian in Benjamin West's painting of his death, had none, while his light infantry were not committed to battle. His line was formed of six regular battalions—from left to right the 58th, 78th Highlanders, 47th, 43rd, 28th, and the Louisbourg Grenadiers—with the 15th in second line and the Royal Americans and 35th protecting the left and right flanks (military traditionalists will identify these by their Victorian names—the Louisbourg Grenadiers excepted—as the 2nd Northants, 2nd Seaforths, 1st Loyals, 1st Ox and Bucks, 1st Glosters, 1st East Yorks, 2nd and 3rd Kings Royal Rifle Corps, and 1st Royal Sussex; their descendants exist in the British Army today). Deep in rear stood the 48th (2nd Northants) as a reserve. Against them Montcalm opposed the regular regiments of La Sarre, Languedoc, Béarn, Guienne, and Royal Roussillon in the centre, with Quebec and Montreal marines on the right flank and the Montreal and Trois Rivières marines on the left. He had no reserves at all.

Both lines stood astride the Grande Allée, which, then as now, crossed the Plains of Abraham to enter the city walls at the St. Louis bastion. The British right rested where the nineteenth-century prison, today a museum, now stands. It is an odd sensation to take the exit from the exhibition and to find oneself, as I did after asking for directions, exactly on the spot where the Louisbourg Grenadiers were deployed 235 years ago. One moment one is in an artistically darkened vault, the next in the open air which, on 13 September 1759, reverberated with the crash of musketry and the cries of wounded men. On the St. Lawrence side of the Grande Allée the ground today is much as Wolfe and Montcalm saw it, though probably clearer of vegetation. It speaks of municipal mowing. On the other the open plan has disappeared under housing, typically late-Victorian North American, with heavy *rundbogenstil* porches and steeply gabled roofs. The northern end of the line of battle ran between what today are the Avenue Cartier—how symbolically appropriate of an event that was to topple New France—and the Avenue de Salaberry.

Beyond those suburban streets the ground drops away to the St. Charles River down a second escarpment matching that up which Wolfe's men climbed from L'Anse du Foulon. This is a topographic feature not mentioned in any account of the battle which I have read. Yet it is of the greatest significance. The twin escarpments, only a thousand yards apart, make the Plains of Abraham into the tabletop it is, and so dictated the nature of the battle. They denied both commanders any opportunity for manoeuvre, forced them to engage frontally, and determined that whichever army won the firefight would carry the day.

The battle opened with sniping and skirmishing along the edges of the escarpments on both sides, the French Canadians and Indians trying to break up the cohesion of the British line, Wolfe's flanking battalions making sorties to keep them at a distance. At about eight o'clock Montcalm got his three guns forward and opened fire with grape. In the face of that cannonade, and to reduce the casualties which the sniping from the flanks was inflicting, Wolfe ordered his line to lie down. This was an unusual order, for eighteenth-century generals were normally concerned to present an unbroken front to the enemy, lest they were suddenly charged; it is probably explained by the absence of cavalry, which alone had the mobility to cross ground at speed. Wellington, nevertheless, was to risk it at Waterloo, despite the presence of cavalry, and would doubtless have approved of Wolfe's concern to conserve lives. He would also have approved of Wolfe's personal behaviour. Like his great successor at Waterloo, the young general "moved about everywhere," as Major Patrick Mackellar later reported; he went over to the left, returned to the centre, "but after the action began kept on a rising ground where our right stood"—that was above the St. Lawrence and opposite the Citadel—"from whence he had a view of the whole field."

Wolfe's front rank lay about a thousand yards from the St. Louis bastion when Montcalm's army began its advance, probably at about ten o'clock. On his order, the men sprang to their feet, presenting a solid line of scarlet, with the tartaned Highlanders, the strongest of the battalions, conspicuous on the left wing. The French must have made a splendid sight also, red waistcoats under white surcoats, regimental colours unfurled above, with the blue blocs of the Troupes de la Marine on either flank. Montcalm and some of the French senior officers, unlike their British counterparts, were ahorse. The French were reported to have come on at a run, which was a mistake, since it broke their cohesion. "We had not gone twenty paces," reported Major Malartie, "when the left was too far in rear and the centre too far in front." That was a bad beginning; the secret of success in eighteenth-century fire-power battles was to present a front of musketry exactly parallel to that of the enemy. Worse was to come. Some of the French, a British eyewitness wrote, opened fire at 130 yards, beyond effective range; some of the marines lay down to reload, as if in forest fighting, which further broke cohesion. Wolfe, meanwhile, was withholding the

order to fire. He "had given positive orders," a British sergeant later recalled, "not to fire a Shot until the Enemy should be within Forty Yards
of the point of our Bayonets"; Wolfe had also instructed his men to
charge their muskets with an extra ball.

The order to hold fire seems to have been strictly kept. It is improbable that only a single volley was fired, as legend has it; eyewitness
accounts give the impression that some battalions fired individually as
the French came within range. That there was a single, final volley,
however, is undisputed. Major Mackellar's after-action report states
that "when they had got within about a hundred yards of us our line
moved up regularly with a steady Fire, and when within twenty or
thirty yards of closing gave a general one; upon which a general route
[rout] of the Enemy immediately ensued." The awful effect of several
thousand musket balls fired at close range—what all eighteenth-century
commanders sought to, but did not often, achieve—disintegrated the
French formation. The physical shock was less than might have been
expected; French losses in killed and wounded throughout the action
appear to have totalled fewer than seven hundred. The psychological
shock was total; that transition from *enthousiasme* to *panique*, which
analysts of eighteenth-century battle have identified as its crucial dynamic, was realised at Quebec in its totality. At one moment the French
line engaged the British in equal combat; at the next it was flying to the
rear as a broken force.

It was at the moment of victory that Wolfe suffered his fatal
wound; he had already been hit once in the wrist, an injury he bound
up with a handkerchief, and he may have suffered a second injury from
a spent round. As the French broke and ran, he was hit in the chest
while standing in front of the Louisbourg Grenadiers, perhaps about to
lead them in a charge. Death followed quickly—his corpse was taken
aboard HMS *Lowestoft* at eleven o'clock—but not before he had given
the order for the 48th Foot to head off the French fugitives at the
bridge across the St. Charles River. It was a heroic death, and it was to
be endlessly commemorated—both in the British literature of empire
and in one of the most famous of historical paintings, by the Pennsylvanian Quaker Benjamin West. The work was revolutionary, for, by de-
picting the death scene as a classical *pietà*, the deposition from the
Cross, with Wolfe's body in the attitude of the dead Christ and his officers as the attendant disciples, West violated a canon which reserved
that composition to religious art alone. Here was the beginning of a

mythologisation of secular heroes that was to provide establishment artists with a principal theme down to our own days.

Montcalm, French Canada's mythologised hero, was mortally wounded in the retreat, of which Wolfe heard as he expired. Hit by grapeshot by one of the two British cannon, he was held up in the saddle by three soldiers until he could be got into the city. Like Wolfe, he had already been wounded twice, but he lingered a whole day before he died; his body was interred in a shell crater in the grounds of the Ursuline Convent. Meanwhile the fugitives from the battlefield succeeded in getting across the St. Charles, thanks to a stand made by the Canadian militia, which held up the Highlanders, and reached the encampment at Beauport. There Vaudreuil, who had wholly lost his nerve, ordered an immediate retreat to Montreal. Picking up Bougainville en route, Vaudreuil did not halt until he was thirty miles from the scene of the disaster.

What remained of the garrison of Quebec within the walls closed the gates and prepared for a siege; when the ration state was reviewed, however, all but one of the senior officers—a man of the mettle of La Bombardière herself, Captain de Fiedmont, who wanted to "reduce the ration again and persevere in holding the place to the last extremity"— voted for capitulation. The gates were opened to the British on 17 September. It was not the end of the fighting at Quebec. In the following year the Chevalier de Lévis, the forthright commander of Montreal, gathered up the remnants of French Canada's army and returned to challenge the British occupiers. They were few in number, but the general, James Murray, who had fought on the Plains of Abraham, was a headstrong man. On the appearance of Lévis, he made the same impulsive decision to give battle as Montcalm had done, marched out on 18 April 1760 to exactly the same piece of ground, the Buttes à Neveu, as Montcalm had occupied seven months earlier on 17 September, and was tossed back into the city quite as precipitately. The casualties in this second Battle of the Plains were even heavier than in the first—259 British and 193 French dead as against 58 British and about 500 French—but the defeat could not alter the result Wolfe had achieved.

Nothing, in fact, could now alter the course of events in Canada. The only initiative which might have allowed the continuation of the struggle was the arrival of a French fleet with men and supplies. A battle on the other side of the Atlantic had precluded all chance of that. On 20 November 1759, Admiral Edward Hawke's blockading squadrons had intercepted the Brest fleet, the only one remaining to France, brought it to action in Quiberon Bay, and, in the most daring of all British naval victories, defeated it in gale-force winds. Two French captains, who had kept their lower gunports open and all canvas set, sailed their ships under in tumultuous seas. Five other ships were burnt or run aground.

Without reinforcements, Vaudreuil, Lévis, and Bougainville could do no more than play out their losing hands. The three-pronged campaign against them—along the familiar Mohawk and Richelieu–Champlain corridors and along the St. Lawrence itself—was slow to get under way, but by mid-July Murray, who had successfully withstood a siege at Quebec after the second Battle of the Plains, was on his way upriver towards Montreal. In mid-August a British advance began down the Richelieu River, before which Bougainville beat a retreat. Simultaneously Amherst, whose point of departure was Fort Oswego at the head of the Mohawk corridor, began to proceed by boat from Lake Ontario down the St. Lawrence. The three forces converged on 7 September outside Montreal, where Vaudreuil, Lévis, and Bougainville, who had been driven inside, rapidly recognised the inevitability of surrender. The capitulation was signed two days later and the remnants of the army was embarked without arms—they had burnt their regimental colours—to sail back down the St. Lawrence past Quebec to old France. New France was no more.

It is not difficult to conjure up, from the heights of Quebec above the river, a shadowy vision of that doleful retreat. But then visions crowd in upon the historical imagination of the visitor to the old city as perhaps in no other place of similar size anywhere in the world. We must not exaggerate. This is not Rome or Athens or Istanbul; Dufferin Terrace is not Seraglio Point, the St. Lawrence not the Golden Horn, the St. Louis bastion not part of the walls of Theodosius. Quebec is not a meeting place of civilisations, not a crossroads of history. Yet it is precisely because the place itself was—and remains—so tiny, the drama played out there so compressed in time, the outcome so clear-cut, the cast of characters so small, their tragedy so final, that the poignancy is so persistent. In a few minutes of walking between French Canada's pantheon of heroes in the Place d'Armes and the green swells of the Plains of Abraham, the whole history of a people is comprehended; in the swivelled gaze from the ramparts of the Parc Montmorency, so too is much of their culture and historical geography. At one's back rises

the spire of the basilica, where fussy hats and marital hissings over entry to the pew recall instantaneously the atmosphere of Sunday in
provincial France; the fortress walls of the seminary of Quebec next
door lower with the gloom of French classroom education, slippery
grey graticuled paper, dusty dictionaries, grading on a scale of one to
six, the awful brilliance of the star pupil, terror of failure in the oral
exam; under the dome of the post office, small bureaucracy flourishes
in a scribble of countersignings and blotching of purple rubber stamps
which only the French know how to raise to the level of social theatre.
Yet, not a thousand yards from this familiar Frenchness of the France
of here and now, or certainly of the France of my boyhood, for Quebec
lingers engagingly a little behind the times, there opens the mouth of
the St. Charles River, where in 1535 Jacques Cartier harboured his
ships and his men raised the first French fort in America in a country
that belonged to the Indians.

A thousand yards across the river, where Wolfe was to build his
battery at Pointe Lévis in 1759, the dark forest then led southward into
territory Frenchmen would not settle for another century. It would be
Champlain, navigating his way down the broad estuary that leads to
the Atlantic, still grey, brooding, and mysterious in a Canadian winter,
who would begin to penetrate the menacing interior. Champlain has
his monument in the Place d'Armes; he has his most extraordinary
memorial in the confection of the Château Frontenac, which stands on
or near the site of his habitation that became the residence of Canada's
French governors. To remember Champlain, bold voyager and warrior
and master cartographer, is to think, however, not of the exit eastward
from Quebec to the Atlantic but of his journeys to the west. That way
lay the New France he wanted to discover, and the route he took up
the St. Lawrence to the Great Lakes and along its tributaries into the
land of the Ottawas was the beginning of an extraordinary French
odyssey. That way lay the network of canoe passages and portages,
painstakingly decrypted by four generations of fur traders, missionaries, and soldiers, many known by name, the vast majority anonymous or forgotten, which were to take La Salle to the mouth of the
Mississippi and the Vérendryes to the prairies and the approaches to
the Rockies.

Theirs is a history of discovery as dramatic and certainly as gallant
and enterprising as any in the record of the European exploration of
the world; their encounter with harsh climate, natural dangers, and of-

ten hostile peoples has few parallels. The America of the French explorations, even more than the Africa of the Victorians, was a dark continent, hiding its secrets from all but the most persistent, and instantaneous in its punishment of the foolhardy and the unprepared. The distances covered by those whose base rested at Quebec or Montreal—five hundred miles to Sault Ste. Marie, a thousand miles to Lake of the Woods, fifteen hundred miles to the Saskatchewan River—were then unprecedented for journeys into unrecorded territory and were scarcely equalled later by the explorers of Australia or rainforest Africa. Yet, in the end, everything does return to Quebec. It was there that the epic of French America began. It is here that it concluded in defeat and heartbreak. *Je me souviens*: "I remember"; that is the motto of the province and the city. The memories press hard, above all on the narrow acres of rolling grassland—in winter truly Voltaire's *quelques arpents de neige*—of the Plains of Abraham. Is there anywhere in the world a more dramatic battlefield—the sombre ramparts of masonry, built and rebuilt by French and British, that close the landscape on the city side, the sharp geometry of the Grande Allée first marched by the Régiment de Carignan-Salières in 1665, the swell of the ill-famed Buttes à Neveu, the sudden fall of the escarpment on the southern edge, the heavy, relentless, seaward outpourings of the St. Lawrence at its foot? I know of none—not Waterloo, not Naseby, not Austerlitz, not even Gettysburg. Here occurred what French Canada to this day calls *la Conquête*. I came, I saw, I left, conquered by emotion.

THREE

....

The Fort at Yorktown

IT WAS, wrote Robert Rogers, the New Hampshire frontiersman who had founded and led the Rangers in the war against the French, "a conquest perhaps of the greatest importance that is to be met with in the British annals," and he went on to enumerate the reasons for that judgement: "the prodigious extent of the country we are hereby made masters of" was one; "the irretrievable loss France sustains hereby, and the importance it must give the British Crown among the several states of Europe" were others; then "the vast addition it must make to trade and navigation"; and, finally, "the security it must afford to the northern provinces of America."

Rogers had more than a frontiersman's grasp of immediacies. He also had a colonist's sharp nose for future realities. The origins of the American Revolution—the War of Independence, as the British call it, in their disinclination to recognise how world-changing was the civilisation to which it gave birth—is a subject that divides historians a dozen different ways. On one point, however, all agree: that the defeat of France in Canada, by its elimination of the danger of French and Indian attacks on the colonies' frontiers of trade with the interior, and of strategic—if not yet legal—obstacles to settlement across the line of the Appalachian Mountains, sharply diminished in the eyes of the British colonists the value of the redcoat presence in their territories. The redcoat was not yet Tommy Atkins; Kipling's future perception held good none the less. While the French had been at Carillon, with their Indian allies at beck and call, the redcoats had been a thin red line between kidnap, scalping, and massacre. With the French gone, or repelled at

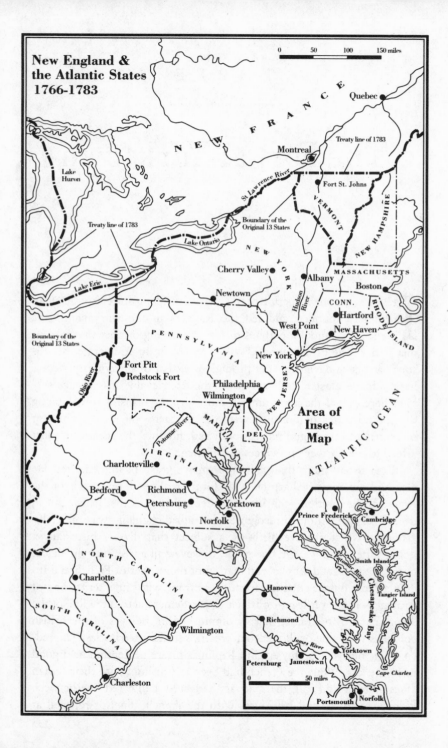

New England &
the Atlantic States
1766-1783

0   50   100   150 miles

Quebec

NEW FRANCE

Montreal

Treaty line of 1783

Lake Huron

St. Lawrence River

Fort St. Johns

Boundary of the
Original 13 States

Lake Ontario

VERMONT

NEW HAMPSHIRE

Treaty line of 1783

Lake Erie

NEW YORK

Cherry Valley

Albany

MASSACHUSETTS

Boston

Newtown

Hudson River

CONN.

RHODE ISLAND

West Point

Hartford

New Haven

Boundary of the
Original 13 States

PENNSYLVANIA

New York

Ohio River

Fort Pitt

Redstock Fort

NEW JERSEY

Philadelphia

Wilmington

Area of
Inset
Map

Potomac River

MARYLAND

DEL

Charlotteville

VIRGINIA

ATLANTIC OCEAN

Bedford

Richmond

Petersburg

Yorktown

Norfolk

NORTH CAROLINA

Charlotte

Prince Frederick

Cambridge

SOUTH CAROLINA

Wilmington

Hanover

Potomac River

Smith Island

Tangier Island

Chesapeake Bay

Richmond

Charleston

Petersburg

James River

Jamestown

Yorktown

Cape Charles

0   50 miles

Portsmouth

Norfolk

least to the far line of the Mississippi, their Indians were reduced from a danger to a mere menace; after the defeat of Pontiac's rebellion (1763–65) in the aftermath of the Seven Years War, a revolt by the Indians of the Northwest against a new British arrogance, to less than that. The forts had changed hands. Those formerly of New France were now, if not abandoned, occupied by British or colonial garrisons and so outposts of an Anglo-Saxon power that dominated security, settlement, and commerce throughout Atlantic North America. Thitherto military relationships in the region had been manifold: Britain versus France; settlers versus Indians; British settlers versus French settlers; or some combinations of these. The Seven Years (the French and Indian) War had ranged France, its regular army and fleet, the French Canadians, and their Indian confederates against Britain, its army, the Royal Navy, the colonists, and their Indians. Henceforth, and unless France rediscovered the strength to challenge Britain once again for rights of empire in Canada—which even at the time appeared improbable—relationships were reduced from complexity to simplicity: Britain and her colonists versus such Indians as took issue with the dominance the Anglo-Saxons now exercised between the Atlantic and the Mississippi.

In practice the relations were not to prove simple. Abandoned by their French protectors—for, despite their long history of differences, the French had always been an ultimate support to the tribes in their resistance to English intrusion into their lands—the Indians took fright. Pontiac's rebellion of 1763 was the chief, though not the only, outcome. To it the British reacted by forsaking diplomacy and instituting a policy of repression and punishment, greatly resented by the Indians, who did not and could not regard themselves as subject to imperial authority. Yet, showing another side of their imperial role, the British also succeeded in provoking resentment among the colonists by declaring in 1763 that the watershed of the Appalachians, for so long a physical barrier to their attempts to penetrate the interior, should now become a legal one. The eastern half of the Mississippi basin was to be reserved to the Indians and closed to settlement, precisely at the moment when, thanks to the explorations and trailblazing of pioneers like Daniel Boone, practicable ways throughout the mountains—the "gaps"—had been found, and the first long-distance roads cleared. As if that did not promise trouble enough between London and the more enterprising of the colonists, the British government ensured that it would attack the interest of them all by imposing taxes intended to pay retrospectively for the costs incurred in lifting the French military menace from the northern and northwestern frontiers.

A strategic simplification therefore came to threaten political complication. As we can see with hindsight, it threatened war; and when war came, it proved to be a very complex war indeed. Politics made it so; geography did as well. The war was not only to be protracted in time, from 1776 to 1781, a long war by any reckoning. It was also to extend for an extraordinary distance along America's Atlantic seaboard, from the estuary of the St. Lawrence to that of the Savannah River 1,600 miles away, and to reach inland to places like Cowpens 250 miles from tidewater. The patchwork of battlefields and campaign trails that resulted is bewildering to Europeans—perhaps to Americans also—since their picture of the War of Independence is formed by schoolbook memories of Lexington, Concord, and Bunker Hill, three sites separated from each other by only a few miles of ground and water around the seaboard city of Boston. What on earth, the European traveller asks himself as he stumbles in the course of some Greyhound or Trailways or rented car journey on an errand wholly unconnected with historical revisiting, can have brought the combatants of the American Revolution to southern New Jersey, or the environs of Kennedy Airport on Long Island, or the back country of North Carolina, or the enchanted city of Charleston, or the green hills of the Hudson Valley, or indeed to already thrice-besieged Quebec? Why did the war between King George III and his American subjects intrude so often upon territories already fought over, sometimes more than once, by the contestants in conflicts over and done with; why, at Savannah or Charleston or Yorktown, did it bloody ground that was bloodied again in the War Between the States of 1861–65? America is not Europe, where space is at a premium and the ways men—and armies—take between places are predetermined by the routes the legionary road-makers surveyed and engineered in the first century A.D. Land is freein America. Space, not time, is the dimension in which the American exists.

What, then, were the forces at work which so often diverted the warriors of 1776–81 into the same tracks as those taken by their predecessors in the French and Indian Wars and would also be followed by their successors in the Civil War? Waterways are a partial but not complete explanation, for rivers and lakes and portages were not the key to movement within English-speaking America to anything like the extent that they were in French Canada. It was already by 1776, at least in New England, a widely deforested land served by an extensive road network and negotiable by man on foot or a horse quite freely over most points of the compass. What attracted soldiers this way rather than that was less a recognition of what was navigable or passable, which is the paramount sense in the wilderness, than knowledge of a secondary geographic pattern that man had already planted in the landscape, a pattern yielding the necessities and even comforts of life, that of townships, markets, agricultural centres, trading posts, and forts.

Forts, I have come to realise, have been a crucial determinant of my discovery of the traces of America's wars, for it is invitations to lecture at military academies that have so often taken me across the Atlantic and, in America, military academies usually occupy the sites of former fortresses. Not so in Europe. The Dutch military academy at Breda, it is true, occupies a bastioned fortress of the Spanish wars, and the former Spanish military academy at Toledo was originally housed in the medieval Alcazar, which sustained a famous siege by the Republicans during the Civil War in 1936. European fortresses, however, being designed to defy artillery by the thickness of their enormous walls, provide miserable accommodation; accordingly the continent's two premier academies, St.-Cyr in France and Sandhurst in England, were founded in, respectively, what had once been a royal boarding school for well-born girls and a purpose-built country mansion. In America, by contrast, the extemporised timber and sod structures left over from the wars of the eighteenth century would never have made suitable dwellings for a student body; most, indeed, went quickly back to nature. The sites they occupied, however, having been chosen because they commanded lines of communication and thereafter often remained in military use, naturally offered themselves as locations for military colleges when, during the nineteenth century, the governments of Canada and the United States were founding such institutions. Hence the existence of the U.S. Military Academy at West Point on the site of the redoubts built to deny the Hudson to the British in 1778 (there the traces of the earthworks have been carefully restored, so allowing the academy's British liaison officer to commemorate the bicentennial by hoisting the Union Jack over Fort Putnam at dawn on 4 July 1976). Hence also the location of the Royal Military College of Canada, Kingston, near the site of Fort Frontenac, built by France in

1673, and of the Collège Royale Militaire at St. Jean, where a fort, still
faintly discernible, to guard the head of the Richelieu River was built
by the Carignan-Salières Regiment in 1665. Much further south, the
magnificent waterfront campus of the U.S. Naval Academy (established
in 1845) covers the site of Fort Severn, constructed to protect the head
of Chesapeake Bay as part of the United States' First System of coast-
wise fortification, begun in 1794.

Invitations to lecture have taken me to all these places over the last
fifteen years, and I now keenly regret my neglect of the opportunities
those visits offered to deepen my understanding of America's strategic
geography; the significance of the sites, except in the case of West
Point, where the least military-minded must grasp at a glance its command of the Hudson River narrows, simply did not strike me at the
time. Not that the academies failed to make an impression. At St. Jean,
so close to French Canada's metropolis in Montreal, it was the Frenchness of the institution that struck; bilingual though it is, I heard French
spoken oftener than English, by cadets and officers whose looks and
mannerisms reminded me more forcibly of my visits to St.-Cyr than to
any of its sister academies in the English-speaking world. The spirit of
the Régiment de Carignan-Salières still breathed over the place, and the
dark blue of the cadets' uniforms vividly recalled that of the Troupes
de la Marine who campaigned with, or against, war-painted Indians in
the surrounding pine forests two hundred years ago. Kingston, by contrast, is pure British imperial. The pillared façades of the city's public
buildings have their counterparts in the Royal Mint outside the Tower
of London, the old British Embassy at Constantinople, the Palace of
the Order of St. Michael and St. George on Corfu, and, indeed, in Old
College at the Royal Military Academy Sandhurst. Kingston's Royal
Military College even outdoes, in some ways, Sandhurst's Britishness.
Watching cadets parade there, I saw them perform a drill movement I
knew only from sepia Victorian photographs—it has long been abolished in Britain—while I listened to a running stream of criticism from
a sergeant in bottleglass-brilliant boots of their minor imperfections in
marching. He hated, he told me after the parade, the adoption by
Canada's army of the naval salute—"the wave, I call it"—he hated the
universal green uniform, he hated the use of common ranks—"How
can the captain of a ship be a colonel?"—he hated the disappearance of
polished brass—the metal of his pacestick glittered with burnishing—
he hated rubber soles, non-iron shirts, nylon uniforms, and being mis-

taken by civilians for an airman. Kipling and he would have got on like a house on fire: "Ship me somewheres east of Suez, where . . . a man can raise a thirst" were almost the next words I expected to hear at the crescendo of his relentless tirade. Spiritually he belonged with the Royal Canadians who had gone to fight the Boers for Queen Victoria; his cadets were unlikely to be allowed to forget that her great-great-granddaughter was Queen of Canada or that he had learnt his drill at the depot of her Foot Guards.

Annapolis carries the visitor back in time also, though to a different age and ethos altogether, that of the United States' fledgling navy of fierce frigate captains and foreign adventure. Its cadets in their gold-buttoned shell jackets—is there a more handsome naval uniform in the world?—actually seem to have been plucked from John Paul Jones's quarterdeck, while the tomb of that terrible scourge of the Royal Navy, which lies under a dome reminiscent of nothing so much as that covering Napoleon's at Les Invalides, lends an anomalous hint of menace to the academy's idyllic Ivy League campus. Yet is it anomalous? The USN is a fighting navy. Its roll of battle honours may perforce be shorter than the Royal Navy's but it is quite as extensive. There is no ocean in which it has not waged war, no continent in which it has not harboured its ships, few coasts on which it has not landed its own Marine Corps or the soldiers of the United States Army. Barbary corsairs, slaving schooners, and Confederate blockade runners were the enemies of the Old Navy of pre-dreadnought years, the German High Seas Fleet and the Japanese Combined Fleet those of the New Navy of the twentieth century. In its victories it is outdone by no other navy and equalled by few: the surprise of Midway was as complete as that of Nelson at the Nile, the risk taken at Coral Sea as bold as that of Hawke at Quiberon Bay, the triumph of Leyte Gulf even greater than that of Trafalgar. Its tradition of victory dates, moreover, from its origins; not for it the need which obliged the German naval pioneers to inculcate a code of death or glory: Stephen Decatur and John Paul Jones had established that at the start. How appropriate, I thought, as I watched the U.S. Naval Academy's élite of future nuclear submariners, on their way to a physics examination, tossing quarters into the grinning mouth of USS *Tecumseh*'s figurehead—"the God of 3.5"—that the captains-to-be of the most powerful navy in the world should seek to propitiate the old sailing men who have bequeathed its totem of oceanic admiralty to this quiet Chesapeake backwater.

Yet Annapolis looks outward; square-riggers still rip down here from the historic collection of wooden ships at Mystic, Connecticut, while cadets navigate outward each weekend to Capes Charles and Hatteras under sail. On a visit not long ago I took the helm of an Annapolis professor's cutter on a beat down-bay to the Eastern Shore of Maryland, following the course of frigates long ago to the open ocean. West Point looks inward. George Washington believed, indeed, that it was the key, if not to a continent, then at least to the strategic geography of the thirteen colonies of 1776. Because of its position, sixty miles north of New York City and 120 miles south of Albany at the first upstream narrowing of the Hudson, he called it the "Key to America." Writing to General Israel Putnam in December 1777, he said, "The importance of the Hudson river in the present contest, and the necessity of defending it, are subjects . . . so well understood, that it is unnecessary to enlarge upon them. The facts at once appear, when it is considered that [the Hudson] runs through a whole State; then it is the only passage by which [the British] from New York, or any part of our coast, can ever hope to co-operate with an army from Canada; that the possession of it is indispensably essential to preserve the communication between the Eastern, Middle, and Southern States; and further, that upon its security, in a great measure, depends our chief supplies of flour for the subsistence of such forces as we may occasion for, in the course of the war, either in the Eastern or Northern Departments, or in the country lying high up on the west side of it [i.e., along the Mohawk corridor leading to Lake Ontario]."

Everything George Washington meant, the visitor to West Point can appreciate from Trophy Point, where the barrels of cannon captured from the British, Mexicans, and Spanish stare across at what used to be the battery on Constitution Island; any passing cadet will indicate how a chain—some of its links are preserved in the academy museum—closed the river to British warships, just as the Byzantine emperors closed the Golden Horn to the Turks by a chain in the fifteenth century. Unlike theirs, the West Point chain worked. It did indeed "perfectly fulfil the object which is proposed, that of hindering the enemy's remounting of the North [Hudson] River." As the historian of West Point's fortifications, Marguerita Herman, has pointed out, it "achieved its first strategic object . . . it permitted Washington and the Continental Army to defend the Hudson with minimal troops, even though the British controlled New York, while shifting the main army to operations elsewhere—particularly to the South and to Yorktown in 1781.' "

It is indeed to the southward that the casual traveller is most likely to stumble upon landmarks of the Revolutionary War. Others, of course, intermingle with the battlefields of King William's, Queen Anne's, and King George's wars, for the colonists campaigned in the Mohawk and Champlain corridors and even essayed the untried approach to Quebec via the Kennebec and Chaudière rivers in 1775, their first offensive of the war. The traces are less prominent than those left by the Anglo-French struggle, however, even though they overlie them, whereas in Massachusetts, New York, New Jersey, Virginia, and the Carolinas they are noticeable and numerous. It was in southern New Jersey and across the state line with Pennsylvania that I found the historical markers that most puzzled me, in Princeton and Trenton and at Washington's Crossing on the Delaware River. What on earth, I asked myself, was Washington doing here, in what is now one of the most tranquil—expensively tranquil—areas of the United States? The road from Trenton to Princeton is lined with meticulously restored colonial houses—named after the original owner, as is the custom thereabouts, and dated sometimes from the seventeenth century—and at Lawrenceville passes the gates of the famous prep school. In Princeton itself the battle markers start at Mercer Street, now a thoroughfare of fine Greek Revival houses, while a stone's throw away stands Nassau Hall, the centrepiece of the university and in January 1777, when His Majesty's 54th Regiment mustered in it, the only building on the campus. I spent a whole semester in 1984 working in a room just across the way, as a visiting Fellow, without discovering that Nassau Hall had been a British headquarters or that Washington had chased the redcoats out of it, without even establishing what had brought him thither or where he had fought the battle.

Everything seemed in the wrong place, too far away from the seedbed of the American Revolution in New England to connect with its significant events. However, I caught a sharper aftertaste of the conflict when, on a cold Saturday afternoon in February, I was driven from Princeton along the valley of the Delaware, high in flood, to Washington's crossing at McKonkey's Ferry. There is a bridge there now, one end in Mercer County, New Jersey, the other in Bucks County, Pennsylvania, but the atmosphere remains authentically eighteenth century, with some empty and tumbledown single-storey cottages, brick-pathed to their front doors, edging the little green on the Pennsylvanian side.

The place keeps a mournful, desolate air which speaks of the hardships suffered by the Continental Army in those backwoods during the harsh winter of 1776–77; the river, too, though narrower than Lutze makes it look in the famous painting of its crossing by Washington—I came across a version a year or two later in the State Department, hanging outside the Secretary of State's door—had a cold, grey, menacing surface, all too easily imagined choked with ice as we see it under the prow of the boat on which Washington rests one booted, resolute foot, on his way to battle at Princeton. Still, my knowledge of the events of the Revolutionary War remained too incomplete to help me associate that genuinely Early American spot with the events which gave the colonies their independence.

So it was also with the traces of the Revolutionary War I had come across earlier in the Carolinas. In North Carolina in February 1976 I followed quite unwittingly much of the route taken by the British under Cornwallis against Nathanael Greene and David Morgan in 1780–81, though in the reverse direction. I had been lecturing at Duke University, Durham, and at the University of North Carolina at Chapel Hill, one of the most beautiful of all stopping places on the American lecturing circuit. There had been a late snowfall in Chapel Hill, followed by a day of sharp, clear sunshine which brought the members of the men's and women's fraternity houses on to Chapel Hill's elegant main street to bombard each other, and the passing traffic, with a barrage of good-natured snowballs and high-spirited shrieks. The English graduate student who had been assigned me as an escort confided that he had chosen Chapel Hill as the place to do his doctorate because, after a reconnaissance, he had identified it as having the largest concentration of good-looking girls at any East Coast university. I saw what he meant and wished him well.

Shortly afterwards I was being driven away from Chapel Hill's human beauty and landscaped charm into its harsh Appalachian hinterland. For hour after hour we made our way along the foot of grey-brown pine-clad hills, reminiscent of forested southern Germany, but bleaker, poorer, less populated, the odd shanty clinging to the slope above the road marking how sparse was settlement in this infertile back country, through Hillsboro, where Cornwallis had marched his army in another February 178 years earlier, and Greensboro, near which he had fought the battle of Guilford Court House against Greene on 14 March 1781, to Winston-Salem and then to our destination, Boone, deep in the Appalachian heartland through which Daniel Boone had hacked his way to the bluegrass of Kentucky in the 1760s. Boone had found this country a wilderness, and even in the late twentieth century a sense of the wilderness waiting to return still clung about the city of Boone. It had the look of a frontier town. It was full of wide, vacant lots and makeshift buildings, with fingers of forest poking down from the overhanging mountains into the bedraggled commercial centre. Academically, too, it was an outpost, where students who were the first members of their families to have gone to college were taught by professors in exile from a larger academic world. They found it a struggle, some confessed, to convey to their pupils any understanding of times and places beyond the mountains and the here-and-now. Even the drama of the Appalachian past seemed to lack reality amid these worn-out, worked-over, second-growth hillsides.

Yet at least they were served by good roads, highways to the outside world, of which there had been none when Cornwallis was beating these forests in pursuit of Greene after the Battle of Camden in August 1780. I picked up their trail when I left Boone by car for Hickory, in a drizzle of sleet from low clouds that filled the tops of the valleys. At Hickory, where I was to take the aeroplane, cloud fogged in the airport, so Air Carolina sent me on to the next airfield, at Charlotte, by taxi. My driver was a grizzled old mountain man, ex-preacher, extrucker, grandfather of sixteen, full of mountain wisdom and unpreacherly language, who, finding Charlotte fogged in also, stoutly offered to drive me out of North Carolina and clear across South Carolina to my destination at Charleston. Only the thought that he might not make it back in time to do his midnight mail run deterred him from the adventure, and it was with evident regret that he delivered me to the Trailways depot. Here was someone, I thought, as we made a warm goodbye, with whom Daniel Boone would have been on instant terms. Still, I am devoted to Trailways, to whose gentle rhythm I have slept over hundreds of miles in the backways of the American South, and so it was that I slept my way down the valley of the Santee River to Columbia, twice crossing Cornwallis's northward line of march, to reach Charleston in the small hours of the next morning. On my way I had passed by the Revolutionary War's Forts Motte and Watson and left far on my right hand the upcountry battlefield of Ninety Six— ninety-six miles from the Cherokee village of Keowee—where Captain George Chicken, Indian fighter, had killed a buffalo in 1716 and Thaddeus Kosciusko, the Polish hero of the American Revolution, had besieged a British garrison in May 1781 for nearly a month.

The siege of Ninety Six connected with the British occupation of Charleston in 1780–81, but in a way that, again, I did not understand. I had known the city since my first undergraduate visit to the United States, but associated it entirely with the Civil War, which had begun there with the bombardment of Fort Sumter in its harbour. Its significance for the British-American struggle eluded me. My destination was the Citadel, the Military College of South Carolina, and it was cadets of the Citadel who, manning a battery on Moin's Island, had fired the shots which marked the first hostilities between South and North in January 1861. The Citadel, however, had not existed at the time of the Revolutionary War and is today a major source of officers for the armed forces of the United States, while the city, ironically, is now a favoured retirement place for its generals. Mark Clark, the liberator of Rome in 1944, was living on its outskirts when I made my 1979 visit. I was sent to see him and found him still as eagle-profiled and concerned for his military reputation as he had been in his glory days in Italy in the Second World War. General Westmoreland was a resident also. I sat beside him at an official Citadel lunch, where he, too, revealed a sensitivity about his reputation and talked at length in justification of his years in command in Vietnam. It was a relief to turn to my neighbour, an elderly gentleman of immense distinction of appearance and manner whose string of Dutch names—Cortlandt van Rensselaer Schuyler—revealed him to be a scion of the Hudson River aristocracy, and the descendant of two of Washington's generals—Philip Schuyler, defender of Lake Champlain against the British in 1776, and Robert van Rensselaer, commander of the militia on the Mohawk River in 1780.

Cortlandt van Rensselaer Schuyler was senior to both Westmoreland and Mark Clark in appointment—he was, indeed, then the last surviving general officer of the pre–Pearl Harbor era—but, like them, a West Point graduate. Inevitably we fell into conversation about the place and I told him how deep an impression my visits to it had made on me, particularly because of its difference from my own military academy in Britain. Sandhurst's dreamy parkland, acres of mown lawns, colonnaded vistas, and soft, creamy façades are the unlikeliest setting I know or can imagine in which to train young men for war. Classical languages, perhaps, or philosophy, or the fine arts—any of those would be appropriate to that sylvan spot; tactics, strategy, drill, musketry, bloodshed seem to have no place at all amid Sandhurst's bowers and arbours. West Point, by contrast, I said, breathes the martial spirit. Its architecture—the great riverside cliff of the old riding school, the harsh outlines of the cadet barracks, the monolithic blocks of the administrative buildings that march along the plain—is grimly purposeful, the dining hall in which four thousand cadets are simultaneously served lunch at noon is a machine for eating; the monumental chapel, where the largest organ in the world thunders out warrior hymns, is a cathedral to the Lord Mighty in Battle; even the contours of the Hudson hills seem to have been sculpted into military uniformity, while the woodland which covers them is regimentally cut and coppiced. Order dominates the landscape, and the ordered landscape dominates its human inhabitants who seem filled with a sense of being there for one purpose alone—to teach or learn the disciplines of war.

General Schuyler conceded that the four years he had spent at West Point as a cadet between the wars had indeed so disciplined him that little in his experience of war itself, when it came, had surprised him by its arbitrary harshness; when every inch of self, he said, has been subjected to the regulation of a higher, institutional will, the individual loses the capacity to protest against the cruelties and unfairness of the battlefield. I remembered a tour of the West Point graveyard I had been given by a graduate not long returned from the Vietnam War. There, amid the graves of other graduates killed in the Mexican and Civil and world wars, he pointed out the headstones of fellow cadets who had served with him; under one lay a body he had escorted home in the aftermath of the Tet offensive to deliver to a widow. He recalled the first day of Tet, its confusion and danger, his effort to rejoin his unit, his urgent enquiries of other soldiers as to which roads were blocked and which not, his perilous journey across the battlefield, his arrival to discover his comrades locked in combat with an unseen enemy, his questioning about who still lived and who had died, his heartbreak at the news that a close friend was among the fatalities. It was that close friend by whose grave we stood; the widow was now his own wife.

Here was the home of a warrior society; that was what I had been brought to understand at West Point, which is itself a place of war, chosen if not used, in the United States' struggle for independence. A sense of the centrality of West Point to America's military history returned to me strongly as I sat in the Citadel's luncheon room, next to Westmoreland, a former Academy superintendent, and Schuyler, a rep-

resentative of the Hudson Valley families who had battled the British
so doughtily in the years of revolution. It was not an anomaly, however, that the Citadel represented an alternative, anti-Federal tradition,
for by one of those strokes of cultural comprehension at which the
United States is so adept its history, too, had been incorporated into the
national mythology. The warriordom of the South has a double aspect.
The firing on Fort Sumter, the mustering of the chocolate-box Blues
and Grays and Greens and Rifles and Ladies' Guards and their rapid
transformation into seasoned and fiery campaigners, represent a defiance of government by Washington; the patriotism of the South, in all
America's wars save that between the states, the readiness of its sons to
volunteer, their over-representation in the armed forces of the United
States, represent a principle of loyalty through military service which
has no equal in any other region. In my blinkered European way I had
long thought of the War of Independence as one fought by the hard-
headed, mercantile, seaboard colonists of New England against the
hard-headed, mercantile, seaboard Old Englanders across the Atlantic.
I remembered that the Hancocks and the Adamses and Alexander
Hamilton were New Englanders or New Yorkers; I neglected to remember that Washington, Jefferson, the four Lees, and Patrick Henry
were Virginians and Francis Marion a South Carolinan. I had overlooked altogether that the culminating campaigns of the War of
the Revolution had been fought in the Carolinas and Georgia. I had
forgotten that its battle of decision, Yorktown, had been fought in
Virginia.

In Charleston, therefore, were brought together for me the chrono-
logical and geographical extremities of the War of Independence: its
offensive beginning only three weeks after the battles of Lexington
and Concord, in an attack from the north along the Hudson–
Champlain–Richelieu corridor against the borders of Canada, which
remains a realm of the royal house that lost its first empire in that war;
its conclusion, at the end of a year of marching and countermarching
through the tobacco and cotton lands of the South, at Yorktown, a
place scarcely a day's journey, at contemporary speed of travel, from
the spot where John Smith, with royal authority, had fortified the first
place of permanent English settlement in the Americas at Jamestown in
1607. North, South, I knew both ends of the theatre of campaign well.
It was the web of interconnections between them that I lacked the
knowledge to draw together in my mind. I could visualise the small

New England battles with which the war opened, little different as they must have been from other contemporary gunpowder battles in Europe—or on the Plains of Abraham. I could equally visualise how the siege of Charleston in 1780 must have worked, for its defence and attack conformed to the pattern of dozens of cannon and musket sieges conducted throughout the maritime empires of approximately even date in the eighteenth century. What I failed to understand was how the loose ends of the war had eventually been knotted at Yorktown. Equidistant though it was between the seedbed of the war in Massachusetts and its subsequent focus at Charleston, Yorktown had remained a military backwater throughout the six years of conflict. What had determined that that remote and tranquil place should see the Revolution's culminating act? I determined to find out.

The War in the North

Lexington, Massachusetts, is not the place "Where the embattled farmers stood / And fired the shot heard round the world." That is at Concord, a few miles up the road. It is, nevertheless, unarguably the scene of the first shedding of blood between the regular soldiers of King George III and his disaffected colonists at the outset of what was to grow into the War of the Revolution. I happened upon the spot quite unintentionally. Simon Schama, who had not yet written *Citizens*, his best-selling history of the French Revolution, suggested on one afternoon of a visit I was making to Harvard that I drive out to see the house he had just bought following his migration from Cambridge, England. I am glad he did. The house was Frank Lloyd Wright-ish, built, in a manner known only to Americans, partly of magnificent natural materials, partly from the bedrock itself: an outcrop of granite half-filled while supporting the conservatory through which we entered, and a hillside spring trickled in a channel through the floor. I was rapt with admiration. On the way back, I asked, "Where are we?" "Lexington," he said. "This is the village green where the battle happened."

It is still recognisably a village green of the English sort, triangular between a fork in the road out of Boston, with some of the eighteenth-century houses, the Buckman and Monroe taverns and the Meeting

House, remaining. Boulders have been placed to mark the spots where the colonists—"Minutemen"—and British regulars stood, and so they also mark where the first American casualties of the war—eight Minutemen killed, nine wounded—fell. Who were the Minutemen, I wondered, and how had this sad, divisive, and unnecessary—I liked to think—but, as it was to prove, irreversible event come about?

I was to acquire the answer only several years later, as a result of a meeting far away and from an unlikely source. John Galvin, the American general serving as Supreme Allied Commander Europe, had invited me to stay at his official residence in Belgium. At the crossroads outside a monument marks the spot where the British fired their first shots of the First World War in the battle of Mons, but the general had asked me there for a purpose unconnected with 1914. He was going to conduct me on his celebrated battlefield tour of Waterloo, a struggle of which I had written an account he wanted to go over with me on the ground. The fire power of his escort, deployed in a convoy of advance and back-up cars, would, I reflected, as we drove between La Haye Sainte and Hougoumont and back again, have significantly altered the balance if offered either to Wellington or Napoleon on 18 July 1815. When we parted he pressed on me a little book, inscribed to "someone who knows both sides of this battle." He had, he said, spent most of his year as a student at the U.S. Command and General Staff College, Fort Leavenworth, writing it. It was called *Minute Men: The First Fight—Myths and Realities of the American Revolution.*

The myth of the American Revolution is that the armed colonists were peaceful men who sprang to arms—shotguns and squirrel rifles—when oppressed beyond bearing by British misrule. The reality which General Galvin's scholarly monograph revealed—John Galvin is that unusually American combination of professional soldier and academic historian—was quite different. The New Englanders had developed both a warlike outlook and a legal military organisation in the earliest period of settlement. The danger of attack by Indians made them warlike; the military organisation had followed them from England. There, under Elizabeth I, the Muster Law of 1572 had required her subjects to form and train in units of militia against the danger of a Spanish invasion. The militia principle survived the defeat of the Spanish Armada, but its practice attenuated; both Crown and Parliament had to improvise armies for the English Civil War of the seventeenth century and, though revived again in the eighteenth and surviving until the early twentieth, the British militia acquired a sleepy, half-comic reputation. In America, by contrast, it was a frontline force. The Elizabethan Muster Law provided a model; by 1643, when the United Colonies of New England were formed for mutual defence, the colonists were actually arming and training themselves to take the field at short notice. In 1645 the Massachusetts Council passed a regulation ordering militia commanders "to appoint out and to make choice of thirty soldiers of their companies in ye hundred, who shall be ready at half an hour's warning upon any service they shall be put upon by their chief military officers."

Service initially was against Indian raids, of which the Pequot War of 1636–37 in the Connecticut River had given a foretaste. King Philip's subsequent war of 1675–76 in Connecticut, Rhode Island, and Massachusetts sent a wave of shock throughout the northern colonies. Terrifying though they were when on the warpath, the Indians, however, never threatened the extinction of the colonies by their own efforts. It was their alliances with the French which made them formidable, and it was therefore directly against the French that the colonists' military efforts were made: by William Phips in 1689–90, by Francis Nicholson in 1711, by William Pepperell in 1745, by George Washington in 1754, and by John Johnson and William Shirley in 1755. From the 1690s onwards the militias of the northern frontier in particular began to acquire real competence in forest warfare, together with a readiness to turn out rapidly for duty in all seasons. As the conflict with the French intensified during the eighteenth century, the militias of the increasingly prosperous New England and Atlantic colonies were meanwhile developing into a semi-regular force, expensively equipped and capable of mounting autonomous operations against the enemy as they did at Louisbourg in 1745.

The extinction of the French threat by British worldwide victory in the Seven Years War caused an abrupt decline in the militias' fitness to fight. Drills were neglected and musters poorly attended, while energetic men did not put themselves forward to be officers. Officers already holding rank lapsed into lethargy; many of them were conservative stay-at-homes who valued the standing brought by their association with the royal government. They acted as a check, both positive and negative, on the hotheads and firebrands, increasingly irked by the insensitivities of the royal governors and the high-handedness of long-distance rule from London. As early as 1772, Boston was co-ordinating a campaign of resistance to new laws which increased taxes, violated colonial charters, and restrained trade. Without local means to oppose the representatives of the Crown and its armed forces in America, however, protests were mere words. The dissenting colonists required a force of their own, and in a local military revolution of 1774 they set about founding one. In September the dissidents in Worcester County, Massachusetts, a centre of military activism since the days of King Philip's War, voted to require the senior officers of the militia to resign their commissions, to be replaced by others of stouter stuff. Each county town was to select a third of its men between sixteen and thirty years of age "to be ready to act at a minute's warning," and each was also to appoint a committee "to supply or support those troops that shall move in any emergency." The Worcester resolutions were to provide a model for military reorganisation throughout the colonies.

This showing of a fierce face to the King and his officials did not presage war, any more than Ulster's swearing of a covenant and raising of a volunteer force was to do at the beginning of the twentieth century. It was an expression of dissatisfaction and a warning against further tampering with established legal practice, not a considered preparation for rebellion. Most colonists remained "loyal," distinguishing "King," whose authority was legitimate, and "ministers," whose misrule was not, even after the first acts of defiance had been committed. Misunderstandings, poor communications between America and England, local misjudgement by royal officials, interference by colonists, and above all the absence of any legal vision of a changed relationship between mother country and its overseas dominions were more to blame for the outbreak of war in 1775 than deliberate intent. Retrospectively, it is all too easy to see how the American Revolution might have been averted; the fact is that it was not and that thereby the most productive civilisation the world has ever known was brought into being. Its military roots and antecedents therefore deserve the close attention General John Galvin has given them.

Moreover, military reality underlay the fiscal disagreements which are usually charted as the steps by which colonists and Crown proceeded to conflict. Victory has a price, as every empire has discovered. The defeat of the French, though resolving a crisis, thereby devolved on Britain a responsibility which its enemy had thitherto largely discharged single-handed: controlling the Indians of the interior. The disappearance of the French threw the Indians into a panic, manifested in

Pontiac's rebellion of 1763, which caused the British Crown to respond with two measures, each ultimately a source of further conflict, though with the settlers instead of the native inhabitants. One was the Proclamation of 1763, which reserved the land west of the Appalachian crestline to the Indians, thereby denying to the most energetic and adventurous of the colonists the new land they were seeking for agriculture and commerce (the subsequent southward extension of the boundary of Canada to the Ohio country exacerbated the resentment the colonists felt); the other was the decision, necessitated by the strategic burden that domination of Atlantic America imposed, to maintain a large military garrison in the region.

No sooner was the Seven Years War over than the British government found itself confronted with the need to find nearly half a million pounds a year, then an enormous sum, simply to pay for its overseas military establishment. The British were already the most heavily taxed people in Western Europe, and the threat of this additional impost aroused outcry in parliament. The response of the landowning and mercantile representatives on whom it would fall was predictable: since it was in America that the heaviest military costs were incurred, the colonists should make an appreciable contribution to what ultimately was a benefit supplied to them without charge by the Crown. Hence the Sugar and Stamp Acts of 1764. These were opposed from the outset by the provincial assemblies and, when their reasonable objections were ignored, were largely disobeyed. They were not merely disobeyed—by evasion and by large-scale smuggling in defiance of royal customs collectors—but actively opposed. The large colonial cities—Boston and New York—were the scene of riots and mob violence, provoked not because the voters were people liable for the prescribed taxes but because they were the targets of another arm of the imperial military system, the impressment service of the Royal Navy. Poor colonists, exempt from or only indirectly subject to tax, thus lent their support to the rich colonists who were the local objectors, through a mechanism which conscripted them to do duty at sea in a navy which, in the last resort, was an instrument of restriction of free trade at the point of entry.

By 1774 the British government had serious trouble on its hands. In that year a Continental Congress, a successor to the earlier Stamp Act Congress which had successfully denounced that legislation, met at Philadelphia in September; only Georgia among the thirteen colonies failed to send delegates. It promulgated a remarkable doctrine, a fore-runner of that which united British Liberal Imperialists in the late nine-teenth century, which would, if accepted in London, have indeed averted the Revolution, but for which British royal and parliamentary opinion was as yet unready: "that the colonies were co-ordinate members with each other and Great Britain of an empire united by a common sovereign, and that the legislative power was maintained to be as complete in each American parliament (the colonial assemblies) as in the British parliament." To give force to their resolution the delegates agreed not to import British goods on the terms imposed and to set up a Continental Association to enforce non-importation. In response the British parliament voted in February 1775, not long after news of the colonists' defiance had reached it, a Restraining Act which forbade them to trade both with Britain and with its other dominions, including the West Indies, with which their richest commerce was conducted. It was widely recognised in both Lords and Commons that the measure ordained war, yet a majority was found for it none the less. That was in the face of the most prescient of the warnings uttered: "To conquer a great continent of 1,800 miles [the length of the American seaboard]," said Lord Camden, "containing three millions of people, all indissolubly united on the great Whig bottom of liberty and justice, seems an undertaking not to be rashly engaged in. . . . What are the 10,000 men you have just voted out to Boston? Merely to save General Gage from the disgrace and destruction of being sacked in his entrenchments. It is obvious, my lords, that you cannot furnish armies, or treasure competent to the mighty purpose of subduing America . . . but whether France and Spain will be tame, inactive spectators of your efforts and distractions is well worth the considerations of our lordships."

Neither France nor Spain would, when the opportunity offered, find themselves able to resist taking revenge on an enemy, currently in extreme strategic difficulty, who had robbed them of so much territory, in India, the West Indies, the Mediterranean, and the Americas themselves; Canada, Gibraltar, Madras, the list was long. All that, in 1775, lay several years in the future. In the immediate present, Lord Camden's warning concerned only a small part of the great continent of America, Massachusetts, where resistance to the Restraining Act was most resolute, and, in particular, Boston, where the presence of a large force of British troops made a confrontation most likely. In warfare, force tends to attract force. During the winter of 1775 and the spring of 1776, the militia companies of the towns around Boston had been stockpiling powder and ball and withdrawing supplies from the King's magazines to those of their own. They had also been drilling with renewed enthusiasm, smuggling cannon into their possession, setting up an intelligence network to report on British movements, and agreeing on signals to give warnings of any move by General Gage to pre-empt resistance. Thomas Gage, Governor of Massachusetts (the colony was royal, as were all except proprietary Pennsylvania and Maryland and chartered Rhode Island and Connecticut, which elected their governors), was no incompetent. He had fought at the victories of Fontenoy and Culloden and acquitted himself bravely in Braddock's battle on the Monongahela, had served as Governor of Montreal, and between 1760 and 1770 had commanded all British forces in the western hemisphere. He understood the American mind, was liked by American people—he was married to a New Jersey lady—but had formed a misjudgement about their probable reaction to the royal policy of repression. He thought a show of force would outface the hotheads, bring the sympathisers to their senses, and lend heart to the loyalists. He had altogether under-estimated the resolve of the Minutemen and the level of their military preparedness.

The extent of his misjudgement was to be shown on 18 April 1775, when he issued his order for a composite force of seven hundred men to leave Boston and march to seize the militia's stores before they could be dispersed to safe hiding. A meeting of the provincial Congress of Massachusetts had already resolved, if the British marched, "to oppose their march to the last extremity," but had just agreed to adjourn for two weeks. Gage, advised by a loyalist delegate, Benjamin Church, saw his opportunity and decided to take it. On the night of 18 April, parties from the 4th King's Own Regiment, 23rd Royal Welch Fusiliers, and 42nd Royal Highlanders (Black Watch) slipped out of their barracks by a back door, hoping to avoid watching eyes, and embarked in boats to march to Concord, sixteen miles inland, "with the utmost expedition and secrecy . . . where you will seize and destroy all artillery, ammunition, provisions, tents, small arms and all military stores whatever." Boston, before the infilling of marshes and shallows of the last two centuries, was then almost an island, and Gage had chosen to send his men by water because spies might thus be deluded about their destination. It was another under-estimation, in this case of the pervasiveness of the resisters' intelligence network. Paul Revere, a leading member of the conspiracy, had positioned himself so as to observe British movements and, seeing them embark, had himself rowed, also with muffled oars, to where he could mount a fast horse and gallop off ahead to warn the Minutemen of the British approach.

The British landed at Charlestown, on the north bank of the Charles River, and marched off through Cambridge in the dark of the April night. Their route took them up what is now Massachusetts Avenue, past the campus of Harvard University and Radcliffe College, on to State Route 2A and so towards Concord. The men were marching light, but the distance was considerable, and at the twelve-mile mark, when they reached Lexington, they were already tiring. It was early morning, the sun was up, the day was crisp and breezy, and on Lexington Green in front of them the British saw, by one of their officer's reports, "near 200 of the rebels; when I came within about one hundred yards of them, they began to file off towards some stone walls on our right flank." In fact the Minutemen numbered seventy-seven, under Captain John Parker, a Lexington man who had fought in the French and Indian Wars. He seems to have intended not much more than a symbolic resistance to the British advance, for he did not actually bar the Concord road, deploying his men to its side rather than across it. The British commander, Major John Pitcairn, certainly did not intend to open a firefight; there is a belief that he wanted to surround and arrest the Americans. Before he could deploy his troops out of marching column into enveloping line, however, the damage was done. Someone—British, American, no one knows—had pulled a trigger, and the firing instantly became general. Within a few minutes, ten at most, eight Minutemen lay dead and nine wounded; one British regular had been lightly touched.

The aftermath is briefly related. Pitcairn and his men pressed on the next four miles to Concord, where they were stoutly opposed and turned back. The Minutemen, alerted by Revere, other scouts, and the news of the Lexington fight, had turned out in numbers large enough not only to defend themselves and their arsenals but to harry the redcoats home almost every step of the way. Three were killed at Concord bridge, more as they were sniped from behind cover on the road to Lexington, while at Menotomy (now Arlington) nearly two thousand militiamen raked the retreating column from both sides of the road. By the time it reached Charlestown on the evening of 19 April, it had lost 273 killed, wounded, or missing. The Americans had lost forty-nine

killed and forty-six wounded but won a major action. Losses on both
sides were too large to be written off as the result of a mere riot or local tumult, of which there had been several in the previous decade.
Lexington and Concord, particularly Concord, meant war. It now
unrolled.

The advantage was with the rebels. Gage had had an immediate
and a subsidiary object in staging his march. The immediate aim was
to seize the arms, the subsidiary one to stake out a line of control in the
higher land above Boston. He had failed in both, and it was now the
turn of the rebels to take the high ground and bring Gage's Boston garrison under siege. There is high ground in Boston proper, notably at
Beacon Hill above the Common, lined with streets of sober, stock-brick
Georgian houses among which the modern London visitor might well
feel himself back at home in Gower Street or Bedford Square. Across
the harbour and the Charles River, however, Dorchester Heights and
Bunker or Breed's Hill offer positions which command both the city
and the approaches to it. By 29 April 1775 all this ground was in rebel
hands, and soon fifteen thousand militiamen ringed the city. A second
Continental Congress meeting at Philadelphia in June deemed them to
constitute the Continental Army, and the soldier who made the chief
impression at the congress, George Washington, was elected general
and its commander-in-chief.

Washington, aged forty-two in 1775, had had a frustrating military
career. His honour had been compromised in 1754 at Fort Duquesne,
his ardour had been blunted on the Monongahela, his hopes of prefer-
ment from the militia to the Crown's regular forces had been disappointed; he had expressed the desire to "be distinguished . . . from the
common run of provincial officers," but it had done him no good.
Now, passed over by royal officers whom he had dearly wished to join
on an equal footing, he was to be given the chance of showing himself
a better soldier than they. He was not to arrive at Boston in time for
the first pitched battle of the war. That took place at Breed's Hill (commonly called Bunker Hill) on 17 June, when General William Howe, a
veteran of Louisbourg and Quebec, unwisely attacked a fortified American position which had been thrown up overnight within cannon shot
of Boston harbour. The soldiers of the Continental Army were to prove
great diggers—in that sense they were embattled farmers—and good
fighters from behind earthworks. Howe, who might have starved the
defenders of Breed's Hill into surrender, decided on a show of force,

ferried two thousand redcoats across the harbour, threw them into a
frontal assault, and lost five hundred killed or mortally wounded to
American musketry. It was here that the phrase "Don't fire until you
see the whites of their eyes" became famous. Washington, who would
become a master of the musketry battle at a later stage, inherited the
Bunker Hill musketeers' triumph as the first prop to his assumption of
command on 3 July 1775.

There was little he could do at once to build on their victory. If he
was to turn the British out of Boston, he needed more and better soldiers—those he inspected on arrival he found "dirty and nasty," and
anxious to go home—and, above all, cannon. Cannon were being
brought from Fort Ticonderoga, captured in May by the future traitor
Benedict Arnold and Ethan Allen's Green Mountain Boys. Until they
arrived, which they would in November, Washington could only wait;
he took up residence in the Wadsworth House at Harvard, the residence of the college president, and considered plans for action
elsewhere.

That must be against Canada, the only part of North America
where the British still maintained a force that could intervene against
the rebellion. Arnold's and Allen's attack on Ticonderoga had been no
more than a raid which had succeeded through a lucky surprise. An offensive into Canada would be a weightier undertaking, demanding a
logistic effort perhaps beyond the capacities of an improvised army. It
was decided, nevertheless, to make the attempt. Ironically, geography
determined that the campaign must be mounted against precisely those
centres which the French had defended so stubbornly during the Seven
Years War and follow, in one case at least, exactly those routes so
much fought over in the preceding century and a half of North American warfare. That was the Champlain–Richelieu water corridor to
Montreal. The Continental Congress, informed that there were only
550 British troops in Canada and that the French might be willing
to throw in their lot with the conquerors' new enemies, commissioned
General Richard Montgomery to lead an amphibious expedition northward from Ticonderoga. Success would depend upon speed and
surprise.

Surprise was not achieved; Sir Guy Carleton, the British Governor
of Canada, got wind of the preparations Montgomery was making and
himself began to build boats and stockpile supplies near St. Jean at the
point where the Richelieu flows into the St. Lawrence, so as to block

Montgomery's egress. In great haste, Montgomery rushed his twelve hundred men to the old French fort on the Ile-aux-Noix twenty miles below St. Jean, where he laid a boom across the river to stop Carleton's boats if they appeared. He then advanced on St. Jean and laid siege to the fort, whose remains can be seen at the Collège Royale Militaire. The garrison was small, but Montgomery was unskilled in siegework and was short of ammunition. Abandoning the siege temporarily, he advanced on the old French fort at Chambly, built by the Carignan-Salières Regiment in 1665, took it, replenished his stocks, returned to St. Jean, where the garrison was now so short of food that it was obliged to surrender on 2 November, and then, in the deepening Canadian winter, set off for Montreal. Carleton had used up what troops he had in attempting to reinforce St. Jean and Chambly and was forced to flee from Montreal to Quebec in the face of Montgomery's advance, which was now turned against Quebec itself.

By extraordinary feats, another American force had arrived at Quebec ahead of him, following a route which, unusually, had not before been put to military use. It was led by Benedict Arnold, the captor of Ticonderoga in May, who had prevailed on Washington at Boston in August to let him attempt it. The route had been mapped during the Seven Years War by the chief engineer of the Braddock expedition to the Monongahela, Captain John Montresor, who was therefore known to Washington already. His map showed that, in theory, a military penetration to the St. Lawrence opposite Quebec could be made up the Kennebec River, which flows into the Atlantic near Portland, Maine (then part of Massachusetts). By ship from Boston, a force could debark at the river mouth, boat up to a twelve-mile stretch of ground called the Great Carrying Place, portage there through three small lakes to the Dead River, then ascend by boat for thirty miles to Lake Megantic and so into the Chaudière River, which debouches into the St. Lawrence at Pointe Lévis, from which Wolfe's batteries had bombarded Quebec in 1759. The length of the whole route was 250 miles, but Montresor's map showed that boats would have to be carried for only twelve.

Arnold, with a thousand men and food for forty-five days, set off from the old trading post, Fort Western, on 25 September 1775, in a flotilla of two hundred hastily built boats. The first stage of the journey to Fort Halifax (modern Winslow on U.S. 201) went smoothly enough, but Montresor had under-estimated the obstacles the river itself presented. Rapids and waterfalls have been engineered out of the Kennebec's course in modern times. In the eighteenth century it was a turbulent watercourse, and the expedition found itself forced to portage boats weighing over four hundred pounds, together with sixty-five tons of stores, at tiringly frequent intervals. The banks of the river were alternately rocky or swampy and increasingly uninhabited; beyond modern Norridgewock there were no settlements at all before Canada. Near modern Brigham, Arnold stopped to build a hospital for his increasing number of sick, then attacked the portages to the Dead River, which took five days to traverse. His numbers had fallen to 950 and food stocks to starvation level; men boiled their moccasins to make soup, ate shaving soap and hair pomade, and slaughtered Captain Henry Dearburn's pet dog for a mouthful of meat "without leaving any vestige of the sacrifice." Even after passing the Great Carrying Place, many portages remained, both before reaching and then along the Chaudière. Not until 8 November did the 675 survivors of this wilderness anabasis reach the St. Lawrence.

There then ensued a parody of the battle of 1759. The British garrison of Quebec was too weak to prevent Arnold from crossing the river to land at Wolfe's Cove and ascend to the Plains of Abraham. Arnold's force, even when joined by Montgomery's from Montreal, was too weak to undertake a siege. Carleton, who had made his way in disguise to reach the city ahead of Montgomery, prudently avoided Montcalm's mistake of coming out to fight. Arnold therefore decided on an assault of the walls in a blinding snowstorm on 21 December. The escalade was a disaster: Montgomery was killed, Arnold wounded, and their little army retired into miserable winter quarters outside the city, in which it remained until May 1776. With the arrival of British reinforcements at the breaking of the ice in the St. Lawrence, its position became untenable and the survivors fled for home via the Richelieu–Champlain route.

The American effort to secure a strategic perimeter at the outset of the Revolution was thus ended. True, Howe had been forced to evacuate Boston on 17 March 1776, after a bookseller-turned-colonel, Henry Knox, had brought down enough cannon from Fort Ticonderoga, dragged by sledge over the snows, to arm a fort on Dorchester Heights which overlooked the harbour. Howe merely transported his army to Halifax, Nova Scotia, however, thus strengthening the position of the British in Canada. They now enjoyed, indeed, most of the advantages the French had always sought in the long years of imperial struggle, and others in addition. They were in control of the mouth of the St. Lawrence, "gateway to a continent," and of its lower reaches, would physically control the Great Lakes as soon as they deployed garrisons in the old forts, had men in the Forks of the Ohio, oversaw the northern exits from the Richelieu and the Mohawk, and absolutely commanded—in the absence of any American naval force—the seaward approaches to the short rivers of the Atlantic Coast, all the way from the Hudson (New York was considered loyalist), past the Delaware and the streams discharging into Chesapeake Bay, to the Santee, near Charleston, South Carolina, and the Savannah in Georgia. The danger that the rebellious colonists faced, therefore, was that of confinement between the ocean and the Appalachians, and of convergent attacks into that area from Canada and from the great coastal cities actually and potentially under British occupation—New York, Baltimore, Georgetown (modern Washington), and Philadelphia—which would cut their north–south line of communications and expose them to defeat in detail. Enthusiasm for the rebellion, the great dominion of Virginia excepted, was notably weaker in the South than the North; it was significant that those of Benedict Arnold's men who reached the Chaudière were known to the local French as *les Bostonnais*. In the summer of 1776 the Revolution, despite Washington's success in chasing Howe away to Halifax, risked ending as no more than a Massachusetts revolt.

That it should was exactly the intention of George III's government in London. Lord George Germain, who was appointed Secretary of State for the Colonies in November 1775, was taking advice from many quarters. One decision had already been taken for him: rather than keep troops landing in Canada, an expedition had been sailed for Charleston, where a show of force was thought to be all that was necessary to hold the Carolinas and perhaps overawe Virginia. The expedition was to prove a fiasco, but that lay in the future. Elsewhere Germain decided to cut New England off from the middle colonies, New York, New Jersey, and Pennsylvania, to get control of upper New York, so as to tap the supposed loyalism of the Canadians, and to impose a tight blockade of the colonial seaports. John Burgoyne, one of Howe's subordinates at Boston, had set forth the key to the strategy in a telling memorandum: "I have always thought Hudson's River the most proper part of the whole continent for opening vigorous operations. Because the course of the river, so beneficial for conveying all the bulky necessaries of an army, is precisely the route that an army ought to take for the great purposes of cutting the communications between the southern and northern Provinces, giving confidence to the Indians, and securing a junction with the Canadian forces. These purposes effected, and a fleet upon the coast, it is to me morally certain that the forces of New England [i.e., the Continental Army] must be reduced so early in the campaign to give you battle upon your [Howe's] own terms, and perish before the end of it for want of necessary supplies." In extension of this scheme, a flotilla of boats was to be built with which Carleton in Canada could take command of the Great Lakes, while he and Howe might then descend from the lakes and the upper Hudson to take the rebels in Massachusetts from the rear.

What this grand design lacked was troops, exactly the problem, in a different form, that was pressing the Continental Congress. Britain's difficulty was to assemble regulars and transport them across the Atlantic, Washington's to enlist, arm, and train amateurs who could face regulars on something like equal terms. Both sides were, in a sense, in the market, Washington for militiamen who would enlist or patriots who would volunteer, the British for foreign contingents which could be hired to supplement the ranks of the King's army, greatly depleted since the end of the Seven Years War. In 1775 it was hoped that Catherine the Great would land 30,000 Russians; by January 1776, treaties had secured 18,000 German troops from Hesse, Kassel, Brunswick, and other small princely states. Nearly 30,000 Germans would serve in America throughout the war. At the outset, however, neither side could count on any large force. Howe began the campaign of 1776 with no more than 25,000 troops on hand or promised, Washington with about 19,000. His advantage was that he could keep his men together to oppose the British wherever they chose to strike; their disadvantage, identified by Lord Camden before the war had begun, was that the sheer size of America dwarfed their means to dominate it. If they dispersed the army, it risked being swallowed up in the enormous spaces of the colonies; their best hope was that Washington would agree to fight a continental, not a guerrilla, war and respond to their strategy.

So—with barely averted consequences of disaster for the Revolution—it turned out. Howe, waiting at Halifax with the army withdrawn from Boston, planned in the spring of 1776 to descend on New

York and so split the rebellious North from—the British believed—the generally loyalist South. Washington, in anticipation, had gone to New York in April, where he wrote to his brother on 31 May, "we expect a very bloody summer of it." His troops followed and began to entrench positions on Manhattan, Governors Island, and Long Island. General Charles Lee had been planning the works since January, but not with an easy mind. "What to do with the city puzzles me," he wrote on 19 February. "It is so surrounded with deep navigable waters that whoever commands the sea must command the town." He did what he could to deny use of the East River to the British, by building batteries on Brooklyn Heights, and at King's Bridge at Harlem, then the only dry crossing to the mainland, but he feared that the Continental Army might be trapped in Manhattan. That was indeed the fate Washington escaped by the skin of his teeth; his escape was to lead to the string of little winter engagements in the back country of New Jersey in 1776–77 which seem to the uninformed traveller so disconnected with the course of the war, and to the harsh sequestration at Valley Forge from which the subsequent resurgence of the Revolution was to flow.

Strange to think today of the megalopolis of New York as a field of military manoeuvre. The points of encounter are buried beneath the suburban streets of Brooklyn Heights and the concrete of Harlem. Almost the only open spaces remaining from the campaign of 1776 are Greenwood Cemetery and the Cemetery of the Evergreens, passed in a rush by transatlantic passengers on their way to John F. Kennedy Airport, covering what were then the marshes beyond the village of Jamaica. New York itself was a city of only twenty thousand people, its northern border running along Chambers Street, where City Hall now stands. Between it and Harlem, ten miles to the north, the surface of the island was largely farmland, but some was forest and rocky outcrop—as it remains in Central Park—and much of it swamp. Infilling has doubled Manhattan's habitable size since 1776.

Lee's fortifications were dug so as to use the line of Brooklyn Heights as a barrier against a British advance; the forts in rear were designed to stop the British fleet running the narrows. Howe did not attempt to do so. Having dropped down to Sandy Hook, the entrance to New York harbour, on 29 June, he made Staten Island his base, camping his troops among its tranquil Dutch farmsteads; the army which, under General Sir Henry Clinton, had tried but failed to capture Charleston, South Carolina, arrived to join him on 1 August, raising his numbers to 25,000. During this leisurely prelude to action there had been two developments of critical importance: the Continental Congress had made a Declaration of Independence at Philadelphia on 1 July, and Howe, with his admiral brother commanding the fleet, had, in the capacity of peace commissioners to which they had insisted on being appointed by the King, met but failed to agree on terms with a delegation of revolutionaries. The Conference House where they negotiated still stands near the Outerbridge Crossing connecting Staten Island with New Jersey.

Now it could only be war to the finish. Howe was ready by mid-August and decided to confront the Americans in the Brooklyn positions. It was a grave mistake of strategy; had he forced the narrows, seized King's Bridge and sent ships to patrol Long Island Sound, the whole of Washington's force, the Revolution's only real army, would have been marooned on two offshore islands. Instead he attempted a shorter encirclement, aiming to pass above the northern shoulder of Brooklyn Heights, along the line of the modern Brooklyn-Queens Expressway, towards what is today Prospect Park, taking Washington from the rear. It nearly worked. On 22 August, fifteen thousand British and Germans were rowed across from Staten Island, landed near Coney Island, and panicked the defenders into flight. In the course of the next three days the British advanced to Washington's main line of resistance and their right wing actually got behind it, via Jamaica, almost as far as Flatbush. The Americans fled in disorder to their last line of defences. Had Howe pressed on against his demoralised opponents on 28 August he might have ended the war there and then. Fortunately for the Revolution, memories of Bunker Hill and of how resolutely the rebels had defended their earthworks on that battlefield deterred Howe from pressing his advantage. While he ordered his own men to dig earthworks, Washington held a council of war, summoning a contingent of fishermen from Marblehead, Massachusetts, who were serving in his ranks, and had them row the survivors of the Continental Army across New York Bay to Manhattan.

Washington lived to fight another day, but his army's position was still perilous. Howe's correct strategy at this stage would have been to bypass Manhattan by the East River, which his fleet controlled, and tranship his vastly superior force to the mainland across King's Bridge from Harlem, into what is today the Bronx. Instead he again attempted a short rather than a long encirclement, debarked men on 15 September at about modern East 32nd Street, only to have Washington slip past him up Broadway. Howe caught up and at one stage his advance guard was marching parallel with Washington's up the line of modern Park Avenue, with what is today Central Park alone separating them; had Howe wheeled left, the decisive battle of the American Revolution might have been fought in the vicinity of today's expensive apartment houses on Central Park West. The Americans, however, managed a spurt, reached the Harlem Heights, where Manhattan island sharply narrows, and pitched their advance line along that of modern 125th Street. There for three weeks Howe and Washington sat and stared at each other.

Why Washington sat out the confrontation defies analysis. Even a short encirclement, Howe's favoured manoeuvre, would have trapped him in the Harlem pocket. Wait he did, nonetheless, until Howe took the correct decision, boated troops to the mainland above King's Bridge and ordered them to capture its approaches from the mainland side. On the map, Washington was trapped again, in worse circumstances than ever. Brave delaying actions by parties of American riflemen saved him on 12 October; when Howe landed more troops at New Rochelle, a little further north, on 18 October, Washington had more troops in position and they fought a successful defensive battle, allowing him, far too late by any prudent military calculation, to gather his men for a precipitate retreat across King's Bridge, from which they reached White Plains on 22 October. Then, on 28 October 1776, in the heart of modern New York City's rich and leafy suburban overspill, Howe launched what should have been a climactic assault on his enemy's position, but the Americans had again thrown up the sort of improvised earthworks he had learnt to fear at Bunker Hill. When his first assault failed in the face of an American cannonade, he retired to prepare a more deliberate attack. He also considered it necessary to deal with two American strong points in his rear, Fort Washington on Manhattan and Fort Lee on the Palisades across the Hudson, guarding what today are the eastern and western approaches of the George Washington Bridge. By the time he returned to deal with the main business, the Americans had slipped out of their White Plains entrenchments, marched beyond Jarrytown to Verplanck, and crossed the Hudson by ferry into what is still the wild country of Bear Mountain State Park.

I first came this way in the fall of 1957, driving to visit the country house of John Houseman, the great film producer, to whom I had been given an introduction. The grandeur of the Palisades, starting sheer out of the Hudson, and the tangled woodlands round Bear Mountain startled me by their reminder of how close the wilderness stood to the world's greatest metropolis; the same sensation has returned often since, whenever I stand with my back to the forest and see the pinnacles of New York scraping the skies across the Hudson a dozen miles away. In 1776, however, Bear Mountain was not wild enough for Washington. "If overpowered," he said as he beat his retreat southward into New Jersey, "we must cross the Allegheny Mountains." It was nearly to come to that. On 20 November, Howe sent his subordinate, General Lord Cornwallis, across the Hudson after Washington, who cleared Newark on 30 November as Cornwallis's advance guard entered the town. Breaking the bridges of the short New Jersey rivers, the Hackensack, Passaic, and Raritan, behind him, Washington got to the Delaware at Trenton on 7 December. He had sent orders ahead for a fleet of boats to be assembled and for those not needed to ferry his army to be destroyed; when Cornwallis arrived on 9 December, the remnants of the Continental Army, six thousand out of the nineteen thousand with which Washington had begun on Long Island, were safe in Pennsylvania, while Cornwallis had no means of sustaining the chase.

The two parties to the war were now in strategic equilibrium. Howe, controlling New York and with his army and fleet intact, retained the freedom to strike at Washington wherever he could be found, but needed to find and fix him if a decision to the war was to be concluded. Washington, though his numbers were severely depleted and proving difficult to restore, could use the barrier of the Delaware as a screen behind which to manoeuvre against the British weak spots. He had a vulnerability, which was the open city of Philadelphia, seat of the Revolution's government on the lower Delaware; if, however, he could divert Cornwallis from it, the war might still be kept alive without that retreat behind the Allegheny Mountains to which he felt himself being driven after his escape from White Plains.

This balance of advantage and disadvantage was to dictate the course of operations in the Middle Atlantic region throughout 1777 and 1778. Operating in a corridor only some hundred miles long and fifty wide between Philadelphia and New York, the two armies feinted, sidestepped, attacked, and retreated as opportunity offered. In December 1776, just after his flight over the Delaware, Washington recrossed the river, at what today is commemorated as Washington's Crossing. He fell on Clinton at Trenton on 26 December and pursued him to Princeton, where he won a second small battle on 3 January 1777. He then trekked across the Raritan to Morristown, on the Passaic, to wait out the winter in the New Jersey back country; he was to return there, after his arctic ordeal of 1777–78 at Valley Forge, behind Philadelphia, for the winter of 1778–79. Spring and summer were a period of inactivity, as Howe tried to tempt Washington out into the open; despairing of the attempt, he chose suddenly to use his amphibious power, sailed his army from New York in July, landed at the head of Chesapeake Bay, forced battle on Washington behind Philadelphia, his weak spot, at Brandywine Creek on 11 September, took Philadelphia, beat Washington again at Germantown, just north of the city, on 4 October, and harried the remnants of the Continental Army to Valley Forge, on the Schuylkill River, which flows into the Delaware below Philadelphia; today the Pennsylvania Turnpike runs past the memorial park.

The crucial actions of 1777 took place, however, not in the Middle Atlantic states but far away in upper New York, along lines of strategic manoeuvre which had been trodden, boated, and portaged since the beginning of European warfare in North America. The New York campaign of 1777 was, indeed, an uncannily exact repetition of those of 1758 and 1760 by the British and Americans against the French, with the difference that it was now the British who were based in Canada and their direction of advance—from, instead of towards, the St. Lawrence and the Great Lakes—was southward, not northward. The plan to bisect the rebellious colonies via the Hudson from Canada had, of course, been implicit in London's scheme of reconquest from the start. It had been delayed for want of troops, by over-optimistic beliefs in the degree of loyalism in New York, and by hopes that Howe, from his central positions in New York City and New Jersey, could achieve the desired result single-handed. It had also been a necessary first step that American control of upper Lake Champlain should be broken; but Carleton, Governor of Canada, had achieved that in a landlocked naval battle, fought with fleets of purpose-built ships, against Benedict Arnold on 11 October 1776. By the spring of 1777 the way was clear. All that was lacking was the impulse to start. Who should be blamed for the failure to supply it is much disputed. Howe, whose relocation to Philadelphia had taken him away from the scene of action, was a bad communicator; Carleton, who might have got things going in 1776, was disgruntled at being replaced in military command of Canada by General John Burgoyne; Burgoyne had spent the critical months of early 1777 in London. By the time he got to Lake Champlain with seven thousand troops in June, the campaigning season was far advanced. The auguries were not good.

Still, he counted on Colonel Barry St. Leger, whose mission was to advance from Lake Ontario down the Mohawk corridor towards Albany, to create an effective diversion; and he was sure his force was large enough to sweep aside the American militia and take Albany himself. After its loss to the British in 1664, the Dutchman Peter Stuyvesant had written that "whosoever, by ship or ships, is master of the river, will in a short time be master of the fort." Burgoyne began the campaign as the master of the waterways above the navigable Hudson and had no doubt he would soon be at Albany and shortly afterwards at New York City.

It was not to be. Burgoyne's failure and failing, akin to those of McClellan in the peninsula below Richmond, Virginia, eighty-five years later, was to be both over-prepared as well as under-assured of his ability to sustain the force he had at his command. Because the forts of the corridor, Ticonderoga in particular, lay in his path, he brought an enormous train of artillery, 138 cannon, with him; because the superabundancy of timber supplied by the Hudson wilderness threatened the danger of the Americans throwing up successive lines of barricades against his advance down the narrow valley, he declined to proceed without assembling the means to move it, a stockpile of thirty days' supplies. "All his wants," wrote a contemporary, "were owing to his having too great an abundance." Ticonderoga, which, since its building in 1755, had been French, British, and American, fell easily to the British artillery on 6 July. Then the delays began. Schuyler, Burgoyne's opponent, falling back towards Fort Edward on the Hudson, created inundations as he went, felled trees across the road, and broke bridges; the British had to build forty as they followed. The great green of the American forest supplied them with the materials, but also Schuyler with what he wanted to place new obstacles in their path. Burgoyne was also forced to detach troops to protect his rear as he moved southward, for volunteers were joining Schuyler in numbers. It was not until 29 July, three weeks after taking Ticonderoga forty miles away, that he reached Fort Edward, and his difficulties, rather than decreasing as he

got near his objective, were compounding. St. Leger's expedition down
the Mohawk River from Lake Ontario was stopped at Fort Stanwix,
guarding the first portage near modern Rome, New York, in early August. The Americans, moreover, were starting to fight back. On 16 August a party of foragers detached by Burgoyne to look for urgently
needed supplies were defeated at Barrington, east of the Hudson in its
Hoosier tributary. On 22 August, Benedict Arnold, marching up the
Mohawk, relieved Fort Stanwix and frightened St. Leger back into
Canada. By early September, Burgoyne's numbers and supplies were
depleting rapidly, as his soldiers deserted and those who remained ate
up what was in hand. Carleton, who might have sent large reinforcements from Canada, nursed his grievance and sent few. A strong offensive had imperceptibly dwindled into weakness, and Burgoyne faced
isolation in the Hudson forests.

He concluded that his best hope was to put the barrier of the Hudson between himself and the increasing number of New England militiamen who were rallying to the fight. On 13 September, therefore, he
crossed to the west bank and marched south towards Albany, where he
hoped both to revictual and to receive reinforcements from Henry
Clinton, the general Howe had left in New York to guard his main
base. Both hopes were in vain. The Hudson highlands at West Point
were too strongly held by the enemy for Clinton's small force safely to
risk a passage up the river; reports suggested that Albany was empty of
supplies. Clinton did his very best to get up to Burgoyne in his positions at Saratoga (modern Schuylerville); indeed, he got as far as
Kingston, but his message urging his fellow general to march towards
him was intercepted; they were still separated by eighty miles of wild
country. Bereft of news, Burgoyne havered. He was confronted by one
of those American entrenchments now so familiar to the British, attacked it on 19 September at a point called Freeman's Farm, and was
repulsed; he now entrenched his own position, in the hope that Clinton
would appear. When he did not, Burgoyne made a second assault, at
Bemis Heights, was counterattacked by the ferocious and ubiquitous
Benedict Arnold, fresh from his success on the Mohawk, and pinned
against the west bank of the Hudson. His splendid little army had been
reduced to a strength of 3,500, and even that small number faced starvation, while the well-supplied Americans outnumbered him. On 14
October, with the gold-and-scarlet warning of an approaching American winter colouring the forest around them, Burgoyne and his officers

entered into negotiations for a capitulation with their opponents. Terms were agreed on 17 October, allowing the British and the German troops to march away as long as they returned to Europe and took no further part in the war. Thus the campaign of 1777 ended in a forthright American victory; to their control of New England, won in 1776, was now added that of New York and the Canadian border.

The irony was that the British ought to have won the campaigns of 1776–77. The strategic advantages which the French had always enjoyed—control of the St. Lawrence and Great Lakes, dominance of the head of the Hudson and Mohawk corridors—were theirs. The military advantages the French had never enjoyed—the presence of a large regular force onshore and of an unchallengeable fleet offshore, supported by a string of excellent bases at Newport, Rhode Island, New York, and Philadelphia—were theirs as well. So, too, was the support of a large proportion of the population among which their army operated. There had been nothing but enmity for the French in British America, while at least a third of the colonists during the Revolution remained loyal to the Crown and a third neutral. Moreover, once the loss of Massachusetts had been accepted, the theatre of operations was reduced to a perfectly manageable size. No more than eighty miles separates New York and Philadelphia, from which Morristown and Valley Forge, Washington's winter refuges, are each only twenty miles inland. Washington, admittedly, was a master of cat-and-mouse marching; but in a test of strength he was the mouse and Howe the cat. The suspicion is that had Howe and his soldiers had the stomach for winter warfare shown by Benedict Arnold on his march up the Kennebec to Quebec in 1775, Washington would indeed have been driven beyond "the Allegheny mountains" and the Revolution would have been overwhelmed by American climate and distances.

As it was, Washington profited from the disaster of Saratoga to sit out the third winter of the war at Valley Forge and to begin the campaign of 1778 on strategic terms that were quite suddenly and utterly transformed. In February, France had seized the opportunity for revenge presented by Britain's difficulties to sign a treaty with the American revolutionaries, promising alliance in the case of war with Britain. As the British recognised, war was now the French purpose, and they found themselves forced to disperse both their fleet and their army to guard against danger in the West Indies and the Mediterranean, where Spain was also moving towards hostilities. In May, Howe, dispirited by his failures, very much of his own making though they were, resigned command in America, to be replaced by Clinton. Clinton had been in Philadelphia only a day when, on 9 May, orders arrived from London that he was to evacuate Philadelphia and concentrate his forces at New York, so that a surplus could be found to reinforce the West Indies and Florida; Florida, ceded to Britain by Spain after the Seven Years War, was an obvious target for reconquest.

Since the reinforcement required ships as well as men, Clinton found his fleet depleted precisely at a moment when Britain's three-year-old command of American waters was threatened by the sailing of a large French squadron across the Atlantic. All military prudence argued for evacuating Philadelphia by sea, but, since there were insufficient warships to protect what transports could be had, the army would have to march by land. Winter and spring in Philadelphia had been pleasant; it was, and remains around Society Hill, a European city of well-ordered streets, decorous architecture, and fine public buildings. It was also, in 1778, full of loyalists, three thousand of whom were judged to be potential victims of revolutionary vengeance. When their number was added to the eight thousand troops of the garrison, and the five thousand horses which Clinton required for his own further operations and dared not leave to Washington for his, the departing forces needed over twelve miles of road simply to move in a single column. It presented a highly vulnerable and almost indefensible target—as Braddock's long column had been at the Monongahela or Elphinstone's would be on the retreat from Kabul in 1842 or that of the French expeditionary force during the abandonment of the Vietnamese northern highlands in 1950. Clinton sensibly declined to follow the militarily compromised route through Trenton and Princeton, scene of Washington's successes in December 1776 and January 1777, instead striking eastward towards the coast along a bad road through swampy terrain. Washington, abandoning Valley Forge, raced after him in the boiling heat of a New Jersey June, which killed some British and German troops by sunstroke, but unwisely entrusted the advance guard to his subordinate, Charles Lee. When Lee caught up with Clinton's rearguard near Monmouth Courthouse (at Englishtown, just west of U.S. 9) on 28 June, he made the mistake of attacking off his line of march without deploying properly. Clinton turned in a trice, pressed the Americans against a natural obstacle, savaged them, and disengaged to complete the march to Sandy Hook at the mouth of New York harbour a week later. It was a classic example of how roughly regular troops can handle under-trained opponents—despite Baron von Steuben's use of the drill book at Valley Forge the previous winter, under-trained the Continental Army still was—in the open field. At Sandy Hook, Clinton found Admiral Howe, who had brought the fleet up from Philadelphia, and it sufficed to transport his men back to the safety of New York. Washington, following by land, arrived at White Plains on 30 July. Nearly two years of campaigning between the mouths of the Hudson and the Delaware had restored the armies to the positions they had held in the Independence summer of 1776.

The War in the South

After Monmouth Courthouse there were to be no more major battles in the North and indeed scarcely any more serious fighting in the Revolutionary War. During 1779 the British mounted a counteroffensive in the lower Hudson, designed to interrupt the flow of supplies from the Revolution's main bases in Massachusetts and Connecticut to Washington's army at White Plains. They took Stony Point, just short of West Point, which Kosciusko had been fortifying with chains and redoubts since April 1778, but it was recaptured by Anthony Wayne, a young Pennsylvanian tanner turned general, in July; an attempt to surrender West Point to the British in September 1780 by Benedict Arnold failed when his papers were found on Major John André. André was hanged as a spy; Arnold, the disgruntled Faust of the Revolution, its most ferocious soldier and most ambitious zealot, escaped to the British, who granted him general rank. He escaped to fight another day against the Americans' French allies in the West Indies.

There was also to be a long passage of arms in the wild Old Northwest, south of Lakes Michigan, Erie, and Ontario, which had been so fought over by the French, British, and Americans in King George's and the French and Indian Wars. The American loyalist Sir John Johnson, son of the Sir William who had terrorised the borders of French Canada in the 1750s, took up the terrorisation of the Mohawk River region, with his Indian ally, Joseph Brant, during 1778–81, causing Washington to detach a force under John Sullivan to pacify the region by counterterror in an expedition up the Susquehanna River in

1779. A little earlier the remarkable American patriot George Roger Clark had embarked almost single-handed on an effort to wrest the Ohio country from the British and their Indian allies. Starting from the Forks of the Ohio (Pittsburgh) in May 1778, he was to carry war against the British and their Indian allies as far away as St. Louis, at the junction of the Missouri and Mississippi rivers, seven hundred miles from Philadelphia, where independence had been declared, and Vincennes on the Wabash, one of the Ohio's great tributaries that rises south of Lake Erie. Vincennes had been taken by a British party under Henry Hamilton, who led it down from Detroit on a winter march of seventy-one days—worthy of the French and the Americans at their toughest—in October–December 1778. Clark, who was acting on the authority of the state of Virginia, which regarded the Ohio as part of its dominion, had already been in Vincennes, after boating the length of the Ohio from Fort Henry (Wheeling, West Virginia), and had gone on to take the former French forts of Chartres, Kakaskia, and Cahokia, the latter now a suburb of St. Louis, Missouri. Hearing of Hamilton's arrival, Clark, believing the British "could not support . . . we should be so mad as to attempt to mark 80 Leagues through a Drowned Country in the Debth of Winter," led his party back for seventeen days, at one stage wading a twenty-mile flood in the Wabash Valley, to surprise Hamilton and force his surrender. The number present at the Vincennes encounter was tiny—two hundred Americans, seventy-nine British—but Clark's triumph was to be confirmed at the peace which ended the war, thus planting the frontier of the United States on the banks of the Mississippi.

These distant campaigns, crucial though Clark's role was in determining the future political geography of his country, contributed nothing to settling the outcome of the war. That was being decided far away in territory as yet—the abortive 1776 descent on Charleston excepted—uncontested: the rich coastal cities of the South and their cotton and tobacco backlands. Britain had long contemplated carrying the war into the Carolinas and Georgia—Virginia, with its high concentration of rivers and vast hinterland, was a tougher nut—because they were, in Piers Mackesy's phrase, "in many ways the soft underbelly of the rebellion." The population of 750,000 whites lived in fear of a slave population of 300,000, which was suspected of sympathising with the British; many of the whites were themselves loyalists none the less. Geography, too, seemed to favour the sort of amphibious force which the Crown controlled. Because the South lived by the export trade, possession of the ports could throttle its livelihood, while the interior offered few of those natural obstacles—wide rivers and mountain ranges running parallel to the coast—which the Americans had proved so adept at using to their advantage in New England and the Middle Atlantic. The "Low Country," as Southerners call the region today, is a continuous belt of almost unobstructed plain, a hundred miles deep and five hundred long, running from Chesapeake Bay to the swamps of northern Florida. Though heavily wooded and, in the eighteenth century, poorly provided with roads, the terrain is not difficult to traverse at any season of the year, while there is no severe winter to confine armies to quarters in the colder months.

The lowland South, indeed, remains to Europeans one of the least alien of North America's regions. Its landscape has a Mediterranean quality—the soft, friable soil, the hot and tangy pinewoods, the relentless insect noise put the European visitor in mind of the southern reaches of the Rhône Valley—while its social character is less unEuropean than that of any other part of the United States. The strong division between classes, the dominant rurality, the intense regionalism within the region itself, are familiar; so, too, are the femininity of its womanhood, the alignment towards the sea, the sense of disassociation from the rest of the continent, the weight of history. History cannot have weighed so heavily in the eighteenth century—the South's obsession with its past is a legacy of the Civil War—for it was then a young country, but most of the other likenesses with Europe were already present. It is easy to believe that the British considered the South a far more promising theatre of operations in which to bridle the Revolution than the hard, cold, high, narrow, and fanatical Northeast.

The keys to the South were two: the extravagantly beautiful coastal cities of Charleston and Savannah, the first commanding the magnificent natural harbour at the mouths of the Ashley and the Cooper rivers, the other the estuary of Georgia's only significant river, also the Savannah, which furnishes an axis of movement into the foothills of the Appalachians that define the lowland South's western boundary. British strategy for 1779 was directed to the capture of these two places, in the belief that they could be used as bases around which loyalists in Georgia and South Carolina would rally and from which offensives could be launched to extirpate revolution in North Carolina and then Virginia, its ideological heart, which had produced the Stamp

Act and Independence resolutions and the Declaration of Rights, which had supplied more troops to the Continental Army than any state except Massachusetts, and which had borne George Washington, its military leader. Britain certainly had no thought that an expedition into the South would draw it into a war in the backland, that that war would be lost, and that the defeat would lead to the loss of its American empire. So, however, would the pieces fall.

The campaign into the South began in December 1778. When Clinton was ordered to evacuate Philadelphia and fall back on New York he was also ordered to send a force to Savannah under Archibald Campbell, which arrived off the city on 29 December. The strong French fleet, commanded by Admiral Jean Comte d'Estaing, which had been in American waters since July, had departed to engage in the alternative campaign in the West Indies, so that Campbell's voyage passed unobstructed. The Savannah garrison had thrown up the usual American timber obstacles, between the swamps then surrounding the city, but it lacked both skill and heart and was easily overwhelmed by Campbell's rough Highlanders. They were soon joined by a force under Augustine Prevost from East Florida. The British, unlike the Americans, succeeded in turning Savannah into a true stronghold, and from it they waged a wide and largely profitable war through South Carolina in 1779. In January, Campbell marched up the Savannah to Augusta, on the approaches to the Appalachian hill country, and raised a large force of loyalists; the Americans had successes against it but failed to recapture Augusta; Prevost failed to take Charleston, against which he marched via Beaufort in May, but when d'Estaing and his fleet arrived off Savannah, to which Prevost had by then returned from Charleston, the French admiral, a sizeable French army, and several hundred Americans not only failed to penetrate the city's defences but suffered a humiliating defeat.

D'Estaing now departed for Boston, leaving the way clear for Clinton to add his strength to the Southern operation. In November 1779 he brought down the garrison from Providence, Rhode Island, the last British enclave in New England, to New York, left a rearguard to hold the city, and took his main force of 8,500 men south to besiege Charleston. Calling first at Savannah to put his expedition in order, Clinton sailed for Charleston on 1 February 1780. It had recently been fortified by a group of French engineers, including Pierre-Charles L'Enfant, the future architect of Washington, D.C. Clinton took his time about investing the place, so that large groups of North Carolinans and Virginians, sent by George Washington at the urgent appeal of Charleston's defenders, were able to make their way into the city while the British waited offshore. Seven hundred and fifty Virginians, who had marched five hundred miles from New Jersey in twenty-eight days—a feat of endurance akin to that of General John Nicholson's force in the march from Mardan to Delhi in 1857 during the Indian Mutiny—arrived within the Charleston lines on 6 April.

By then, however, Clinton was ready to pounce. The strength of the American defences lay in a line of entrenchments dug between the Ashley and Cooper rivers which enclose the peninsula on which Charleston stands. Charleston is a small city, which is one of its charms, and thus wholly indefensible against an enemy which commands the surrounding waters and the isthmus to its rear. Clinton already commanded the waters, got easily on to the isthmus, and, soon after opening a bombardment with his vastly superior artillery, convinced the defenders that they could not sustain the defence. It was a mercy that the British did not, as they had at Quebec in 1759, make the interior of the city their target, for its enchanting Barbadian double-verandaed wooden houses would have burned in a trice. The surrender of 12 May 1780 spared one of the glories of Atlantic civilisation; chance spared it again in the years 1861–65. The tender attention of its citizens, and the encompassing waters which protect its edges from the attack of suburbanisation, combine today to present a vision of how perfect a thing the English-speaking rich of the eighteenth century could make a city.

With the two strongholds of Charleston and Savannah now in his hands, Clinton returned to New York, leaving General Cornwallis and the hard-riding cavalry colonel, Banastre Tarleton, to pacify the Carolinas and carry war into Virginia. Cornwallis very quickly fixed upon a strategy. It was to raise a force from the large number of loyalists believed to be willing to serve in the back country and meanwhile to set up a cordon of posts 150–200 miles inland on which the campaign of pacification could hinge. These, at Camden, Rocky Mount, Cheraw, Hanging Rock, and Ninety Six, were all located on the headwaters of the two rivers which reach the Atlantic north of Charleston near Georgetown: the Santee and the Great Pee Dee. Their secondary function was to force an American army attempting the recapture of Charleston to concentrate against any one of them in order to open its line of advance. The strategy was both orthodox and, in the circumstances, correct. Congress had appointed Horatio Gates, with Baron de Kalb one of the Revolution's emigré supporters, to command in the South. He was not Washington's choice and he mishandled the campaign. Catching up with de Kalb from North Carolina, Gates decided to march on Camden, the most important of Cornwallis's posts, through Cross Creek, into the Cape Fear River, rather than by the easier and more northerly route by Charlotte. The Cross Creek country was swampy, barren, and infested with British sympathisers. It was a hungry and tired American army, therefore, that reached Camden on 15 August, after a march of nineteen days, and it was in no state to fight the British regulars which Gates attempted to surprise next morning. Though outnumbered, the British easily panicked Gates's militiamen into flight; harried by Tarleton's cavalry, Gates's army disintegrated. All that was left of the Revolution's presence in South Carolina after the Camden defeat were the partisan bands led by Francis Marion, Thomas Sumter, and Andrew Pickens, whose raids against the British and their sympathisers caused bloodshed and misery but could not of themselves alter the balance of power in the theatre.

The initiative, indeed, now passed to the British and might have remained with them, had Washington not got his way with Congress and appointed to succeed Gates a general who had served him well in the northern campaigns and in whom he had confidence, Nathanael Greene. Greene's year in the South, from his appointment in October 1780 until the British collapse at Yorktown in September 1781, was a mixed passage. He was defeated as often as he was successful; but he was relentless, he made the best of the resources he had, including the assistance of the American irregulars, and in the end he wore the British down, as good a way of achieving victory as by decisive battle in the open field. The essence of his success lay in using the enormous distances over which the campaigning was conducted—Cornwallis was forced to march over five hundred miles in four months of the beginning of 1781—to exhaust the small force deployed against him—the opposed armies each numbered below five thousand men—and then to move sharply to the counteroffensive when the opportunity offered. Once Cornwallis's field army had been put out of action, the British posts could be picked off at leisure, thus bringing the Carolinas under American control without the cost of bloody engagements on the battlefield.

Greene had, nevertheless, to fight at the outset, and made a poor fist of it. His subordinate, Daniel Morgan, dealt a shrewd blow against Tarleton on 17 January 1781 at the Battle of Cowpens in the distant upcountry of South Carolina, Cornwallis having foolishly divided his force, but, when Cornwallis turned on him, he had to beat a hasty retreat as far away as the unfordable Dan River, a tributary of the Roanoke in southern Virginia. Trying his luck again, Greene sailed out in February 1781 as far as Guilford Court House, on the headwaters of the Cape Fear River, near Greensboro, North Carolina. There on 15 March he met Cornwallis in pitched battle, one of the fiercest of the war, and was defeated. He had chosen his ground well, however, placing his first line on open farmland, his third in the woods behind. When the British, excited by their success in dispersing the militiamen in front, reached Greene's seasoned Maryland and Virginian Continentals in rear, the redcoats were drenched with steady musketry. Cornwallis saved the day only by firing his artillery on foe and friend alike. When the smoke cleared, Greene began to withdraw but Cornwallis was in no state to follow. His force had lost a quarter of its strength and he was short of supplies. He fell back to the Cape Fear River, hoping supplies might be brought up it, but the enemy commanded the steep banks and none came. So he marched downriver to Wilmington, North Carolina, which he reached on 7 April, after another 150 miles on the road, and there decided that the Carolinas had overcome him. Greene was now in his rear and he feared defeat at the river crossings if he turned back, precisely what he had hoped to inflict on the Americans when he had pegged out his line of posts north and east of Charleston the previous autumn. The commandant at Charleston was willing to send boats to bring him down, but that would have meant delay and the abandonment of his horses, so precious in the South's wide spaces. On 25 April, therefore, Cornwallis set off by land for Virginia's Chesapeake Bay country, having written a scheme for future operations. It was eerily prophetic: "I am quite tired of marching about the country. . . . If we mean an offensive war in America, we must abandon New York and bring our whole force into Virginia."

Behind him Greene embarked on a systematic campaign against the British posts on the rivers, fighting actions near Camden (Hobkirk's Hill) on 25 April 1781 and at Eutaw Springs on the Santee in September. Both of these he lost, but the effect was to drive the British in on Charleston, drawing the detached garrisons behind them; Ninety Six, which sustained a month's siege in May and June, had then to be abandoned, and Augusta also. By the autumn of 1781 Charleston and Savannah alone remained as British Southern strongholds. In the Floridas, which Britain had acquired from Spain in 1763, the Spanish, who had entered the war in 1779, profited by the over-extension of her enemy's armed forces—now committed in India, Africa, the Mediterranean, where the Great Siege of Gibraltar was raging, the West Indies, the Atlantic, and home waters, in which the infant American navy was raising havoc—to claw back the coastal towns and river forts then lost. Baton Rouge, the modern capital of the state of Louisiana, held by a scratch garrison of five hundred, fell in August 1779 to an expedition led by Bernardo de Galvez, Governor of Spanish Louisiana, and Natchez, on its high bluff above the Mississippi, shortly after; he then turned to the Gulf towns of Mobile and Pensacola. He took Mobile from the rear, having ascended the river on which it stands from Mobile Bay, in March 1780. After returning to Havana to gather reinforcements, he moved against Pensacola in March 1781, besieged Fort George, and forced its surrender on 8 May. The whole of West Florida—the seaward sections of the modern states of Louisiana, Mississippi, and Alabama—were thereby returned to Spain, which retained them until the sale of all the Floridas to the United States in 1819. These were not Britain's only setbacks in the South.

Lord Camden's pre-war forecast of the difficulties of carrying war into a region of "1,800 miles" had thus been far exceeded by 1781. If the fronts in Canada and the Ohio country, in the Gulf, and along the lower Mississippi are counted in with the Atlantic coast of the thirteen colonies, Britain had in fact been campaigning around a strategic perimeter of over 3,000 miles in length, and often over exterior rather than interior lines, which greatly increase distance. If the distances over which the French had attempted to exert power in the wars of King William, Queen Anne, and King George and in the Seven Years War seem great, those over which Britain was operating between 1775 and 1781 were greater still, so much so, indeed, that comparisons with other extended strategies are hard to find. From Portsmouth, Britain's main home naval base, to New York is 3,000 miles; from New York to Charleston another 650; from Charleston to Augusta a further 150— 3,800 in all. The United States, campaigning against Germany in 1945, was operating at an extreme outreach of 3,500 miles from New York, against Japan in the Solomon Islands in 1942 again at 3,500 miles from Honolulu. Alexander the Great in the Punjab was 2,500 miles from Macedonia, the German army at Stalingrad only 1,500 miles from Berlin. Britain's achievement in sustaining a war at such long range deserves recognition, all the more because she was simultaneously conducting other campaigns as far away as West Africa and southern India.

The scale of the American war, measured in number of men on the ground, might be judged minor also, for the total of British and mercenary troops sent to America between 1776 and 1781 did not much exceed sixty thousand. Proportionately the naval effort made was far greater, for the mobilisation of transport to ship and supply the army, and of men o' war to protect the convoys, was the largest yet seen in any campaign; but it was men on the ground who counted, and by 1781 there were no more forthcoming. By contrast, American militiamen, even regulars, continued to come forward in numbers, and since July 1780 there had been a French army under Rochambeau at Newport, Rhode Island. Clinton retained seventeen thousand soldiers in and around New York but was effectively marooned there because British naval strength had now fallen to a level which could not guarantee safe protection to a troop convoy in the face of the French fleet in American waters. In any case, he lacked the will to move, instead asking Cornwallis to send troops to reinforce him.

Cornwallis in Virginia had troubles of his own, troubles which were to attract into the state most disposable troops remaining in the war and so determine that it should become its culminating and decisive theatre. His troubles had begun, paradoxically, with the arrival in Virginia of the renegade Benedict Arnold on 3 January 1781. Arnold had sailed from New York on 20 December and, after delays at sea, had landed at Hoods Point on the James River on 3 January. His orders were to cause destruction, raise loyalist recruits, and prevent the Virginians from taking measures to defend themselves, all of which he did to such effect that in February, Washington, still at White Plains, felt alarmed enough to send the Marquis de Lafayette overland to oppose him. Lafayette marched down the traditional route through New Jersey and Pennsylvania to Head of Elk at the top of Chesapeake Bay, found enough small ships to carry him to Annapolis, the capital of Maryland, and then resumed his overland march to arrive in Richmond (not then the capital of Virginia) at the end of April. Anthony Wayne followed him from Pennsylvania, arriving on 10 June, and a force of Virginian riflemen under William Campbell three days later.

This was not to Cornwallis's liking. He had left the Carolinas because he despaired of restoring order in those states. Now he faced a growing concentration of American forces in tidewater Virginia, geographically a far more difficult region over which to establish control. Unlike the open and poorly watered Carolinas, Virginia is broken up by rivers and estuaries into a complex of estuaries, inlets, and intermediate peninsulas, any one of which is a potential refuge for an enemy or a trap for a pursuer deprived of waterborne means of escape. The Chesapeake, from Elton at its head to the Atlantic exit at Norfolk, is some 175 miles long on the north to south axis. Into its western shore drain four rivers that flow off the Appalachian chain, the Susquehanna, the Potomac, the York, and the James; the headwaters of the James are known as the North and South Anna rivers, while into the James flows the Appomattox, on which Petersburg stands. Several of these rivers are navigable for seventy-five or a hundred miles above their estuaries: the Rappahannock as far as Fredericksburg, the Potomac to above Alexandria, near modern Washington, D.C. In the political and economic geography of eighteenth-century Virginia, the peninsula between the York and the James rivers—the "Peninsula" of the Civil War—was the key area. On it stood Williamsburg, then the state capital, as well as the vanished remains of Jamestown, the first place of permanent English settlement in North America. At its head was Richmond, already an important commercial centre for the agriculture and industry of the state. The shores of the peninsula were lined with the oldest plantations of the colony, while across the York and the James stood the most important of the tidewater harbours at Gloucester, Norfolk, Portsmouth, and Suffolk. It was a region made by nature for the strategy of march, countermarch, and amphibious advance and withdrawal, rich in water communications, protected from the ocean by the great arm of Maryland's Eastern Shore, well provided even in the eighteenth century with passable roads, and offering a friendly army copious supplies of food and riding and draught animals.

Cornwallis might have played a strategy of march and countermarch to advantage during 1781, for the main American force was still immobilised far away at White Plains outside New York, where Washington's primary concern was to persuade Rochambeau at Newport, Rhode Island, to join him in an offensive against Clinton on the lower Hudson. For much of the summer, indeed, Cornwallis did succeed in moving about Virginia at will; he arrived at Petersburg from Wilmington, North Carolina, by an overland move on 20 May and spent much of June and July chasing Lafayette from place to place, subjecting Anthony Wayne to a sharp defeat at Jamestown Ford on 6 July, while his freebooting subordinate, Banastre Tarleton, raided as far as Charlottesville, Thomas Jefferson's seat and the meeting place of the Virginian legislature underneath the Blue Ridge Mountains, in early June. There were now five thousand American troops in Virginia but seven thousand British, and Cornwallis retained the initiative.

It was taken from him not by the enemy but by his own superior. Clinton, a less able and more timorous general, had rightly failed to comprehend any rational strategic purpose in Cornwallis's abandonment of the Carolinas for the much more difficult and less profitable campaigning ground of Virginia; he now wrongly decided that he was at greater risk than Cornwallis, to whom he sent a series of orders during June and July, all confusing and often contradictory. He demanded that Cornwallis weaken his force to strengthen his own position by fortifying a harbour in which he could be supported by the British fleet. This despite the fact that Clinton's situation in New York was unassailable, that a large French fleet under Admiral de Grasse had sailed from France for the Caribbean, that the British fleet in the western hemisphere was weakened by commitments in the West Indies and the need to send ships for repair in British ports, that Clinton had conceded freedom of strategic manoeuvre to Washington by his unwillingness to venture outside his New York base, and that the immobilisation of Cornwallis in the Yorktown peninsula might, could a British fleet not reach him, lead to his destruction.

So it was all to turn out. Clinton's series of letters effectively put Cornwallis on the defensive, while he might have been acting offensively; worse, they tied his force to a fixed point. On 6 July, while marching from Williamsburg to Portsmouth, from where he was to ship troops to New York, he inflicted a final defeat on his opponents when he caught Wayne's pursuing vanguard at the Jamestown Ford (now Green Spring Battlefield) and beat him back with loss. Then more letters arrived cancelling the order to reinforce New York but ordering him to fortify Old Point Comfort at the top of the Yorktown peninsula opposite Hampton Roads, the great anchorage off Norfolk where a British fleet was expected to rendezvous later in the year. Cornwallis found Old Point Comfort indefensible, and, as Clinton also required other fortifications to be built at Yorktown itself and at Gloucester opposite, commanding the narrow entrance to the York River, he set off thither, arriving by water on 4 August. Lafayette, following cautiously at a distance, took up a position at West Point, where the Pamunkey and Mattaponi rivers combine to form the York. Cornwallis's engineers meanwhile began to throw up lines of earthworks around the little riverside settlement of Yorktown to protect it from the landward side.

With the initiative in his hands, Washington now moved to profit by it. His eyes were still on New York, but an armed reconnaissance against its defences on 21 July convinced him that they were too strong to be carried. That was Rochambeau's view also; he and Washington had agreed at a meeting at Wethersfield, Connecticut, on 21 May to concentrate their forces and the French had arrived at White Plains, after a march of 220 miles in eleven days from Providence, on 18 June. What to do next? The American forces were divided and, in the view of both Rochambeau and Washington, "at the end of their resources." The British retained three seaboard strongholds: at New York, Yorktown, and Charleston. The only light on the strategic horizon was the temporary naval weakness of the British and the equally temporary naval superiority of the French in American waters. If Admiral de Grasse's fleet could sail from the West Indies to support the American armies before Britain found the ships to re-establish her control of the American coast, great things might be achieved. Time was short, however, and the choice of the point of concentration crucial. As late as August, Washington still hoped that de Grasse would help him crack New York's defences. Then the French admiral sent word on 14 August that he had a different objective. He was sailing for the Chesapeake with twenty-nine warships and three thousand troops and would remain there until 14 October, when he would have to return to the Caribbean. This made up Washington's mind. "Matters now having come to a crisis," he wrote in his journal, "and a decisive plan to be determined on, I was obliged, for the shortness of Count de Grasse's promised stay on this Coast, the apparent disinclination in their Naval Officers to force the harbour of New York and the feeble compliance of the States to my requisitions for Men . . . to give up all idea of attacking New York; and instead to remove the French Troops and a detachment of the American Army . . . to Virginia."

The removal was a formidable logistic exercise. In two months at most, Washington would have to displace from a distance of 450 miles, make a junction with de Grasse, and carry a strong defensive position at Yorktown in the teeth of a resolute enemy's resistance. Washington set off at once, the French following, down the familiar route through New Jersey to concentrate at Princeton. They were at Trenton on 30 August, whence, failing to find sufficient boats to use the Delaware for onward movement, they marched to Philadelphia, which they passed through on 2 September, to reach the top of Chesapeake Bay at Head of Elk on 6 September. By then they had heard the heartening news that de Grasse had arrived in Chesapeake Bay; the timetable, however, was still at risk, for insufficient boats were found to ship the whole force onward. While siege stores were sent forward by water, some troops had to be marched to Annapolis and Baltimore, and Washington himself proceeded overland to Williamsburg. Not until 26 September was the whole force—Washington's New York contingent, Rochambeau's French army, Lafayette's and Wayne's Virginian contingents, and de Grasse's reinforcement—assembled on the peninsula, the waterborne elements having come down Chesapeake Bay to land at Jamestown, Burwull's Ferry, and College Landing near Williamsburg. The contestants in what was to prove the decisive confrontation of the war were now all grouped in an area about twelve miles square; American and French numbers were about seventeen thousand, British about seven thousand, and the need to resupply alone would determine that an outcome could not be long delayed.

The thumbscrew of time had been tightened for the British by the failure of their fleet, under Admirals Graves and Hood, to break through the French cordon at the mouth of the Chesapeake between 5 and 9 September. Outmanoeuvred and outnumbered, by twenty-eight to nineteen, Graves and Hood retired to New York, leaving de Grasse, now joined by the Newport squadron under Commodore de Barras, in control of Virginian waters. Since the only other naval force remaining to the British on the American side of the Atlantic lay in the West Indies and numbered ten ships, Britain had conceded command of the sea at the decisive point to the enemy, an almost unprecedented and rarely to be repeated lapse of strategic grip by the Royal Navy. The concession was to spell the end of the six-year-long effort to reimpose royal rule over the American colonies.

At Yorktown, Cornwallis had enclosed the few streets of the little town with a double line of entrenchments, redoubts, and batteries in a circuit some two miles round, the ends resting on the York River; the outer line was formed of individual strong places, the inner of continuous trenches. It was an orthodox eighteenth-century field system, of the sort that had served men in America before: at West Point, which had deterred attack, and even at Bunker Hill, overrun though the earthworks had been. At Yorktown, however, Cornwallis's system was to be subjected to attack by professional siege engineers, who included Louis Duportail and Jean-Baptiste Gouvion, both graduates of the French military engineering school at Mézières. They swiftly threw up a chain of exterior earthwork "parallels," from which the preparatory bombardment could begin; from them forty heavy guns and sixteen mortars, enough to overwhelm Clinton's puny artillery, opened fire on the evening of 9 October. In the first day some 3,600 solid shot and shells fell on the British positions; Cornwallis immediately concluded that "against so powerful an attack [he could] not hope to make a very long resistance." He had already abandoned all his outworks, except those known as Redoubts 9 and 10 and Fusiliers' Redoubt, which stood on the water and guarded his weakest spots, but by 14 October the enemy siege engineers had pushed forward a second parallel which brought these under direct bombardment; that night they were taken by storm in a bloody assault. Cornwallis's soldiers could still show fighting spirit, for on 16 October they sallied out and spiked eleven enemy guns; but he himself was so dispirited that he tried that night to evacuate the garrison into the subsidiary entrenchment at Gloucester across the York River. When a sudden storm scattered the boats, he accepted that he was beaten and made preparations to offer his surrender. Next morning, 17 October, the request for parlay was beaten on a drum, a blindfolded officer was taken into American lines, and terms discussed. They were written next day in a building called the Moore House on the waterside and at two o'clock in the afternoon of 19 October 1781 the British marched out to lay down their arms, surrender their colours, and pass into captivity. This was not to be a Saratoga; Cornwallis's army was not permitted to take ship for home. Yorktown, the unexpected and unavoidable battle, was to be ended as a complete American victory and an ignominious British defeat.

It was not the end of the war in the "great continent of 1,800 miles." Clinton, arriving from New York off Yorktown five days too late, returned to that base, where the British would stay until 25 November 1783. Savannah would remain in British hands until 11 July 1782 and Charleston until 14 December; indeed, many of the forts in the west, including Detroit, would remain in British hands until 1797. Nathanael Greene meanwhile extinguished the last pockets of resistance in the South, though as late as August 1782 the Americans of Kentucky suffered a Canadian and Indian raid, which Daniel Boone helped to repulse. Nor was it the end of the larger war. Britain remained at war with France and Spain and at the Battle of the Saints, between the West Indian islands of Dominica and Guadeloupe, inflicted a shattering defeat on de Grasse's fleet on 12 April 1782; the victory was reinforced later in the year when the siege of Gibraltar was lifted and the Royal Navy's control of the western Mediterranean was decisively restored. Despite these strategic alleviations, the significance of the surrender at Yorktown could not be denied. Britain had lost an empire and a new nation had been created, which would shortly embrace a policy of high-minded detachment from the strategic and military entanglements of the old world across the Atlantic. The United States had fought a war to win its liberty, but its Founding Fathers sought no wars in America's future. Washington's independent United States would be left with scarcely an army or navy at all and its people to depend on the remoteness and expanse of their enormous national territory as its defence. The notion that a war might arise between the states themselves was unimaginable. The thought that the upturned earth of the trenches and redoubts at Yorktown, already returning to nature in the spring of 1782, might be fought over again by soldiers who all called themselves American defied imagination itself.

FOUR

....

Fortifying
the Confederacy

YET, when war did arise between the states in 1861, it was not
many months before it found its focus at Yorktown, exactly at
the spot surrendered by the British to Washington eighty years
earlier. It is an odd sensation to scramble over Redoubts 9 and 10, now
so carefully conserved by the National Park Service and labelled to
commemorate the desperate hand-to-hand struggles of the night of 14
October 1781, in the knowledge that the humps and declivities felt under one's feet may not have been delved by redcoats at all but record
the reworking of the British defences by Magruder's grey-coated soldiers in the spring of 1862. This is bloodied ground, of that there is no
doubt; but it is ground twice bloodied, first in the struggle for America's independence, then in the war to found a more perfect Union; of
exactly who did what and when on the double battlefield of Yorktown,
the upturned soil gives the visitor no clue at all.

I came to Yorktown in 1992 by a circuitous route, deliberately chosen because I wished to impose discovery of new territory upon old familiarity with places already visited and routes travelled before. I began
in Richmond. It was that city which General John Magruder was seeking to defend in the spring of 1862. It had also been my entry point to
the South when I started on my great American journey in the summer
of 1957. Then it had been Richmond's *Gone with the Wind* charm
which had left the impression, the pillared severity of the state capitol
in its formal gardens, the traces of Federal elegance in the terraces
across the square; but I had been in a hurry, hastening on to see the
battlefield of Petersburg and to reach the Carolinas, and I saw scarcely

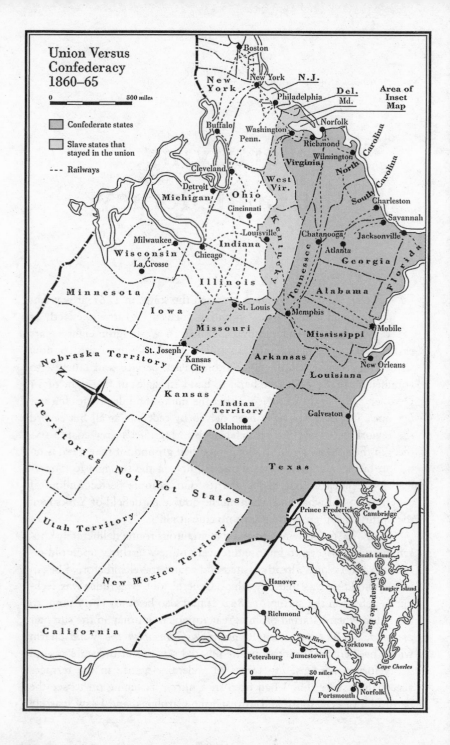

Union Versus
Confederacy
1860–65

0   500 miles

■ Confederate states

□ Slave states that
stayed in the union

--- Railways

Area of
Inset
Map

Boston
New York
New York
N.J.
Philadelphia
Del.
Md.
Buffalo
Washington
Penn.
Norfolk
Richmond
Wilmington
Virginia
North
Carolina
West
Vir.
Cleveland
Detroit
Michigan
Ohio
Cincinnati
Kentucky
South
Carolina
Charleston
Savannah
Louisville
Chatanooga
Jacksonville
Milwaukee
Indiana
Chicago
Atlanta
Georgia
Florida
Wisconsin
La Crosse
Tennessee
Alabama
Illinois
Minnesota
Iowa
St. Louis
Memphis
Mobile
Missouri
Mississippi
Nebraska Territory
St. Joseph
Arkansas
New Orleans
Kansas
City
Louisiana
Kansas
Indian
Territory
Galveston
Oklahoma
Territories
Not Yet States
Texas
Utah Territory
New Mexico Territory
California

Prince Frederick
Cambridge
Smith Island
Hanover
Tangier Island
Richmond
Chesapeake Bay
James River
Yorktown
Petersburg
Jamestown
Cape Charles
Portsmouth
Norfolk
0   50 miles

more of Richmond than its ceremonial centre. On another, unintended visit, a freak January storm which had closed the airports from Washington southward had driven me on to Trailways and at Richmond snowed me to a dead stop. A midnight trudge through the snow in search of lodging had shown me nothing at all of the city but left the reminder that even in the South a winter campaign could be as harsh as in Pennsylvania.

In 1992 I had leisure to explore. I took my time. It was worth the delay. At St. John's Church, where in 1775 the firebrand Patrick Henry had made his inflammatory "Give me liberty or give me death" speech, I attended Episcopalian Sunday eucharist. Roman Catholic though I am, I always find myself drawn when abroad to the places of worship and the services of the Anglican Communion. It is the claim, almost part of the creed of the Church of England, that it is the "Church of the English," and the claim has powerful cultural force. I feel it strongly. I have felt it in the stark and now often desolate Gothic boxes left by the British in their Indian cantonments where stucco peels from the façade and headstones lean at crazy angles in the untended dust of the graveyard. I have felt it in the neat, discreet Victorian All Saints' and Christ Churches, built for rich summer congregations, to be found in the shadow of the better hotels on the French and Italian rivieras. I have felt it strongly, of all places, in Jerusalem, where the pitch-pine pews, over-coloured stained glass, and lists of former incumbents in St. George's cause a pang of homesickness I cannot distingush from religious emotion. English Catholicism is deeply English; the echo I catch there of Hymns Ancient and Modern, of the Book of Common Prayer, and of metrical psalms, which all the English of whatever Christian denomination carry in their inner ear, arouses in me a rush of piety that does not come even in Christianity's most sacred place at the Holy Sepulchre.

At St. John's the predictable sensations returned. This was almost England. Steep, cobbled, tree-shaded streets of Georgian or Regency houses—Colonial or Federal though Americans might call them—surround a graveyard of old brick, mown grass, and elaborate tombstone inscriptions, and a decent, steepled eighteenth-century church which might stand in any prosperous London suburb, Hampstead or Highgate or Clapham, of equal date. Only the murmur of pigeons and the faint chill cast by shadow on the hottest English day lacked to complete the illusion. Inside the similarities were even more exact: box pews, a three-decker pulpit, and, beside the flags of the United States and the state of Virginia hanging in the apse, those of the colony of Virginia, George III's United Kingdom, and the Episcopal Church. The liturgy of the Book of Common Prayer was recited with dignity, a devout congregation took communion at the altar rails, deeply familiar Anglican hymns were sung at the entry and the recessional. I repeated the words of the Creed and the Lord's Prayer in a spirit of heartfelt fellowship with the American Anglicans in the pews beside me.

There was much else that was English about Richmond's eastern district: terraced housefronts, neat front gardens behind cast-iron railings, high brick walls hiding the sanctuaries of grandees long dead. The atmosphere, if anything, was of the moneyed urban England of my childhood, where families had occupied the same address for generations, neighbours called only with warning and then with ceremony, and the lower social orders intruded but as tradesmen or servants. The atmosphere carried me back in time, but to places I knew very well. When I left East for South Richmond, as I did after Sunday service to head for the Yorktown peninsula, the transition was not from one period of my life to another but between continents. In the streets around St. John's Church I might have been in some genteel part of my home country; in the wasteland below the James River, I was in Africa. This was not because South Richmond is black, though black it is and poor as well; there are great tracts of poor, black America in the Northern cities which are not African at all but have their highrise, concrete counterparts now, alas, in Europe also. South Richmond, by contrast, instantly recalled to me those endless, shapeless, gap-toothed, one-storey, cinderblock, corrugated, clapboard sprawls which Africans attach as if by cellular redivision to the city centres which the Europeans have planted wherever wealth is to be found in the continent. I have traversed their interminable highways—in South Richmond it is the venerable U.S. 1—in Banjul (formerly Bathhurst) in the Gambia, in Harare (formerly Salisbury) in Zimbabwe, in Nairobi, in Pretoria, and in Johannesburg. It is an unvarying townscape, part *bidonville*, part open-air market, part salvage dump, part car repair shop, part wayside eating place, part improvised sports field, part *terrain vague*. It has characteristic features, among which are wide dusty roadside verges, tumbledown fencing between plots, regular succession of half-completed permanent buildings, abandoned in mid-construction for want of money, materials, or municipal permission, an extraordinary variety of eccentrically hand-lettered signs advertising food, entertainment, professional and commercial services, second-hand goods for sale, spare parts, insurance, undertaking, necromancy, beer, lodging, or merely the stray thoughts or observations upon life of residents and bystanders.

A uniform ingredient of the scene both in Africa and in the Southern states is the sectarian, go-it-alone churches—of Antioch, Judah, Jerusalem, God's Disciples, Bible Christians, True Gospel, Whole Baptism, Testament, Pentecost, Holiness, God in Christ—which promise, within their shanty walls, every variety of religious experience from Coptic episcopacy to the priesthood of all through the gift of tongues. Here is an extraordinary and inexplicable domestic *koine*, for the ancestors of the black Americans who live in places like South Richmond were kidnapped from Africa long before its modern, suburban sprawls sprang up, while few in modern times have made and returned from a transatlantic crossing. What is the determinant? It cannot be cultural, for black Americans are very American indeed. Perhaps it is climatic; perhaps it is the availability of space, of which both Africans and Americans have more than any other inhabitants of the fertile zones; perhaps, incorrect though the thought is, the determinant is ethnic. Who can say that the preference for the temporary and makeshift, a preference akin to that of Central Asians for the mobile or collapsible, was not something which Africans brought with them in their enforced translation to the Americas and which persists? There was so much that was taken from them by their white enslavers and so much which was alien that was imposed. Can it be that their replication of the contemporary African townscape represents an expression of choice, of historical memory, and of that submerged but persistent rebellion against their uprooting which is the abiding legacy of slavery?

The affinities are too obvious to ignore. My route through South Richmond, though my destination was Yorktown, was taking me to the region where slavery in English America began, for in 1619 the first cargo of Africans was imported into the original English foothold on the continent at Jamestown. Jamestown can be reached from Richmond by road. I chose instead to approach it by water, as the English who came to settle had done in 1607, sailing from the Atlantic between Capes Charles and Henry into Chesapeake Bay. I could not retrace that route, but my second-best was still arresting. Leaving Richmond behind—here as almost everywhere in the United States, the abrupt transition from the densely built-up to the deeply rural surprises the European—I drove through farmland and forest along State Route 10 by Burrowville, Spring Grove, and Surry to the ferry at Scotland. A tremendous tropical storm descended as I passed the signposts to tidewater plantations, and the head of the James estuary was still crowned by towering thunderheads as we set off at speed across the channel. I love ferries, take them wherever they can be found, and treasure memories of crossings in the Sea of Marmara from Turkey-in-Europe to Asia, from Gourock across the Clyde to Dunoon, from La Rochelle to the Ile de Ré, from Cyprus to Beirut during the Lebanese civil war, from Canakkale to Gallipoli, from Kyle of Lochalsh over the sea to Skye.

The Scotland–Jamestown crossing is but a spit in the wind in the American scale of things but a dramatic maritime excursion for an Englishman across a waterway wider than any found at home. Surely the waterfront cannot much have changed since the *Susan Constant*, *Discovery*, or *Godspeed* nosed their way in from the ocean nearly four hundred years ago? The outline of some enormous industrial construction—power station or refinery—cleaves the horizon away towards Richmond. Nearer at hand and on every side the forest descends unbroken to the shore, blue-green, lush, silent, and mysterious. The mystery deepens within the remains of Jamestown itself. Travel in America accustoms one to the phenomenon of the abandoned place, the town that once was and is no more, but the eeriness of human relinquishment is heightened here by the oldness of what is left: the tower of a church that might rise over any English village, the windowless brick carapace of a gentleman's mansion, which an inscription records was burnt by Cornwallis's soldiers in 1781, burnt by Union troops in 1862, burnt by accident in 1895. It had made a stronger effort to survive than most habitations in America from which a settled population had departed to try its luck elsewhere. Jamestown, however, had never had luck on its side. Riverside fevers, failure of crops, and Indian raids had harried its inhabitants near to extinction at times; a ponderous graveside sensation weighs on the visitor as he makes his way from the excavated foundations of one seventeenth-century dwelling house to the next in the narrow grass-sown strip between the encompassing forest and the sodden foreshore of the estuary. Jamestown must always have been, as it certainly now is, oppressed by a feeling of being hemmed in, of subsisting as nothing more than a remote toehold at the extremity of seaborne communication with the Old World. This can never have seemed, as Quebec dramatically looks, the gateway to a continent. It remains what it was when the English debarked, a tidewater backwater, offering neither welcome nor escape. It is not surprising that by 1699 it had fallen into decay and that the Governor of Virginia had migrated to the higher, drier, better surroundings of Williamsburg a few miles inland.

Yet Jamestown discloses one relic for the historian, particularly the military historian, guaranteed to fire the imagination, particularly an imagination attuned to the power of geography in this continent to impose and reimpose fortification at the same spot. Jamestown, of course, had been fortified—against Indians, perhaps also against the Spaniards who roved as far north as the Chesapeake in the sixteenth century and founded a short-lived mission, Ajacan, near or at Jamestown itself— but the fortications fell constantly into decay, as visitors complained in 1610 and 1617. Jamestown's real strength was that it was almost an island, its strategic significance that it commanded the first good landing at the point where the James River narrows from the sea; hence the Scotland ferry. It was an obvious and necessary spot for the Confederates to fortify again once war came to the Chesapeake in 1862, and they did so. Adjacent to the tower and forlorn unroofed nave of Jamestown's church stands a typical little Civil War quadrilateral earthwork, much overgrown now, as dank and gloomy as an earthwork of the English Civil War might be if any as well preserved had survived, and testimony both to the topological sense which had caused John Smith and his companions to choose Jamestown Island as a point of entry to America in 1607 and to the determination of the South to defend its capital and heartland against a Union offensive in the aftermath of the easy victories of 1861.

The little Jamestown earthwork opened my eyes. Again, I had not realised before I came to see for myself how militarised the whole of the Yorktown peninsula was, how much fought over, how bloodily contested. The placenames that commonly occur in the military history of this part of Virginia are few: Yorktown, Richmond, Petersburg. I had never heard—I might be excused—of the Jamestown Fort, but less excusably I had never heard either of the battle of Williamsburg, and I made no connection at all between Fortress Monroe, the base and starting point for the northern offensive against Richmond, and Old Point Comfort, which Cornwallis had declined to occupy as a defended place guarding Hampton Roads in 1781. It was time to explore further.

From the causeway that joins Jamestown island to the peninsula I turned westward towards Richmond to survey the countryside through which redcoats and revolutionaries had manoeuvred against each other in the spring and summer of 1781 and McClellan's men had pushed their way towards the city in May 1862. This road crosses Green Spring Battlefield Park, where Cornwallis turned and savaged Anthony Wayne's men on 6 July 1781, and then runs alongside the line of great plantations, Sherwood Forest, Westover, Berkeley, Shirley, whose properties stretch down to the banks of the James. These are rich men's houses, as grand as the grandest manor houses in England, approached by tree-lined avenues, filled with fine eighteenth-century furniture, and surrounded by the extensive outbuildings that go with a large estate in a productive countryside. Two are the residences of Presidents—Tyler at Sherwood Forest, Harrison at Berkeley, which Virginians also claim was the place of the first celebration of Thanksgiving in 1619; it was one of McClellan's headquarters in 1862, and at it his subordinate, Daniel Butterfield, composed the haunting "Taps," played every evening at American military posts when the flag is lowered. Less visited—there is an irritating tourist industry atmosphere at Berkeley, birthplace of Robert E. Lee's mother, where the guides wear colonial dress and lapse into mechanical guidebook patter at the sight of a visitor—is Westover church, half hidden by forest across the meadows from State Route 5. It satisfies all the criteria of the seeker-out of Anglican atmosphere in the Communion's distant parts: shadowed interior, Georgian gothic round-headed windows, box pews filled with buttoned hassocks, tablets listing the Ten Commandments on each side of the altar, over it the arms of George III of England embroidered on damask under a carved Hanoverian crown. The location is sylvan, secluded, and isolated, yet carefully tended, and the building yields, at the moment of entry, an authentic English village church smell, compounded of mouse droppings, decaying hymnbooks, and sepulchral dust, the universal odour of Anglican sanctity. It was not a surprise to read that it had been vandalised by Union troops in 1862.

The parish was established in 1619, but the church in its present form was brand-new when Cornwallis passed by Westover in 1781 on his way to Point of Fork on the Upper James and then back again to Richmond and Williamsburg. It was thither I turned to follow his route. Williamsburg, rescued from decay and a twentieth-century sort of vandalism by John D. Rockefeller in 1926—a garage in the centre advertised itself by a placard reading TOOT-AN-CUM-IN—is much derided. Purists dismiss it as Disneyland with taste. Certainly there is much that is modern masquerading as old, notably the Governor's Palace, which is new from the ground up. There is plenty of old Williamsburg, none the less, and that has a used and lived-in look which conveys an authentically colonial feel. The College of William and Mary is, after all, the oldest degree-granting institution in North America after Harvard, has been at work since 1693, and its buildings abut quite naturally on to the restored streets. The brick paths that border them have the same higgledly-piggledy look as those in Gilbert White's famous vicarage garden at Selborne, where he was writing his *Natural History* while Williamsburg was a seat of colonial government; the forge, if tidier, is much as I remember blacksmiths' forges in the West Country of my boyhood, where there are old-fashioned shops today even more cluttered with obsolete saleables in illegibly labelled pigeonholes than their reconstructed lookalikes which line Duke of Gloucester Street at Williamsburg. The interior of the parish church, recovered from crass Victorianisation by the Rev. Dr. Goodwin at the beginning of the century, is heavy with the atmosphere of three hundred years of worship, but its most arresting historical association is with the 1862 battle; after it was over the floor was covered with wounded soldiers brought in from the surrounding fields, including many of the four hundred Confederates too badly injured to be evacuated by the retreating army.

The Confederates had by then already retreated ten miles from their original positions at and south of Yorktown, some of them following the line of the Colonial Parkway, built in the 1930s as a New Deal enterprise to alleviate local unemployment, which links the three historic places, Jamestown, Williamsburg, and Yorktown. Uncluttered by building of any sort, it carries the visitor through towering forest swiftly and rather mysteriously to the site of the British surrender of 1781. Little evidence of that survives; by contrast, there is a moving reminder of another foreign presence, that of the French. The United States has been generous in the tribute it pays to those who helped win its victory. Near Fusiliers' Redoubt, at the waterside above the York River, are listed the names of the 320 Frenchmen who died in the siege and of the regiments from which they came, Beaujolais, Bourbonnais, Brie, Foix, Gâtinais, Picardie, all historic provinces of France, the Irish emigré regiment of Dillon, and the Royal-Deux-Ponts, whose soldiers' German names reveal its origins in the border regions won from the Habsburgs in Louis XIV's wars. For anyone who has visited the military sites of New France, there is an odd feeling of *revanche* about this quiet little spot, a counterpoint to the poignancy of the memorials on the Plains of Abraham and in the old city of Quebec. "This monument is dedicated to the sailors and soldiers of the French Expeditionary Corps who died for the independence of the United States during the Campaign of Yorktown." France has, after all, left its military stamp upon the continent, by an act which determined that the British victors of 1763 should not long enjoy their triumph on the St. Lawrence.

The exact site of the French monument is marked by the National Park Service as French Trench, though traces of that earthwork have disappeared. Elsewhere they are meticulously preserved, as is everything in the Service's care. What a magnificent institution it is, unequalled in the world. I have talked to its young officers—those who meet visitors seem always to be young college graduates—at dozens of places across the United States, from the battleship graveyard at Pearl Harbor to restored Fort Sumter, target of the first bombardment of the Civil War, in the harbour at Charleston. I invariably experience the oddest sensation when I do: that here are the representatives of an organisation most closely akin to one of the colonial services of the vanished British or French Empire. That has something to do with their crisp khaki-drill uniforms, the faint snap of military discipline about their manner and movements, but more with the sense conveyed of their membership of a body with a continental mission, dedicated to the conservation of a cultural empire's history, human and natural. They might indeed be seen as the Federal government's district commissioners, for they work often in the country's wildest places, and as ethnographers, forest officers, archaeologists, geologists, cartographers, exactly as colonial servants did in days of empire.

Great though the achievements of the colonial services were in the sphere of field research and conservation, however, those of the Park Service are far greater in scale and quality. Its battlefield parks in particular surpass all others in the care with which the remains are preserved and explained to the visitor, and Yorktown is an excellent example. I have only one quibble. The Park Service treats it as a battlefield of 1781. There are no references on the ground to the operations of 1862, and so no clues as to how the Confederates reused the old earthworks to make their defences against the Union invasion of the tip of the peninsula. Use them they did, none the less; indeed, Magruder also extended his position across the York River into Gloucester on the opposite point a thousand yards away, just as Cornwallis had done, with the same object of denying the enemy the chance to run shipping up the York towards the head of navigation at West Point, in his war. Magruder's defences, however, were much more extensive than Cornwallis's had been. They ran right across the peninsula from Yorktown along the sluggish and swampy Warwick River to reach the James in an area called Mulberry Island. Eight miles in length, they consisted of batteries at each end to command the rivers, rifle pits, and redoubts in between guarding the only two roads that led to Richmond, and a chain of inundations that rendered the valley of the Warwick nearly impassable.

When McClellan saw the obstacle Magruder had constructed, he wrote to his wife for books on the Anglo-French siege of Sebastopol, which had taken place only eight years earlier and at which he had been present as an observer. "I cannot turn Yorktown without a battle," he explained to a brother officer, "in which I must use heavy artillery and go through the preliminary operations of a siege." He was correct in his anticipations, but too casual about the difficulties. His army, which had started to debark at the tip of the peninsula on 22 March, began operations against the Yorktown lines on 4 April but did not pass through them until a month later on 4 May. Why had it taken so long? What, more important, was the plan which had brought McClellan to the site of Cornwallis's surrender in the first place? Why, when North and South confronted each other across hundreds of miles of dry land, from the District of Columbia to the borders of Indiana, had the Union's chief general decided, as the British had done eighty-six years earlier, to set about reducing rebellion by amphibious invasion?

American Geography and the Civil War

McClellan's transhipment of the main Union army from the outskirts of Washington to the shores of Chesapeake Bay a hundred miles southward came about through his desire to strike at "the heart of the enemy's power in the East." That, however, is not an explanation of his strategy. "On to Richmond!" had been the cry in Washington in July 1861 and also in McDowell's army that had marched out of the Union capital towards the Confederacy's—recently transferred from Montgomery, Alabama—to do battle with Beauregard. The battle—at Manassas Junction on Bull Run Creek, a tributary of the Potomac on which Washington stands—had, however, not gone well. It had ended, indeed, in Confederate victory. The North, stronger in every way, in numbers, in industry, in agricultural production, in liquid wealth, in extent of territory, suddenly found itself not on the offensive but the defensive. It was Washington, not Richmond, that was at risk after Bull Run, and the Confederates were to sustain the threat for the next eight months, not only by keeping an army in being within thirty miles of Washington but by cheekily closing the Potomac's outlet to Chesapeake Bay with batteries sited downstream at Occoquan and Aquia creeks; they even interdicted upstream navigation by keeping hold of Leesburg, not only a river town but also the terminus of the railway from Alexandria, Washington's twin city, in the Potomac Valley. At a time when rivers were still as important as the novel railways as means of communication, the two often sharing routes for railway engineering reasons, the South thus blocked the Federal capital's access both to the Chesapeake, its outlet to the Atlantic, and to the head of the Shenandoah Valley, the great strategic corridor which marches parallel to the fertile and settled lowlands of Maryland and northern Virginia, the cockpit of the Civil War.

At the very outset, therefore, the South had disrupted the North's opening, overall, and long-term strategy, which was to gain control of the Confederacy's seaward and internal borders—roughly the Atlantic and Gulf coasts, the Mississippi and Ohio Rivers—and then to crush it by concentric offensives. This "Anaconda" strategy, as it was called, was conceived by General Winfield Scott, victor of the war against Mexico of 1846–48 and general-in-chief at the outset of the War Between the States. Its attraction to the government of President Abraham Lincoln was that it promised to be relatively bloodless, a major consideration when the Union lacked troops and, besides, still hoped to end the conflict by reconciliation rather than slaughter. In April 1861 the army of the United States numbered only sixteen thousand and it was largely deployed in the Far West, garrisoning the forts which protected the settlers who were already making their way across the Mississippi or Missouri to claim "free" land in Indian territory. North and South were urgently raising larger armies, and in both regions there were numbers of pre-war volunteer units—Zouaves, Blues, Grays— which could be put into the field. Until armies of hundreds rather than tens of thousands could be enlisted, equipped, and trained, however, conventional campaigning in the European style was beyond the power of either contestant. Hence the attraction of the Anaconda Plan to the North. It had other advantages. Though a third of the United States' regular officers had "gone with their states," so effectively joining the Confederacy, almost the whole of the navy remained under Federal control, and so did some of the key coastal fortifications, including Fortress Monroe at Old Point Comfort on the Yorktown peninsula, Forts Taylor and Jefferson at Key West off the tip of Florida, and Fort Pickens at the north of Pensacola Bay, near Mobile, Alabama; giant brick or masonry mastodons of the Third System, built at enormous expense between 1815 and 1860 (Fort Jefferson was still incomplete), they were designed to resist siege for fifteen to fifty days. The makings of a maritime squeeze on the Confederacy thus lay to hand, once the navy could organise itself to impose a blockade of the South's major points of seaboard entry at Chesapeake Bay, Charleston, Savannah, and New Orleans.

In retrospect, the Anaconda Plan can be seen as an equivalent of those earlier strategies, devised by the French against the English, by the British and the American colonists against the French, and by the British against the American revolutionaries, to use the geography of the continent as a means of imposing control over one of its regions. France at the end of the seventeenth century set out to confine the English to the Atlantic seaboard by using its ownership of the St. Lawrence, Great Lakes, and Mississippi water chain as an ultimate stop line, from which its own troops and Indian allies could mount short-range offensives along the subsidiary rivers—Richelieu, Mohawk, Ohio—to harass the outlying settlements and check attempts by the much more numerous colonists of New England, New York, and Virginia to acquire land on their northern and western borders; within the water chain, they had counted on their familiarity with what would be called "the Old Northwest" to block the gaps through the Appalachians, thus ensuring that the English colonies would remain coastal enclaves, without access to the riches of the interior.

French strategy had failed for two reasons: want of numbers—of both settlers and soldiers—to match those in the English colonies and want of sufficient naval strength to hold the mouth of the St. Lawrence, the "gateway to a continent," and to carry war against Britain's naval bases in Nova Scotia, New England, and New York. As a result, the immensely strong geographical position of New France had been reduced piecemeal, first by the British capture of Louisbourg in 1758, then by the "rolling up" of the St. Lawrence line, via the Mohawk and the Richelieu, finally by Wolfe's amphibious attack on Quebec, culminating in his victory on the Plains of Abraham.

British strategy between 1776 and 1781 reverted to that pursued by the French during King William's, Queen Anne's, and King George's wars, with the difference that command of the sea, exercised for most of the War of the Revolution by the Royal Navy, conferred advantages that France had not then enjoyed. Britain's hope was that through the use of the St. Lawrence–Great Lakes line, which it continued to control, attacks could be mounted into the hinterland of the rebellious colonies, that New England and New York in particular could be separated from the rest by bisection along the Hudson–Lake Champlain–Richelieu route and that, from strong sea-supplied bases in the coastal cities—Boston, Newport, New York, Philadelphia, Charleston, Savannah—their armies of regulars could bring the amateur Continental troops to battle, defeat them, and reduce the Revolution step by step. The strategy was absolutely correct but failed for reasons which the French would have recognised all too well, and for others particular to circumstances. Want of numbers was paramount. Though the British troops always exceeded their enemies in quality, they could rarely achieve preponderance at a decisive point, and they were often too weak absolutely to exercise power over the enormous distances at which the sheer scale of North America required them to operate. Thus the advantages conferred by their possession of Canada were negated by their inability both to protect it and to find an offensive surplus with which to strike down the strategic corridors into the American rear. On the contrary, it was the Americans—Benedict Arnold in his Kennebec River expedition to Quebec in 1775, Arnold again on the Mohawk in 1777, George Rogers Clark by his penetration to the Mississippi in 1778–79—who showed the initiative in the great spaces of the interior, where the British were never at home. When they did attempt a long-range expedition, by General Burgoyne down the Lake Champlain route in 1777, American superiority in warfare "American-style"—earlier it would have been called "Indian"—brought the enterprise to a halt.

Britain's determination to retain the great colonial seaports failed also for want of numbers. Its army in America was strong enough, when supported by the Royal Navy, to hold two or three at the same time—New York, Charleston, and Savannah, for example, in 1780–81—but never all six of the key points together. As a result, the blockade was never impermeable, which meant that George Washington had always had an open doorway to the sea at one or more points—Boston after 1776, Newport, Rhode Island, as well after 1779—through which supplies and eventually French troops could be landed to join him. Throughout the Revolutionary War, moreover, he had played against the British the technique earlier employed by the French to confine their enemies to the Atlantic seaboard by use of a natural obstacle. Theirs was the line of the Appalachians; Washington, operating east of the Appalachians on the coastal levels, had sheltered behind the Delaware and the little tributaries of the Hudson, the Raritan, and the Passaic, rivers which provided cover for his base camps and for his evasive marching and countermarching that held the British at bay and occasionally exposed them to surprise attack, as at Trenton and Princeton. It was at best a delaying, not a war-winning strategy; but when in 1781 the Royal Navy temporarily lost control of American waters to the French, at a moment when the British generals' want of numbers ashore had also lost them control of almost all of the interland, the pieces suddenly fell into Washington's hand. The natural boundaries of the theatre of operations and most of its entry points— the Mohawk and Hudson corridors, Boston, Newport, the mouth of the Chesapeake—were in the Americans' hands or commanded by their French allies. The British zone had effectively been bisected, in that Clinton in New York could not come to the rescue of Cornwallis at Yorktown at the critical juncture. The result was that their war for America fell apart in their fingers.

It might have been, if reflected upon, a promising augury for the Union, which in 1861 occupied a position not unakin to that held by Washington's armies in 1780. True, the British had then retained their New York stronghold. New York State, New England, New Jersey, and Pennsylvania, however, had been cleared, the Ohio and Illinois country was American, and only the Carolinas and Georgia were under British control; Virginia was disputed territory. A sort of Anaconda was working, therefore, to Washington's advantage, and, when French sea power came into play on his side, the vice would be closed. Since, in 1861, the Union also dominated Ohio and Illinois, absolutely controlled New Jersey and Pennsylvania, had a foothold in Virginia and enjoyed as a given the naval superiority only brought to Washington by the retreat of the Royal Navy from American waters in the summer of 1781, it might have seemed that the South's position was too precarious to be maintained.

Against the analogy of 1780, however, might be argued that of 1812–14, when the British had attempted to break into what would become the territory of the Confederacy—in retaliation for the United States' efforts to break into Canada by the familiar river and lake routes—by amphibious expedition and had failed at the points of entry. True, they had burnt the city of Washington, but they had been deterred by Baltimore's defences and at New Orleans had suffered a resounding defeat. All this implied that the Confederacy would be a tough nut to crack. Careful analysis reinforced the impression. Geographically the Confederacy was very strong indeed, commanding magnificent natural frontiers. Admittedly it was, industrially, commercially, and demographically, at a severe disadvantage to the Union: its white population was only 5.5 million, while the North's was 22 million; its railway density was half that of the North's; in 1860 it had produced only 3 per cent of the nation's firearms, 6 per cent of its cloth, and overall only one-ninth of the whole United States' industrial output, all the rest coming from the burgeoning factories of the twenty-two Northern states. Commercially, moreover, it depended for income upon the export of cotton and tobacco, into markets which were closed to it in the North by the war itself and in the outside world by blockade or embargo, not effective at the outset but threatening eventually to be very constricting indeed.

On the other hand, while the Confederate landmass offered four avenues of strategic penetration to its Northern neighbour, none was an easy option. On the Atlantic and Gulf coasts the same difficulties presented themselves to the Union as they had to the British in the War of 1812–14, notably the fortified closure of the lower Mississippi at New Orleans. In the interior, meanwhile, a chain of Confederate strongpoints on the upper Mississippi and its dependent rivers, particularly the Cumberland and Tennessee, blocked ingress from the states of Indiana and Illinois. North Carolina and Kentucky appeared to offer a gap east of the Mississippi which led into the Southern heartland, by-passing Virginia; but no north–south railways ran that way, indeed no railways at all, and few navigable north–south rivers either. On the contrary, the region was blocked off from the North by the diagonal line of the Appalachians, rough, unpopulated terrain and a formidable defence to the "low country" of the Carolinas and Georgia, offering few gaps, as the French, British, and colonial Americans had all found in their time, for movement either towards the great internal basin or, more important, to the North and towards the Atlantic seaboard.

"On to Richmond," the easy slogan of the summer of 1861, had not therefore been a false exhortation after all. Given the closure of the coasts, the closure of the Mississippi, and the obstacle of the Ap-palachians, the only geographically open frontier between North and South indeed lay in the narrow strip between the Shenandoah Moun-tains and the Potomac, scarcely fifty miles wide. It was not after all so surprising that a trifling stream like Bull Run—crossed in one second today by a commuter's car on Route 66 in or out of the District of Co-lumbia—could, if defended stoutly by patriotic Southerners under gen-erals like Joseph E. Johnston and Stonewall Jackson, close definitively the North's main axis of advance into the South's enormous territory. Enormous it was; with a coastline almost 2,500 miles long, from Chesapeake Bay to the Mexican border, an east-west span of 1,500 miles, and a north–south depth of 600 miles, the Confederacy had a land area of 750,000 square miles, as large as that of modern France, Germany, Italy, Spain, Portugal, and Great Britain combined. As a mili-tary commentator writing in *The Times* of London in 1861 remarked, the North's task, if it espoused an offensive, was to "reduce and hold in permanent subjection a tract of country nearly as large as Russia in Europe." He went on to conclude that "just as England during the rev-olution had to give up conquering the colonies so the North will have to give up conquering the South."

Not only did the South have strong natural frontiers. Its interior also presented a complex of geographical difficulties to an invader from almost any direction. There was, first of all, the railway problem. Though 30,000 miles of track had been laid within the United States by 1860, more than 20,000 miles of that ran in Northern territory. There, moreover, it formed several large east–west trunk systems, in particular those from Boston to Chicago via Buffalo, Toledo, and De-troit on the Great Lakes, from New York and Philadelphia to Pittsburgh on the Forks of the Ohio, and thence to Chicago again, and from Philadelphia to Cincinnati, Ohio, and St. Louis, Missouri, where the Missouri and Illinois rivers join the Mississippi. Chicago, Detroit, Pittsburg, and St. Louis, all former French fur-trading and strategic ports, are familiar from the wars of the seventeenth and eighteenth centuries. Southward from the trunk routes, however, there were few branches into the Confederacy and none which formed trunk routes. The only useful connections were at Louisville, Kentucky, from which lines ran down to the Tennessee cities of Nashville and Memphis, and at Washington, D.C., from which the line ran to Richmond and then to Wilmington—Cornwallis's bolthole in 1780—in North Carolina. The South's railways served the South only; that they did so inadequately was no help to the Union. Not until it could get an army to Chattanooga or Atlanta in the South's heartland would it be in a position to dominate the Confederate network and turn its use to its own purposes; and that eventuality was not to occur, after much bloody fighting, until the very end of 1863.

Then there was the road problem. A scheme for a system of national highways had been drawn up as early as 1808, the "Gallatin Plan," but cost always impeded its realisation and, with the coming of the railways, the need for long-distance communication by road, still a medium for the foot traveller or riding, pack, or draught animal alone, was overtaken. Lengths of National Turnpike, linking Washington with St. Louis and the state of Maine with Georgia, existed, but there were long gaps, to say nothing of execrable surfaces. Moreover, roads were still conceived as part of an internal waterway-portage system, harking back to the wilderness days of the eighteenth century. Roads commonly served "heads of navigation" on the rivers, as indeed local railways did, rather than superimposing their own long-distance pattern of communications on geography, as expected by the traveller today.

As a result, there were no strategic avenues of advance by road leading into the Confederacy open to the Union in 1861, nor would there be any throughout the course of the war. That state of affairs invested the alternative communications medium of internal waterways with the greatest importance, since the steamboat was in many ways superior to the steam train as a long-distance carrier, while the ramifications of the Missouri–Mississippi–Ohio river system offered a multitude of branchings that penetrated the Confederacy from many directions; many, moreover, had been improved by canalisation before

1860 and had been interconnected by canal construction. Once again, however, detailed analysis revealed that the majority of long-distance water routes—the Erie Canal linking Albany with Buffalo in New York, the Wabash and Erie Canal linking the Ohio River with the Great Lakes, the Illinois and Michigan Canal linking Chicago with the Mississippi—lay in Union territory. There were four canals in the South, but the Southern rivers, the Mississippi itself excepted, were all short for navigational purposes; only the Cumberland and the Tennessee, tributaries of the Ohio and so of the Mississippi also, reach for any useful distance, and they terminated for purposes of navigation at Nashville and Chattanooga respectively. The waterway map revealed in consequence that an enormous area of the Confederacy, embracing most of the upcountry of Georgia, the Carolinas, Kentucky, Tennessee, Alabama, and Virginia, could not be reached by water or indeed by railway or road. This area formed what might be called a National Redoubt, irreducible by any offensive effort that the North might contemplate directing against it.

So, "On to Richmond"; but how? That was the burning question in Washington in the summer of 1861, in the aftermath of the humiliating setback at Manassas thirty miles to the south. Far away in the west, the Union was opening a campaign at St. Louis on the Mississippi and Louisville, Kentucky, on the Ohio which, by January 1862, would put the formidable but as yet unknown Ulysses S. Grant into action at Cairo, where the Ohio and Mississippi join. It would be the start of a campaign that would open up the head of the Mississippi to a long-range Union offensive, culminating eighteen months later in the victory of Vicksburg and the extension of the North's control along the whole length of the river from New Orleans, which Commodore Farragut would capture in 1862, to Memphis, Tennessee. That triumph was unanticipated and unforeseeable in the months after Bull Run. The war appeared to have its focus on the doorsteps of the national capital, not in the interior of the United States, and what President Lincoln, his government, Congress, and Northern public opinion demanded was a scheme of things that would begin to beat the Confederate Army of northern Virginia back to its starting place. What form should such a scheme take?

The South itself had determined that the North's response to secession should be offensive or invasive through its own aggressive conduct at the opening of the war. Reason argued for a different Southern strategy altogether. Given the Confederacy's strong natural frontiers, enormous size, and intermittent connection with the national communication system, there were the best of reasons for standing on the defensive, guarding the key points of northern Virginia, the head of the Mississippi, New Orleans, and the Cumberland or Tennessee rivers, while building up a navy to protect the coastline and interrupt blockade, and at the same time pressing by sober diplomacy for recognition abroad. Jefferson Davis, the Confederate President, seems at the outset to have sympathised with this Fabian approach, which would have used time as a weapon and worked towards disheartening the Union while accustoming the outside world to the existence of two Anglo-Saxon Americas rather than one alone. Confederate Fabianism, Professor James McPherson has suggested in his magnificent history of the war, was defeated for two reasons, both of which bit at the start: the first was strong political and public opposition within the seceding states to the exposure of any part of Confederate territory to a Union offensive; as a result, available troop strength was dispersed in small armies at a variety of points, including the Gulf and Atlantic coasts, not all of which were threatened at the outset. The second was Southern hubris; Southerners, with some reason, thought themselves a warrior people, to whom a strategy of wait-and-see was an indignity. Persuaded that they could beat any number of Yankees in fair fight, they sought battle in the belief that favourable decision must flow from it. "The idea of waiting for blows, instead of inflicting them," the *Richmond Examiner* declared in September 1861, "is altogether unsuited to the genius of our people. The aggressive policy is the truly defensive one. A column pushed forward into Pennsylvania or Ohio is worth more to us, as a defensive measure, than a whole tier of seacoast batteries from Norfolk to the Rio Grande."

There was a confusion of purpose here; the South could not at the same time stage successful offensives and protect its whole perimeter: "he who defends everything," Frederick the Great had said, "defends nothing." During 1861–62 it did mount a series of successful offensives and counteroffensives, at Manassas, at Ball's Bluff on the Potomac above Washington, at Wilson's Creek far away in the west, and, above all, in the Shenandoah Valley, where Stonewall Jackson bemused, bamboozled, and consistently beat his Northern opponents in the months April–June 1862. Meanwhile, however, the North was accumulating solid, strategic gains around the South's water frontiers precisely because of the Confederate want of those "seaboard batteries"—though of effective naval strength also—whose value the *Richmond Examiner* had comprehensively dismissed. The gains were not the outcome of any tit-for-tat policy of retaliation, but a function of the maritime element of the Anaconda Plan. Impermeable blockade required more ships than the United States Navy could hope to find at the outset, though it added to their number by every means possible—building, requisition, conversion—throughout 1861–62. It also required active means to close the point of navigable entry into the Confederacy's 3,500 miles of coastline; they included "ten major ports and 180 inlets, bays and river mouths," Professor McPherson has calculated. It was these on which the North set about laying its hand during 1861–62.

Its first success came in August 1861 at Cape Hatteras, South Carolina, and it was of great significance. America's Atlantic coast is a surprise to Europeans, particularly to those from western Britain and France, who expect the edge of a continent to end in steep cliffs descending abruptly to the sea. Between Maine and Florida there are scarcely any cliffs at all, only dunes, swamps, and forested lowlands against which tidewater laps, a coast often separated from the ocean itself by chains of offshore islands. The gradual transition from dry land to the deep is particularly marked off the northern coast of North Carolina, which lies behind a chain of barrier islands and is approachable by large ships only through the gap at Cape Hatteras. By securing the Cape, it could be seen, some two hundred miles of Confederate coastline might be sterilised against military use; on 29 August a Northern amphibious force battered the Cape's half-completed forts, Clark and Hatteras, into surrender and so achieved that purpose.

In November the success was repeated at Port Royal, south of Charleston, South Carolina, where two Confederate forts protected the entrance to the largest natural harbour on the Atlantic coat. It had not been developed commercially, for it lacked a navigable river connection with the interior, but it made a fine anchorage for blockade runners and would do, conversely, for Union ships on blockading duty. Again, the defences were overcome in a single day's bombardment, and another stretch of coastline was thus denied to Confederate use. The process continued. Ship Island, between Mobile and New Orleans, had been captured in September. In January 1862, General Ambrose Burnside led an amphibious expedition to Roanoke Island, the site of the abortive English settlement of the sixteenth century north of Cape Hatteras, overcame resistance, took control of Albemarle Sound, which provided Richmond with an alternative exit to the Atlantic, and went on to capture all its ports and those in Pamlico Sound behind Cape Hatteras as well, including Beaufort and New Bern, the latter of extra importance because from there rail links led into the interior. Finally, in April, Union sailors and soldiers achieved the most remarkable of all these seizures of coastal strongholds in their attack on Fort Pulaski at the mouth of the Savannah River. The fortress, built from 1829 onwards, was one of the monsters of the Third System, specially reinforced in rear with giant timber baulks to help absorb the shock of shot striking the outer face of its immensely thick walls. This enormously expensive method of construction proved no use at all against the North's newly developed rifled artillery. In two days, ten batteries set up on an adjoining island—they were named for such leading Union generals as Grant, Sherman, Burnside, Halleck, and McClellan—and firing at ranges of up to three thousand yards, broke the carapace open, while shells from heavy mortars devastated the interior. Local Confederate forces lacked both the artillery to counter-bombard and landing craft to launch troops against the Union gunners. The operation was a perfect demonstration of the North's amphibious freedom of action which, by this offensive, completed its acquisition of a chain of coastal footholds and protected anchorages running from Fortress Monroe at the mouth of Chesapeake Bay to Mobile in the estuary of the Alabama River. At the outset of the amphibious campaign, the United States Navy had retained only two Southern bases from which to conduct a blockade, Fortress Monroe and the offshore island of Key West. By its end, it was the South which was left with only two Atlantic ports, Wilmington, North Carolina, and Charleston, South Carolina, the pivots of Cornwallis's campaign before Yorktown eighty years earlier.

The North's amphibious offensive was not maritime alone. It was riverine as well; the logic of North American geography, which had determined so much of the course of the continent's earlier wars, impressed itself on the strategy of the Civil War at an early stage. While Fort Pulaski was coming under attack on the Atlantic coast, Commodore David Farragut, who would become the North's foremost admiral, was launching another amphibious assault on the two great Third System works at the mouth of the Mississippi, Forts Jackson and St. Philip. Unlike Pulaski, these were not battered into submission, but boldly bypassed in a night attack after days of bombardment; when Farragut reached the city of New Orleans the following day, 25 April, he debarked marines to seize it while the garrison of the forts mutinied and surrendered. The fall of New Orleans was a crippling blow to the Southern war effort, not so much because it closed another exit to the sea, though that was bad enough, but because it positioned a Northern striking force at the entry to the Confederacy's largest internal axis of manoeuvre. Scott's Anaconda Plan required the bisection of the South along the line of the Mississippi, chiefly to deprive the cotton and to-bacco states to the east—the Carolinas, Georgia, Alabama, Mississippi, and Virginia—of the livestock resources of Texas and Arkansas. An an-cillary outcome of such a bisection, however, would be to provide the North with a line of departure from the eastern bank of the great river—at the railheads of Memphis and Vicksburg and along such trib-utaries and sub-tributaries as the Ohio, Tennessee, and Cumberland rivers, which led into the Southern heartland from the western direc-tion—from which a succession of parallel offensives could be securely mounted.

These offensives had already begun when Farragut seized New Or-leans, largely thanks to the initiative of the unknown Ulysses S. Grant, a disgraced West Pointer to whom the Civil War had offered the chance to remake his military career. The North's desperate need for trained officers brought him the colonelcy of a volunteer Illinois regiment; his efficiency in command of it rapidly elevated him to lead a brigade. Grant had an extraordinary interest in topography—his private store of maps had been called into use during the Mexican War of 1846–48 to supply a lack at headquarters—and an uncanny eye for country, which he could read as if by feel; "I will take no backward step" was one of his favourite remarks, and he would usually choose to ride his way through a wilderness to his objective after a false start rather than begin again. He seems to have deciphered the strategic geography of the western theatre at a glance. Albert Sidney Johnston, the Confeder-ate commander of the Western Military Department, had fixed upon Columbus, Kentucky, as the key to his theatre. It stands on the Missis-sippi just below the confluence with the Ohio and not far from the points where the Ohio is joined by the Cumberland and Tennessee rivers. Where those two are at their closest he had built two forts, Henry and Donelson, to block any Northern penetration downriver, while at Columbus on the Mississippi itself he had constructed a

"Gibraltar of the West." The importance of this cordon of forts lay in its denial to the Union not only of the water routes leading southward, but of the southerly rail connections as well, particularly the long lateral route running parallel to the front between Memphis on the Mississippi and Bowling Green, Kentucky, and the spurs from it which led to Nashville and Chattanooga, Tennessee, Corinth, Mississippi, and Decatur, Alabama.

Grant, on his own initiative, thrust a wedge into this cordon in September 1861 by seizing Paducah, where the Tennessee joins the Ohio; then, after, winning a small diversionary battle at Belmont in Missouri, he addressed himself to the main issue, Confederate control of the Ohio–Mississippi river system. His superior was Henry Halleck, whose headquarters were at St. Louis, far upstream; Halleck's jealousy of his fellow general Don Carlos Buell, based at Louisville on the Ohio, and his own wait-and-see attitude deterred him from action; "too much haste will ruin everything," he told Lincoln in January 1862 when urged to get a move on. Grant needed no such urging. During January he talked Halleck into letting him and the commander of the river flotilla of armoured gunboats, Andrew Foote, embark on an offensive against Forts Henry and Donelson by land and water. Steamboats brought Grant's troops to Fort Henry on the Tennessee; Foote's ironclads bombarded it from the river. On 6 February, the garrison fled overland to Fort Donelson, only twelve miles away on the Cumberland. By 14 February, Foote had got four of his gunboats, which had to steam up the Tennessee to the Ohio before steaming down the Cumberland to the scene of action, in position, and their fire, concerted with that of the army, quickly brought the Confederate commander, Simon Bolivar Buckner, to ask for terms. There had been hard fighting and he thought himself entitled to fair treatment, all the more because he had helped Grant with money during Grant's dog days ten years earlier. His old comrade coldly replied that "no terms except an immediate and unconditional surrender can be accepted," thus bringing Confederate resistance to an end, winning a name for himself as "unconditional surrender" Grant, and implanting an abiding ethic in the American style of making war.

This loss of Forts Henry and Donelson broke Albert Sidney Johnston's western cordon apart, unlocked the Cumberland and Tennessee system to the Union, and led in short order to the abandonment of the "Gibraltar of the West" at Columbus, guarding the upper reaches of the Mississippi, and to the capture on 8 April of its subordinate down-stream fortress at Island No. 10. Union progress was now relentless. Fort Pillow, further downstream, was abandoned in the face of the Union's river flotilla on 4 June; two days later Memphis, one of the largest cities on the Mississippi and the junction of three railroads, fell too. On 25 May the Confederates had also been forced to abandon Corinth, the rail centre on the track midway between Memphis and Chattanooga, thus leaving the flanks of the Appalachians as the only barrier against the advance of the Union's western armies into the heartland of the Confederacy; as Nashville, the state capital of Tennessee, had fallen to Don Carlos Buell without a fight on 23 February, almost the whole of Kentucky and Tennessee—that land beyond the Cumberland Gap which Daniel Boone had roamed in the 1770s—had passed under Union control.

The only check to the Union's steamroller advance into what had formed so much of the Old Northwest had been imposed in early April at a tiny place called Shiloh, far down the Tennessee River, known to the Confederates as Pittsburg Landing. There Grant, in the first great battle of his career, had won a victory, but at terrible cost. Believing after his string of successes that he had the Confederates on the run, he prepared to attack Albert Sidney Johnston without making allowance for the possibility that Johnston might be preparing to attack him. That, however, was the case, for Johnston had determined to protect the rail centre of Corinth at all costs. On 6 April he took Grant by surprise in the broken, wooded, and swampy country around the isolated Shiloh church—a nightmare landscape for a general, since small creeks and streams cut through it from a dozen directions—panicked many of his soldiers, inflicted heavy losses, and threatened to reverse the whole course of the western campaign thus far. It was only because Grant kept his nerve, took advantage of the defensive opportunities this unchosen battlefield offered, used the artillery in his gunboats to bombard the Southern positions, and committed his reserves correctly on the second day of battle that he was able to retrieve the situation. On the evening of 7 April, Johnston decided to withdraw, but he had so exhausted Grant's army that it was unable to follow. When the casualties were counted, they were found to total nearly twice those suffered in all the major battles of the war yet fought.

Geography and logistics had worked to the North's advantage up to that point. What Shiloh made clear was that as the North more closely approached those regions of the Confederacy for which it had to fight if it were to survive, guts on the battlefield rather than skill at the map table would bring decision. The South would fight desperately in Tennessee to hold the barrier of the Appalachians against the Union's western armies: that was to be proved on the Stones River campaign, at the battles of Chickamauga and Chattanooga in 1863, and in Hood's madcap counteroffensive towards Franklin and Nashville in 1864. It was to be proved more immediately on the Mississippi. Farragut's seizure of New Orleans in April 1862, which postdated Grant's bloody victory at Shiloh, led swiftly to the capture of Baton Rouge, Louisiana's state capital, and the beautiful riverside resort of Natchez, but thereafter progress up the Mississippi was checked. In June Farragut got up to Vicksburg, but artillery on the high riverside bluff there prevented him from establishing a proper link with Foote's gunboats which had come down to the city via Memphis; a locally constructed Confederate ironclad, CSS *Arkansas*, temporarily won local command of the river and Farragut retreated downstream to await a Union success on land. There were to be several diverse attempts, including the cutting of a canal at the neck of the Mississippi loop on which Vicksburg stands, but none succeeded. Right into the summer of 1863 Vicksburg was to stand as an apparently impregnable fortress on the great river, frustrating all efforts by Sherman and Grant to take the city or bypass it to east or west. Geography—the meanders of the Mississippi and its tributaries, its commanding bluffs and its impenetrable swamps—had here worked to the Confederacy's full advantage.

Vicksburg was eventually to be brought to capitulate. In the spring of 1862, however, that outcome lay over a year in the future. When Lincoln contemplated the strategic situation of the Union at the beginning of April, he could form only the following picture, by no means a wholly gloomy one but conforming patchily to the Anaconda Plan of the early months of the war.

In the west, thanks to Grant's initiative, the head of the Ohio–Cumberland–Tennessee river system was under Union control and a start had been made at using those waterways to penetrate the state of Tennessee, threaten the Chattanooga–Memphis rail link, and menace upper Alabama and Mississippi. In the Gulf, the ports of Mobile and Pensacola—where Fort Pickens had been held for the Union from the outset—were under Federal control, while Farragut was about to begin his successful assault on the mouth of the Mississippi. Along the Atlantic coast, all major ports, harbours, inlets, estuaries, and fortresses were in Northern hands and denied to Confederate use, except for Charleston and Wilmington in the Carolinas. Chesapeake Bay was stoppered by a Federal presence at Fortress Monroe, while the United States Navy, though it could not intercept all blockade runners, commanded the eastern seaboard. The isolation of the South from the outside world seemed, therefore, to be well under way. The North did not look to be at risk of attack, as long as the line of the Potomac River could be held secure. The Confederates had retreated generally to the parallel Rappahannock and Rapidan rivers forty miles to the south. McClellan's arguments that he should be allowed to transfer the army by sea from Washington and Alexandria for an attack on Richmond, though they had alarmed Lincoln from the start, at length prevailed. Beginning on 22 March 1862, McClellan set about shipping 100,000 men, 300 pieces of artillery, and 25,000 animals in 400 transports down Chesapeake Bay to the tip of the peninsula between the York and James rivers, guarded by Fortress Monroe at Old Comfort Point. This spur of rich, old-settled land would henceforth in American military history become "the Peninsula."

The Peninsular Campaign

McClellan's plan for the Peninsula was straightforward: to put a superior army as close as possible to Richmond, the Confederate capital, and break his way through its defences by a combination of strategic outmanoeuvring and material outnumbering. He had originally intended to land at Urbanna on the Rappahannock, the next river northward from the York; when Joseph Johnston, his Confederate opponent, fell back, thus aborting the chance to land in his rear, he had fixed upon Old Point Comfort instead. The plan nonetheless remained the same in essentials and retained its virtue of simplicity: strike for the enemy's capital.

There were to be three impediments to its achievement: a Southern secret weapon, a Confederate diversionary campaign, and McClellan's own prevaricating and procrastinating character.

The South's secret weapon was an ironclad ship, formerly the USS

Merrimack, rebuilt as the CSS *Virginia*, whose appearance on 8 March 1862 threw all Northern schemes to attack Richmond by sea into disarray. The *Merrimack*, as history knows her, was a cut-down frigate fitted with an iron penthouse mounting ten guns. Its construction had consumed most of the output of the Tredegar Ironworks in Richmond, the South's main, indeed almost only, foundry for several months. She was sailed as soon as she was ready and in her first day of action sank two conventional Union men o' war and threatened three others with the same fate. That spelled doom also to McClellan's gathering fleet of transports and the cancellation of the Peninsular campaign before it began. When *Merrimack* came out of Norfolk—the South's naval base opposite Fortress Monroe but inside Chesapeake Bay—on the following day, 9 March, she seemed set to finish off the rest of the Federal fleet and then cruise at leisure in those inland waters, devastating any armada that McClellan or Lincoln sent southwards. That might well have been the outcome; but, by perhaps the most remarkable technological coincidence in the history of warfare, the North had the week before sailed an answer to *Merrimack* from Brooklyn Navy Yard and got her into Hampton Roads on the night of 8–9 March. *Monitor* was almost as makeshift as the Southern ironclad, an armoured turret on a steam-powered raft, but she matched her in fire power, fought her to a standstill on 9 March, and so secured Federal command of the Chesapeake for the duration of McClellan's land campaign. It had been touch and go.

Lord Palmerston, when he had seen the first British ironclad, the sleek, sinister *Warrior*, lying at anchor beside Britain's bluff old wooden ships of the line soon after her launching in 1860, had called her "a snake among the rabbits." *Merrimack* and *Monitor* were both too ungainly to be called snakes; the first was never to venture into the open sea, the second foundered soon after her famous first encounter of the ironclad era. While they were giving battle, however, a real master of the snake's mesmeric technique with rabbits—his motto was "always mystify and mislead the enemy"—was preparing to attack the flank of the Union armies in the Shenandoah Valley.

Stonewall Jackson's manoeuvres, which generations of American and British staff college students have subsequently studied for strategic inspiration, were to be an essay in the pure use of terrain for which there are few parallels in military history; campaigns that perhaps bear comparison are Wellington's backing and filling between the Portuguese frontier passes in the years 1809–11 and Rommel's "now you see me, now you don't" dodging among his own minefields in the Western Desert in 1941–42. Jackson, godfearing, hypochondriac, professorial, resembled neither, except in dedication to his profession, and he had much less practical experience of war than either. He enjoyed, however, a cardinal advantage in confronting his Northern enemies: he knew the ground on which he was to fight intimately. His years on the faculty of the Virginia Military Institute in Lexington, which is actually inside the Shenandoah Valley, had familiarised him with its southern end; he was further aided, Professor McPherson points out, "by local spies and scouts, who knew every foot of the country"; and "he had spent many hours studying . . . maps drawn by his brilliant topographical engineer Jedediah Hotchkiss."

The valley—for military purposes its length may be taken as some 120 miles—is a region of great, still unspoilt natural beauty which runs from the confluence of the Shenandoah with the Potomac at Harpers Ferry, scene of John Brown's anti-slavery demonstration of 1859, southwestward into the greater Appalachian chain beyond Staunton. It has no natural outlet in that direction and lacked, therefore, any strategic value to the Northern armies. At its Potomac exit, however, it menaced Washington from a flank and with its "gaps" or passes through the Blue Ridge Mountains which form its eastern side, the Rockfish Gap, the Swift Run Gap, and the Manassas Gap, it offered sally ports through which a Confederate force could fall upon a Union army operating in the coastal lowlands between the Blue Ridge and Chesapeake Bay. Moreover, it is not a simple trench; behind the front range of the Blue Ridge but before the main mass of the Appalachians lying to the west run the intermediate Massanutten Mountains, dividing the North Fork of the Shenandoah from the South Fork, and again pierced by their own "gaps" and passes. The valley, in short, is a ready-made Tom Tiddler's ground, presenting a resourceful general with the opportunity to play hide-and-seek, up one side of the Massanutten, down the other, through the gaps, and back again, for as long as his enemy would tolerate the game.

This is countryside I have known for nearly forty years, from my first visit to the theatrically beautiful University of Virginia at Charlottesville in 1957. It was my earliest encounter with the high civilisation of the South, and the impression it made has never faded. Here, in physical form, were the aristocratic argument for the slave system, the

Palladian grace of Thomas Jefferson's plantation at Monticello, the scholarly seclusion of its great library and that of the university itself, the serpentine walls of the mown university gardens, the wide-rolling, white-fenced pastures of the Albemarle County horse estates. It is a countryside of stifling noontide heat, but also of cool verandas, dark shadows, old shade trees, wealthy ease, discreet service, and the ever-ready offer of the evening mint julep. Close at hand are the magnificent vistas of the Skyline Drive, which follows the crest of the Blue Ridge, while below it rise and fall the green slopes of long-tended grazing farms in the Shenandoah Valley itself. For all its richness, this is still sparsely settled country. Not long ago, half a lifetime after I first came here as an undergraduate, I drove northward along Interstate 81 from Lexington, home town to the serene campus of Washington and Lee College and the spartan stronghold of the Virginia Military Institute—surely even in Stonewall's time, the cadets must have enjoyed a little more ease of life than they do today?—and confounded myself with the thought that this lovely and tranquil land had in 1862 been the scene of breakneck marching and countermarching by Union and Confederates and of bitter battle at the little towns of Forest Royal, Winchester, Cross Keys, and Port Republic.

Stonewall Jackson's problem is easy to describe, its solution almost as difficult to relate as it was to realise. With an inferior force—never many more than eighteen thousand—he had to outface two larger Union armies dedicated to doing battle with him, that of General Nathaniel Banks in the valley itself and General John Frémont's across the mountains in West Virginia, and at the same time mount such a threat to Washington that he would deter President Lincoln, who was temporarily acting as commander-in-chief, from releasing a third army, McDowell's, to join McClellan in a convergent attack on the Confederate capital of Richmond a hundred miles to his east. All this, moreover, though he had few cavalry and, as always with Confederate forces in the field, lacked transport, food, and every sort of military supply. His solution to his problem was starkly simple: to run his soldiers as harshly as he ran himself, to march them so fast from strategic point to point that they earned the name of "foot cavalry," to live off the land, to drub the Union forces wherever found but, above all, to so "mystify and mislead" that the enemy always fought divided and never succeeded in uniting against him. ———

Thus, starting in the far south of the valley on 8 May, he won a

small victory over Frémont's army at the place confusingly called Mc-
Dowell (today on U.S. 250) on the slopes of the Shenandoah Mountains. Then, dropping back into the valley proper, he force-marched his
troops northward via Harrisonburg (today Interstate 81) to New Market, jumped through a gap in the Massanutten Mountains to Luray (on
U.S. 340), and advanced to Front Royal. There he won a small victory
on 23 May, so alarming the Union troops that Banks retreated first to
Winchester (now in a loop of Interstate 81), where he was beaten
again, and then all the way to Harpers Ferry.

The appearance of Confederates in fighting mood at a place only
sixty miles up the Potomac from Washington alarmed Lincoln in exactly the way that Jackson—and Robert E. Lee, who was acting in effect as Confederate chief of staff—hoped that it would. Lincoln
cancelled his plans to send McDowell forward from Fredericksburg to
assist McClellan in the Peninsula and ordered him to turn against
Stonewall instead. From Fredericksburg to the nearest of the valley
"gaps" at Front Royal is only fifty miles, three, perhaps two days'
march. From Front Royal to Frémont's current position on the other
side of the valley was a good deal less than fifty miles. Jackson, at the
moment McDowell turned, was forty miles to the north, which meant
forty miles the wrong side of safety. A trap was being sprung in his
rear, and every map table calculation suggested that he would be
caught in it. Map table calculations did not make allowances for Jackson's powers of manoeuvre when he was in a hurry. Turning like lightning, and using what cavalry he had as an advance guard to hold
Frémont at a distance from his planned line of retreat, he passed
through Winchester for the second time on 31 May, only a week after
he had fought his battle there and only two days after he had been at
Harpers Ferry. He had escaped the immediate trap, but Frémont was
marching to pursue him down the west side of the Massanutten Mountains, and another Union force, under James Shields, was marching
down the east side, so that he could not tarry. He pressed on to Harrisonburg at the foot of the Massanutten Mountains, where he left his
subordinate Richard Ewell to fight Frémont at Cross Keys on 8 May.
He could at this point have beaten an honourable retreat out of the
Shenandoah Valley through the Blue Ridge Mountains via Brown's
Gap and made his way to Richmond to join Joseph Johnston, since he
had now fully accomplished his mission of disrupting the Union concentration against the Confederate capital; but the spectacle of a di-

vided Northern force—Frémont west of the Massanutten Mountains at Cross Keys, Shields east of the mountains at Port Republic—was too tempting to ignore. On 9 June, he arrived opposite Shields at Port Republic, defeated him in a five-hour battle, collected Ewell, organised his train of fifteen thousand troops, two thousand prisoners, and heavily loaded wagons of booty into a column of route, marched through Brown's Gap out of the valley, and there shortly took the rails to Richmond.

It had been an astonishing month. Jackson's army had marched some 350 miles between its starting and finishing points, fought five battles, all victories, kept three armies divided, menaced the Federal capital, thrown the enemy's strategy into disarray, and got off scot-free, causing the commanders of seventy thousand Union soldiers to wonder how a general, whose force had never exceeded eighteen thousand, could so completely have mystified and misled them.

Jackson's will-o'-the-wisp manoeuvres galled all the more because they cast so unfavourable a light on the pedestrian evolutions of his old fellow cadet of the West Point class of 1846, George B. McClellan, in the Peninsula. More galling still was the fact that McClellan had an opinion of himself, while Jackson appeared to have none. History would make of Stonewall a figure of romance: the nickname itself, won at the first Battle of Bull Run, was part of it, the valley blitzkrieg its substance, his tragic death—shot by one of his own sentries at Chancellorsville after his brilliant flank manoeuvre which decided the battles—would crown it; the poignancy of his dying words, "Let us cross over the river and rest under the shade of the trees," would live as his epitaph. Their enigmatic beauty supplied Ernest Hemingway with the title for his least-understood novel. Yet, while Hemingway's central figure was meant to be a romantic hero, Jackson was quite the opposite. Modest and self-effacing, he owes his romantic reputation to history, not to self-seeking.

McClellan was everything that Jackson was not, vain, vainglorious, opinionated, worldly, self-satisfied, ostentatiously busy—but also dilatory and self-doubting. He was a splendid organiser, on the principle of doing everything himself and delegating to nobody, but his gifts were for solving problems presented to him by unsatisfactory subordinates, not by active and contentious enemies. He was a great fault-finder—with his predecessor as general-in-chief, Winfield Scott ("a dotard"—Scott was seventy-six, McClellan thirty-five), with Gideon Welles,

Secretary of the Navy ("a garrulous old woman"), with William Seward, Secretary of State ("incompetent little puppy"), with Edward Bates, the Attorney General ("an old fool"), and with President Lincoln ("a well-meaning baboon"). He found no fault with himself. If he were to be compared with other famous American generals, it could be said that he resembled MacArthur in his arrogance and George C. Marshall in his hauteur, but that he lacked, as events would prove, the former's dynamism and the latter's strength of character. He was a hollow man who, though events would find him out, refused to confront his own failure and preserved his self-esteem to the very end of a career which encompassed defeat in the field and defeat in electoral contest for the presidency as well.

Grant, a senior at West Point in McClellan's freshman year, confessed in the aftermath of the war that "[he] is to me one of [its] mysteries." So he might well have found him. Grant was a tanner's son who managed to fail at the military academy, fail in the army, fail in business, fail in farming, and succeed only when war offered him the chance to deploy his gritty skills of decision, self-control, and selection of the enemy's weak spot. McClellan had, until elevated to high command, succeeded at everything. His family was rich, he had graduated second in his cadet class, he had won golden opinions in the Mexican War. He had been sent as an official observer to the Crimea, a plum appointment, but had left the army to become vice-president of the Illinois Central Railroad, of which Lincoln was the attorney, and then president of another. When appointed to the second most senior post in the United States Army in May 1861, he accepted the title of "Young Napoleon" conferred on him by the newspapers as if it were his due. When in November, deferring to congressional pressure, Lincoln appointed him to the post both of general-in-chief, formerly held by Winfield Scott, and of commander of the Army of the Potomac, but with the warning that the dual responsibilities "will entail a vast labour for you," McClellan complacently riposted, "I can do it all."

He could certainly organise large-scale military movement. When he eventually persuaded Lincoln that the correct strategy for 1862 was to transfer the Army of the Potomac to the Peninsula, the movement went like clockwork. A fleet of 113 transports of every variety, including transatlantic liners and Hudson River pleasure craft, had been chartered to carry 121,000 men, 14,500 horses, 1,200 wagons, the guns of forty-four artillery batteries, and a vast quantity of stores to

Old Point Comfort. The whole force was moved from Annapolis, Washington, and Alexandria in less than three weeks and found camps prepared for it inland of Fortress Monroe near the devastated town of Hampton behind the spit of land on which the great stronghold of Fortress Monroe stood. The value to the Union of the retention of the fort in 1861 now revealed itself. Since the next defensible position was at Yorktown, twenty miles up the river, where General Magruder had in fact planted the Confederate position, the intervening space was a sort of no-man's-land in which McClellan could deploy his army at leisure before beginning the advance on Richmond. The great natural bastion of Quebec had offered Wolfe no such advantage.

McClellan, indeed, had almost every advantage, most of all a huge preponderance of numbers over the Confederates. He had been less than frank in his assurances to Lincoln that Washington was adequately protected; the President had given him leave to reposition the Army of the Potomac from the outskirts of Washington to the shores of the Chesapeake—potentially at Urbanna on the Rappahannock River, actually to the Peninsula—on the strict understanding that he should "leave said city [Washington] entirely secure." McClellan had compiled figures to show that 73,500 men would remain. In fact, he had double-counted some men, and included the forces detached to operate around the Shenandoah Valley, so that the true figure was under 30,000. Lincoln's staff—he was temporarily acting as commander-in-chief, having rightly judged that McClellan could not direct the Peninsular campaign as well, to the latter's intense annoyance—consequently "agreed in opinion that the capital *was not safe*." By then, 28 May, it was too late for second thoughts, because the Peninsular campaign was under way.

Fortunately, McClellan had grossly over-estimated Confederate strength. At the end of 1862 he was insisting that Joseph Johnston had 150,000 men around Manassas, when the true figure was nearer 40,000. It says something about McClellan's egotism that he nevertheless persisted in arguing for stripping Washington of troops and striking at Richmond via the Chesapeake as the current strategy. Lincoln had seen things the other way: that Johnston might respond to an offensive against Richmond not by falling back to defend it but by mounting his own offensive against the unprotected Washington. Had he had the numbers, Johnston might well have done so. As he actually commanded less than a third of McClellan's estimate—which had been prepared by the Pinkerton detective agency—it was he who felt over-exposed at Manassas, and it was his consequent decision in March to fall back to the more secure line of the Rappahannock and Rapidan rivers, fifty instead of twenty-five miles south of the capital, that objectively robbed McClellan's Chesapeake venture of risk.

Napoleon had said generals should be lucky. McClellan was extraordinarily lucky right up to the opening of the campaign: lucky that Johnston did not have the strength the intelligence reports alleged, lucky that the *Monitor* turned up in the nick of time to rescue the fleet off Fortress Monroe from destruction by the *Merrimack*, lucky that Jackson's brilliant manoeuvres in the Shenandoah Valley did not panic Lincoln into diverting more of his troops in that direction, lucky even that Johnston withdrew behind the Rappannock when he did, for, though that put the Confederate main army closer to Richmond, it scuppered the Urbanna plan, which, involving as it did the need to cross two, if not three, rivers by a sodden and inadequate road network, would almost certainly have left him floundering.

Then McClellan proceeded to dissipate all the luck he had been given. Instead of proceeding up the Peninsula as soon as his advance guard was ready to march in the first week of April, he began to see difficulties. He had already been warned by the navy that the presence of the *Merrimack* at the mouth of the James River denied that water route to him as a means of shipping men and guns forward towards Richmond; he himself decided that he could not break into the York River past Gloucester unless he diverted troops to attack the Confederate batteries there, which he was unwilling to do because it broke the principle of keeping his army concentrated. When on 5 April he discovered that General John Magruder was not merely encamped at Yorktown, as he believed, but had thrown a line of defences across the whole Peninsula from the York to the James, he took fright. He began at once to over-estimate the force opposed to him—by 7 April he was informing Washington that he would soon be faced by 100,000 men, when the real number was about 30,000—and to exaggerate the natural strengths of the Confederate position, the badness of the roads leading to it, and the width of the Warwick River behind which some of Magruder's entrenchments ran. Magruder had only 3,000 men per mile to defend ten miles of front, far too few to oppose a determined assault at a particular point, but exaggerated his numbers by marching units up and down and staging demonstrations by fire. McClellan took the display for reality, declared that he was opposed by a major force, and announced that he must sit down to conduct a siege. By 7 April he had learnt that Lincoln had diverted troops—McDowell's corps—towards Stonewall Jackson in the Shenandoah Valley; he took that as a reason, while sending forward his own heavy guns along the bad road from Fortress Monroe, to demand both more guns and more troops, pleading that "my force is possibly less than that of the enemy."

Lincoln judiciously replied with the reminder that he himself had "always insisted, that going down [Chesapeake] Bay in search of a [battlefield], instead of fighting at or near Manassas, was only shifting, and not surmounting, a difficulty—that we would find the same enemy, and the same, or equal entrenchments, at either place." This gentle reproof stung McClellan not at all. An expert in sieges as he conceived himself to be—he was a siege engineer by training and had been a spectator at the Anglo-French siege of Sebastopol nine years earlier—he settled down to a siege of the old Yorktown position as if he had all the time in the world. Cornwallis had succeeded in defending his, admittedly shorter, lines at Yorktown for only three weeks in 1781. The Confederates were to hold out for a month and then get clean away, the reason for that being a strange inflexibility that settled upon McClellan: having decided upon siege as the means to carry the Yorktown line, it seems as if he thereafter dismissed all others. His programme envisaged the assembly of over a hundred heavy guns including 200-pounder cannon and 13-inch mortars, together capable of delivering seven thousand pounds of shot and shell in a single discharge, and he settled himself to await that moment. When on 16 April his subordinate William F. Smith captured a portion of the enemy lines at Lee's Mills, McClellan declined to exploit the success.

His mentality, and therefore the likely development of the campaign, had been discussed two days before by his opponents in a remarkable council of war at Richmond, at which President Jefferson Davis and Generals Robert E. Lee, Joseph E. Johnston, and James Longstreet, all of whom had known him in peacetime days, had pondered strategy. The sharpest judgement was made by Longstreet, who predicted that the cautious McClellan would not attack before 1 May. So it was to turn out, almost exactly. McClellan, after a month of demanding more men and guns and meticulously positioning the very many he had, finally set the date for his great assault at 5 May; but two days earlier, when he sent one of his balloons aloft to observe the enemy's positions, they were found to be empty. During the previous night, Johnston had evacuated his trenches, hitched in his guns, and set off up the Peninsula's bad roads for Richmond forty miles away.

Moving sometimes as slowly as a mile an hour—but the Confederates were impeded as much—McClellan's leading division caught up with Johnston's rearguards where the Peninsula's two main roads joined just short of Williamsburg. With forethought, Johnston had prepared there a secondary position between Cub Creek and College Creek, tributaries respectively of the York and the James. It held well during a day of fighting on 5 May, in which the Union army suffered twice the Confederate casualties, so well that Johnston was able to slip away, leaving his earthworks empty. This, counting Manassas in March as well as Yorktown, was the third time he had disengaged without detection, and his manoeuvre succeeded as well as it had before. McClellan did not press a pursuit but proceeded with the methodical advancement of his superior force, part by road up the northern bank of the Chickahominy River, which bisects the upper Peninsula before flowing into the James above Williamsburg, part by river up the York, which Johnston's simultaneous evacuation of Gloucester and Yorktown had now opened. McClellan moved first to West Point, the objective of his aborted Urbanna plan, and then up the Pamunkey River, one of the York's feeder streams, to White House, almost due east of Richmond and only twenty miles from it; but the advance had taken another fifteen days, during which Johnston had succeeded in further strengthening the earthwork defences around Richmond and finding more troops to man them. By the last week of May his numbers had reached 60,000, to oppose the 105,000 McClellan had concentrated on the far bank of the Chickahominy.

The Confederates had also had another success, which was definitively to close the James River as an avenue of approach to the Confederate capital. The abandonment of Yorktown had meant not only that of Gloucester but also that of Norfolk, the great naval base opposite Fortress Monroe, and it entailed as a result the withdrawal of the Confederate fleet. *Merrimack* had proved too cranky to make the voyage; the world's first fighting ironclad had had to be scuttled and burnt off the Elizabeth River, which leads into the wilderness of the Dismal Swamp. The other ships, including an unfinished ironclad, were got up as far as Richmond, and the James behind them was then blocked with scuttled ships and felled trees. The real obstruction, however, was Fort Drewry, an earthwork built on a bluff the previous year, from which eight heavy guns commanded a mile of the James southwards from modern Bensley. The area today is scruffy exurbia, neither quite town nor country, sandwiched between Interstate 95 and the river, and patchily wooded. The fort—known to the Union as Fort Darling—still stands, however, thanks to the National Park Service, and from its parapet the strength of its position is instantly recognisable. Throughout the Civil War it served as the Confederacy's naval academy, and a miserable time the cadets must have had, crammed into its cramped surroundings; today it seems to be favoured as a weekend trysting place for middle-aged couples, clearly more interested in each other than in the Park Service's recorded descriptions of the drama that unfolded at its fort on 15 May 1862.

Early that morning five Union warships, including the redoubtable *Monitor*, got up to within six hundred yards of the bluff, which stands 110 feet above the water, and one, the ironclad *Galena*, anchored broadside-on downstream to engage the fort with all its guns. It was not to prove a fair fight. In the age of smoothbore cannon, ships had been at a disadvantage in gun duels with land batteries, but the appearance of rifled ordnance had changed that. Deprived, however, of the ability to manoeuvre, as the Union ships were by the narrowness of the river, and dominated by the height of Drewrys Bluff, the flotilla found the odds reversed. *Galena* was hit forty-four times in the three-hour cannonade and disabled; *Monitor*, which had accompanied her, could not elevate her guns sufficiently to engage at all; the ironclad *Naugacket* burst a gun; the unarmoured gunboats dared not come within range. As the Northern squadron dropped back defeated, a Confederate shouted down at *Monitor*, "Tell the Captain that is not the way to Richmond."

Richmond lies only five miles north of Drewrys Bluff; a Union breakthrough past the fort up the James would have brought riverborne guns to bear not only on the city's heart but also on the freight yards and rail junction of five lines, as well as the Tredegar Ironworks, the Confederacy's chief source of cast and forged metal. It had been a narrow squeak. The reverse for McClellan was decisive, none the less; his way to Richmond now lay from only one direction: across the Chickahominy River, which guards the city's eastern and northern approaches. He had arrived on the far bank of the river on 20 May and lined his army up on a front between the little town of Mechanicsville and the Chickahominy crossing place of Bottom's Bridge nine miles to the south. Richmond was only six miles west of his most advanced positions and though protected by earthworks—those at Chickahominy Bluff just off U.S. 360 remain almost in their original state—lay open to a swift attack. Yet again over-caution assailed him. The Confederates, expecting battle in the open field, battle at the gates of their capital which might decide the issue of the Civil War once and for all, were concentrating troops by all means and at utmost speed. McClellan, the siege engineer, had determined another course. The sight of Magruder's earthworks at Yorktown had decided him that he must conduct a siege there. Johnston's earthworks on the Chickahominy brought him to the same conclusion. While Johnston gathered reinforcements, and Jackson's sleight-of-hand in the Shenandoah Valley continued to deprive McClellan of McDowell's forty thousand men, the Union engineers east of Richmond were turning White House into a great logistic base and rebuilding bridges, some four hundred yards long, to bring the battering train of 200-pounders and 13-inch mortars across country from the York River's head of navigation. The work would fritter away over a month of the high campaigning season.

In the interval, the Confederates did not remain idle. While Lincoln urged McClellan to action and McClellan renewed demands for McDowell's corps to be sent to him—though McDowell was, in this last week of May, marching urgently to protect the Potomac crossings against Jackson's lunge up the Shenandoah Valley—Joseph Johnston was contemplating how he might strike a blow that would set back what he imagined to be McClellan's timescale. The most advanced of the Union troops could see Richmond's church spires and hear the church bells chiming the hours; Johnston presumed it could not be many days before he was forced to give battle at a grave disadvantage in numbers. When news—wrong in detail, right in substance—reached him on 30 May that McDowell had turned away to chase Stonewall Jackson, Johnston therefore decided—with a strong prod from Jefferson Davis, fretting in the Richmond White House—to fight a spoiling action. The heavy rains that had dogged all movement for the second month of the Peninsular campaign had swollen the Chickahominy, isolating one of McClellan's corps on the wrong side of it. It—Keyes' corps—was to be the target.

Even these short Virginian rivers can turn nasty in spate. I had the luck to see the Rappahannock after a single day of heavy rain in September 1992 and have not forgotten the sight: a mass of brown water, boiling yellow over the boulders that choke its bed at Fredericksburg, was rushing to the Chesapeake, tossing broken trees about and lapping the woodlands that edge its banks. The Chickahominy is a slighter river, but a month of rain had washed away the bridges that crossed it, leaving Keyes's corps with a real obstacle at its back. The Confederate troops that appeared to oppose it on 31 May, moreover, in a battle the North would call Seven Pines and the South, Fair Oaks, had a clear advantage of numbers—51,000 to 33,000. All was set for a victory. The outcome was lamentably different. Johnston was a good general—he had won the first battle of the war at Bull Run and would be the last Confederate commander to surrender in April 1865—but he failed to keep a grip of events and was let down by subordinates who misunderstood his orders. Perhaps his orders were not clear; he operated the Prussian principle of outlining his intentions and leaving his subordinates to execute them as they saw best. In an army like the Prussian, whose senior officers had trained together at the war academy, the system worked well; but the training of the Confederacy's officers was uneven, sometimes wholly deficient, and too often negated by individual temperament. James Longstreet, Johnston's principal subordinate, was notably erratic and temperamental. On 31 May at Seven Pines he misheard or misunderstood his orders, took the wrong road, decided to bridge a swollen stream he might have forded, wasted time so doing, fell into argument with a fellow divisional commander over precedence in using the bridge, and thus succeeded in confronting the Northern troops not with a concentration of force but with a succession of piecemeal attacks. Seven Pines should have been a Confederate victory. It turned into a sort of Union success, its main outcome being a change of command, for in his effort to retrieve the situation by personal intervention, Johnston strayed into the fire zone at Fair Dales, astride the railway line McClellan was using to bring his siege train forward, took a bold stance on a hillock, and was knocked off his horse by shell splinters. He was too badly wounded to continue serving Jefferson Davis as director of operations and was replaced at once by Robert E. Lee.

Lee, today the romantic hero of the Civil War to Northerners and Southerners alike, still had his reputation to make. Indeed, in the summer of 1862 his name did not stand high in the South. His campaign in West Virginia in 1861 had failed so badly that that homeland of crotchety backwoodsmen and squirrel hunters, defiant fighters for liberty in the War of the Revolution but proud of the poverty that kept them from owning slaves, proclaimed reverse secession and went over to the Union to found a new state. Richmond newspapers had then called him "Granny Lee" and "Evacuating Lee": now McClellan, hearing news of his appointment, characterised him as "cautious and weak. Under grave responsibility . . . likely to be timid and irresolute in action." A finger should not be pointed in retrospect; but during the next month—the third month since the Peninsular campaign had been opened—it was to McClellan that both North and South looked for action, and of action he gave no sign at all. Everything was against him. The roads were sodden; the bridges were down; the railroads needed rebuilding; the battering train of siege guns was not in place; the Seven Pines battle had disorganised his army; McDowell was still not with him (though one of his three divisions arrived during June); above all, he was dangerously outnumbered. On 25 June he telegraphed Washington to say that the "rebel force" stood at "200,000. . . . I shall have to contend against vastly superior odds . . . If [I am] destroyed by overwhelming numbers . . . the responsibility cannot be thrown on my shoulders."

In fact, though Lee had, by massing every man in the northeastern theatre, including at last Stonewall Jackson's valley army, succeeded in raising his numbers near Richmond to 90,000, McClellan still outnumbered him with 105,000; moreover, by cautiously pushing forward to the headwaters of the Chickahominy River, the Northern army was no longer divided by the watercourse as it had been before Seven Pines, and occupied an excellent position from which to attack. More Northern soldiers than ever were able to see Richmond's spires and hear their bells, only a thin earthwork and a screen of troops away; but still McClellan refused to move. In the end it was the "timid and irresolute" Lee who took the decision for him. Informed by galloping J. E. B. Stuart, one of the last of the Western world's cavalry swashbucklers, that the Union right flank at Mechanicsville was "in the air"—that is, neither rested on a defensible position nor was supported by an adjacent force—he decided to open a wide turning movement, around and then behind the Union army, on 26 June.

Ironically, he was to be forestalled, by what McClellan was now describing as one of a series of "partial attacks" designed to advance his artillery into a commanding position. On 25 June, McClellan sent forward troops from his right wing to skirmish across the old battlefield of Seven Pines and seize a piece of woodland known as Oak Grove, from which he planned to advance his heavy guns to high ground at Old Tavern and there open the bombardment of Richmond's defences. Because Lee was preparing major operations which were intended to take place the following day on exactly the same sector, McClellan's short-range advance bumped into part of the Confederate main deployment, and the encounter flared into a small battle that lasted the whole of the day. At the end, McClellan declared himself satisfied with the result, which brought him the ground he wanted, though at the cost of six hundred casualties. What he did not know was that this little engagement, now known as the Battle of Oak Grove, was to be the first in a week of continuous fighting, collectively to be called the Seven Days Battles, 25 June–1 July, which would culminate in the collapse of all his plans and the ignominious retreat of the Army of the Potomac to its original theatre of campaign in northern Virginia.

It is easily possible today to drive the whole circuit of the Seven Days Battles between breakfast and dinner. I did so in the late summer of 1992, though I had allotted much more time to what I planned as a preliminary reconnaissance. My exploration was a salutary reminder that there is no substitute, in the writing of military history, for going to see for oneself. Thirty years before, I had taught this campaign to my class of cadets at Sandhurst, and the cartographic image of the events of the last week of June 1862 remained impressed on my mind: 25 June, Oak Grove; 26 June, Mechanicsville; 27 June, Gaines's Mill; 28–29 June, the Union retreat to the James River and the actions at Peach Orchard, Savage Station, and White Oak Swamp; 30 June, Glendale and Frayser's Farm; 1 July, Malvern Hill. These are battlefields that looked widely separated on the maps I was using, the wonderful maps prepared by Ed Krasnoborski for that magnificent publication *The West Point Atlas of American Wars*. Years later I met Mr. Krasnoborski in his drawing office at West Point. I had specially asked to do so, for I rightly esteemed him to be a prince among mapmakers. I had imagined that he would occupy extensive, well-lit premises and command a large staff. I found him alone in a small windowless room, perched on a high stool at a tilted board, quite happy to be disturbed at his work but faintly bemused by my enthusiasm for what he did. Every word of my thanks was justified; there is still nothing to compare with *The West Point Atlas,* which remains the *Gray's Anatomy* of Western military history.

Yet, for all the clarity of the Krasnoborski maps, I had not properly grasped from them the special relationship between one place and another; despite the scale of miles at the bottom, they made everywhere look further apart than it actually was. This optical illusion does not affect military historians only; it is so well known among soldiers that they commonly ask each other, without embarrassment, at the map table, "Have you seen the ground yourself? What does it look like: How far [they usually mean in time] is X from Y?" The mistake I had made was the last: because McClellan's battles with Lee around Richmond had lasted seven days, I had imagined that their circuit would take almost as long. Setting out in my rented car from Chickahominy Bluff for Beaver Dam Creek, one of the most fiercely contested sections of front in the battle for Mechanicsville on 26 June, I had expected an hour of driving. I found it just round the corner. Gaines's Mill, fought the following day, was three miles down the road; the course of the retreat to the James, which lasted two days and involved four actions, runs along only eight miles of modern roadway; Frayser's Farm and Malvern Hill lie on the five miles of road—Virginia State Route 156— south of White Oak Swamp. Stops to inspect the sites and to read the series of splendid historical markers—grey-painted cast-iron columns put up by the Virginia State government in the 1930s—protract the tour. My reconnaissance—I was to drive over the route several times again later—lasted, however, a good deal less than a day. It was a vivid lesson in the difference between travelling time and campaigning time, and in the human inclination to take from a map what one expects to see, not what it is designed to tell you.

McClellan, in the immediate aftermath of his small success at Oak Grove, fell into different but familiar misapprehensions. "I shall have to contend against vastly superior odds," he telegraphed to Washington that night. What had alarmed him were reports of troop movements into Richmond, which he took to be the Confederate army in Mississippi marching up to join Lee. It was a phantom army on a phantom journey. The only troops arriving were Jackson's, from the Shenandoah Valley, but they were coming from the west, not the south, and by fits and starts. Jackson's muddled intervention in the Seven Days Battles temporarily undid much of the reputation he had won along the Shenandoah. At least McClellan had grasped that he was to be attacked; instead of contemplating a counterstroke, however, he issued orders to prepare for a retreat to the James—what possessed him to think of such a move, when his main base, constructed with great labour and containing mountains of stores, lay on the York River defies explanation—and warned his corps commanders to prepare to defend their entrenchments. "I wish to fight behind the lines if attacked in force." Here was timidity become almost paranoiac. A general in command of a superior force in an attacking position could think of nothing better to do with his troops than dispose them in entrenchments—which ought not to have been dug in the first place—astride the headwaters of the Chickahominy and await a weaker opponent's offensive.

It was late coming and should not have discountenanced a man of resolute will. Lee had fixed on Mechanicsville, five miles north of Richmond, as his centre of effort, intending there to turn McClellan's extreme right flank, which Jackson was approaching from a northerly direction. Mechanicsville then was not a town at all but a collection of buildings at a crossroads; a contemporary photograph shows some pleasant clapboard houses on a dirt road running through unfenced and worn meadow. McClellan had posted few troops there, and, as 26 June drew into afternoon, none of them expected to be attacked that day. When at four o'clock they were suddenly charged by Confederate infantry, they took fright, legged it to the rear, and did not stop until they found shelter in the nearest friendly entrenchments, which defended the eastern bank of a little tributary of the Chickahominy, Beaver Dam Creek. There, in what remained of the day, one of the nastier small battles of the Civil War was to be fought out until the smooth waters of the creek ran red.

Beaver Dam Creek is, I think, the most sinister little battlefield I have ever visited. Just to the north, at the top of a Park Service track which drops down to a concreted parking place, State Route 156 crosses the creek on a high modern bridge; it is just too far away for the sounds of the trucks using it to reach the visitor's ear. What I heard was the croaking of swamp birds and what I saw were willows, goldenrod in flower, poplars, and a scattering of those dead, grey, branchless trees standing up from the water in the swamp bottom so distinctive of American wetlands. The setting is intensely green and lush, the vegetation so dense that the battlefield, except in a slot to the north where the truck route shows through the trees, is entirely shut off from the outside world. The creek itself, though quite fast-flowing, is almost hidden under sedge and cresses. It may be about ten feet wide; the whole battlefield, from the bank down which the Confederates attacked to the higher bank on which the Union troops, a division of Pennsylvanians, awaited them behind timber stockades, is perhaps 150 yards across. It was a warm, deserted, oddly beautiful bowl of stillness when I saw it on a fine September noon; on the afternoon of 26 June 1862 it must have been a place of sudden horror.

The Pennsylvanians, 9,500 strong, were on the east bank, hidden on rising ground among trees, through which gaps had been cut to open fields of fire for their artillery; on the west bank, where the visitor stands today, more trees had been felled to form an entanglement. As so often in North American warfare, the abundance of timber was to influence directly the outcome of the fighting. A Confederate artilleryman judged the Union position to be "absolutely impregnable to a front attack." The Southern infantry, North Carolinans and Georgians, attacked none the less. They were repulsed and attacked again—and again. A Georgian carrying his regiment's colour had to wrap it round the staff to get through the entanglement; next day he found ten bullets in the fabric and another in the wood. "We were lavish of blood in those days," a Confederate general later wrote of a battle which was their first for many of his soldiers, "and it was thought to be a great thing to charge a battery of artillery or an earthwork lined with infantry." There were six Union batteries of thirty-two guns opposite the Confederates at Beaver Dam Creek. By the end of the afternoon's fighting, which Lee directly commanded himself from the western bank, 1,484 Confederates had been killed or wounded. The 1st North Carolina lost 142, including its colonel, lieutenant colonel, major, and six captains; the 44th Georgia lost 335 men, 65 per cent of its strength. It had been a terrible day; "nothing could be heard in the black darkness of that night," a survivor recalled, "save the ghastly moans of the wounded and the dying." It had also been Robert E. Lee's first battle as a commanding general and it had profited the Confederacy nothing at all.

A robust enemy would have profited from this local success to press home the advantage, or at least to reconsider plans for retreat. McClellan did no such thing. Though Jackson had signally failed to intervene at Mechanicsville, to the north of which he hovered about in uncharaceristic inactivity, while the grim battle of Beaver Dam Creek was fought to a close, his presence confirmed McClellan in all his fears of being outmanoeuvred and outnumbered. On the night of 26–27 June he ordered Fitz-John Porter, commanding the corps which had held the Beaver Dam Creek position, to fall back four miles to another line on high ground, behind Powhite Creek and Boatswain's Swamp, south of a tiny place called Gaines's Mill. The position was strong, but by retreating further down the Chickahominy, where the river widened, while leaving his army astride it, he risked physically dividing his force. The retreat also surrendered a long stretch of the railroad—the Richmond and York River—by which he had planned to bring his siege artillery forward from the landing place at White House on the York. These circumstances, avoidable though they were, were the justification for the decision, already half-formed in his mind, which he now definitively took to retreat to the James River. He called it "shifting his base of operations"; but, as he had an excellent base on the York and none on the other river, he was unarguably abandoning the offensive and embracing withdrawal.

Given that McClellan was going, he did so with efficiency. Indeed one of the foreign observers attached to his army, the Comte de Paris, noted that he showed "a firmness of decision" in issuing orders for retirement that he had never shown in the advance. Retreat in the face of the enemy was a technical problem; echoing the classic masters, McClellan now called it "one of the most difficult undertakings in war." Since, however, it could be done by the rule book—the rules laid down that a general should fight a firm delaying action while clearing the routes to his rear, evacuating the army's train of transport, and then falling back behind strong rearguards—and adherence to rules calmed, we may surmise, the anxieties to which McClellan's mind was prey whenever he had to grapple with the uncertainties of pressing forwards into ground controlled by the enemy, he solved the problem very efficiently. His engineers had built and rebuilt four bridges over the Chickahominy: the Grapevine Bridge and, named for their constructors, Alexander's, Woodbury's, and Duane's. The position McClellan had ordered to be held between Gaines's Mill and the Chickahominy covered all four. It rested on a plateau between Gaines's Mill and the Chickahominy, some forty feet high, two miles wide, and a mile deep, and much of it heavily wooded.

There is an extraordinary calm about this piece of the Peninsula battleground today. Perhaps the woodland is denser now than it was then—nineteenth-century photographs generally show, outside the swampland, a more open Peninsula—and it certainly presses hard against the escarpment on which Porter's troops took their stand to repel the Confederates on 27 June 1862. At the Watts House, one of the few scattered dwellings which occupied the tabletop of the plateau above Boatswain's Swamp, the forest so closely surrounds the farm and its mown enclosure that nothing of the outside world intrudes at all, no sound or sight of the twentieth century. Unlike Beaver Dam Creek, where a miasma of past blood-letting hangs in the hot air of the little amphitheatre, the Watts House clearing is a clean, cool, and tranquil place, with no hint of old violence about it. Yet the Battle of Gaines's Mill, part of which was fought on the lip of the ground that falls away here to the stream below, was a far longer and bloodier action than that of 26 June. In the opening stages, the two sides were more or less equally matched: Fitz-John Porter's corps, separated from the rest of McClellan's army by the Chickahominy, faced part of Lee's army, the rest of which was also south of the river. Porter, however, had a marked superiority in artillery, twenty batteries to nine, and over a hundred guns to less than fifty; on the other hand, while McClellan was leaving Porter to fend for himself, Lee was counting on Jackson to reinforce his line and so achieve a preponderance of numbers.

The oddity of the situation was that Lee did not grasp the moral superiority he enjoyed. He had no inkling of McClellan's collapse of will, imagined that his opponent was still fighting to protect his line of communications with the great Union base at White House on the York, and had not detected from any source of intelligence that Mc-Clellan was intent on retreating to the James River and so effectively on giving up his offensive altogether. Had he done so, he would have pressed events. As it was, he failed to get the battle going at full swing until noon, failed to energise Jackson, who was still behaving as if combat-fatigued by the Shenandoah Valley campaign, and so failed to bring all available force against the plateau on which the Watts House stands until late afternoon. Porter and his men showed a determination in defence which McClellan had abandoned altogether. While they rode out the storm of repeated Confederate attacks across Boatswain's Swamp and up the wooded slopes beyond it, McClellan was commanding the battle from south of the Chickahominy by telegraph in a bizarre anticipation of the generalship of the First World War. An aide who came forward on horseback found Porter watching the stream of wounded making their way back from the firing line, while Confederate shells dropped near him. "We're holding them but it's getting hotter and hotter" was all he said. When the aide returned to McClellan's headquarters, he found only the telegraph office still operating, the tents packed, horses saddled, wagons loaded, and McClellan sitting silent by himself on a tree-stump, awaiting the outcome.

Porter very nearly won the Battle of Gaines's Mill. His 35,000 men, who included several units of the tiny pre-war regular army, fired volley after volley, salvo after salvo, throughout the long hot afternoon, inflicting terrible casualties on each Confederate regiment that approached their earthworks. The 1st South Carolina Rifles lost half its strength killed and wounded, 309 men. The 20th North Carolina lost 272, the 4th Texas 253. The colour of the 7th North Carolina changed hands five times, as those carrying it were shot down in turn; thirty-two bullet holes were later found in the fabric. When bullet hit flesh, but particularly bone, the effect was terrible. Both sides were using some variant of the Enfield rifle, which threw a solid cone of lead, half an inch in diameter and weighing a full ounce, to a range of four or five hundred yards. The small-calibre bullet of the high-velocity rifles of the First World War would travel farther but usually made a neat puncture wound. The ball of the old smoothbore musket of King George's War would kill in close-range combat but otherwise, if it hit, would often track along a bone without breaking it or lodge in muscle; some of the Southern troops at Gaines's Mill were still carrying smoothbores. The Enfield bullet, by contrast, being both large and fast-moving, could do catastrophic damage, destroying large volumes of tissue or reducing bone to shattered fragments. To suffer wounding in a battle like Gaines's Mill, therefore, was not a passport off the battlefield, but might mean disablement for life or, indeed, death in the immediate aftermath.

Until mid-afternoon on 27 June, the weight of casualties fell on the Confederates. Lee had been finding the troops, however, to thicken his front, while McClellan sent almost none, though he had many to spare. At one stage he promised "the whole army" but released only two brigades, one-tenth of his available force; nor did he go to Fitz-John Porter's battle line himself. Lee, by contrast, and Stonewall, who had at last arrived, put themselves squarely behind the centre of the firing line as the light began to fade, urging their subordinates to carry the Union position at whatever cost. Some 35,000 men were now ranged against each other on either side, but in the Union line the heat and losses of the day were beginning to tell. So, too, was the burden of defence. The Confederates, buoyed up by the spirit of the offensive, gradually began to overcome. It would never be agreed which of the Confederate formations eventually achieved the break. When it came, in the centre of the line, the collapse was so rapid and widespread that credit for victory was difficult to apportion. An index of the scale of the Northern defeat was the number of guns lost, twenty-two pieces or nearly a quarter of the artillery, a clear indication that the retreating Union infantry passed through their own battery positions too rapidly for the gunners to hook in the teams and get the guns away. Only the descent of darkness, in which the attacking Confederates held fire for fear of hitting each other, saved Porter's corps from complete rout.

Had Jackson's Shenandoah Valley troops intervened in mid-afternoon, as Lee intended and expected, all would certainly have been up. Porter's troops would have been pushed against the Chickahominy and been slaughtered or forced to surrender. As it was, they pressed over the bridges in the dark and got back to the main position, where the sixty thousand men McClellan had not committed to their assistance waited about their campfires. In the interval before the pursuing Confederates cut the wire, he got off to Washington one last self-pitying telegram. "I have lost this battle because my force was too small. I again repeat that I am not responsible for this. . . . The Government has not sustained this army. . . . If I save this army now, I tell you [the Secretary of War] plainly that I owe no thanks to you or any other person in Washington. You have done your best to sacrifice this army."

A staff officer in the Washington telegraph office sensibly censored the last two insubordinate sentences, leaving Lincoln, still unapprised of the full extent of McClellan's moral collapse, to assure him of his continuing support. McClellan meanwhile was busying himself at the engineering work which he did best, covering the crossings of the Chickahominy with battery positions, having trenches dug, and directing the bridging of White Oak Swamp, the tributary of the Chickahominy which stood between him and the landings on the James River to which he planned to make his final retreat. Bridging was an operation at which the Army of the Potomac was now skilled. It had bridged to bring the railroad forward from White House and bridged the

Chickahominy. At high speed its bridging columns now constructed two crossings, one in the remarkable time of two hours. Across them throughout 28 June the Union army pulled back. It remained a formidable fighting force. Though it had lost 894 killed, 3,114 wounded, and 2,829 captured, Lee's losses were higher. He had given no prisoners, but his dead totalled 1,483 and his wounded 6,402, from a smaller army. He continued to misinterpret McClellan's intentions, not crediting that he could be in full retreat and believing that he might either recross the Chickahominy lower down and resume the offensive against Richmond or stand where he was and fight to regain the rail link to White House. It was only when a cavalry patrol brought news that Union troops had destroyed the railroad bridges in their faces and set White House ablaze that he grasped the truth and organised his army to press the Northerners in their retreat.

A series of small battles fought on 29–30 June on the roads south to the James River were the result. They form a confused episode, which the modern traveller follows with difficulty, for the armies were deployed to fight to the left and right of the roads, which therefore usually cross the lines at right angles. In some sectors the countryside is open, particularly at Savage Station on the old Richmond and York railroad, where the ground is bumpy, abandoned-looking heath rather like some nasty patch of the Western Front in France. In others the woodland is dense—is this second growth, invading old, worked-out farmland, as one suspects?—and along the watercourses the vegetation is very thick and lush. Yet the whole area is also strangely uninhabited, without town, village, or even farmstead to give a traveller bearings. Richmond is only ten miles away to the northwest, but this landscape seems to have no social or economic connection with it at all. In Europe the surroundings of a major city would be dotted with small centres of habitation, a pub or bistro or *Wirtschaft* every mile or so to offer hospitality. Henrico County is eerily deserted, only the odd gas station–cum–country store at a crossroads giving any sign of human settlement at all. The traveller here can easily go hungry and thirsty, as I did, and all the more readily understand why the American tourist in the European countryside is so charmed by the wayside inn, the husband-and-wife *estaminet,* the beer garden in a forest clearing. America might be like that, had time allowed; Europe's pattern of settlement reflects centuries of slow, short-range movement by horse or wagon or on foot, which required frequent stops for refreshment, sustenance, fodder, or stabling. In much of America, by contrast, the railroad often antedated the trunk road, and then the appearance of the motor car robbed the neighbourhood halting place of point. Those that existed in places of old settlement like the Peninsula must have disappeared over the last century, leaving nothing to replace them but those charmless caravanserais of Wendy's and Burger King restaurants, filling stations, and efficiency-unit motels into which the weary vacationer falls by default at the end of a day's driving. It is one of the greatest oddities of life in the richest country in the world that its hinterland is so bereft of civilisation's small comforts.

I did not pick up clear traces of the course of the Seven Days Battles again until I passed Glendale, now little more than a country store on State Route 156, and approached Malvern Hill, the site of the last battle of the Seven Days. On the way I had found Grapevine Bridge over the Chickahominy, almost destroyed in the May flood, rebuilt by McClellan's engineers, then destroyed by his engineers in the retreat from Gaines's Mill, then rebuilt by Stonewall Jackson's engineers, today a graceless county engineer's concrete span on Route 156. I had also found Savage Station, which McClellan briefly made his headquarters on 28 June, and White Oak Swamp, where the Union fought its main delaying action on 29 June; a wet wilderness in 1862, its banks have been drained today and it is little more than a sedate stream south of a modern railroad track. On the spot where Confederate and Union soldiers were busy killing each other 130 years earlier, I found an auction sale in full swing at a decrepit farmhouse, with neighbours bidding enthusiastically for tattered hymnbooks, Marshall Field catalogues, and long-superseded items of hand-agriculture equipment; an enterprising confectioner was selling ice-cream out of a small truck to a crowd seated on folding chairs on what might once have been a lawn, rapidly going back, as everything does in America, to secondary forest.

· These were brutal and bitter battles none the less. During the rearguard actions of 29 June at Savage Station and White Oak Swamp the Union army lost nearly two thousand men and the pursuing Confederates nearly a thousand. The next day, 30 June, there was a pitched battle at Glendale and Frayser's Farm, fought by McClellan to cover his taking of position on the feature he had correctly identified as the spot where he could deploy his superior numbers to fight an action that would halt his pursuers and allow him to get the army to safety down the James River. That spur was Malvern Hill, the highest elevation on the Peninsula, which covers the roads leading to the landing places on the river behind the ancient Shirley, Berkeley, and Westover plantations. The army of the North would make its escape through a spot called Harrison's Landing opposite Bermuda Hundred, where another Union attempt on Richmond mounted from Fortress Monroe would fail in 1864. During 30 June McClellan at first retreated to the river bank, where he lost touch with his own telegraphic link to the army five miles away and then, without appointing a subordinate to deputise for him in command, boarded the *Galena,* one of the gunboats which had fought the artillery duel with Fort Drewry on 15 May. As it cruised about the river firing on Confederate troops ashore, McClellan was in a strange state of elation; an observer who appreciated how complete his demoralisation was noted that, underneath, he was "a man . . . cut down. . . . He was unable to do anything."

His army had much to do. Some of it was still leaving the battle-field of White Oak Swamp, getting the long train of wagons on to the Quaker Road (today State Route 156) that leads to the James, and felling trees to impede the Confederate retreat; that American plethora of timber was once again playing its part in an operation of war. The rest of the army was assuming positions in which to defend the retreat to Malvern Hill, both against Jackson's troops pursuing it on the direct route south down Quaker Road and to form a flank against the rest of Lee's men, who were angling in from the left. The centre of the position was at Glendale, the crossroads where I stopped to refuel but failed to find lunch on Saturday, 26 September 1992, but the focus of the fighting was to lie at a nearby homestead, Frayser's Farm. This is high, dry, rather sandy countryside, where tall-standing corn intermingles with forest, fine but empty country now and not much changed, it appears from contemporary descriptions, since 1862. The Confederates certainly complained of the difficulty of spotting the enemy among the trees—two days earlier the 1st U.S. Sharpshooters had skirmished "Indian-style" in the woodlands along the Chickahominy—and now Union riflemen and artillery batteries took a heavy toll as their opponents pressed forward in an effort to cut their retreat to Harrison's Landing.

The results of the fighting can be found in the Glendale National Cemetery, in between Glendale itself and Malvern Hill, from which the bodies of those killed the next day have been brought also. They lie under little white rounded markers, inscribed with the barest of information—name, regiment, date of death. The starkness, matter-of-factness, of the cemetery took me aback. Glendale was the first American military cemetery I had visited, and I expected something more like those built and maintained by the Commonwealth War Graves Commission in France, in Flanders, and, indeed, in almost every country in the world. The British—and the soldiers of the Commonwealth and Empire who died with them in the wars of the twentieth century—are scattered wide. I have found War Graves Commission cemeteries wherever I have travelled, as tourist, correspondent, or historian, from Lebanon, where I was covering the civil war in 1983, to South Africa, where I went to investigate the Namibian war in 1984, to Pakistan, which I visited during the Afghanistan War in 1985; in Germany, in Israel, in Turkey, where the dead of Gallipoli lie within sight of Homeric Troy, in Australia, in Canada, and in the United States itself.

Commonwealth war cemeteries signal themselves from a distance. First, there are the indications of a gardened landscape—a mown verge to the roadside, a stretch of park wall in stone. Then, above the wall, there is a glimpse of flowering shrubs and of garden sculpture, a memorial stone, a cross, a classical gateway. Inside, the ideal English garden unfolds, roses, rosemary, bay, myrtle, and shaven turf, across which stretch the rows of white Portland headstones, carved with a cross, the regimental badge and title, the name, the age, and the date of death of the fallen soldier. At the bottom of the stone is space for a family inscription, two lines that read all the more poignantly for the effort made, often by simple people, to cram heartbreak into no more than a dozen words. The British war cemeteries move the visitor readily to tears, as they were intended to do. Edwin Lutyens, Britain's greatest modern architect, designed the monuments, Rudyard Kipling wrote the inscriptions that appear everywhere, from the Arctic to the South Pacific: "Their Name Liveth for Evermore"; "A Soldier of the Great War Known unto God." Death and beauty intermingle in a cunningly contrived Arcadia, eloquent of the ease with which the British fall into romantic communion with the ideas of self-sacrifice and love of country.

Other countries do things differently. The central point of the French national war cemeteries is the tricolour, symbol of liberty, equality, fraternity, floating above a field of white crosses, symbol of France, eldest daughter of the Church. The Germans bury their war dead among sombre evergreens in terrible mass graves; at Langemarck in Belgium, site of the slaughter of the German student volunteers of October 1914, 36,000 bodies, the same number as were killed in battle in the seven years of the Vietnam War, lie intermingled in a single plot no bigger than a stage on which Wagner's *Twilight of the Gods* might be sung; those who stand at its edge are brought to wonder at what dark forces underlie the German urge for dominance over the Old World. America's military cemeteries arouse different emotions altogether. The headstones are so small, the landscape which surrounds them so little interrupted by the digging and clearing which preceded their planting: this is a place, the visitor feels, which might go back to nature in a generation, as so much that is human interruption of the vastness of America has already gone back. I have found cemeteries elsewhere in the United States already relapsing into the wilderness: at Durham, Connecticut, where garter snakes have made their habitation among the elaborate, overgrown headstones of soldiers of the Revolution; at Princeton, where a tiny graveyard of Washington's battle of 1777 is reverting to scrub and briar.

Glendale, I felt as I walked over its rough-cut grass, was fated for the same forgetting. Its headstones commemorated an America which belongs to the past, an America of exclusive Anglo-Saxonism and simple state patriotism. The list of names I noted, though it contains a sprinkling of Irish and German, is preponderantly English of the two centuries of colonial settlement: Wilson, Burton, Atkins, Pottle, Hall, Cole, Lawrence, Wheldon, Long, Angell, Tarbell, Prosser, Denson, Goodrich, Tibbets, Cleeland, Coombs. There are Lawrences and Coombses in my Wiltshire village in England where, the parish record books testify, they have been born, married, and died since the sixteenth century. I feel little doubt that genealogy would establish a connection. Americans and Canadians come to our churchyard each year to peer at gravestones and mark names in their notebooks of family history. What I was doing at Glendale, as I walked among the tiny headstones, was pursuing a similar quest; but while our Coombses and Lawrences spread themselves over no more than a dozen or so square miles in places called Witham Friary, Milton-on-Stour, North Brewham, Marston Bigot, the American Coombses, Lawrences, and fellow settlers from the old country who lie at Glendale had come with their regiments to fight and die for the Union from places as far away as Michigan, Wisconsin, Maine, Utah, and California. The English are a people of fierce local loyalties; hereabouts villages only a mile apart

PENINSULA

ABOVE: Richmond, the
capital of the Confederacy,
1861

McClellan

Robert E. Lee, after the
Confederacy's defeat,
1865

The Battle of Williamsburg

TOP: "Stonewall" Jackson

BOTTOM: The Battle
of Malvern Hill

TOP: The Union retreat to Harrison's Landing

BOTTOM: McClellan faces Lincoln,
after the failure of the Peninsular campaign,
October 1862

TOP: The ruins of Richmond in 1865,
with the Capitol in the skyline

BOTTOM: The Virginia State Capitol today

TOP: Plains Indian hunting buffalo,
by George Catlin

BOTTOM: Indians catching wild horses,
by George Catlin

TOP: Cheyenne village on the Great Plains, c. 1870

BOTTOM: Custer in the uniform of his own design

Sitting Bull,
chief of the Hunkpapa Sioux

Custer with his Crow Indian scouts
before the Battle of Little Bighorn, 1876

Otto Becker's reconstruction of Custer's Last Stand;
the landscape remains much the same today.

CUSTER KILLED.

DISASTROUS DEFEAT OF THE AMERICAN TROOPS BY THE INDIANS.

SLAUGHTER OF OUR BEST AND BRAVEST.

GRANT'S INDIAN POLICY COME TO FRUIT.

A WHOLE FAMILY OF HEROES SWEPT AWAY.

THREE HUNDRED AND FIFTEEN AMERICAN SOLDIERS KILLED AND THIRTY-ONE WOUNDED.

SALT LAKE. U. T., July 5.—The correspondent of the Helena (Mon.) *Herald* writes from Still water, Mon., under date of July 2, as follows:

Muggins Taylor, a scout for General Gibbon, arrived here last night direct from Little Horn River and reports that General Custer found the Indian camp of 2,000 lodges on the Little Horn and immediately attacked it.

He charged the thickest portion of the camp with five companies. Nothing is k ... n of the operations of this detachment, except their course as traced by the dead. Major Reno commanded the other seven companies and attacked the lower portion of the camp.

How news of the disaster reached the nation: the *New York World*, 6 July 1876

Temporary graves
on the Little Bighorn battlefield

insist on their difference from each other. The English of Michigan and Maine who lie at Glendale had preserved that emotion but invested it in the vast tracts of the continent their settler ancestors had taken as home. There will be no real sadness if Glendale eventually goes back to nature. That would be in the spirit of the English escape from the narrow constriction of their Domesday fields to the wideness of the New World, where space enlarges the individual and his progeny, and time and history are dimensions to be left behind.

Glendale, a little clearing in the forest, holds the bodies of 1,192 soldiers, mainly Northerners, who died on 30 June or 1 July 1862. The majority were killed at Glendale and Frayser's Farm, a day of fighting in which McClellan's undirected army was at a disadvantage. At Malvern Hill, McClellan had the battlefield he wanted: Andrew Humphreys, his topographical engineer, wrote of "the splendid field of battle on the high plateau where the greater part of the troops, artillery etc. were placed." It has been called an American Waterloo, and there are indeed similarities: the Union position on the high ground, bisected by a good road, the long fields of fire sweeping down towards the positions from which the enemy had to launch an attack, and the strong flanks. Malvern Hill is, if anything, a better position than Waterloo, where Napoleon had high ground of his own on which to position artillery to oppose Wellington's, whose flanks were protected by some broken ground on the left and the orchards of Hougoumont on his right. Two streams, running through dense woods, absolutely define the Malvern Hill position, funnelling any enemy attack into a corridor no more than a mile wide. All this is grasped instantly by the visitor's eye, which sees a landscape that can have changed little in 130 years. "It was as beautiful a country as my eyes ever beheld," wrote Lieutenant Charles Haydon of the 2nd Michigan. "The cultivated fields, interspersed with belts and clusters of timber . . . wheat was in the shock, oats were ready for harvest, and corn was waist high." It was strikingly beautiful when I saw it in the late summer of 1992; then the corn had been cut and the fields burnt golden by three months of sun, but the woods stood tall and silent on each hand, their dark depths only hinting at the stream bottoms they concealed, and the Quaker Road down which McClellan's men had marched to deploy across the plateau and range their batteries on the crest was as empty as a country lane in the West of England. Not a sound broke the drowsy, noontide air, and not a sign remained to warn that on 1 July 1862 this had been a terrible place, except for the National Park Service's little marker and the recording machine's description of how, on the morning following the battle, enough of those wounded "were alive and moving to give the field a singular crawling effect."

McClellan should have won every fight he fought on the Peninsula. He did win Malvern Hill. He was, moreover, present in person. The morning of the battle, as at Waterloo, and the early afternoon were occupied with a great artillery duel. The Confederates might have given as good as they got, had they brought forward all the guns available, but for no good reason, except poor staff work, they did not. As a result, their two "grand batteries" positioned left and right of the Quaker Road (today at places off State Route 156 just south of Glendale Cemetery) were gradually overwhelmed by the greatly superior concentration of Union artillery on the Malvern Hill plateau. By three-thirty, when McClellan arrived after another morning cruising in the James aboard USS *Galena,* Lee had accepted that he was not going to win by gunfire and had sent forward his infantry. The point of assault was entrusted to Lewis Armistead, who had come bottom of the West Point class in which McClellan graduated one from the top and who was to die a year later at Gettysburg placing his hand on the muzzle of a Union cannon on Cemetery Ridge. He might have died at Malvern Hill; terrain and tactical situation were not dissimilar. In the event, his brigade was so devastated by Union gunfire that it was driven to ground and dropped early out of the battle. Its advance was succeeded by a succession of others, launched as fast as troops could be put into action. Lee's problem was not, as it had been earlier in the Seven Days Battles, to find formations. All stood ready to hand, including Stonewall Jackson's men; the problem was to find space on which to deploy them. In the tunnel of fire the ground and the Union positions contrived, the Confederates were reduced to mounting one narrow frontal assault after another, at fearful cost and without productive effect. Lee, who had placed himself in the centre of his battle line, tried to open the engagement to the flanks, but, even had his men succeeded in finding a way over the two streams that hemmed them in, Turkey and Western Runs, it seems doubtful that the pattern of the fighting could have been altered to productive effect. The battle had acquired a momentum and logic of its own, rather as the dreadful trench-to-trench assaults of the First World War were to do. As darkness fell, a last Confederate charge reached the summit of Malvern Hill, forcing one Union battery to limber up and retire. The gun line itself held firm, however, and under its unrelenting cannonade the Confederate line fell back. When one of his subordinates proposed making a last attempt on the iron front of Union batteries, Stonewall replied, "I guess you had better not try it, sir." It was the admission of defeat.

Next morning the two sides, separated by the "singular crawling effect" of a no-man's-land full of wounded survivors, counted the cost. Lee's army had lost over 1,000 dead, McClellan's, which had fought largely an artillery battle, about 400. The toll of wounded was very high also, more than 4,000 Confederates, nearly 2,000 Union. Altogether, the Seven Days Battles had caused 36,000 casualties, and the total for the Peninsular campaign as a whole, from the landing at Fortress Monroe to the final evacuation, would reach 56,000. This from a force, it was later calculated, which approached a quarter of a million combined, North and South.

All for nothing, too, from the Union point of view. On the morrow of Malvern Hill, some of McClellan's subordinates raged against his determination to behave as a defeated general. Phil Kearny, commanding Third Corps, announced that "I, Philip Kearny, an old soldier, enter my solemn protest against this order for retreat. . . . I say to you all, such an order can only be prompted by cowardice or treason." Kearny was indeed an old soldier. He had lost an arm in the Mexican War in 1847 and, as a freelance, won the Legion of Honour with Napoleon III's Imperial Guard fighting in 1859 at Solferino and Magenta. In the Peninsula he had had the eerie experience of picking up an echo of Washington's victory over Cornwallis when, on reconnaissance beyond Fortress Monroe, he was told by an aged plantation slave of his memory of hearing cannon firing at Yorktown in 1781. What Washington had achieved he believed McClellan could do also. Richmond lay only ten miles from the battlefield; with resolute will—and the soldiers were willing to fight—McClellan might have used the victory of Malvern Hill to march on the Confederate capital, carry the defensive lines around it, and end the war. McClellan would have none of it. Apparently oblivious of what his subordinates felt, he retired aboard the *Galena* and issued orders for retreat to Harrison's Landing eight miles away along the river road. He had reconnoitred it as a safe haven in person, while he might have been commanding in battle, and was determined to withdraw the Army of the Potomac into it rather than exploit his success.

He insisted, particularly in his Independence Day address to the army on 4 July, that the move was a change of base, as he had been insisting to Lincoln since the second of the Seven Days Battles, and he made the new base very strong. Into a space only a mile deep and four miles long, flanked by Herring and Kimmage's creeks, backed by the James River, which Union gunboats controlled, and fronted by a hastily dug line of strong earthworks and battery positions, he crowded all ninety thousand men of the Army of the Potomac, with their stores and guns. Lee, after one look at it, declared it to be impregnable. McClellan's claim that it represented the culmination of a strategic redeployment cut less ice with his soldiers. "We are at a loss," wrote Sergeant Edgar Newcomb of the 19th Massachusetts, "to imagine whether this is strategy or defeat."

It was defeat in every sense, of course, except McClellan's willingness to admit it. For the next six weeks he protested to Washington that his plans remained entirely offensive, that he only needed more troops to make victory a certainty, and that his new plan was another change of base: to cross the James to the south bank, advance on Petersburg, the rail junction twenty-five miles below Richmond, entrench himself there, await a convergent attack by other Union forces on the Confederate capital, and so complete its capture. Lincoln came to Harrison's Landing on 8 July to hear McClellan's assurances that victory was still possible—given 100,000 men—and Henry Halleck, the new general-in-chief, came on 25 July. That hard-headed professional heard McClellan out, demonstrated that if, as he insisted, Lee now had 200,000 men—pure fantasy, as with all McClellan's intelligence assessments—the Confederates would defeat both the Army of the Potomac and any other marching to co-operate with it, and gave him a stark choice: either resume the advance on Richmond from Harrison's Landing with such local reinforcements as were available or quit the Peninsula for good. McClellan seemed to accept the ultimatum; but, as soon as Halleck was back in Washington, he telegraphed him with further alarmist estimates of Lee's strength and demanded yet more reinforcements if he were to move. Halleck had now heard enough. McClellan, he said, "does not understand strategy and should never plan a campaign." On 30 July he wired the order to begin evacuating from Harrison's Landing the Army of the Potomac's sick, of which unhygienic conditions in the crowded encampment had produced thousands; on 3 August he issued the command to abandon the Peninsula altogether and bring the army north again to open a fresh campaign in upper Virginia in combination with the forces McClellan was demanding should be sent to him.

So the great army began its withdrawal down the river road, today State Route 5, across the Chickahominy, past Williamsburg and Jamestown, through the old Yorktown lines it had besieged so laboriously in April, across the ground on which it had concentrated in March, to Fortress Monroe, there to embark for Aquia Creek and Alexandria on the Potomac. It was the completion of the rondo which had begun almost six months earlier. Then the army had taken ship with every hope and much objective indication that Richmond was about to fall into its grasp. By September, it would be Washington that lay under threat, with Lee north of the Potomac, Harpers Ferry in Confederate hands, and a desperate battle about to be fought at Sharpsburg near Antietam Creek; its result forced Lee to withdraw to the Rappahannock, that *de facto* military frontier between South and North, but the Union effort to secure a bridgehead across it at Fredericksburg in December ended in defeat and repulse; 1862 was not a good year for the Union cause in the eastern theatre of war.

The landscape around Fredericksburg, that charming little town of grey-painted clapboard houses on narrow, tree-lined colonial streets, bears the evidence of the long ensuing struggle along the hilly banks of the Rappahannock to this day. Trenches follow the defensible contours, protected here and there by restored timber *chevaux-de-frise,* and battery positions can be discerned among the enveloping woodlands. It is only a few minutes' drive northwestward to the battlefield of Chancellorsville, scene of Lee's supreme act of generalship and of Stonewall Jackson's death in April 1863, and entrenchments follow one all along the road. General Hal Nelson led me along the route in 1992, elucidating with brilliant clarity each step of the campaign, from the rapids, which make Fredericksburg the head of navigation on the Rappahannock, to the unbuilt railroad track along which Jackson drove his battle-winning flank march on the day before he died.

Yet the memory of this narrow theatre of war that remains most strongly with me is of the shoreline that binds it so closely together: the low, lush, overhung banks of the Chesapeake at Annapolis, from which part of McClellan's army sailed for the Peninsula and along which I navigated in 1983 in a naval academy professor's sloop; the upper reaches of the Potomac under eighteenth-century, brick-built Alexandria, opposite Washington, where the main body embarked; the densely forested York River; the long, sloping sward beneath Shirley and Westover plantations at Harrison's Landing, where McClellan lingered after the Seven Days while his thousands of men and horses trampled the light, yellow sandy soil to pulp; the dank, gloomy defile of the James River at Drewrys Bluff, high-water mark of his attempt upon the defences of Richmond; and above all, the grass-grown hummocks of the Yorktown redoubts opposite Gloucester, defending nothing now but the delicate beauty of a forgotten colonial seaside place, but in 1781 and in 1862 the focus of giant military enterprise. "These frowning battlements," General John Magruder had told his army in the days while he was awaiting McClellan's assault, "are turned in this second war of liberty against the enemies of our country." Too flowery; but the recurrence of decisive conflict on "these very plains of Yorktown," as he called them, re-emphasises the dominance of the shape and size of America over the wars that its inhabitants fight within it. The French conquest and loss of Canada had begun and ended on the great headland of Quebec; the American struggle to win their liberty from the British had begun with an assault on Quebec and ended on the headland between the York and the James, where the English had planted their first place of settlement coevally with Champlain's arrival in the St. Lawrence; the first great Northern assault on the stronghold of Southern power had begun at Yorktown and petered out in a withdrawal past the original English Jamestown colony; but the culminating act of the Civil War in 1864 would open with a return to the battlefields of the Seven Days at White Oak Swamp and Malvern Hill and a transhipment of much of Grant's army up the James to the vicinity of Harrison's Landing and an advance to Petersburg to begin that investment which McClellan had claimed was the object of his "change of base" but which he lacked the resolution to initiate.

Two and a half centuries of the European presence in North America had seen much warfare, but the spaces of the continent had been touched by little of it. The sea and its inlets, the great rivers and their tributaries—St. Lawrence, Mississippi, Ohio, Tennessee, Cumberland, Hudson, Mohawk—the Great Lakes by which they are fed or into which they run, appear in hindsight more significant altogether as determinants of events than any of the human players who acted out the drama of campaign in the narrow corridors made available by nature for their efforts. A few Americans whose intelligence attuned them to accept the smallness of man before the vastness of nature in the New World displayed an ability to work with, rather than against, its forces: Samuel Champlain, with his instinctive grasp of the unity of the lakes, the St. Lawrence, and the Hudson, was one; George Washington, with his understanding of how the hinterland could be used as a barrier against the settled littoral, was another; Benedict Arnold, who possessed a fierce determination to exploit difficulties of weather and terrain as a means of surprising his enemies, was a third; perhaps the greatest of all was Ulysses S. Grant, whose ability to carry in his head a mental map of the Civil War's nodal points made him the master of manoeuvre between them. Most of the rest, however, those who approached warfare in America in terms of European strategy or tactics, owed the defeats they thereby suffered to their failure to comprehend how fundamentally different the New World was from the Old. No one was more guilty of that fault than McClellan. What remained of the warfare to be fought in America would be directed by pupils and subordinates of Grant, whose gifts were for generalship over wide spaces and in the continent's interior. "I will take no backward step" was his watchword in the harshest and most impenetrable of terrains. In the era of Grant's presidency which followed the Civil War, America's step lay forward, across the wide Missouri and into the heartland of European America's last enemy, the native Americans of the Great Plains. That was where the final battles on American soil were to be fought.

FIVE

....

Forts on the Plains

I FIRST SAW the gateway to the Great Plains, just as I first saw the gateway to New France, on a day of intense cold. Both gateways stand high above mighty rivers, that of New France above the St. Lawrence at Quebec, that to the Great Plains above the Missouri at Fort Leavenworth. An aeroplane had brought me to Leavenworth from the beginnings of spring in the Carolinas, from Charleston via Charlotte to St. Louis, the old mid-point of the French Empire—whose water routes connect with the Great Lakes and Canada, with the Illinois country, with the Dakotas, and with New Orleans and the Gulf—to Kansas City. There the end of winter showed a bleak and desolate landscape. Patches of tired snow lay about on the eastern banks of the river; the grass which it did not cover was seared lifeless by months of wind from the north. The far bank of the Missouri, rising in a line of low bluffs above the wide flow of leaden water, stared bare and brown at the visitor arriving from the Atlantic side. No shred of vegetation relieved the escarpment to promise any awakening from the iron sleep of winter. There was a hint of building on the skyline. The only other evidence of man's passage this way was a great incised scar, hundreds of yards wide, climbing the far shore from the water's edge to the crest.

"That was the way the wagons went" was my host's answer to my question. Roger Spiller, part-Cherokee, professor of military history at the U.S. Army's Command and General Staff College, had stopped the car on the way from the airport to survey the approach to America's other half, the half that begins on the Mississippi–Missouri and leads fifteen hundred miles westward to the Pacific Coast of Oregon and Cal-

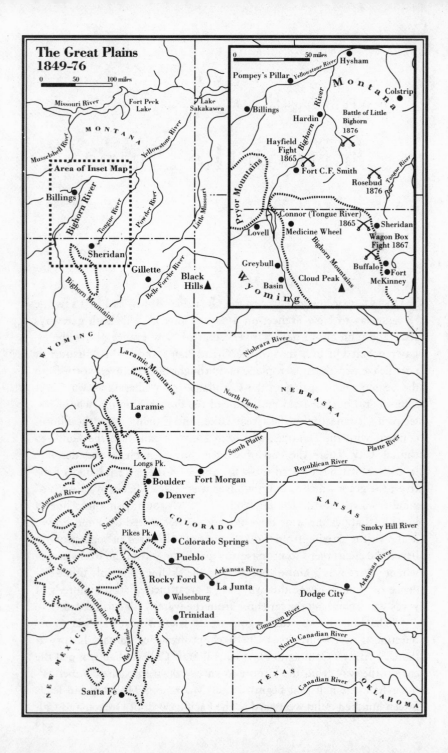

The Great Plains
1849–76

0   50   100 miles

Missouri River
Fort Peck Lake
Lake Sakakawea

MONTANA

Musselshell River
Yellowstone River
Little Missouri

Area of Inset Map

Billings
Bighorn River
Tongue River
Powder River

Sheridan
Gillette
Belle Fourche River
Bighorn Mountains

Black Hills ▲

WYOMING

Laramie Mountains
Niobrara River

NEBRASKA

North Platte

Laramie

South Platte

Longs Pk. ▲
Boulder
Fort Morgan
Republican River

Denver

Colorado River

COLORADO

KANSAS

Sawatch Range

Pikes Pk. ▲
Colorado Springs
Smoky Hill River

Pueblo
Rocky Ford
Arkansas River
La Junta
Arkansas River

San Juan Mountains

Walsenburg
Dodge City

Trinidad

NEW MEXICO

Cimarron River
North Canadian River

Rio Grande

Santa Fe

TEXAS

Canadian River

OKLAHOMA

Inset Map

0   50 miles

Pompey's Pillar
Yellowstone River
Hysham

Montana
Colstrip

Billings
Hardin
Bighorn River

Battle of Little Bighorn 1876 ⚔

Hayfield Fight 1865 ⚔
Fort C.F. Smith

Rosebud 1876 ⚔
Tongue River

Pryor Mountains

Connor (Tongue River) 1865 ⚔
Sheridan

Lovell
Medicine Wheel

Wagon Box Fight 1867 ⚔

Greybull
Bighorn Mountains
Buffalo
Fort McKinney

Basin
Cloud Peak ▲

Wyoming

ifornia. "They crossed here, the people going west after the Civil War, and hauled their wagons up the bluff to the interior of the fort. Then they set off across the plains, on the Santa Fe Trail to Texas or the Oregon Trail to California and the Northwest. The trails divide about eight miles inland. Either way they had half a continent to cross."

I stared in bemusement at the scar for a long time. There is such a scar on the western flank of Salisbury Plain, which I can just glimpse a mile away through the beeches and oaks beyond my study window; but it is only a few dozen feet wide and was cut into the chalk by Bronze Age people four thousand years ago to guard the emergence of an ancient pack route from the Somerset Levels through the thickets of Selwood Forest to the dry uplands that lead to Stonehenge. Alfred the Great brought his army that way in the ninth century A.D. to defeat the Danes at the battle of Ethandune. Drovers used it within living memory to herd their flocks of sheep to summer grazing from the wetter ground at the plain's foot. Today it survives only by careful conservation, and in its heyday it was never more than one link in a route perhaps a hundred miles long. Beside the Leavenworth wagon scar, it is scarcely better than a scratch in a tiny, prehistoric landscape. Its significance is local and now almost forgotten. The Leavenworth scar opens the story of the greatest event in modern American history, the departure of the migrants, from the temperate, forested territory of the Atlantic east to the Great Plains, the Rocky Mountains, and the Eldorado of the Pacific coast.

It was with the greatest excitement, therefore, that I crossed from the outskirts of Kansas City—by a trick of nomenclature a place in the state of Missouri—to Kansas proper, the territory of the Kansa Indians, via the bridge that now spans the river, and entered the gates of Fort Leavenworth. I had come, inevitably, to give a lecture, to the students of the Staff College, whose buildings have long ago overflowed the boundaries of the original fort. They contain today one of the most magnificent military libraries in the Western world, a thousand earnest students, eager for military advancement, and the School of Advanced Military Studies, training the cream of the crop to be the army's future thinkers; in 1990, General Schwarzkopf turned over to them the task of outlining the strategy for Operation Desert Storm. It was odd to think of the plan for the most complex air-ground-sea campaign in the history of warfare being hatched eight thousand miles from the scene of action and on the site of an old Indian-fighting fort half a continent distant from salt water. Yet some traces of the old fort remain. It was to these, as soon as my duty was discharged, that I turned my attention.

The fort had been founded in 1827 by Captain Henry Leavenworth as a base for soldiers detailed to protect merchants trading overland from Missouri into Mexico, which then occupied the whole of the modern United States' Southwest. He had come from Fort Jefferson at St. Louis, where a few of its fine Federal buildings still stand on the high ground of the eastern bank; they make a favourite backdrop for high-school prom photographs. The sight of radiant and extraordinarily good-looking young people in evening dress posing before the Cyclopean masonry of the old magazine remains for me a snapshot of the promise of American life. Leavenworth's commission had been to find a site at the mouth of the Little Platte on the eastern shore, but he found no suitable place. Twenty miles down the Missouri, however, he was attracted by the bluffs in the west bank, landed, pitched camp, and had a rough stone wall hastily built as a protection against the local Indians.

By one of those now familiar coincidences, he had hit upon a place previously fortified by Europeans. In 1744 a French engineer called Chevalier Pierre René Harpin de la Gautrais had selected the Leavenworth bluffs as a suitable location for a trading post among the Kansa Indians, built a stockade eighty feet square, and named it for the Governor of Louisiana, François Pierre Rigaud de Cavaignal. For a while it flourished as the usual sort of centre for rowdy, fur-seeking *voyageurs*, but the Indians soon began to drift away to better hunting grounds, while the French garrison departed in 1753 to campaign against the British in the widening war for Canada. By 1764, two years after France had ceded Louisiana to Spain, the fort was abandoned, and it soon fell into decay.

It did not disappear altogether from human ken; in July 1804 the Lewis and Clark expedition, en route to Oregon and the Pacific from St. Louis, camped on an island nearby and a Frenchman in the party—could it have been the legendary Charbonneau, husband of Sacajawea, the Shoshone girl they were to liberate from the Minnetarees the following year?—remembered that there had once been a French fort on the spot; the expedition's journal of 2 July 1804 records that "the situation of the fort may be recognised by some remains of chimneys, and the general outline." Thereafter, however, its traces disappeared altogether, taken back to nature, as so much is in America, by the assault of the continent's climate. Despite searches by the Staff College's historians, nothing of it has been found again. The congruences remain compelling; France, Spain, the fur business, the migratory Indians, the British war for Canada, the United States' exploration of its "noble bargain" in the Louisiana Purchase, the trade with Mexico. An American fort is so often a nodal point, both in time and space. Leavenworth, like St. Louis, from which it was founded, knots several regions by water, the Northwest by the Missouri, the Great Lakes and the Gulf by the Mississippi; by land it opened routes to the Great Plains and to the Old Southwest of Mexico and New Spain. In time it connects the government exploration of the Northwest and the region's penetration by the ungovernable mountain men, the mercantile venture to Mexico, its defeat by the American army in 1846, and the cession of the Southwest to the United States in 1848; the settlement of the Great Plains by wagon train and their opening to worldwide export of grain by the building of the railways—the Kansas Pacific and the Atchison, Topeka and Santa Fe railroads start spitting distance away; and, finally, the doleful story of the resettlement of America's native inhabitants, their desultory resistance to the incoming white hordes, their belated decision to fight for their lands, and their ultimate defeat by the United States Army.

Some, if not all, of this is commemorated within the walls of Fort Leavenworth's Memorial Chapel, a small, shadowed place of extraordinary poignancy. I entered expecting the undenominational bleakness of military convention. I found a tiny shrine of warriordom, the aisles pillared with the polished bronze barrels of 12-pounder mountain howitzers, the walls covered with tablets commemorating the dead of campaigns far and near. The image of the old chapel at Sandhurst, Britain's West Point, came instantly to mind. There, in a similarly reverential gloom, brass and marble recall the deaths of officers killed fighting tribesmen on the North-West Frontier of India or the Mahdi's fanatical followers in the Sudan, or drowned in the attempt to rescue comrades, or lost on imperial exploration, or—there is more than one of these—murdered by treachery on peace-making missions to remote hill villages or desert camps. Leavenworth's chapel tells much the same story: "Died from wounds received in battle at Santiago de Cuba, July 1, 1898"; "Congressional Medal of Honor for Conspicuous Gallantry. Davenport Bridge, Virginia, July 5th, 1864"; "Killed near Fort Nio-

brava, Nebraska, while in command of a detachment pursuing horse
thieves and deserters"; "Drowned in attempting to save the life of a
brother officer, Camp Supply, Arizona, 1872"; "Died at Cape Sabine,
Grinness Land, Greely Polar Expedition"; "Killed in action August 4,
1918, near Ville-Savoye, France, while gallantly leading his battalion";
"Died at El Obeid, Egyptian Sudan, April 20th, 1941"; "Killed in action at Carrizal, Mexico, 1916. Engagements Philippine Insurrection,
San Miguel, San Isidro-Parañaque, Las Piñas–Santa Cruz, Erected by
his classmates"; "Lost in plane crash off Okinawa, Ryuku Islands, 26
August 1946." These little tablets are a reminder of something a European easily overlooks: that the United States Army, just as much as the
imperial armies of France and Britain, has a worldwide history of service in Latin America, China, and Africa, as well as in Europe and the
islands of the far Pacific. There is an echo here of "Taps" sounded in
distant cantonments, of the rattle of Springfields in the Philippine
boondocks, of the creak of saddle leather beyond the Rio Grande, of
the muttered complaints of men in campaign hats and canvas leggings
settling into their stride on the dusty road from Tientsin to the Forbidden City.

   Mentally I saluted them, men whom duty had taken far from home
to die in places where George Washington had passionately believed
American soldiers had no business; but the principal emotion Leavenworth's Memorial Chapel left with me was of intimacy with battlefields
closer at hand. For every commemoration of a death suffered beyond
the seas there were a dozen others inflicted on the Great Plains, along
the edge of the Rockies, or on the desert frontiers of Mexico: "Mortally wounded in action near Nacori, Mexico, during an attack on his
command of Indian scouts by a force of Mexicans, January 11th,
1886"; "Died of wounds received in action with hostile Indians";
"Killed in action with hostile Apache Indians at Cibicu Creek, Arizona,
August 30th, 1887"; "Killed in the line of duty by Apache Indians at
San Carlos, Arizona, erected by his classmates of the USMA, and the
officers of his Regiment"; "Killed in action with Bannock Indians";
"Died of wounds received in action with Indians"; "Killed while in the
field against hostile Indians"; "Killed in action with hostile Indians,
Sierra San Mateo, New Mexico"; and, the longest list of all, that begin-
ning "In Memoriam Officers 7th Cavalry, Little Bighorn, Montana,
June 25th, 1876, Lieutenant Colonel George A. Custer, Brevet Major-
General, USA" and ending twelve names later with "2nd Lieutenant

William Van W. Reilly." The U.S. Army's chief mythic episode in its war with native America has its spiritual consummation under the steep-pitched eaves of the Memorial Chapel. It had had its beginnings nearby also, for the 7th Cavalry had wintered at Leavenworth throughout the 1870s, years when its mission was intimately bound up with the human drama that left the great churned-over scar on the face of the escarpment above which the chapel stands. The scar—will it last as long as the scratchings of the Bronze Age people on the green flank of Salisbury Plain at Whitesheet Hill?—remains as the single most graphic relic of the westward movement, while the saga of the 7th Cavalry is read and read again by Americans as a commentary on the story of emigration, settlement, conflict with, and final victory over, the original inhabitants of the continent in their struggle to preserve a way of life for which the urgent modern world could make no room. What began so tentatively at Fort Leavenworth in the 1820s would be settled for ever fifty years later by the Indians' doomed act of defiance on the banks of the Little Bighorn twelve hundred miles to the west.

Emigration and the Great Plains

The Great Plains, in the popular imagination, began as an empty land, empty, that is, of anything but buffalo and Indians. The Great American Desert was what two early government explorers, Zebulon Pike— of Pikes Peak—and Stephen Long, called it. Horace Greeley, who urged "Go West, young man!"—he meant California—wrote in 1859 that the Great American Desert was a reality and that "every day's sun is extending it." That, alas, was to prove true in the dry years which reached one of their peaks in the 1930s when Steinbeck launched *The Grapes of Wrath* at the social conscience of America: " . . . the sun shone redly, and there was a raw sting in the air. During the night the wind raced faster over the land, dug cunningly among the rootlets of the corn, and the corn fought the wind with its weakened leaves until the roots were freed by the prying wind and then each stalk settled wearily sideways toward the earth and pointed the direction of the wind. The dawn came, but no day. In the gray sky a red sun appeared, a dim red circle that gave a little light, like dusk; and as that day advanced, the dusk slipped back toward darkness, and the wind cried and whimpered over the fallen corn. . . . The people came out of their houses and smelled the hot stinging air and covered their noses from it. . . . Men stood by their fences and looked at the ruined corn, drying fast now, only a little green showing through the film of dust. The men were silent and they did not move often. And the women came out of the houses to stand beside their men—to feel whether this time the men would break."

The farmers who were broken by the dustbowl, however, were the victims of eighty years of soil-stirring, during many of which the winds had brought rain and the settlers had flourished. The Norwegians of Rolvaag's *Giants in the Earth*, another great novel of plains life, found "the finest soil you ever dreamed of—a veritable land of Canaan." It was the promise of "a nameless, blue-green solitude, flat, endless, still" which brought them from Europe, up the St. Lawrence, then to Minnesota, and finally to the Dakotas to make a new life. Yet the plains they found in the 1870s had already ceased to be empty; fingers of settlement were creeping out into the best land, that watered by the rivers which flow into the Missouri and Mississippi; indeed, modern scholars deny that the plains had been "empty" in the European sense even before the promise of "free" land had begun to draw Scandinavians and Germans, Czechs and Russians westward, any more than Canada west of the Great Lakes was empty in the eighteenth century. The *coureurs de bois* and then *voyageurs* had already begun to make sense of the wilderness, to form Indian alliances, to interbreed, to overwinter, to spin a filigree of increasingly permanent habitation at a time when French Canada's centre of gravity remained fixed in the St. Lawrence. In the same way, the region between Spanish America's Texan and Californian boundaries and Anglo-Saxon America's frontier on the Mississippi had already been penetrated by the early nineteenth century by transients of many callings, traders, trappers, hunters, proto-ranchers and cattlemen, missionaries, and soldiers. The Great Plains of the buffalo and the Indians who lived in symbiosis with the herds had lost their isolation years before Captain Leavenworth arrived to plant his bridgehead on the west bank of the Missouri; perhaps their isolation had gone two centuries earlier, when the first horse escaped or was stolen or bargained away from its Spanish owner and passed into Indian hands. It was the coming of the horse on to the Great Plains that initiated their opening to the outside world, transformed their age-old culture, and imposed a unity on the vast region not possible of attainment during the millennia when movement by foot, on the trail of the herds, was the only means of traversing its vast distances.

Today the Great Plains are held to lie within the boundaries of all or some of ten states of the Union: Montana, Wyoming, Colorado, New Mexico to the west, North and South Dakota, Nebraska, Kansas, and Oklahoma to the east, and the vast expanse of Texas to the south. Geographers discriminate more precisely, particularly between the short-grass and long-grass plains, which lie respectively west and east of the hundredth meridian, a boundary between uncertain rainfall, which may inflict years of drought on the short-grass farmers, destroy their economies, and threaten the destruction of the ecology itself, and the higher and more certain rainfall of the belt nearer the Mississippi–Missouri. The plains together form a zone of high land, raised by the silting of the Continental Divide by aeons of precipitation which has created a west–east gradient, five thousand feet high at the foot of the Rockies and petering out on the Missouri into the bluffs on which Fort Leavenworth stands. The west–east distance across the gradient is some five hundred miles, between Leavenworth and Pikes Peak, but from south to north, comprehending the Great Plains extension into the Canadian prairies, more than fifteen hundred miles. Within this expanse of 750,000 square miles of level and treeless territory—it is the treelessness of the plains that is their distinguishing characteristic—geographers recognise some significant subdivisions. On the west bank of the Mississippi–Missouri, immediately behind Leavenworth, for example, the countryside does not differ significantly from that of the Middle West: rolling hills, belts of forest, smaller and larger river valleys, none of it unfamiliar to the visitor from Western Europe. It is beyond the hundredth meridian, roughly the line of the western boundaries of Arkansas, Kansas, Nebraska, and the Dakotas, that the terrain takes on its steppe character. Below the Platte River, which enters the Missouri near Omaha, Nebraska, and forms the north–south division between better and worse farming land, the land falls into three strips—Low Plains, High Plains, and the Upland Trough—which, running east–west, resemble each other in offering grass cover of varying richness to the farmer and rancher in Nebraska, Kansas, Oklahoma, and Texas. Above the Platte, in the Dakotas, Wyoming, and Montana—Montana, one and a half times the size of the United Kingdom, today has only 750,000 inhabitants—climate and soil combine to confront the settler with vast areas of inhospitable land. The high, rich

Black Hills of Dakota teem with game which hides in their dense forests; elsewhere there is much badland and barren river valley amid this dry hill territory. Buffalo roamed where it could, and the Indians preyed on it, but the northwestern Great Plains threatened heartbreak to farmers who hacked arable fields from its semi-arid surface.

Many who came that way in the mid-nineteenth century were, of course, bent not on staying but on pressing forward, through the Rockies, to the promised Arcadia of California and Oregon. Geography largely determined the routes they should take. While the Santa Fe Trail was chiefly a human creation, pieced out to connect the Leavenworth bridgehead with the termination of the Old Spanish Trail from California at Santa Fe itself, the line of the California and Oregon trails was fixed by the discovery of the South Pass, the easiest way through the Rockies in what today is southwestern Wyoming. It was only on the other side that they diverged, the Oregon Trail northwestward towards the valley of the Columbia River and Vancouver, the California Trail southwestward along the line of the Humboldt River (today Interstate 80) and so across the Sierra range to San Francisco.

There are many names associated with the penetration and exploration of the plains, the Rockies, and the Pacific coastland, and there must have been many unknown to us who took a hand in the work as well. Some were the leaders of government-sponsored expeditions, some were capitalist entrepreneurs, some missionaries, some bravados or toughs, some unlettered hunters or trappers, some traders, some free spirits who, like Daniel Boone, heeded the call of the wild. First and in many ways most remarkable was Francisco Coronado, who, at the behest of the Spanish governor of Mexico, set out northward in 1539 with a party of several hundred and during the next four years journeyed a thousand miles northward into southern Arizona and then another thousand miles eastward into Oklahoma, probably into Kansas as well and possibly into Nebraska and Missouri. On the Brazos River in Texas his tracks approached those of the marauding Hernando de Soto, who was simultaneously crisscrossing the Southeast and was the first white man to see the Mississippi. Coronado, however, established no permanent line of march inside the American Southwest, nor did Spain appear to want one. Juan de Oñate, who travelled as far as Kansas in 1601, almost single-handedly created New Mexico in the following decade. But the Crown's efforts were devoted to consolidating and exploiting its empire in Mexico proper. Missionaries—Franciscans, Dominicans, Jesuits—breached that policy by their efforts, during the seventeenth and eighteenth centuries, to convert and civilise the Indians, particularly the sedentary Pueblo Indians, in New Mexico, Arizona, and California, but the extension of the Hispanic cultural frontier into what today is the southwestern United States had no official impetus behind it.

The Spanish colonial government was energised into a more positive policy only by foreign threat, the arrival of Russian traders and trappers on the Pacific Coast, the creation of French Louisiana. Spain's response to the Russian approach towards California was pre-emptive: to survey its coastline as quickly as possible in 1769–70 and plant forts (*presidio* was the Spanish term) at the strategic spots, such as Monterey and San Francisco. On the Gulf the Spanish were more timid. The appearance of French traders and explorers in Texas, particularly the Mallet brothers in 1739–40, who got as far as Santa Fe itself, prompted the Spanish Crown to establish fortified settlements and encourage missionary effort. After 1762, however, in which year Louisiana passed from France to Spain, the effort of policing a frontier constantly assailed by warlike, horse-riding Comanche and Apache proved too onerous to be sustained, and in 1772 it was decided to fix the frontier in Texas on a line of new *presidios*, running from Natchitoches on the Red River (today in the state of Louisiana) across the Saburie River to the Alamo at San Antonio and then to Laredo on the Rio Grande. The royal order was to leave Texas north of the line "to nature and the Indians."

Exploration of the Great Plains was therefore to be exclusively an Anglo-Saxon enterprise, though a freelance as well as an official one. What the La Vérendryes and Mallets had found on their adventures to the Black Hills and the Rockies did not tell the United States government enough about the land it had bought from France. What Thomas Jefferson, then the President, sought in particular was the discovery of "the most direct and practicable water communication across this continent [to the Pacific] for the purposes of commerce." In May 1804, therefore, he despatched two young officers—Meriwether Lewis, a graduate of the College of William and Mary (so near to Yorktown), who had been his private secretary, and William Clark, brother of George Rogers Clark, who had won the Illinois country for the United States in the year of Yorktown—to ascend the Missouri and find a way into the West. They carried out his instructions to the letter, leaving St.

Louis in May 1804, passing the future site of Fort Leavenworth soon afterwards, arriving at the Forks of the Missouri in Montana in July 1805 and on the Pacific, at the mouth of the Columbia River, in November after a terrible passage negotiating the high land above the headwaters of the Columbia and having constantly portaged their canoes to reach their destination. On the way back, they divided their parties, Lewis returning via the upper Missouri, Clark by its tributary the Yellowstone—Custer's future campaigning ground—rejoining each other in modern North Dakota. Lewis had had a frightening brush with Blackfoot Indians, the most warlike of the Sioux, but their return downriver to St. Louis was largely uneventful; they knew the way and were greeted as familiars by Indians they had met on the outward voyage.

Three other official explorers, Zebulon Pike, Stephen Long, and John Frémont, who went respectively to the Rockies in 1805–6, to Texas and Mexico in the years 1817–20, and to Nevada and California in 1846—all started from or near St. Louis—added considerably to knowledge of the geography of the United States. Pike saw and named his peak—that ugly, red, boulder-strewn pinnacle of the Rockies first pointed out to me because the headquarters of the North American Air Defense Command lurks in its bowels; Long, who climbed Pikes Peak, which Pike had declared unclimbable, explored the Platte, Arkansas, and Canadian rivers and helped to popularise belief in an overland route from the Mississippi into the Southwest; Frémont, who followed that route in part, is better known not as an explorer—though he captained four expeditions—but as an instigator of the 1846 Bear Flag Revolt in California, which led to the incorporation of the territory as a state of the Union in 1850, and as a leading Civil War general.

Indeed, after Lewis and Clark, it was freelance, not official, explorers who must be accorded the credit for opening up the West. They include John Jacob Astor and the employees of the American Fur Company, who, encouraged by Lewis and Clark's success, pioneered another overland route to the Northwest which did—by its use of the South Pass through the Rockies—blaze a section of the Oregon Trail the later settlers would use. On the far side of the Rockies, in California and Oregon, which were the objectives of the earliest migrants in the 1840s and 1850s, it was again fur trappers and traders who ranged widest and brought back the most important topographical information. Loosely known as the mountain men, they looked the part, bearded, skin-clad, armed to the teeth. Their numbers in their heyday of 1820–40 never seem to have exceeded six hundred, though they were difficult to count: many, as the *coureurs de bois* had done, spent a lifetime, commonly a short lifetime, in the wilderness, returning to the settled frontier but occasionally and appearing to view only at the annual rendezvous—equivalent of the old French Canadian fur fairs—where pelts were sold, tales told, and whisky drunk in quantities which often bankrupted and sometimes killed the revellers. The names of the best-known mountain men belong to the Western legends. Some, like Jim Bridger and Old Bill Williams, were fiercely independent, sometimes lending their services to government or fur company, more often wandering where spirit and instinct for profit took them. Others, Jedediah Smith, Peter Skene Ogden, Joseph Walker, were more purposeful in their adventuring, more formally attached to official or commercial expeditions, and better at reporting their discoveries. Ogden submitted detailed reports, while Smith, recognised as the greatest of all explorers of the Far West, pioneered the first practicable routes to California, both beginning at the Great Salt Lake in Utah, one leading to San Gabriel, the other to San Francisco itself.

The mountain men were travellers above all, ever in search of untrapped rivers and then of traders who would purchase their take. In the way of commerce, traders came looking for trappers when they had accumulated enough to make the buyers' journey worth while. This was the origin of the rendezvous system, flourishing between 1823 and 1839, but reminiscent of similar gatherings on the boundary between wild and tamed land from the beginning of history; Huns, Turks, and Mongols had come to the edge of the steppe to trade with civilisation for a thousand years in the age of Rome and Byzantium. A common place for the mountain men to meet the fur buyers was Green River, a tributary of the Platte in Wyoming, on the way to the South Pass through the Rockies. Ray Allen Billington, the great historian of the West, describes how "shortly after the first of July the caravan of trading goods arrived from St. Louis. The mountain men always rode out to meet the mile-long line of laden mules, yelling like demons as they greeted the merchants who were willing to ensure the wearisome journey for profits of 2,000 per cent on their investments. They asked eagerly for year-old news first, then watched greedily as the merchandise was spread before them. Trading came first . . . then the flat casks of alcohol were tapped . . . eventually both the alcohol and the mountain

men were exhausted. Those who had gambled away their guns and
horses pledged the next year's catch for new supplies, and all stumbled
away into the wilderness, their year's earnings squandered in a few
days of barbaric dissipation."

Even while the rendezvous system was in full swing, however, some
traders were seeking advantage over others by setting up permanent
centres of trade out on the plains. Usually simple stockades, but more
often sunburnt brick (adobe), for timber was hard to come by outside
the river valleys, those posts quickly acquired the name of "fort"—Fort
Union, Fort Laramie—and a number were destined to blossom into
permanent centres of population. Lewis and Clark had built forts on
their way, one at the Mahdan villages on the Missouri near modern
Bismarck, North Dakota, and another, Fort Clatsop, at the mouth of
the Columbia River in Oregon. The North American Fur Company
built Fort Astoria nearby in 1811, while the Hudson's Bay Company,
during the decades when Oregon Territory existed as an uneasy Anglo-
American condominium, built Forts Vancouver and Hall. Its example
encouraged the construction of Fort McKenzie on the upper Missouri
in 1824, of Fort Union at the confluence of the Yellowstone—future
Custer country—with the Missouri in 1827, and of Fort Laramie, on
the North Platte, in 1828. Foremost among all these private-enterprise
forts, however, was Bent's Fort, later Fort William, built in 1833 on the
Arkansas River near modern La Junta, Colorado, a hundred miles east
of the Rockies. Between 1834 and 1852, when its owner abandoned it,
it was the centre of trade on the southern plains and was visited by
such American grandees as Francis Parkman, historian of the French-
English struggle for the continent, and President Thomas Jefferson
himself.

Bent's Fort was a rip-roaring place in its day. "In the corral," wrote
an English visitor, George Ruxton, in 1847, "leather-clad mountaineers
. . . gamble away their hard-earned peltries . . . St. Louis Frenchmen
and Canadian *voyageurs* are pressing packs of buffalo skins. Indian
squaws, the wives of mountaineers, strut about in all the pride of beads
. . . happy as paint can make them. . . . Against the walls groups of Indians too proud to enter without an invitation, lean, wrapped in their
buffalo robes, sulky and evidently ill at ease to be so near the whites
without a chance of fingering their scalp locks; their white lodges shin-
ing in the sun, at a little distance from the river banks; their horses
feeding in the plain beyond." Its day, however, was short. By the 1860s

the army had assumed responsibility for fort-building on the plains and was extending chains of posts westward along the river and overland routes pioneered by trappers, traders, explorers, and settlers in the first half of the century. The chains had their lodgements on the Missouri and Mississippi—at Fort Smith, established in 1817, where the Arkansas joins the Red River on their way to the Mississippi; at Fort Atkinson, established in 1819 at Council Bluffs on the Missouri; at Fort Snelling, where the Minnesota joins the Mississippi, also established in 1819; and, of course, at Fort Leavenworth. These were formal government foundations. From them in the years after the Civil War, the army built in the northern plains, along the line of the California and Oregon trails, Forts Kearney, McPherson, and Mitchell, militarised the old Fort Laramie of fur days, and protected the trail north-westward—here known as the Bozeman Trail—by Forts Fetterman, Phil Kearny, and C. F. Smith. On the Santa Fe Trail from Leavenworth the line of forts ran from Fort Riley in Kansas via Fort Dodge to Fort Union in New Mexico, where the way leads under the last outcrop of the Rockies and so to California across the desert. Many other forts were built along the river systems, on trail branches, and near Indian stamping grounds, and, as the railroads began to be built west of the Mississippi, new forts were planted along their tracks to protect engineers and the travellers who followed in their wake. In 1871 the chairman of the Board of Indian Commissioners explained frankly to Red Cloud, the great Sioux chief, that the policy was for "the Great Father to put war-houses all through the Indian Country." The general commanding the Department of the Platte, Edward Ord, put it more bluntly: "Building posts in their country demoralises them more than anything else except money and whiskey." By 1881 there were more than a hundred forts in the West, besides many which had been abandoned or had grown into civil settlements.

Some still survive as military centres, Fort Riley, Kansas, home of the 1st Infantry Division, foremost among them. An unprepossessing town clings to its gates. Within the boundaries of the training area, however, some feel of the terrain which the army and the settlers confronted in Indian days persists. This is not yet the Great Plains—too wet, too hilly, too wooded. It had to be crossed, nevertheless, by the pioneers. I wondered, as I went "down range" in a Huey helicopter in 1987 to watch an all-arms exercise, what they made of it. "Remember," my escorting officer said to the pilot as we clambered aboard, "the idea is to make the number of landings equal to the number of take-offs." As we swooped and turned, the surface of very rough country passed my field of vision through the open door, yellowy-reddish scrub, small birches and pines, little swampy bottoms. We landed to watch an infantry platoon firing its anti-tank weapons by electronic simulation at a troop of armoured vehicles, and their platoon leader ran up to salute and tell the major delightedly how many hits had been scored. A West Pointer, bristling with the sort of good officer qualities I recognised from my years of teaching at Sandhurst, he was a handsome young black lientenant. A hundred years earlier, the only black soldiers hereabouts were the enlisted men of the 9th and 10th Cavalry and 24th and 25th Infantry, the "buffalo soldiers" of the U.S. Colored Regiments. He joined us for a cup of coffee served off the back of a tracked carrier half-bogged by the side of a soggy creek. Inhospitable now, the surroundings must have been even more bleak and inhospitable when the army took up post here for a real military purpose, in 1866. Fort Riley, founded in 1853, was still building, and its first garrison was formed by the newly raised 7th Cavalry, commanded by George Custer.

What brought Custer and his men to Fort Riley was the need to protect the railhead of the Kansas–Pacific railroad, begun near Fort Leavenworth 136 miles to the east in 1863 and now pushing towards Denver, Colorado, at a pace of 90 miles a year. Other railroads were paralleling its progress, notably the Union Pacific from Council Bluffs, while roads which started in California, such as the Central Pacific, were reaching back through the Sierras, to join them. When the Central Pacific met the Union Pacific at Ogden, Utah, in May 1869, the continent was spanned—as it had been by telegraph in 1861—by a continuous system leading, east of the Mississippi–Missouri, to Chicago, Baltimore, and New York.

There is a European misconception, long held by me but shared, I suspect, by many Americans, that the westward expansion of population in the United States, "Manifest Destiny," was incremental: that it began with the crossing in the eighteenth century of the Appalachians, proceeded to the line of the Mississippi–Missouri, broke that barrier in the mid-nineteenth century, progressed to the Rockies, and ended eventually in California, where the pioneers found no one but some gold-rushers and the scattered Hispanic subjects of New Spain's missions and *presidios*. Nothing, of course, could be less true. Like the Russians, who reached the Pacific at Vladivostok long before they had fully explored Siberia and subdued the nomad tribes of Central Asia, the Americans first populated their rich Pacific West—more often by ship to San Francisco than by wagon overland—and then found other reasons to filter back into the Great American Desert. The search for mineral wealth, particularly gold, was one; the need to get cattle north from the open ranges of Texas to the westward-reaching railroads and the stockyards of Chicago which they served was another. Sodbusting on the sea of grass was almost an afterthought. I exaggerate, but there is just enough truth in the thought to bear pondering.

Two experiences in eastern Kansas, on the threshold of the Great Plains, made me ponder. One was a visit to the Eisenhower Presidential Library in Abilene, where the victor of the North-West Europe campaign of 1944–45 grew up. I venerate Dwight Eisenhower. He personifies the American army which I remember coming to save my country in 1942. He also personifies to me the ideal of America: a poor boy, born to God-fearing parents in the continent's heartland, who by hard work and the practice of simple virtue rose to lead his country and eventually the world. Abilene, 164 miles east of Leavenworth on the railroad, is a backwater now; the curators of the presidential papers, kindly offering me lunch, could find nowhere better than the sort of authentically American eating place I remember fondly from my first youthful visit: plastic tabletops, glass sugar-shakers with metal caps, coffee plonked down before orders taken, and a choice of meat loaf or hamburger. What impressed me most about the town was the display of school books on which Eisenhower was raised. In 1904, when the high school was built, it was teaching French, German, and Latin—Eisenhower got a B—as well as algebra and geometry; forty years earlier the place had been wilderness.

What should have impressed me was its history. Between 1867, when it was "a small dead place of about one dozen long huts," and 1872, it was the cattle capital of America. A cattle dealer called Joseph McCoy, the "real McCoy" of proverb, succeeded in 1867 in clinching a deal with the Kansas Pacific to transport cattle to Chicago. They were driven up from Texas along the Chisholm Trail—three others running parallel would later join the Union Pacific, Missouri Pacific, and Atchison, Topeka and Santa Fe railroads at Cheyenne, Wyoming, Dodge City, Kansas, and Sedalia, Missouri—corralled, loaded, and railed northward to the meat-packing yards on the Great Lakes. But Abilene was the first of the cow towns. "More than four hundred miles north of the Red River and nearly a thousand miles from the Nueces Country (New Spain's old northern border), [it] was to become the commercial capital of Texas . . . to know in prosperity a lustiness and a greed which would make it a legend wherever cattlemen stopped to talk . . . In Abilene the Texas cowboy was discovered and first became a distinct type, and here he first displayed for a national audience those extremes of temperament that make him a hero."

Abilene's cattle glory was long done when Ike grew up there; what he learnt of it he must have done later, much as I did in front of the cinema screen showing *Red River* or *The Plainsman*. Yet Abilene and Texas nevertheless connect in Eisenhower's life, for he was born not in Kansas but near the start of the Chisholm Trail at Denison, on the Red River, where a farm bankruptcy had driven his father to seek work while Ida, the wonderful, sunny, Bible-quoting mother of the extraordinary Eisenhower brood, was pregnant with Dwight. Farm bankruptcy: an introduction to that event in the settlement of the plains was the second experience which made me ponder my mistaken understanding of the movement westward. On a free afternoon at Fort Leavenworth in February 1979, I was taken by a colonel on the faculty, Gordon Rogers, to tour its immediate hinterland. He showed me where, eight miles west of the fort, the California and Oregon trails divided; he showed me white-tailed deer grazing in herds on rough ground exactly as they did when the leader had to keep an ear cocked for Indians; he showed me a rough little rural settlement where every pick-up with a young man at the wheel had a .30/30 slug inside the cab; most important, he showed me the abandoned settlements of those who had moved on.

Colonel Rogers was a farmer himself. He had bought land and planned to retire to it when his thirty years in uniform were up, so he understood the rhythm of ploughing, grazing, and stock-rearing. His farm, nevertheless, would be at best a help to his pension. Stopping by an abandoned church and school, Catholic, American Gothic, clapboard and paint, he told me a story of farming which federal pensions did not subsidise. These, he said, were the relics of settlers of the 1880s. They had bought their sections or quarter-sections, built and ploughed, sowed and harvested. For a while they had prospered, pieced a community together, hoped for the future. Then times had turned against them, or better times had promised elsewhere, and they had left, perhaps for California, perhaps for the Great Plains proper in the years when the winds brought rain. No one had succeeded them: the relics of their little effort at wider culture were crumbling away, while their sections had been bought up and subsumed in larger holdings. Not even here was the land rich enough to bring small men a secure living; out on the plains, in the dry years, if they chanced their second luck there, times must have been worse. I thought of Dwight Eisenhower's father. He had never got his Abilene farm back after his bankruptcy but taken work in a creamery—what a descent from longhorn, trail-driving cattle days—beaten Latin into his boys with a strap, and barely lived to hear how his hardscrabble life had carried them to the threshold of place and fame in the world. Only Ida, the Bible her rock, had survived to see the homestead virtues she had taught her sons turn them into great men.

A little of what I feel about the Eisenhower epic I was able to transmit in 1986 to an audience at Kansas State University in Manhattan, the stop before Fort Riley on the old Kansas Pacific line. I had been honoured by an invitation to give the Eisenhower Memorial Lecture. Ironically, however, I found that the interests of the history department did not lie with the westward movement at all. The lady who drove me about the campus had succumbed to the fashion for women's studies, while the chairman was an American member of the great Monumenta Germaniae Historica at Frankfurt-am-Main, the seat of medieval scholarship in the German-speaking lands. It was doubtful whether his interests extended to the Eisenhowers' origins in the Pennsylvania Dutch Mennonite community of the eighteenth century, let alone to the story of their migration to Kansas in the nineteenth. Yet the Eisenhowers epitomise the story of the movement to the plains. Kansas had been legally opened for settlement in 1854. After the Civil War, the Eisenhowers, still German-speaking, decided to take up the promise made by the railroad companies of cheaper land westward for their children, sold up, loaded their goods at Harrisburg, and, with three hundred other Mennonites, crossed the Missouri and bought a quarter-section, 160 acres, in Dickinson County, just where the Flint Hills of eastern Kansas give way to the Great Plains. If they crossed at Leavenworth, as they probably did, their wagon wheels must have deepened the scar on the bluff; there was no bridge for the railroad until 1872.

Yet the Eisenhower story is not truly typical of the settlement. For one thing, Jacob, Ike's grandfather, came with money. He had sold up

in Pennsylvania for $8,500 and bought a full farming outfit; his Men-
nonite party was described as "one of the most complete and properly
organised . . . that ever entered a new country." Moreover, Jacob prospered. He gave each of his children on marriage, daughters as well as
sons, a farm of 160 acres and $2,000 in cash. Ike's father's bankruptcy
was the result of a business failure, not of drought. Secondly, the Eisenhowers were ahead of their time. Most of those who crossed the Missouri immediately after the Civil War were bound for California and
Oregon, and many of them were gripped not by land hunger but by
gold fever. The discovery of gold in California caused the great Forty-
nine rush. There were subsequent rushes into Nevada and Colorado in
1859, into Montana and Idaho in the period 1861–66, into Wyoming
in 1867, and into the Black Hills of Dakota in 1874; that last gold rush
was to precipitate the events that led to the Battle of the Little Bighorn.

Most of this gold-rushing went westward, but some came back
eastward, led by rushers who had tried their luck in California, failed
there, and crossed the mountains to try again. Whichever way they
came, the numbers involved were enormous, 100,000 in Colorado in
1859, far exceeding those who were beginning to try for a living from
the land. Much deterred the early farmers. Until 1862 their access to
"free land," that in the public domain, was limited by the requirements
to pay cash either for the whole of a claim or a part of it. After the
Homestead Act of 1862, a settler who paid $10, worked his quarter-
section of 160 acres for five years, and then made another small pay-
ment acquired title to it. The Homestead Act, passed in the same year
as that abolishing slavery, founding land-grant colleges and granting
rights of way for a Pacific railroad, is rightly regarded as a landmark in
making the United States a free and rich country. Nevertheless, there
were pitfalls. The Homestead Act favoured, if unintentionally, the rich
over the poor, while the railroad legislation took much land coveted by
would-be farmers out of the public domain.

There were other deterrents to settlement, intrinsic to the plains
themselves. Many who came, particularly those from the temperate,
forested states, failed to understand that they were entering territory
utterly unlike eastern America. It lacked timber, it lacked water, and it
lacked a settled climate, which meant that farmers would lack fences
and food, would need to irrigate if they could not acquire bottom land,
and could not count—outside the delusive decades of higher rainfall—
upon regular crop yields; unless near a railway or navigable river, they

would also lack markets and so both supplies of trade goods and the cash to purchase them. The promise of free land was tainted. What it offered the homesteader was not riches—those would come later to the big men with machinery, capital, and the wide spreads wealth could buy—but bare subsistence. Jacob Eisenhower prospered because he came early, brought money, and got land in the Kansas River Valley. Those who came in the next decades and took sections on the high plains had to scratch for existence and often gave up the struggle. It is not surprising that the most successful of the pioneers of 1870–90 were often not native Americans from east of the Mississippi, though these were the majority, but immigrants from Europe's harsher climates, Scandinavia and the Steppe, who were used to extremes of climate—hot summers, bitter winters—and to tilling difficult soil. Those from Russia, with their experience of ploughing dry grassland, adjusted quickest of all.

America's industrial genius would eventually offer solutions to most of the problems of plains agriculture. Against cyclical drought—which afflicted the plains from 1881 to 1904 and again from 1917 to 1939—it could offer only palliatives; but barbed wire, invented in 1874, gave the farmer cheap fencing against free-ranging cattle (and provided Hollywood with the plot for dozens of western movies, including *Shane*, the supreme classic of the genre), while, by the 1890s, tube wells and metal windmills were raising water cheaply even on the high plains, and deep-shared metal ploughs and spring harrows were cultivating the fine dust seedbeds essential to grain-growing in dry conditions.

All these developments lay years in the future, however, when the first settlers chanced the luck offered them by the Homestead Act of 1862. They faced a deterrent to settlement in the Great Plains quite separate from their aridity, tracklessness, intimidating vastness, want of companionship, and extremes of heat and cold; quite separate from the threat of blizzard, drought, and insect plague; quite separate from the threat of difficult childbirth or life-threatening accidents hours, even days, from medical attendance. They faced the threat of death at the hands of the horse-riding High Plains Indians.

The Indians of the Great Plains

The Indians of the Great Plains may be thought among the most remarkable of all the world's warrior peoples. Between the middle of the
seventeenth century and the end of the eighteenth century, they acquired two quite disparate instruments of warfare, the horse and the
gun, assimilated them into their culture, and combined their use into
terrifyingly effective military practice. It is difficult to think of any
other pre-literate ethnic group which has made so rapid and complete a
transition from primitive to sophisticated warriordom in so short a
space of time.

The nomadic peoples of the Euro-Asian steppe, Scythians, Huns,
Magyars, Mongols, and Turks, learnt how to carry offensive warfare
against the civilisations which surrounded its edge, Rome, Byzantium,
the Islamic Caliphate, and Han China, using the horse and the composite bow—a weapon not inferior to early firearms—with deadly effect.
The process by which the steppe dwellers evolved from marginal herdsmen to makers and breakers of empire was protracted and remains obscure. Before 2000 B.C. the horse of the Old World was a poor thing,
valued by humans as meat rather than a mount. It was, indeed, too
weak in the back to be ridden at all. About 2000 B.C. however, muta-
tion and selective breeding produced an animal strong enough to pull a
load, and soon afterwards appeared the ancestor of today's riding
horse. By about 1500 B.C. there also appeared the composite bow; but
not until nearly a thousand years later did individual riders learn
how to use the bow from horseback and so combine into a single
man–horse weapon unit all the elements which make up what historians call "the cavalry revolution." The process which was to lead to the
overthrow by the world's first true horse people, the Scythians, of the
world's first great empire, Assyria, was, therefore, nearly fifteen centuries long.

The process is not to be admired. The horse peoples in the two
thousand years in which they flourished, between the Scythian on-
slaught in Assyria in the seventh century B.C. and the Turks' victory
over Byzantium at Constantinople in A.D. 1453, were the enemies of
true civilisation. They were, nevertheless, a force in the world which no
account of its history can ignore. Equally, no history of America can ignore that of its native inhabitants. Their fate was ultimately tragic,

though sentimentality should not blind us to a record of savagery inflicted as well as savagery suffered; but their history is also one of extraordinary adaptation to the arrival of a civilisation which nothing in their past had prepared them to confront. From that confrontation they unerringly selected the two novelties best designed to facilitate their struggle for existence, in the Southwest the horse, in the Northeast the gun. When Indian horse culture and Indian gun culture met and overlapped, as they did on the Great Plains at the end of the eighteenth century, a warrior way of life was born which was to impede and distort the Manifest Destiny of Europeans to possess the continent for nearly a hundred years. It is the unparalleled rapidity with which America's Indians brought a "cavalry revolution" to its military history which elevates them to a special place in that of the world.

The horse came twice to America, first at some irretrievable period before the opening of the Bering Strait separated it from Siberia, then when Cortés brought his seventeen chargers to Mexico in 1517. In the interim the ancestors of the Amerindians who crossed from Asia to Alaska twelve thousand years ago had hunted the native American horse out of existence, probably in the first millennium after their arrival. The disappearance of the American horse, supposing that it might have evolved into a riding animal, determined that the way of life of the continent's earlier inhabitants moved nowhere faster than at foot's pace and in many regions settled into sedentary forms. That was to be the case on the fertile lakeside and river valleys of Mexico and the Southwest. In the forests of Atlantic America, hunting, trapping, fishing, gathering, and scavenging provided subsistence, except where breaks in the tree cover permitted peripatetic agriculture. The pattern persisted also on the Pacific Coast and, in marginal forms, on the mountain slopes and the edges of the frozen northern hinterland. It was on the Great Plains, however, that there developed a way of life distinctively American, unlike any other in the inhabited world, for it was only there that was found game in the superabundance that the herds of buffalo represented.

Before the white man came to the plains, it has been calculated, they were roamed by thirty million buffalo, often forming herds which covered as much as fifty square miles of territory. Though large, slow, and small-brained, the buffalo had no natural enemies; unlike Africa, America sheltered no predator strong enough to pull down a ruminant on its grazing ground. Not even the Indian could be counted a real enemy, for the natives of the plains lived by small-scale parasitism on the herds. They were wholly dependent on the buffalo for life. A member of Coronado's expedition of the early 1540s described how "with the skins they build their houses; with the skins they clothe and shoe themselves; from the skins they make rope and also obtain wool. With the sinews they make thread with which they sew their clothes and also their tents. From the bones they shape awls. The dung they use for firewood, since there is no other fuel in their land. The bladders they use as jugs and drinking containers. They sustain themselves on their meat, eating it slightly roasted and heated over the dung. Some they eat raw." Though the Indians would, when they could, organise buffalo "drives," a method of killing known to archaeologists from many regions and from as long ago as 100,000 years B.C., in which the hunters funnelled beasts into a dead end at a cliff's edge, Indian numbers were so small on the plains—the Sioux, most feared of the plains people, seem to have formed no more than sixteen thousand in the 1860s— that even the most successful drive scarcely dented the buffalo stock. Hunting on foot against the flanks of a herd was laborious and time-consuming, requiring great skill in stalking and the use of bow and lance, and yielded even fewer carcasses.

The coming of the horse put the Plains Indian on more equal terms with his prey. By raising the speed of the hunt from four to over twenty miles an hour, it facilitated the "surround," a hunting method in which a section of the herd was cut out by mounted men and ridden down to death by lance and bow. The Indian's mythic relationship with his source of life continued to restrain, nevertheless, the number of buffalo he took, and that might have remained so even after the appearance of the gun. The ball fired by the flintlock musket may actually have been inferior to the arrow as a killing agent against the bulk of a body as large as the buffalo's; and while that was not true of the conical bullet fired by the breech-loading rifle, the rifle did not change the Indian's relationship with the great buffalo herds. They remained the biosystem from which he drew his subsistence, and so a stock to be conserved and valued above every other means of life on the Great Plains.

It was the arrival there of the rifle-bearing white man that changed everything: the white herdsman, driving the cattle columns north from Texas to the railroads, the white farmer staking out his claim on the grassland, above all the white buffalo hunter bent on collecting hides for the tanneries of trans-Mississippi America. The farmers simply wanted buffalo-free land; the herdsmen wanted the buffalo's grass, not knowing or caring that without the buffalo's droppings and eventual decomposition after death the grass would be progressively impoverished; but the hide-hunters wanted the buffalo itself and in the early 1870s were killing three million a year. Both ranchers and farmers applauded that, since the slaughter promised to empty the plains at no cost to themselves at all. It confronted the Indian with the threat of extinction of a way of life so old that he could not imagine a future without it. Herding, farming, hide-hunting: the combination meant war, and not merely war but war to the death.

War between white and Indian had been part of the history of North America since the Europeans had first arrived to settle in the seventeenth century. War had, of course, also been central to the way of life of many of the Indian tribes since time immemorial. Indian warfare, however, generally took forms quite different from those known to Europeans. Like most hunters, gatherers, and itinerant agriculturalists in other pre-literate, pre-metallic societies in Asia, Africa, and the Pacific, the Indians had little conception of territorial acquisition, usurpation, or victory. They fought frequently over women, particularly where female infanticide was practised, sometimes over hunting rights, commonly for prestige and revenge. The very vastness of America and the sparsity of human population—there were only about 600,000 Indians in the future United States when the Pilgrim Fathers landed—imposed no need to fight for those reasons dear to anthropologists: competition for scarce resources or protein shortage. Some Indians fought very little; the Pueblo peoples of the Southwest, settled, village-dwelling farmers, scarcely knew war at all. The forest Indians of the Northeast fought tribe to tribe over farming and hunting grounds, which shifted as soils were temporarily exhausted or stocks of game hunted out, and sometimes with determination and discipline; both the Algonquins and the Iroquois wore bodily protection and came to close-quarter combat. A dominant motive in their style of warfare, however, was the taking of captives, to be adopted into the tribe as a replacement for a casualty if thought worthy, to be tortured to death if not; it was bravery under torture that usually determined the captive's fitness for adoption. Out on the plains, Indian warfare seems, before the coming of the Europeans, to have been a tepid affair. Tribes were few and small in number. They practised the sun dance at the beginning of the year, which invoked a successful season; they raided for women and re-

venge; they staged ritual combats in which "counting coup," the striking of a symbolic blow against an enemy, meant more than killing or
wounding. In an almost infinite land, however, they did not fight for
territory or wealth, because territory was effectively free and wealth
was for anyone fit enough to hunt the buffalo.

Plains warfare was transformed by the coming of the horse. It provided an object worth fighting about, for wealth immediately came to
be measured in horses, which braves set out to steal, stampede, or capture in combat. It also liberated the male from almost all activity except warriordom. The males in all horse societies appear to have been
lazy; on the Central Asian steppe their days were spent idling on horseback as they supervised the grazing of their flocks. On the Great Plains
the Indians were spared even that pastoral responsibility, since the buffalo herds needed no attention at all. Endlessly reproductive and
threatened by no predator except man himself, they needed only to be
followed along their grazing tracks to yield a livelihood. The buffalo
hunt itself required skills of horsemanship and of the use of arms from
the saddle. Such skills, however, were as much military as predaceous,
and, once mastered, as they were by the beginning of the nineteenth
century when the gun had found its way into the hands of the Plains
Indians, they provided a potential for effective war-making not only in
the stylised give-and-take of tribal rivalry but also in the defence of the
hunting grounds against the white encroacher.

Encroachment was not initially a white policy. Indeed, the plains
were first seen as the solution of the "Indian problem" east of the Mississippi, a region inhospitable to whites into which the tribes of the Old
Northwest and the South could be decanted. In emulation of the
Proclamation of 1763, United States policy in the last quarter of the
eighteenth century and the first of the nineteenth was to get the Indians
out of the wooded East and across the Mississippi–Missouri on to the
treeless levels where they would cease to be competitors for productive
land. There were subordinate policies, including those of forcing
hunters to become farmers, and of creating reservations, deemed to be
permanent, within the 1763 Proclamation territory. The relentless desire of settlers for land, however, and their determination to take it
even from Indians who were or became farmers, as did the Five Civilized Tribes—Choctaw, Cherokee, Chickasaw, Seminole, and Creek—
of the Southeast, reduced all Federal policy in the end to one of

removal, through a succession of broken treaties and despite a series of
Indian wars of desperation.

The policy became explicit in 1825 when John C. Calhoun, Secretary of War to President Monroe, proposed removing the eastern Indians west of the 95th Meridian, which meant across the Missouri, and of
making room for them by displacing the Plains Indians further westward still. In 1830 the most notorious of the Indian laws, the Indian
Removal Act, transplanted the Five Civilized Tribes to Arkansas, while
treaties and bribes got the tribes of the Old Northwest into lands adjacent to Fort Leavenworth. The arrangement was not only high-handed.
It also provoked trouble between the Indians themselves, for the easterners not unnaturally found the plains alien to their way of life, while
the displaced westerners objected that the easterners were occupying
their traditional hunting grounds. Moreover, they despised each other:
the incomers thought the plainsmen to be primitive savages, the plainsmen thought the incomers to be interlopers and dependants of the white
man. Far from solving the Indian problem, the creation of what was
called the Permanent Indian Frontier merely shifted it. The administration of the Frontier required the establishment of new forts in Indian
territory and a steady inflation of the number of troops stationed there.

The problem worsened as the settlers began to make their way
across the Permanent Indian Frontier towards California and Oregon
in the 1850s. Though they were not legally permitted and did not seek
to stay in the Great American Desert, they did want secure through-
routes, and that required the Indians to migrate either north or south
of the California and Oregon trails. New agreements about reservations were made, and inevitably broken. Then the roadheads in what
would be called Kansas and Nebraska were "organised" as Territories,
soon to be states, further diminishing Indian land and opening a wedge
into the plains which threatened to widen. The Sioux tribes were assured at Fort Laramie in 1857 of their permanent right to the Dakota
lands, where they had particularly rich hunting grounds in the Black
Hills, but even a corner of those had been usurped by 1860. "By alter-
nate persuasion and force," an agent of the Indian Bureau wrote,
"some of those tribes have been removed, step by step, from mountain
to valley and from river to plain, until they have been pushed half
across the continent. They can go no further: on the ground they now
occupy the crisis must be met."

The crisis was postponed by the Civil War, which effectively interrupted the course of western expansion for nearly five years. Yet even by 1864, trouble was brewing again, largely because of the mining fever which had impelled the first rush to California in 1849. Now it was Colorado, immediately west of Kansas, where word said wealth was to be made, and the stampede of miners to the Rockies provoked the Cheyenne and Arapaho to war. The Colorado militia of locally enlisted irregulars, the sort of force which had made trouble for central authority ever since the Kirkes had taken Quebec from Champlain in 1629, put the tribes down with terrible ferocity in the Sand Creek massacre, the memory of which reverberated among the Indians of the Southwest throughout the next decade, kept them constantly on the warpath but broke the spirit of many individuals. News of the massacre, however, only inflamed the Sioux of the northern plains. Always the most warlike tribe of the region, as their neighbours knew and the French had found, they had already been driven out of Minnesota for rebelliousness. When mining fever engulfed Montana, in their current tribal heartland, in 1864 the Sioux resolved to fight. The immediate cause of trouble was a Federal decision to open a new spur from the Oregon Trail to supply the mining encampments around Bozeman. The Bozeman Trail branched off at Fort Laramie, the old fur-trading post where many of the dishonoured Indian treaties had been negotiated, and was guarded by three new forts, Reno, on the Powder River, C. F. Smith, on the Bighorn River, and Phil Kearny, in between.

Red Cloud, the leading Sioux chief of the time, warned that his people saw the road as a violation of treasured territory. The U.S. Army, which was constructing both it and the forts, nevertheless kept on with the work, though they were constantly attacked and their supply parties regularly ambushed. In December 1865, however, Red Cloud's warning hit home. Lieutenant Colonel William Judd Fetterman, leading a punitive party of eighty-two soldiers against their Sioux tormentors, fell into a trap, and he and all his men were killed.

The Fetterman massacre, which the Indians may have seen as a tit-for-tat for the Sand Creek massacre, brought an end to fighting in the short term but in the long term presaged a greater crisis. The fighting, known as the Powder River War, was ended because Washington decided on yet another revision of its Indian policy. In March 1867, with the garrisons of the three forts virtually under siege, Congress voted to send peace commissioners to the plains with new proposals. Four civilians and three generals reached the West in August and agreed on the terms to be offered, first to the Indians of the southern plains, then to those of the north. In practice, the new policy was no more than a revision of the old—definition of reserves, compensation for land surrendered, and promise of material support to tide the Indians over the change of homeland—with the difference that the territories which the Indians were to hold would be even more constricted than those guaranteed under the previous treaties. The displaced eastern Indians, including the Five Civilized Tribes, were to be confined to the eastern half of what is now Oklahoma, displacing the indigenous Plains tribes, Cheyenne, Arapaho, Kiowa, and Comanche, to the western half. Feasts, smooth talk, and cash payments clinched the deal.

The commissioners then turned to the central and northern tribes. The Shoshoni and Bannock of Wyoming and Idaho, the Ute of Colorado, and the Navaho and Apache of Arizona and New Mexico accepted reservations in those states and territories. The Sioux agreed to proposals which gave them a permanent reservation centered on their cherished Black Hills hunting ground in what is now South Dakota, together with the country astride the Bighorn River in Montana as "unceded" Indian territory. In return the United States ceased work on the Bozeman Trail and abandoned the three forts guarding it.

The government conceived that the West was now pacified. As so often had proved the case before, however, deals concluded with chiefs could not bind their followers. Indian chiefdom was transient, Indian tribal structure fluid, Indian understanding of territorial ownership and alienation at variance with the legalism of the white world. Chiefs were commonly accorded chiefly status precisely because they could inspire young men to war, lead them to victory, and outwit the tribal enemies. Powers of diplomacy were valued in a leader only if they brought advantage. The treaties of 1867–68 made at Medicine Lodge, Fort Laramie, and elsewhere had brought the glister of cash and the white man's goodwill, but on terms which the younger warriors recognised to be greatly to their disadvantage. On the plains, as anywhere else that settled people treated with nomads, two utterly irreconcilable styles of life were brought into conflict. Settled people, particularly people of settled habits seeking to impose them over a nomadic zone, simply cannot comprehend the fulfilment that the roaming existence brings to the migrant pastoralist and the hunter. The settler is a creature seeking the certainties of boundaries, fixed habitation, mine and thine. The nomad,

by contrast, relishes uncertainty, movement, adventure, random re-
ward, chance wealth, and values no possession that does not serve his
restless, rootless, irresponsible habits. To the incomprehension of the
farmer, and even of the rancher who thinks of his stock and his spread
as his own, the nomad regards himself as a superior being, because he
enjoys the greatest of all human endowments, personal freedom and
detachment from material burdens. Nomadism, anthropologists have
concluded, is the happiest of all human ways of life; and because of the
happiness it brings, those who enjoy it react with ruthless violence
against outsiders who seek to limit or redirect it. Much of the history
of the Old World concerns the feckless expectation of nomads that settled and civilised peoples should submit to their depradations, their determination to persist in nomad habits even when their military
ruthlessness made them masters of civilised societies, and the equally
stubborn determination of sedentary civilisations to beat nomadism
back into the remoteness where it originated.

On a smaller scale, and in circumstances which preordained the
nomads to defeat, the Old World history of conflict between nomadic
horse peoples and sedentary civilisation was to be played out in the
New World on the Great Plains in the two decades after the Civil War.
In the aftermath of the Fort Laramie and Medicine Lodge treaties, the
compromising chiefs who had signed the tribal lands away were dis-
owned by their followers, who, by the traditionally shifting loyalties of
tribal life, accepted the leadership either of unreconciled elders, like
Chief Black Kettle, of the Cheyenne–Arapaho confederacy, or of
younger chiefs with fire in their veins. In August 1868 the Southwest
took flame and several thousand Comanche, Cheyenne, Arapaho,
Kiowa, and Apache rode gun in hand across Kansas, Texas, Colorado,
and New Mexico, killing and burning. The greatest of Hollywood
westerns, John Ford's *The Searchers*, begins with the descent of a Comanche band on an isolated Texas farmstead at this time.

By March 1869 this outburst of nomadic violence had been
quelled, largely through the efforts of the young Colonel George
Custer, whose surprise attack on Chief Black Kettle in an encampment
in the Washita Valley, in Indian territory in Oklahoma, on 27 November 1868, resulted in the chief's death and that of a hundred of his followers, as well as the demoralisation of most of the other Indians who
had taken the warpath that season. Two years later, however, trouble
again broke out in Texas and rumbled on, with the usual bloody conse-

quences of burnt homesteads and bushwhacked wagon trains, reaching a climax in 1874 with the deaths of sixty Texas whites. The army then resolved on concerted action, from its posts on the upper Red River—Forts Union, Sill, Griffin, and Concho and Camp Supply—and fought fourteen actions before winter and Indian exhaustion brought an end to the Red River War.

The tide was now turning decisively against the Indians. The army was protracting its punitive expeditions into the winter months, which "hostiles" did not regard as a campaigning season. Hostiles were becoming increasingly dependent on the handouts and cash payments distributed in the reserves, and though many would drift out of the reserves in the summer months when the temptations of the warpath overcame the force of the promises of good behaviour they had given, bad weather and military action usually drove them back again towards the end of the year. Above all, the bottomless resource of the buffalo herds which had supported their way of life since time immemorial was now running out. The penetration of the plains by the transcontinental railroads had split their grazing grounds, put hide-hunting on to a commercial basis, and accelerated slaughter to an industrial pace. The southern buffalo population was near extinction by the time of the Red River War; the northern population was in catastrophic decline also. Deforestation had been the necessary preliminary to settlement in the temperate United States; the buffalo holocaust was the equivalent precondition to the opening of the plains. It was immeasurably easier and it had the direct side-effect of forcing the Indians to choose between acceptance of dependency on the whites through the reservation system or increasingly desperate armed resistance.

In 1875 the Indians of the northern plains were confronted by just such a choice. Under the Fort Laramie treaty of 29 April 1868, the Sioux had agreed to abandon the warpath in return for the grant of a permanent reservation in the Dakota Black Hills, valued precisely because it carried rich stocks of other game than the disappearing buffalo, and the "unceded" territory in what is now Montana, around the Bighorn River and its tributaries, where the buffalo did roam. At the time the treaty lands were not thought valuable to whites. The Bighorn country was too remote for settlement, the Black Hills too steep and wooded for agriculture. By 1873, however, one of the now familiar gold rumours swept the States, identifying the Black Hills as a spot for instant fortune-making. Since it was nearly a decade since the last lucky strike, and the United States economy was temporarily in depression, the rumour had an electrifying effect.

Loners competed with syndicates to get to the Black Hills, only to find that the Federal government barred their way. Soldiers were few, however, prospectors many, and the cordon was broken by hundreds willing to risk Indian anger for the chance of quick riches. In the face of the gold rush, Washington decided on a novel means of observing its treaty obligations, which was to mount an expedition of its own that would explode the gold fable. The soldier chosen as leader was Colonel George Custer. Unfortunately the scientists attached to his column brought back news exactly contrary to that expected: the Black Hills were rich, not only in game but in gold-bearing lodes. It could not be kept secret. Efforts to exclude prospectors by legal proclamation did not work. The government found itself squeezed between its treaty obligations and the gold-lust of thousands of miners. Soldiers hustled them outside the frontiers of the reserve in hundreds, only to find them filtering in again when their backs were turned. By September the government concluded that it could regularise the situation only by prevailing on the Sioux to renegotiate the Fort Laramie treaty. In September 1875, agents conferred with tribes, offering money for the mining rights. The disheartened Sioux of the reservation, those who had chosen to settle for peace and handouts, were prepared to discuss terms. Against the government offer of $6 million, however, they demanded $70 million. The unreconciled Sioux, mainly from the Teton clan within the Sioux confederation, refused to barter at all. As the Fort Laramie treaty stipulated that three-quarters of all adult male Sioux had to assent to an instrument of sale, an impasse resulted.

The government's response was twofold. Recognising, realistically, that it could not control the thousands of miners who ringed the Black Hills, it withdrew its soldiers from the approaches. Hoping, unrealistically, to overawe the Indians by threat of penalty, it ordered all the Sioux to report to the reservation, even from their external hunting grounds where they were legally at liberty to roam, by 1 February 1876. The miners poured through the passes to the Black Hills as soon as the soldiers left. The warrior Indians withdrew to the upper reaches of the Yellowstone River and its tributaries, the Bighorn and Little Bighorn, west of the reservation and outside the cordon of forts encircling their lands, Forts Laramie, Lincoln, Fetterman, Benton, and Ellis, to stockpile supplies and await the war they now knew was inevitable. The penultimate but decisive round of the struggle between red man and white in North America trembled on the point of outbreak.

The Army on the Plains

The United States Army had not been raised to fight Indians and until the Civil War was over had done little Indian fighting. Anthony Wayne, the Revolutionary War hero, had led an army against the forest Indians of the Old Northwest in 1793–94, which made Ohio safe for settlement. A succession of generals had battled with the fierce and wild Seminoles of the Southeast from 1835 to 1842 with little credit to their reputations; exhaustion, not defeat, was what eventually forced the Seminoles to accept "removal" to the plains under the terms which guaranteed them, with all other transplanted Indians, possession of their reservations "as long as waters run."

The fighting against Tecumseh, leader of the Shawnee during the War of 1812–14, and Black Hawk and Red Bird in Wisconsin and Illinois in the 1820s, was largely carried on by local militias, whose land hunger made them more ferocious enemies of the Indians than regular soldiers could ever be. Their training in Federalist days was, in any case, not to fit them for the exhausting and interminable tit-for-tat of savage frontier warfare but for operations against foreign enemies, the British and Canadians and then the Mexicans. The United States' military budget during the early nineteenth century gave priority to the building of coastal fortifications on a European scale, the results of which are the magnificent Third System forts, together with the construction of a ship-of-the-line-fleet and the maintenance of a miniature spit-and-polish army of musketeers and artillerists. The army and navy served their purpose in the war against Mexico of 1846–48, in which one of the major expeditions against the enemy was mounted from Fort Leavenworth down the Santa Fe Trail. Federal strategy in the West during all the years between the formulation of the "removal" policy in 1825 and the end of the Civil War in 1865 was one simply of policing and preserving the Permanent Indian Frontier. Such forts as were built were sited either to define it or to protect the north–south

Federal road, linking the Indian frontier posts, between Fort Snelling in Minnesota and Fort Towson in modern Oklahoma. A few scattered forts were dragged out westward following the line of emigration to California and Oregon but according to no pattern and policy. Until 1865 government policy meant what it said: an America for whites east of the Mississippi and west of the Rockies, and a red America in the "desert" in between.

Peace in 1865 confronted Washington with a changed reality. The move west was suddenly in full swing. Settlers were finding fertile farming ground in the lands of the buffalo and the Indian; roads and soon railways were breaking the oceanic integrity of the plains; the emptiness of the centre between historic Atlantic America and new Pacific America was filling with people who demanded the protection of the government. Piecemeal, forts sprang up along the river valleys on which settlement was centred: on the upper Missouri, Forts Sully and Buford in 1866, Fort Stevenson in 1867; along the Red River, Fort Sill in 1869 (today still the headquarters of the U.S. Artillery); and on the Washita River, Fort Cobb in 1869. The multiplication of forts was heading towards its eventual total of two hundred posts in the West, some properly defensible stockades or adobe outposts, others, where the garrison was larger, conventional barracks surrounding a parade square.

If Federal policy trembled on the brink of radical, inevitably anti-Indian, redefinition in 1865, so too did the Western strategy of its army. In the spring of 1866 General William Tecumseh Sherman, newly appointed commander of the Division of the Missouri, set out on a tour of his territory from his headquarters in Jefferson Barracks, St. Louis. Sherman, like Ulysses S. Grant, was a man made by the Civil War. They shared the same experience of humiliating failure in civilian life during the years preceding the war, of redemption through victorious command, of success achieved through high-handed and ruthless realism. Yet success also in some way diminished both men. Grant failed as President to bring to politics the extraordinary powers of dominance over others which he had displayed as the Union's generalissimo. Sherman revealed in his formulation of a strategy for pacifying the plains something of that disgust with warfare as an instrument of policy which was to overwhelm him in his declining years. "The poor Indian finds himself hemmed in," he testified to Congress. "There is a universal feeling of mistrust on both sides and this will sooner or later result in a general outbreak." Yet as a man who knew the West in its pre-war rawness, when he had unsuccessfully practised law at Fort Leavenworth, he also recognized the intractability of the Indian, his maddening habit of giving his word one day and breaking it the next, his terrible cruelty and rapaciousness. Grant as President initiated a policy of peace-making with the Indians, in which Sherman, appointed his commanding general in 1869, co-operated. Indian behaviour seems nevertheless to have driven him to accept that the only solution to the tribes' constant refusal to abide by solemn agreement was to drive them into a Northern and a Southern reservation and keep them there by force of arms. He also seems to have thought this best achieved by offensive operations, mounted whenever the Indians misbehaved, rather than by progressively constricting their territory by penning them in with a chain of forts, the strategies adopted by the British on the North-West Frontier of India and by the French in North Africa.

Yet comparisons between the imperial strategies of the British and French and those of the American army in the plains are perhaps unfair. In the first place, the enemies of the British and French, Pathans and Kabyles—cunning, tough, and brave though they were—did not approach the Plains Indians in qualities of harsh individual warriordom. Neither of those Islamic peoples could be called "primitives" in the strict sense; as followers of one of the great monotheistic religions, they shared many of the ethical assumptions of their white enemies and knew something of political organisation above the tribal level. Neither statement could be made about the Sioux, the Cheyenne, or their fellows. Anthropologists distinguish between "soft" and "hard" primitivism. The pre-metallic, pre-literate, but benevolent culture of Polynesia characterises the first; the rigorously masculine and individualistic way of life of the Plains Indians the second. The rituals undergone by them in the sun dance, in which the aspirant warrior tortured his muscles and lacerated his flesh in the effort to demonstrate in public his powers of endurance, scarcely have parallels elsewhere in the savage world. It resulted in the Indian warriors acquiring qualities of physical hardness, contempt for pain and privation, and disregard of danger to life which both disgusted and awed the white soldiers who fought them. "The adult Apache," wrote General George Crook, perhaps the U.S. Army's foremost Indian fighter, of the foremost warrior tribe of the southern plains, "is an embodiment of physical endurance—lean, well proportioned, medium sized, with sinews like steel, insensible to hunger, fatigue, or physical pains." What was true of the Apache was also true of the Cheyenne and the Sioux.

Moreover, their very qualities of barbaric individualism almost wholly unfitted them for the poacher-turned-gamekeeper system of service on which the French and British counted to subdue and police their Algerian and Indian frontiers. Their colonial armies enlisted Islamic tribesmen—Turcos and *méharistes* in Algeria, Khyber Rifles and Waziristan Scouts in the North-West Frontier Province—who loyally submitted to European discipline and faithfully obeyed the orders of white officers. The American officers in the plains grasped that they needed such poachers-turned-gamekeepers. In fighting Apaches, General Crook wrote, "regular troops are as helpless as a whale attacked by a school of swordfish"; he recognised that "the only hope of success [against them] lies in using their own methods." Plains Indians, however, would never submit to the disciplining and direction that the French and British managed to impose on the wild peoples of their imperial frontiers. Indians could be inveigled into enlisting as "scouts," usually against traditional tribal enemies and always for cash or other inducements. They could never be persuaded to form regiments of the sort the British and French raised. Their loyalty was for a season or to a person. When times and personalities changed, they melted away, perhaps to disappear into the vastness, perhaps even to turn up on the other side. If an Indian scout did not break faith, he retained the option of dissolving back into the landscape. The only survivor of Custer's Last Stand was a Crow scout who used the colour of his skin as camouflage to make his escape.

The army's inability to enlist Indians as effective regulars would have mattered less had the white infantry and, more important, cavalry regiments been better attuned to warfare on the plains. The post–Civil War army was a poor thing. Under-trained and miserably paid, its soldiers, like Victoria's redcoats, were recruited from the country's unskilled poor. Many were immigrants off the boat, Irishmen and Germans, who had drifted into uniform after failing to find any productive place in the republic's booming economy. A vast proportion, as many as one-third each year, rapidly drifted out again, impelled by harsh treatment, bad food, boredom, and the hard labour of barrack-building and store-humping to desert when the sergeant's back was turned. Redcoats in India and French seven-year conscripts in Algeria did not have that option. Isolation in a foreign land turned them into hardened troopers willy-nilly, perfect in drill, adept at marksmanship, dutiful horsemasters. In Custer's 7th Cavalry, which was to fight at the Little Bighorn in 1876, a quarter of the soldiers were recruits that year, 15 per cent raw recruits. A third of the regiment had joined within the last six months, and, though some had served elsewhere, there were too many unfamiliar faces for it to be reckoned by European officers an effective fighting force. A British cavalry regiment in a similar state of training would have been on the home establishment, working up for active service, not posted to frontier duty in a theatre of war.

If the men were unsatisfactory, so too were many of the officers. Custer's regiment was unusual in containing several of his relatives as officers, but nepotism did not explain the low quality of captains and colonels in others. The truth was that the post–Civil War army, like many others in the aftermath of a great war, retained rank-holders who had avoided risk-taking in combat and shrunk from the risks of making a new civilian career in the aftermath. They were the second-best, often bureaucrats who made their juniors' lives miserable by pettifogging application of the rule-book, because they themselves lived in fear of reproof by penny-pinching, narrow-minded superiors in Washington or at departmental headquarters. Custer was an exception, a *sabreur*— more braggart than beau—who would have been out of place anywhere but at the head of a band of horsemen, however badly trained. He was not an exception in having descended several ranks since his Civil War glory days, when he had worn the star of a brigadier general at the age of twenty-three. By courtesy he was still addressed as "general" after he had reverted to his appointment as a lieutenant colonel commanding the 7th Cavalry, which in his glittering case was fair enough; but too many of the other officers of "brevet" rank in the post-war army were simply inflated leftovers, jealous of past status, jealous of such diminished position and privilege as their shrunken profession left them.

Jealousy and resentment shows in their faces. The soldiers of the Revolution look sternly and steadily out of the frames of their canvases; there is a spry elegance about the tight-waisted, double-breasted warriors of 1812 and 1846; the pathos of anticipated self-sacrifice lights the features of a multitude of young Confederates and of their opponents in dark blue in the fading daguerrotypes of 1861–62; a workmanlike jauntiness surrounds the images of Uncle Sam's campaign-hatted regulars of the Spanish war and carries over into

286 FIELDS OF BATTLE

those of the doughboys of 1917–18; I myself recall the well-cut khaki of the fit, young GIs who swarmed into the English West Country in the months before D-Day in 1944. The officers of the army of the Indian wars, by contrast, look seedy and shady. In their ill-fitting frock coats, scraps of gold lace, Dundreary whiskers, and wrinkled boots, they resemble, in their group photographs, nothing so much as a bunch of carpetbaggers or share-pushers on campaign to relieve honest farmers of their hard-earned dollars. Personally, I find the Indians they fought no more likeable; there is a selfishness about their belief in their right to enjoy the vastness of America quite as unappealing as the standing-upon-dignity of the Civil War relics. Nevertheless, all contemporary observers testify to the physical dignity of braves like Gall, Red Cloud, and Sitting Bull. The efforts of the painters of the plains army, Frederic Remington and Charles Schreyvogel, to glamorise the Indians' shabby opponents strains the credulity of the viewer.

Yet the army of the plains was the only army the United States possessed in the age of Manifest Destiny. Undefended, underpaid, ill-equipped, overstretched, it was the instrument with which white America had to overcome red America if the continent were to be bridged by civilisation from sea to sea. Militarily, moreover, the army had to solve a problem of unparalleled complexity. Nomads everywhere are a menace to civilisation. Hardy, warlike, elusive, they have throughout history tested the powers and discipline of regular armies to the limit. Enormous systems of fortification—the Great Wall of China, the Russian *cherta* lines on the Steppe, the Roman *limes Syriae*—were built over the centuries to contain them and protect the settled lands from their depredations. Almost all nomads, however, have an Achilles heel—flocks of grazing animals that they must protect, oases to which they retire between bouts of raiding, patches of fertile land in which they carry on transient agriculture. The American Plains Indians were unique in that they could sustain their nomadic way of life by parasitism on another nomadic entity, the millions of buffalo in the two vast migratory herds which roamed north and south of the Platte River. As long as the buffalo survived, so would the nomadism of the Indians, for unless cornered in combat, which the unobstructed surface of the plains and their own legendary fleetness in retreat made almost impossible, or constricted within a line of continuous fortification, which the army had neither the money nor manpower to construct and garrison, they could always disappear into the landscape.

By the early 1870s the systematic slaughter of the buffalo diminished year by year their freedom of action; so did the army's adoption of the practice of campaigning in the winter months, when the Indians traditionally hibernated, and of slaughtering their pony herds when found. Neither was a decisive means of imposing control. In any case, neither government nor army sought to extinguish nomadism altogether. In 1866 the Secretary of the Interior, whose department was responsible for running the Indian agencies, wrote that "it has been the settled policy of the government to establish the various tribes upon suitable reservations and there protect and subsist them until they can be taught to cultivate the soil and sustain themselves"; but long experience had taught the unlikelihood of the pony Indians ever becoming farmers. What the government arrived at was a halfway house, a sort of limited nomadism on what were judged generous spreads, the 77,000 square miles of the Sioux reservation, today South Dakota, and the 147,000 square miles of "unceded" territory to the west, today Montana, together exceeding in extent the land area of France or Spain. The Sioux, however, did not want a France or a Spain. They wanted their traditional hunting grounds on the Great Plains, half a million square miles, or nearly one-sixth of the United States; they also wanted their traditional right to war among themselves and against their tribal enemies, while granting themselves the liberty to practise pillage and rapine against whites who violated their territories. They saw, moreover, little wrong in taking what the Indian agents dispensed on the reservations in hard times, flour, sugar, blankets, and in slipping away to the good life outside the reservation when times were better. These transients swelled the numbers of the irreconcilables in an infuriating way and at the most awkward times.

Such a time was 1876, when the great irreconcilables, Crazy Horse and Sitting Bull, a religious intermediary with the Great Spirit of magnetic power over his fellow tribesmen, preached scorn against the weaklings on the reservations—"slaves to a piece of fat bacon, some hardtack and a little sugar and coffee"—and decried the threat of an army offensive. Unfortunately the chiefs had miscalculated. The army was resolved to march if the "roamers" did not report to the reservation by the deadline on 1 February, and when they did not, set its campaign in motion. There were to be three thrusts, all directed at the headwaters of the Yellowstone River, in "unceded" Indian territory, where the intransigent Sioux and their Cheyenne allies had set up their camps.

The Yellowstone, I discovered to my surprise when I bought a Montana state map at Billings Airport, flows eventually into the Gulf of Mexico, via the Missouri, not into the Pacific. I had supposed the famous geysers and blowholes of the national park spouted on the western, not eastern, slopes of the Continental Divide. They seem too geographically exotic to belong on the Great Plains side of the Rockies. Yet I was nearly right. The Yellowstone misses rising west of the Continental Divide by less than ten miles. Then it flows clear across Montana, almost parallel to the Missouri, to join it at Forts Union and Buford and so begin a journey of two thousand miles to the delta below New Orleans. By 1860 the head of steamboat navigation was already well beyond Fort Union on both rivers, giving communication to the army's main western bases at Fort Leavenworth and St. Louis. The strategy for the 1876 campaign, however, did not depend on steamboat for the concentration planned against the Indians. The three columns were to ride or march overland, one under Colonel John Gibbon from Fort Ellis at Bozeman deep in the Rockies, a second under General George Crook from Fort Fetterman on the North Platte River, a way-station on the Oregon Trail short of the famous South Pass through the mountains, and the third under General Alfred Terry from Fort Lincoln at Bismarck, North Dakota. They were intended to converge, from west, south, and east, on the cluster of small tributaries—the Bighorn, Little Bighorn, Rosebud, Tongue, and Powder rivers—which feed the Yellowstone itself. The deployment would bring together a significant proportion of the army's high-ranking officers, including two of its six brigadier generals, but few enough of its 30,000 soldiers. Crook commanded only 800 men, Gibbon 450, Terry 925. When combined, they would total few more than 2,000. The Indian Bureau had assured the army, however, that the Sioux could not put more than 800 men into the field. General Philip Sheridan, the Civil War luminary who succeeded Sherman as commander-in-chief in 1884, had assured Congress in 1874 that "we cannot have any war with the Indians because they cannot maintain five hundred men together for three days; they cannot feed them." Three days, however, is a long time in war, particularly if, as Sheridan admitted, the full fighting strength of the Sioux and their allies might be 3,000 to 4,000. His lofty under-estimates were to have a fatal sequel.

Sheridan counted on winter weather to hold Indian fighting numbers low. The army's new policy of attacking while the snows kept the "hostiles" scattered and campbound had proved successful; but only one of the columns, Crook's, got away before winter ended, and when it did catch some Indians in camp in the Powder River on 17 March, the officer in charge of the advance guard, Colonel Joseph Reynolds, panicked in the face of a counterattack and withdrew. Crook, perhaps the best of the army's Indian fighters, cunning, relentless in the trail, a keen student of Indian ethnology, a champion of the principle of using Indians to fight Indians, honourable in his dealings with them, was furious. He had entrusted the attack to Reynolds perhaps to help that officer out of trouble over some recent shady quartermaster deals. When together they returned to Fort Fetterman, he put Reynolds on a charge. The colonel not unjustifiably complained that his men had been defeated by the weather before the fight began. At times during the march to the Powder the temperature had frozen the mercury in the column's thermometers. Nevertheless, the Powder River hostiles had humiliated the army, lived to fight another day, and, worst of all, kept their herd of ponies on which to ride into battle.

The two other columns failed to take the trail from their forts before the bad weather relented. Gibbon did not leave Fort Ellis at Bozeman until 30 March. He had about two hundred miles to march down the Yellowstone to the mouth of its Bighorn tributary, where today a tiny place called Custer stands east of Billings, and reached it on 20 April. His orders were to stop hostile Sioux escaping northward across the Yellowstone from their encampments, guessed at but not precisely located, on the other side. He did not fulfil them. For nearly a month he patrolled the north bank, skirmishing occasionally with Sioux, who robbed his Crow scouts of their horses, collecting through his chief of scouts, the efficient Lieutenant James Bradley, extensive intelligence of Sioux strength and whereabouts but failing either to move to the attack or to pass on to General Terry the information his command had collected. It is a familiar story from the record of irregular warfare before the age of radio: a local commander putting his own preoccupations, in this case a concern about shortage of supplies, above his duty to transmit his observations of the enemy's movements, perhaps because of the presumption that what he knew must be known also to fellow commanders in the same area, perhaps because he did not recognise the importance of what his subordinates told him. One way or another, Lieutenant Bradley's identification of large Sioux encampments—dense smoke, interwoven pony trails—on 16 and 27 May did not reach General Terry. The Helena *Herald* printed news of the discovery of "500 lodges of Sioux on the Rosebud" on 28 May; but it was collecting information up the line of Gibbon's march from the west. Terry was still to Gibbon's east, outside the *Herald*'s distribution area.

Terry had marched from Bismarck, North Dakota, on 17 May. The 7th Cavalry formed his main force, though Custer, its commanding officer, had rejoined it only at the last moment; during the spring he had been detained in Washington, where his testimony was needed at hearings investigating frontier fraud. Terry's plan was to use Custer's cavalry to find the Indians, whom he then hoped to surround between Custer and Gibbon; Crook's force, which was to mount a second march up from Fort Fetterman, might also arrive in time to take part. The thoughts of all officers were fixed on the importance of stopping the Indians running away, as they almost always did when the army made concerted moves against them. The idea that they might fight was in no one's mind.

All the marches were long—Terry's 250 miles, Crook's 150 miles, while Gibbon had already marched 200—but the theatre of operations on which they were concentrating was quite small, about a hundred miles square. The terrain, however, made it seem large to soldiers who, at the fastest, could ride fifty miles a day and were forever breasting one slope only to see the horizon closed by another; the valleys of the little rivers offered no help, for they were twisty and filled with vegetation. The Indians were impeded admittedly by tentage, pony herds, and families; the soldiers were equally impeded by the wagon trains on which they depended for food. Only the horsemen—the cavalry, the braves—could move unfettered, and they not for long. Sheridan had not been so wrong in his estimate that three days was the maximum period a large Indian fighting force could be kept together in the field. Unfortunately, the same logistics applied to the army. A cavalry regiment like Custer's could either ride free but grow hungry or feed but keep close to its wagons; it could not do both. This obliged a cavalry commander who established contact with a fleet-footed enemy to take risks or lose his quarry, and that imperative was to underlie all that happened in the coming Sioux War.

Good intelligence would, of course, cut through the logistic difficulty; but good intelligence, even with Indian scouts beating the hills in large numbers, was hard to come by. A rumour that Sitting Bull was waiting on the Little Missouri, well east of the concentration zone, caused Terry to send Custer on a quite fruitless reconnaissance in early June. Not until 8 June, when he met the uncommunicative Gibbon at the mouth of the Powder on the Yellowstone River, did Terry get firm news of the Sioux presence on the Rosebud twenty miles to the west. Jumping to the—wrong—conclusion that they were still there, but wanting to eliminate the possibility that they had shifted camp to the Tongue or Powder rivers, he detached Custer's subordinate, Major Marcus Reno, thither. Reno, who went further than ordered, returned with the important information that the Sioux had indeed been on the Rosebud but had since moved further away from the Yellowstone into the hilly country to the southwest. Terry, correlating what he now knew of where the Sioux had been with what he could guess they would not do, which was to move westward towards the reservation of their Crow enemies, rightly decided that they must be somewhere in the Bighorn river system, probably in the valley of the Little Bighorn. That greatly reduced the area of geographical uncertainty and shortened the distances his columns would have to march before finding the Indians encamped. Discarding the orders given to Gibbon and Custer to converge on Rosebud, he summoned them on 21 June aboard the *Far West*, a government-chartered steamer which had succeeded in getting up the Yellowstone from the Missouri as far as the mouth of the Rosebud, the highest head of navigation so far achieved, and issued new instructions. Terry, with Gibbon under command, would proceed along the Yellowstone and then down the Bighorn to the mouth of the Little Bighorn. Custer would ride in a sweep down the Rosebud, proceed across country to the Little Bighorn, and then sweep up the river towards Terry and Gibbon. The Sioux would be trapped.

Unknown to any of the officers who met aboard the *Far West* on 22 June, however, the Sioux had already fought, and very fiercely. Crook's ill-fated third column, which had been turned back by Indian resistance on the Powder River on 17 March, had returned to Fort Fetterman, had set out again on 29 May, and had got up to the theatre of operations in mid-June, but suffered a second setback on 17 June when it had to fight a serious, six-hour battle near the headwaters of the Rosebud. Crook's men had stopped for coffee when they were surprised by hundreds of Sioux. Crazy Horse was in the band, and so were numbers of Cheyenne allies. Luckily for Crook, he had over two hundred of the Indian scouts he so favoured, who held off the first rush while the regulars formed up. When the fighting died down in mid-afternoon, however, Crook found he had lost several score dead and wounded. He reported ten and twenty-one respectively, but his chief scout said twenty-eight killed and fifty-six wounded. The truth was that Crook, who prided himself on his fieldcraft, had been defeated and wished to disguise the fact. He withdrew to base, at modern Sheridan, Wyoming, took no further part in the campaign, and did not get word of his reverse to Terry until too late.

Custer set off, therefore, on 22 June from the mouth of the Rosebud to march up its valley still in ignorance not only of the exact whereabouts of the Sioux but also of the mood that possessed them. He thought his mission was to prevent their escape, so that they could be rounded up and returned to the reservation. He did not know that they were in highly aggressive temper, nor that they had added the second fight with Crook to the success of their first. He did not know that Sitting Bull had presided at a sun dance on the Rosebud in mid-June, where the young warriors had tortured their flesh in demonstration of their courage and endurance and the chief had had a vision of "many soldiers falling into his camp." Above all, he did not know that the numbers of the Sioux had grown from the expected few hundred into several thousand.

Custer's orders allowed him wide latitude. Terry expected him to go far up the Rosebud before turning northward again to meet Gibbon, who should by then have reached the forks of the Bighorn and Little Bighorn and be awaiting him, so that the Indians "may be so nearly inclosed by the two columns that their escape will be impossible." He was reminded, however, of the ration problem—he had food for fifteen days at most, carried on mules—warned to "feel" towards his left, which meant towards the Little Bighorn, and permitted to depart from his orders if he thought that reasonable.

Custer was to see reason to do so. Late on 24 June the trail of Indian pony hoofs he was tracking up the Rosebud turned west, and he decided to follow it. He told his officers that he would pursue it as far as the divide—the separating ridge—between the Rosebud and the Lit-

tle Bighorn, rest his men there while sending scouts over to recon-
noitre, and then move to the attack against the Indian village he expected to find on the far side on 26 June.

My friend Roger Spiller retraced Custer's route from the Rosebud
to the divide in 1992 with a party from the Staff College at Fort Leavenworth. They were looking in particular for a lookout point on the divide called the Crow's Nest, from which Custer and his scouts are
supposed to have spotted the Indian village eight miles distant (the National Park Service marker at the battlefield says fifteen) on 25 June.
They found it. "We found the Crow's Nest," he wrote to me, "by a
form of what I can only call historical triangulation, using the sources,
the maps, the photo [a contemporary photograph of Crook and Scouts
taken just after the battle], and local knowledge. We climbed the hill,
taking perhaps a half hour or more to reach the top. Then we spread
out to see if we could locate a spot that corresponded to the photo. We
found it, on the side where Custer and his scouts would have come up.
. . . [It was] on a hill mass, perhaps a thousand meters high, that jutted
out from the main trace of the divide. . . . All day long we had been
trying to insinuate ourselves into Custer's frame of mind. He did not
know the strength of the enemy or even where they were. . . . He
wanted to engage the Sioux, but he was afraid they would get away.
And why wouldn't he have been anxious? That was the record of most
of his kind. . . . Up on the Crow's Nest, we wanted to test if he could
actually see the eight miles over to the Little Bighorn. Sources said
Custer was up there in the morning, and there was much talk about
visibility and haze. We were there in mid-May, and Custer came a
month later, when the heat works differently. On that day, we could
see. We could see the long brow of high ground on the other side of the
creek (the Little Bighorn) where the Indians' pony herds were grazing
and which had been noted at the time.

"At this point, the question was: if Custer could have seen the
pony herd and all that it implied about the strength of the enemy he
was facing, why was he so crazy to get at them? I thought the answer
was pretty simple. Like so many other colonial soldiers, Custer believed that the discipline and order and fire power of his own force
would easily compensate for lack of numbers. The fight would be a
repetition of his massacre at the Washita River (of Cheyenne in November 1868). . . . He didn't think the Sioux would stand."

Roger Spiller's re-creation of Custer's movements, observations,

and psychology on the morning of what was to be the last day of his
life are both fascinating and convincing. Nevertheless, it demands a
gloss or two. The campaign of 1876 may have been "colonial" in character, in the sense that distances, terrain, climate, and the nature of the
enemy compare with those the British and French had to face in
Afghanistan or Algeria. On the other hand, British and French soldiers
were normally better trained than Custer's, and the locals who accompanied them, Sepoys or Turcos, were many times more numerous and
altogether better disciplined than the U.S. Army's Indian scouts. Moreover, the 7th Cavalry was not only under-trained and under-
experienced; it was also, on 25 June, desperately tired after a march of
thirty miles the day before and ten during darkness. The mule train,
moreover, was lagging, which threatened food supply. If Custer kept to
its pace, he might lose the chance of attack. Exhausted though his
men—and horses—were, the imperative was to press them forward the
eight miles to where drifting smoke of cooking fires in the Little
Bighorn valley and the dark masses of pony herds grazing on the grass-
covered shoulders of the bluffs above indicated that Sitting Bull, his
Sioux, and their Cheyenne allies were in camp.

Custer came to a decision. Some of his scouts reported that the 7th
Cavalry had been observed by the enemy. He would attack at once. Accordingly he divided his twelve-troop, or company, regiment for battle.
These divisions have subsequently been called "battalions," a term
harking back to the age of European pike-and-musket warfare when it
first came into use. One battalion of three companies under Captain
Frederick Benteen was despatched to scout to the south, so as to prevent any Indians retreating towards the headwaters of the river. Another three formed Major Reno's battalion. Custer kept five in his own
battalion and left one to guard the pack train. He intended to move to
the charge as quickly as possible. Reno would move first, towards the
nearest edge of the village, which was not yet in view. Custer would
press on to encircle what he estimated to be the other end of the village. He had the high ground, on the crest of the ridge which fronted
the Little Bighorn valley on the north. The length of the projected battlefield was less than six miles. Half an hour's rapid movement would
place his battalions in positions from which the escape routes of the
Sioux either up or down the river could be blocked. Then their only resort would be to charge against him up the steep sides of the valley
which he dominated from the crest. Indians, we may presume Custer

believed, did not make frontal attacks against disciplined fire power over open hillsides. It was a fair judgement. It was to be proved wrong.

Custer's Last Stand

George Custer was not a nice man. Brave, certainly, bold, dashing, quick in decision, physically attractive, both to men and women, sexually alluring, all that; but nice, no. Niceness is not, of course, a prerequisite quality in a successful soldier. Grant, greatest of American generals, was not nice. The 1st Duke of Wellington, epitome of the English gentleman, was not nice. Washington, mastermind of Revolutionary victory, was not nice. Sherman, hatchet man of the Civil War and Custer's commander on the plains, was not nice. There was about all of those four, however, a redeeming moral quality that makes their lack of niceness beside the point. Wellington fought Napoleon with the relentlessness he did because he thought the Emperor of the French a political charlatan. Washington and Grant fought for the United States because they believed in the principles on which the republic was founded. Sherman fought in order to bring to an end a form of political intercourse, war between the states, for which he had come to feel distaste. For all four, war was no more than a means serving a higher object. The object engaged their moral sense, the means aroused in them an ultimate repugnance.

Custer, by every account, enjoyed war for its own sake. "Oh, could you have but seen some of the charges that were made," he exclaimed to a friend, recalling his experiences in the Civil War. "While thinking of them I cannot but exclaim, 'Glorious War.'" Young, headstrong, successful, and unwounded soldiers have often felt the glory of war. It is the emotion that runs through the *Iliad*; but Homer's heroes, like Alexander's Companions and Bohemund's Crusaders, were the offspring of warrior societies, in which skill-at-arms rode roughshod over higher values. Warriordom survives into our own times: the Gulf War would not have been won did West Point and Quantico and Sandhurst and St.-Cyr not continue to turn out young leaders who snort like warhorses at the scent of blood. There ought to be, however, a difference between the emotions of the young warrior and the old in civilised societies. A young warrior enlists to fight. His senior serves to tame the impetuousness of gallants and braves—the Sioux thought as much—to more sober purposes. Indeed, the role even of the young officer is as much to restrain as to lead; without his exertion of a measure of control over the actions of his followers, combat descends rapidly into mayhem on the one hand and disaster on the other. In that context, the failure of an officer to grow up is calamitous. Custer, the "Boy General," appears never to have grown up. His actions on the plains are tinged with the taint of mayhem. His final essay in command resulted in disaster *tout court*.

Custer was the quintessential bad-boy cadet. At West Point he chose deliberately to be in trouble, since that amused his contemporaries, and passed out thirty-fourth of a class of thirty-four. He had calculated the thinness of the ice on which he skated and just avoided engulfment. "He had more fun," recalled his West Point friend Peter Michie, "gave his friends more anxiety, walked more tours of extra guard and came nearer to being dismissed more often than any cadet I have ever known." Recognising only two positions in the cadet ranking, "head or foot," he opted for foot and gloried in its achievement. War redeemed his West Point record. Within a year of graduation, in June 1861, he had distinguished himself in action by the capture of the first Confederate colours taken by the Army of the Potomac, and had been offered a captaincy on his staff by General McClellan himself.

The serendipity of American warfare never ceases to astonish the European military historian. The continent is so large it defies belief that individuals should so often turn up in the same place and frequently at the same time over and over again. Yet in the history books there they are. Washington managed to be at the Monongahela, as an officer of King George III, at the siege of Boston in rebellion against him, and at the victory of Yorktown which crowned the King's defeat; the only surprise is that he was not at Quebec also. Bougainville was both at Quebec, on the losing side, and at Yorktown, on the winning side, having circumnavigated the globe and given his name to one of the most beautiful of tropical flowering plants in the meantime. Benedict Arnold was at the American assault on Quebec in 1775 and in the King's army during the Yorktown campaign of 1781. Gage was not at Quebec or Yorktown but was at the Monongahela and in Boston for the battles of Concord, Lexington, and Bunker Hill.

So perhaps we should not be surprised after all that Custer had fought in the Peninsular campaign. He had literally seen more of it than most, for he had been chosen to join the balloonist Professor T. S. C. Lowe in aerial observation of Confederate lines. From a height of a thousand feet he had noted, through his binoculars, tents, earthworks, and "heavy guns peering through the embrasures"; he made daily ascents until Magruder withdrew from the Yorktown position to the outskirts of Richmond. Ballooning he nevertheless found alarming; almost everything else about war he did not. Custer was ferociously brave, with the sort of ostentatious bravery that actually diminishes risk in hand-to-hand combat because its display instils fear into opponents. He was always to the front in his cavalry charges, killed men at close range, escaped death himself by a whisker. One of his soldiers killed the great Confederate cavalry leader Jeb Stuart, and he himself not only defeated the formation of his old West Point roommate "Tex" Rosser but captured his kit and tried on his uniform, for all the world like a Greek outside Troy parading in the armour of a fallen Trojan. Custer loved uniforms and cultivated a flamboyant appearance. As a cadet he had thrice been disciplined for wearing his hair or whiskers too long and once for "unauthorised ornament on coat." During the Civil War most of his uniform had been unauthorised—velvet trousers, braided jacket, sailor shirt, scarlet cravat, long jackboots, gilt spurs, and gold lace everywhere—and his hair was positively effeminate, blond locks spilling over his shoulders. He had, nevertheless, risen to command a division, to win McClellan's golden opinion, and to be given by Sheridan, as a present for his bride, the table on which Lee had signed the articles of surrender at Appomattox. Sheridan had bought it for twenty dollars in gold, and Custer rode off with it balanced on his head.

Peace is bad for bravadoes like Custer. Those with sense as well as fire find something unwarlike in the aftermath of a great conflict to occupy their energies. Nathan Bedford Forrest, who had made a fortune before the war in cotton, made another afterwards in railroads; perhaps the Confederacy's greatest cavalryman, he put defeat behind him and devoted himself to capitalism and extremist politics. Baden-Powell, Britain's Boer War darling, took up youth work. Ernst Jünger, Germany's leading storm-trooper of the trenches, became an intellectual. Leonard Cheshire, who won the Victoria Cross as a Bomber Command pathfinder, founded a major humanitarian charity. There is something dysfunctional, in a civilised society, about heroes who cannot kick the heroic habit. Often they drift off in search of other wars to fight, as so

many of the veterans of the Napoleonic Wars did to Greece in its struggle for independence from the Ottomans in the 1820s; sometimes they
become mercenaries, hiring their guns to anyone who will pay; the
lowliest of them may take to crime. Custer eschewed both crime and
mercenarism—though Keogh, who died with him at the Little Bighorn,
had been a soldier-of-fortune in Italy—but he succeeded in getting himself court-martialled at Fort Leavenworth in 1867 for insubordination
and he became a thorn in the flesh of high command and government
in the post-war years, ever ready to allege malpractice against officials
of the administration.

He also spoiled for a fight. His wildest exploit before the Little
Bighorn was at the Washita in 1868, when he surprised Chief Black
Kettle's Cheyenne in camp and fell on them savagely. That they were
"hostiles" there was no doubt; but the 103 dead included women and
children as well as braves. Moreover, the battle resulted in the extinction of seventeen of his own soldiers who, departing imprudently to
chase the fugitives, were killed to a man. Many in the 7th Cavalry did
not forgive their commander for what they saw as a failure to support
his subordinates, and the rancours were to fester as late as the Little
Bighorn itself. He had other fights, notably in the Yellowstone in 1873,
and he won a name as a leading Indian fighter. He never acquired,
however, the reputation either of George Crook or Nelson Miles, the
leading practitioners of plains warfare, never achieved the sort of empathy with the foe which is the mark of the real wilderness warrior,
and never again, after the Civil War, established that psychological as-
cendancy over his own subordinates which is the bedrock of cut-and-
thrust leadership. The impression left by his career in the eleven years
between Appomattox and his death is of increasing discontent and
frustration, depression and decline, relieved by occasional bursts of action, enlivened by forced displays of independence, and alleviated by
passages of adventure, as in his Yellowstone expedition of 1874. In a
different, truly colonial or imperial society, Custer might have gone
on from the Civil War to greater things, as did Bugeaud in Algeria
after the Napoleonic Wars and the Russian veterans of the Crimean
War in the conquest of Central Asia. In the stridently populist, mercantile and farmer society of later-nineteenth-century America—
critical though its tiny army was to its final occupation of the
national territory—Custer could not be more than a servant of forces
greater than himself. Some realisation of his marginal role in the

growing greatness of America shows in the story of his final years.

Still, the old fire awoke on the divide between the Rosebud and Little Bighorn rivers on the morning of 25 June 1876. Near him, he knew,
was the most important encampment of "hostiles" then challenging the
authority of the U.S. government and army. That its warriors greatly
outnumbered the force he did not guess and may not have cared; he
continued to believe, with other plains soldiers, that Indians confronted
by cavalry would run, not fight. He gave his orders: Benteen to scout
the upper Little Bighorn, the rest of the regiment to follow him along
the high ground above it, until the two forces could combine and overawe or overwhelm the Indians below them.

It is an eerie and unsettling experience to come upon the ground
that Custer discovered when in early afternoon his column breasted the
heights above the Little Bighorn and at last got visual confirmation—
clouds of dust, reports of a party of fleeing Sioux—that the Indians
were close at hand. We see now almost at a glance—a few minutes by
car along the Park Service road, by a brief study of the topographic
model at the Visitor Center—what Custer did not see: the length of the
battlefield, about four miles from the point of first contact to the site of
his last stand, and its exact shape, a series of shallow gullies and
ravines running down from the undulating ridge line to the serpentine,
tree-shaded course of the Little Bighorn. We also see what the future
concealed from Custer: the unrolling of the battle, the unravelling of
his command and its final bloody extinction.

Small white headstones, the same headstones that stand in the
mown grass at Malvern Hill in the Peninsula, tell the story. This is a
curiously Scottish landscape, green but also brown, rough underfoot
yet smooth and undulating in the long view, treeless on the tops but
bumpy with small knobs of bushes on the slopes, dry and burnt but
giving a hint of sogginess in the hollows. White stone shows clear
against the ground cover, all the clearer because this is indeed Big Sky
country, the banks of high clouds sailing against the blue in stately convoy towards horizons that lie far beyond the circle of vision. Big Sky
light picks out the headstones, here a cluster, there a straggling line, in
the distance the dot of a single memorial, each marking the spot where
a man died, all starkly inscribed: "U.S. Soldier 7th Cavalry Fell Here,
June 25, 1876."

The Park Service road has been driven to follow the route Custer
rode, but one travels it in reverse direction, beginning at Last Stand

Hill where the battle ended, then down the course of the running battle that unfolded as the Indians raced up the hillside to shoot at the white men riding the ridge, to terminate at the other hill where the companies which had not taken part dug themselves in and survived the on-slaught. A historian's eye interprets the evidence the headstones pre-sent: at Last Stand Hill a dense concentration of men fighting for their lives; here and there along the road signs of an effort to form a firing line; down the forward slopes small clumps where troopers tried to take the battle to the enemy; off in the hinterland individual stones marking the death place of fugitives or stragglers; in half a dozen scat-tered spots small concentrations where isolated groups made last stands of their own. Beaver Dam Creek remains a sinister place, but time has removed from it the physical signs of who died where and when. The Custer battlefield retains its chilling poignancy because each stone tells a story. It is a story of a battle going desperately wrong for the man who initiated it and for the soldiers who followed him into confrontation with savagery.

On my drive back along Custer's route a coyote—could it have been a wolf? I have never seen either in the wild—cleared the road ahead of my car in a single bound and shot off into the undergrowth beyond, a reminder that this is still wild and unsettled country. A little further on, two travellers in Custer cavalry uniform stopped their horses to be photographed by tourists in a leisure vehicle. There were more leisure vehicles at Reno Hill, where the companies which did not follow Custer dug their rifle pits. There a man with a pitted face and cowboy hat took turns with me to peer through the peepholes in the Park Service markers at the Crow's Nest and the site of the Sioux en-campment. We watched some graziers on horseback begin to drive a small herd of brown cattle up the steep rise from the valley floor. A few minutes later, driving back, I met them opening the roadside fence to let the cattle through. That was all the time it must have taken for the Sioux to ride their ponies up from the river bottom to the high ground where the white men were strung out along the ridge line. Disaster came quickly to the 7th Cavalry.

Disaster began not up in the bare high ground but in the verdant valley below. Custer's first order, after he had taken the decision to ride to the attack, was to detach the Reno battalion down a feeder stream of the Little Bighorn, now known as Reno Creek, where they stumbled on a party of Sioux, who rode off in alarm towards the encampment, still hidden by a shoulder of the ridge on the west bank. Custer sent Reno in pursuit, promising that "you will be supported by the whole outfit." While he rode on, Reno crossed the stream to the east bank. At the water the horses stopped to drink, but he got the column moving again at about three o'clock. Soon there were a succession of Indian sightings, for they were approaching the southern end of the camp. Reno sent back first one, then a second man, to warn Custer that the Indians "were strong." An interpreter, Fred Gerard, pointed out to Reno that the Indians were not retreating but coming forward, but was disregarded. As Gerard knew, however, that "Custer was under the impression that the Indians were running away . . . and it was important for him to know that the Indians were not running away," he also told the adjutant, William Cooke, who decided to take the message back on his own account.

As Cooke rode back, Reno pressed on down the valley, now separated from Custer by the river and the tree line; the line of pretty cottonwoods is not wide, but it is, as it was then, quite dense and thickened by fallen branches and undergrowth. Very shortly, Reno ran into the Indians the scouts had reported coming towards them and ordered his men into skirmishing order. This was a drill common to cavalry all over the world. Three men dismounted to open fire, while a "horse holder" led his and their mounts to the rear. One flank of Reno's skirmishing line was out in the flat ground, above which the Indian ponies had been grazing when Custer spotted them from the Crow's Nest that morning; the other rested by the river and under the trees.

For a while Reno's skirmishing tactics held the Indians at bay. Soon, however, they began to filter round his open flank—the end of his line which lay out in the valley—and he began to worry about his ammunition supply. The men were shooting off the rounds they had in their pouches, and the reserve ammunition was up in the heights behind him, with the mule train. After about fifteen minutes Reno decided he was losing the firefight and ordered his men back into the trees; but there the Indians joined them and casualties were suffered. Within half an hour, Reno ordered his men to mount—somehow the horse holders found them—and then, after briefly dismounting them again, perhaps in the hope of forming another skirmishing line, led them upstream at a gallop, mounted Indians intermixed with the fugitives, until they could find a way across to rejoin the main party on the opposite bank. In the disorganisation, many cavalrymen were shot down. By the time Reno reached high ground, 40 of his 140 men had been killed or abandoned and 13 wounded.

While the little battle in the valley bottom had been raging, several of Reno's troopers had time to notice Custer's main party on the high ground above, moving at a trot downstream; some saw Custer wave his hat. Custer saw the commotion of battle down below, for one of his Crow scouts, who escaped the catastrophe, recalled that "we could see Reno fighting. He had crossed the Creek. Everything was a scramble with lots of Sioux." Custer soon knew, moreover, what trouble lay in store, for the adjutant, Cooke, had come up to him and he could see the size of the Sioux host: "camps and camps and camps," remembered a Crow. "There was a big camp in a circle near the west hills." Custer's military sense told him that there was much shooting ahead, for he sent word back "to bring the pack train straight across to high ground—if packs get loose don't stop to fix them, cut them off. Come quick. Big Indian camp."

This order must have been sent at about quarter past three, when the head of his column was halfway down the modern battlefield road, approaching the hollow called Medicine Trail Coulee. Here some of his troopers lost control of their horses, which began to gallop. Custer called out, "Boys, hold your horses. There are plenty down there for all of us." He was still expecting discipline and fire power to prevail, despite the growing evidence of how large Indian numbers were. A little further on he sent a second order to bring up ammunition. Cooke, who had carried news of the Indians' strength up from Reno's valley fight, pencilled a quick—still existing—note to Major Benteen, commanding the rear party, "Come on. Big Village. Bring pack. W. W. Cooke. P. [sic] Bring pacs [sic]." He handed the scrawl to John Martin, an Italian immigrant who had recently anglicised his name from Giovanni Martini, and rode on. Martin, spurring back, met Custer's brother, Boston, bringing ammunition forward. Martin then glimpsed "the command . . . going down into [Medicine Trail] ravine. . . . they were galloping"; he also "saw Indians, some waving buffalo robes and some shooting."

With this report, Custer passes from white history. All we know of his and his soldiers' fate comes hereafter from Indian sources. Their testimony—it includes that of Indian scouts, Indian participants in the battle, and the very late deposition of an Indian woman—tantalises Custer historians by its unconcern for exact chronology, topography, or the relationship of one with the other. Yet in truth, the testimony of Custer's enemies, however exact perfectionists might hope it to be, could add no more than detail to the outcome of their encounter. For Custer, with few more than two hundred men under command, had chosen to ride into a concentration of several thousand Indians, men, women, and children, whose warriors outnumbered the troopers perhaps by ten to one. Some of them were better armed than the soldiers, firing Winchester repeating rifles against single-shot Springfield carbines. All were rested, while the soldiers were physically exhausted, their horses also, while the Indian ponies, hastily collected from the shoulder of the valley bluffs where they had been grazing but minutes before Custer's appearance, were fresh. The Indians, moreover, were in fighting mood. Custer's men may have been fired by the sight of the encampment so long sought, and by Custer's exhortations, but the Indians were not only rebelliously aggressive but frantic to defend their women and children from an attack on the village in which, experience told them, sex and age were no protection against slaughter.

Few against many, therefore, tired against fresh, and, at best, cavalry courage against warrior rage, outrage, and instinct for revenge. It was only to be expected that Custer's unsupported two hundred should go down to defeat and that, in defeat, they should be killed to the last man and their bodies mutilated. The questions are: How exactly did the two hundred put themselves in a position from which they could not extricate themselves by flight? Where and when were they overwhelmed? Why did the unengaged companies of the 7th Cavalry not ride—if not to their rescue, which disparity of numbers probably ruled out—at least to their support?

The broad answer to these questions is that Custer seems to have believed until the very last moment that he was attacking and enjoyed an offensive advantage, both of timing and dominant position, and that the Indians were running away or would do so when his fire power told. When he at last recognised that it was he who was at a disadvantage, of numbers, of isolation, and ultimately of fire power, and that it was the Indians who were attacking him, it was too late. The bare heights of the ridge above the Little Bighorn offered him no compact, commanding position on which to concentrate his soldiers for a rally in which disciplined fire power might have told. He may well have attempted a rally but then tried to hold too long a perimeter and dispersed his troops. He may simply have been caught by superior numbers while his column was in extended order, encircled, and gunned down. Either way, the results proved fatal.

John Gray, a retired physiologist, has dissected the evidence that survives—narrative, archaeological, topographical—in relentless detail and offered a reconstruction of events upon which it seems impossible to improve. It confirms the picture of a headstrong commander, tensed bowstring-taut in his determination to bring back a victory from the Little Bighorn, pressing ever deeper into danger and taking a succession of decisions each one of which heightened the risks he was running until he had no choice of action left except that of dying in a trap of his own making.

Gray's timescale is short, little more than an hour and fifty minutes between the departure of Private Martin towards the rear party with the urgent request for ammunition—"Bring pacs"—and the death of Custer's last survivor in the last stand on what is now known as Custer Hill. Gray discounts disorganisation. Custer, he convincingly proposes, handled his command during some of those two hours in a controlled and military fashion. He had, if not an exact plan, at least an anticipation of how the engagement ought to unroll. Reno, down in the river bottom, would engage the surprised Indians in a firefight and keep them busy at the west end of the village while he and his five companies continued with the envelopment along the high ground towards the eastern end of the encampment. That was his initial decision; then, as he rode further forward and got the extent of the village in view as it unfolded beyond the bumps of the ridge's shoulders, he decided to create a second threat by detaching part of his battalion to ride down the slope and attack it inside the diversion Reno had already created. While this second threat was developing he rode on further, choosing a route on the reverse slope of the ridge, out of the Indians' view, with the object of reappearing above the river at a fordable point and riding down to open a third firefight in the heart of the village itself. By then, Gray surmises, he hoped that his urgent appeals for ammunition and reinforcements would have brought up the rest of the regiment. The Indians, assailed at three points, disorganised and frantic for the safety of their families, and now attacked by Benteen's companies, would then cease to operate as a cohesive force and succumb to the military orthodoxy of Custer's concentrated attack.

This is a convincing reconstruction of what may have passed through Custer's mind. The testimony of Curley, an Indian scout whom

Custer sent back as action quickened, bears it out; Custer's dismissal of all his Indians—three Crows were ordered away as well—at a moment when a European officer would have been counting every rifle is in itself a demonstration of his persisting sense of superiority over the Sioux. Curley, through a later testimony interpreted by an officer, described how part of Custer's force went down to the river, exchanged fire, and then rode back to join the main column on the ridge. "They came down ravine to its mouth. . . . The Sioux could be seen mounting . . . and commenced to fire. . . . the troops fired back, remaining mounted. . . . The troops then turned from the mouth . . . the men in the lead motioning with their hands to go northeast, when [where?] the companies broke from the main column, as if to meet again on the main ridge."

Dr. Gray suggests that what Curley saw was the outcome of a decision by Custer to divide his command about halfway along the modern battlefield road, in order to create a diversion by part of it, opening the second firefight, while he led the rest of his force behind high ground to reappear further westward, nearer the end of the Sioux encampment, at which point the detached troops rejoined him. Archaeological evidence supports the view that two companies, probably E and F under Captain George Yates, went down to the river; Gray suggests that their role was to make a feint, which would hold some of the Sioux there while Custer pushed on to extend what he still believed was an envelopment of the encampment. When Yates rejoined him, at about a quarter to five, near what is now known as Custer Hill, his command may still have been largely intact. Some men had been lost by Yates in the skirmish at the river and others in the ride along the ridge, but he still led a fighting force.

Shortly afterwards, however, a different reality began to break in. Curley, just before he left to ride out of the battle, saw "a hurried conference of officers. . . . [Mitch] Bouyer [a half-breed scout] told Curley . . . that if the command could make a stand somewhere, the remainder of the regiment would probably come up and relieve them. Personally, Bouyer did not expect relief would come, as he thought the other commands had been scared out. Bouyer thought the orders would be to charge straight ahead, drive the Indians from the ravine [below Custer Hill] and try to find more favourable ground." Bouyer was by this stage wounded. His last words to Curley were "You are very young and do not know very much about fighting. I advise you to leave us, and if you can get away by detouring and keeping out of the way of the Sioux, do so, and go to the other soldiers and tell them that all are killed. That man [Custer] will stop at nothing. He is going to take us right into the village, where there are many more warriors than we are. We have no chance at all." They shook hands. Curley rode off and followed a creek "until a tributary took him in a northerly direction. He followed it until he reached the high ridge east of the battlefield, about $1^1/_2$ miles. From this place [he] could see the battle with field glasses. He saw the Indians circle Custer's men."

Curley had ridden away at about ten to five. By twenty past, when he brought his field glasses to bear, the end was less than ten minutes away. In the interval, Custer had abandoned his remaining thought of charging down into the village from the high ground and had spread his companions out to line the ring of little crests that encircled his position, from which fire could be directed down on the Indians now swarming in hundreds not only up the slope from the valley, but round his flanks and out into the open heathland to his rear. "Heap Shoot" Curley had already witnessed from close at hand before he left. "Heap Shoot" now enveloped Custer's men as they made their last stand. Custer's decision to form a front in all directions along the best ground available had been correct; distance robbed it of point. Dr. Gray has calculated the length of the perimeter Custer tried to hold at 1.8 miles, into which two hundred men go—supposing two hundred were still capable of pulling a trigger—fifteen times. Individuals forty-five feet apart, for that is the interval at which the calculation puts them, would have had, with their single-shot carbines, no hope of sustaining an impermeable wall of fire against attackers outnumbering them eight or ten to one. Their line would soon have been penetrated. The gravestones tell the rest of the story.

No doubt, as Indian numbers thickened, the attempt to maintain a cohesive firing line collapsed. Terrified men must have clustered together, opening wider gaps; parts of the line may have been overrun altogether. There are Indian accounts of this final stage, difficult to relate to the ground or to arrange in time. Some speak of soldiers throwing aside their carbines, perhaps because they had been out of ammunition; others of soldiers committing suicide, not unknown in savage warfare when scalping, disembowelling, dismemberment, or transfixing by arrows awaited the disarmed victim. Much of the killing seems to have been done with arrows, though perhaps only after the soldier targets had been shot or ammunition had run out. Stories of Custer's men being overwhelmed by a hail of dropping arrows are unconvincing, since the bow was an effective killing agent only in flat trajectory against a visible target. Haphazard shooting into the general area of the last stand would have missed more often than it hit. In the final minutes, however, tomahawking and knifing, described by several Indian participants, probably did despatch the last survivors. What is certain is that, by about half past five on the afternoon of 25 July, all 210 men of the Custer battalion were dead and most of their bodies lay within the two-mile perimeter on which its commander had tried to make a stand until the help which did not reach him should arrive.

The unfolding and culmination of the ghastly slaughter the eye takes in all too quickly, almost at a single glance, in the final circuit of the battlefield road. The dense cluster of gravestones on Custer Hill is the centrepiece of the Park Service's meticulous conservation of the site; more poignant are the smaller, more distant groupings out in the heathland where the detached companies met their end. They mark the outlines of the most transient fort of American military history, a field position extinguished almost as soon as conceived, not a strong place but a weak place, a mere smear of neural conception, wiped away in an outburst of native American ferocity against the conqueror and tormentor.

The Indians' ferocious emotions were temporarily assuaged by their triumph over Custer at the western end of the camp. Some of the victors dressed themselves in soldiers' uniforms, caught and mounted their horses, paraded in triumph before the women and children who had sheltered during the battle in a ravine on the far side of the Little Bighorn. Others searched the battlefield for weapons and ammunition. The battle was not yet over. Beyond the eastern end of the campsite the companies of the 7th Cavalry not yet engaged—Benteen's three and that protecting the mule train, together with the men of Reno's three companies who had escaped from the fight in the trees at the river— had gathered on the high ground. They were within earshot of the fighting and sight of the dust it threw up. They had received Custer's last messages, including the pencilled appeal to "Bring pacs." It was clear that there was a crisis. Martin, who carried the note, arrived on a wounded horse. One of the company commanders, Captain Thomas Weir, had on his own initiative started forward at the head of his men, other companies following, to go to the rescue. Benteen's heart was not in it, however, nor was Reno's. His first words after his escape were "For God's sake, Benteen, help your command and help me. I've lost half my men."

Reno was the senior officer, and Benteen obeyed. Indians arriving from the victory over Custer soon confronted Captain Weir with superior force, and he fell back on the position his superior officers, Reno and Benteen, had taken up around a hollow in one of the river bluffs. There the companies, some 350 strong, were able to find the compact, defensible position which Custer had sought but not found further to the east where the white marble headstones now dot the heath. During the remaining hours of daylight, spread out in a tight circle around the wounded and the tethered horses and mules grouped in the hollow, they gave back shot for shot against the exultant Indians ringing their firing line. Then, when darkness descended, they began to disappear below the surface, as soldiers do when fire descends, into every shallow scrape that knives, mess tins, and hands could win from the soil. Night had fallen by nine o'clock.

When the sun rose on 26 June the remnants of the 7th Cavalry, companies A, B, D, H, G, K, and M, were entrenched within a shallow earthwork, parapeted by ammunition boxes, saddles, and supply packs. A fort had come into being. Benteen, who had taken effective command, defended it tenaciously throughout the day, striding about to hearten his men when Indian fire quickened, encouraging Reno to counterattack at one stage, at another leading a charge beyond the perimeter himself. This was frontier warfare in classic style. The defence of the entrenchment held through the hot morning, though thirst tormented; at one stage some brave troopers sallied out to the river to bring a few cupfuls of water to the wounded, of whom there were sixty in the hollow. Then in early afternoon the fire of the Indians began to die away. Thirst would have won them the battle, but they lacked the patience to wait and they feared the arrival of army reinforcements. They had triumphed over Custer, they had taken trophies, and now the urge to leave the place of death took possession of them. Perhaps as many as three hundred of their own, out of a fighting force of two thousand, had died. It was time to go, before more were killed on the slopes of Reno Hill, before inevitable retribution arrived. At seven o'clock in the evening the defenders of Reno's entrenchment saw the valley below them fill with smoke, as the Sioux and their Cheyenne allies set fire to the grass, and through it they watched the great encampment of warriors, women, children, and ponies begin to file away southwestward to a new sanctuary in the Bighorn Mountains.

Early next morning, 27 June, the survivors of Reno's fight in the treeline at the river, who had lain concealed for a day and a half, staggered into the position. Then, as the hills lightened, the defenders saw the head of a relief column of the 2nd Cavalry riding up the valley from the east. Soon the steamboat *Far West*, which had supported the expedition, was forced up the Bighorn to its junction with the Little Bighorn at modern Hardin, fifteen miles from the last stand, and the wounded loaded aboard. They were laid on the deck on beds of cut grass; fifty-four hours later, in a burst of speed never to be exceeded in the Missouri river system, *Far West* docked at Bismarck, North Dakota, 710 miles away. The captain hastened to the telegraph office, where the operator tapped into the national network the brief report: "General Custer attacked the Indians June 25 and he, with every officer and man in five companies, were killed."

The message down the wire caused a national sensation. The red man had struck back. White America demanded revenge. It got it. Indian resolution in all the wars with the European invader, from those of the Iroquois with the French in the seventeenth century onward, had always—except in the case of the Seminoles—been short-lived; so that of the Sioux proved. Crook and Terry, the two generals who had planned the Sioux War of 1876, did not at once take up the pursuit of the victorious Sioux. They seem to have been disoriented by the disaster. They certainly exaggerated to themselves the numbers of armed Sioux and Cheyenne roaming the warpath in the Bighorn Mountains. Not until early August, when reinforcements arrived at their camps in the Yellowstone and Powder rivers, did they lead out their punitive expeditions: Terry to the Rosebud River with 1,700 men, Crook to the Tongue with 2,300. By then the Indians, who had quickly hunted out the Bighorn region, were already scattering; some actually reported to the Sioux reservation. Crazy Horse was heading for the Black Hills, Sitting Bull—who may in fact have taken no part in the battle his big medicine inspired—for the Little Missouri. Wherever they went, neither Crook nor Terry could find them, though they floundered about all autumn in their pursuit. In September, however, some Sioux chiefs were brought to sign away the Black Hills, while the aggressive Colonel Nelson Miles campaigned all winter against what Sioux bands he could find in Yellowstone country. His relentlessness and that of other younger commanders paid off. In May 1877 Crazy Horse brought 1,100 Sioux into Camp Robinson, Nebraska, and cast his weapons on the ground in token of surrender; within the year he was dead, killed by his jailers when appearing to defy their orders. On 19 July, Sitting Bull led forty-three Sioux families, all that remained under his leadership, into Fort Buford, North Dakota, and handed his Winchester to his eight-year-old son to present to the commander, Major David Brotherton. "I wish it to be remembered," he said, "that I was the last man of my tribe to surrender my rifle." Then he slipped away into Canada, where whites were fewer—the great settlement of the prairies had not begun—and the authorities less exigent, and where he remained until 1881, when shortage of game and the seepage of his followers back into the United States brought his exile to an end.

That was not quite the end of Sitting Bull's defiance or of warfare in the West. There remained numbers of tribes, of the Southwest and the Rocky Mountains, Nez Percés, Bannocks, Paiutes, Ute, Apache, who had grievances over treaties or who disliked the reservation system or who simply chose to cling to their traditional ways and who accordingly fell into war with the United States during what remained of the 1870s and the 1880s. The army fought them hard, as the memorial tablets in the Fort Leavenworth chapel record; but during those years some of its leaders also came to adopt a protective attitude towards its enemies, to identify with their culture—as far as any white man could—and even to espouse their cause. Soldiers in savage wars were behaving similarly all over the world during the late nineteenth century, in empathy, part romantic, part moral, with the heroic qualities of the warriors they fought. British officers on the Afghan frontier, French officers in the Sahara, Russians in Central Asia, were learning local languages, adopting native costume, studying tribal customs, even dabbling in alien religions. The U.S. Army did not go so far: its officers jibbed at warpaint and shamanism. Some, nevertheless, came to feel an increasing distaste for the corruption that raged in the Indian Bureau, for the greed of cattle barons and mining kings, for the racialism of settler politicians, for the expedient readiness of the Federal government to abrogate its treaty obligations to native Americans. Nelson Miles, the great Indian fighter, was one of them; his advocacy of the cause of Chief Joseph of the Nez Percés resulted in the survivors of the tribe being allowed to return from Canada, where they had taken refuge with Sitting Bull, and settle near their tribal home in the Northwest.

Such officers inevitably were in the minority. The army's central relationship with the remaining "hostiles" during the decade following the Little Bighorn was a campaigning one: in the Nez Percé War of 1877 in Idaho and Oregon, in the Bannock and Paiute wars of 1877–78 in those states and in Nevada, in the Ute War of 1879 in Colorado, and in the Apache War in Arizona, New Mexico, and across the Mexican border in the years 1881–86. Geronimo, most elusive and irreconcilable of the Apache chiefs, was the last of the Indian war leaders whose name was to join those of Tecumseh, Crazy Horse, and Sitting Bull in American folklore. Ironically, on the collapse of his resistance, his Chiricahua Apache were exiled to Florida, from which the expulsion of the Seminoles had been supposed to end the Federal government's difficulties with native America nearly sixty years earlier.

Geronimo was the last defiant, but not the last resistant. In 1890 a new mood swept the Plains Indians, a belief that they could escape their white tormentors and enter a harmonious new world by the adoption of a quietist moral code, expressed through prayer and dance. Beaten people elsewhere had adapted similarly: Sikhism began as a quietist resistance to forced conversion to Islam by devout Hindus of the Punjab. Quietism, however, has a tendency to tip the other way, into militant self-righteousness. The Sikhs became in the nineteenth century the most warlike people in India. There are other tendencies, notably conversion to a belief that mystical practices or symbols will protect cultists against physical harm. In 1905–6 the Africans of Tanganyika rose against the German colonial government in the Maji-Maji rebellion; Maji-Maji magic, they were persuaded, would turn away German bullets. Seventy-five thousand died in the process of discovering that magic was not a weapon of war.

Some Sioux converts to the Ghost Dance cult of 1890–91 both rejected its quietism and conceived a belief that "ghost shirts" were bulletproof. Their frenetic dancing caused alarm throughout the white settlements of Montana, Nebraska, and the Dakotas, and the army was called in. Many of the Sioux were talked back into passivity; a few chiefs, foremost among them Sitting Bull, remained intransigent. On 15 December 1890, soldiers attempting to arrest Sitting Bull, at Standing Rock on the Sioux reservation, fell into a fracas with his followers, at the end of which the old chief lay dead. Two weeks later the soldiers caught up with the last hostiles at Wounded Knee Creek in South Dakota, surrounded them, and, when they refused to be disarmed, opened fire with automatic cannon. Within a few minutes, 150 Sioux were dead, and within the month, native American resistance to white power in the continent was over for ever. Custer had been revenged. The 7th Cavalry paraded its colour to mark the surrender of his rifle by Kicking Bear, the last fighting Indian chief.

"The Ghost Dance," concludes Robert Utley, foremost scholar of plains military history, "was the Indians' last hope . . . [the last act] in the four-century drama of the Indian wars. . . . Accommodation had failed. Retreat had failed. War had failed. And now . . . religion had failed. No choice remained but to submit to the dictates of government. Whether coincidentally or not, in this very year of 1890 the statisticians of the Census Bureau discovered that they could no longer trace a distinct frontier of settlement in the map of the United States. Only three years later a young historian named Frederick Jackson Turner appeared before the convention of the American Historical Association in Chicago to present a paper entitled 'The Significance of the Frontier in American History.' "

Turner's thesis has since become celebrated. In brief, he proposed the idea that it was the frontier which made Americans different from the peoples of other continents. Coming anew to a new world, those with the spirit to abandon the Europeanised coast and push inland found an un-European self-reliance and spiritual freedom through their successful struggle over distance, nature, and danger, of which one was danger from Indian hostility. Self-reliance and the sense of liberty bled back from the frontier to make all Americans innovators, democrats, and wanderers, fiercely nationalistic as individuals but free of the particularistic attachment to a locality or homeland that divided Europeans against themselves. If that were true, it would explain the pitiless relentlessness with which frontier Americans battled against native America for possession of the continent. It would also explain their success. Indians were intensely particularistic, both as social beings and as occupants of territory, but for those reasons incapable of making common cause to defend what they held dearest, their freedom to roam as nomads inside territories they did not claim to own but nevertheless sought to use and enjoy by exclusive right. Against their fragmented resistance, white America was bound to triumph. The only surprise—though this was not part of Turner's thesis—was that they should have resisted so long and so tenaciously.

There are parallels. The Battle of the Little Bighorn is not a unique example of the humiliation of white regulars by indigenous warriors. At three places in Africa during the imperial era, Isandhlwana, Adowa, and Anual, European armies marching on the offensive were surprised by their enemies, defeated, and slaughtered, not in hundreds but in thousands. At Isandhlwana in 1879 the warriors of the Zulu kingdom overwhelmed a British force and killed nearly 2,000 men. At Adowa in 1896 the soldiers of Emperor Menelek of Ethiopia destroyed an Italian army, killing 6,500. At Anual in 1921 the followers of the Moroccan rebel leader Abd-el Krim attacked a Spanish army and left 12,000 dead on the field. Retribution nevertheless followed, instantly against the Zulu and Abd-el Krim, later but no less certainly against the Ethiopians.

Yet, in the longer run, the Little Bighorn stands apart from Isandhlwana, Adowa, and Anual. Zululand, Ethiopia, and Morocco are today self-ruling, or parts of self-ruling, sovereign states which have escaped from European domination and thrown off white empire. Montana, the "unceded" Indian territory of the 1870s, is a state of the Union. I cannot say that I feel things should be otherwise. There is much that is tragic in the story of native America's conflict with the European interlopers, particularly in the treatment of the Indians of the temperate forest lands east of the Mississippi by the young republic; the displacement of the Five Civilized Tribes to an utterly alien environment reeks of racialism. Yet the pretensions of the Plains Indians to exclusive rights over the heartland of the continent cannot, it seems to me, stand. Their claim, the claim of less than a million people, to possess territories capable of supporting not only millions more directly settled, but of still more millions outside America waiting to be fed by those territories' product, is the claim not of oppressed primitives but of the selfish rich. The Plains Indians were indeed primitives; but their primitivism was of the "hard," not "soft," variety. Here were not shy, self-effacing marginalists, like the Bushmen of the Kalahari Desert, the Semai of the Philippine jungles, or the pygmies of the African rainforests, but proud, warrior nomads, who had taken from the Europeans what they coveted as a means to support their way of life, the horse and the gun, and then refused Europeans any share of the lands which horse and gun equipped them the better to exploit.

Little wonder that the European immigrants who made their way onto the Great Plains in the nineteenth century, Slavs of Eastern Europe, Russians from the Steppe, peoples whose history was suffused with memories of oppression by galloping, sword-wielding, slave-taking Hun, Magyar, Mongol, and Turkish nomads, should have felt so little pity in their hearts for those other Mongoloid nomads whose interest in life seemed to subsist in hunting, pillage, and war. If the Indians' fate was to meet head-on in battle people as tough as themselves, veterans of a civil war in which brother had fought brother, Virginians had slain New Yorkers, Ohioans had burnt out Georgians, so be it. There may be a poignant hurrah about the Little Bighorn. I do not echo it.

SIX

······························

Flying Fortresses

S O MUCH of America seen, so much still to see. Since I began this book I have added another two states, Washington and Minnesota, to my tally, but there are still vast patches of personal *terra incognita*. I do not know the desert, I do not know the upper Great Lakes, I do not know the Canadian wheat belt. I pore over the map, immerse myself in photographs, but the reality is missing. Will I have time?

Will I have time in particular to visit the one spot above all others I should like to see with my own eyes, Kitty Hawk, North Carolina? It is off on the Outer Banks, which close Albemarle Sound from the Atlantic, near Roanoke Island, site of the "Lost Colony," the first, mysteriously extinguished, plantation of English settlers in North America. Sand and wind: that is all it offers. It was all Wilbur Wright wanted. "I am intending to start in a few days for a trip to the coast of North Carolina," he wrote to his father, Milton, a bishop of the Church of the United Brethren in Christ, on 3 September 1900, "in the vicinity of Roanoke island, for the purpose of making some experiments with a flying machine."

There is a sublime modesty about Wilbur Wright which makes him one of the most attractive as well as creative of all the world's geniuses. "It is my belief," he went on, "that flight is possible, and, while I am taking up the investigation for pleasure rather than profit, I think there is a slight possibility of achieving fame and fortune from it. It is almost the only great problem which has not been pursued by a multitude of investigators, and therefore carried to a point where further advance is very difficult. I am certain I can reach a point much in advance of any previous workers in the field, even if complete success is not attained just at present. At any rate, I shall have an outing of several weeks and see a part of the world I have never before visited."

No one visited the Outer Banks; almost no one lived there. Fishermen passed that way, and navies. The French and British fleets had manoeuvred off the banks in the campaign that would lead to Washington's victory at Yorktown eighty miles to the north in 1781; the United States Navy had knocked on the head a chain of small Confederate posts behind the banks in 1862. Since that time they had fallen back into forgetfulness. There were no bridges, no ferries, no connections with the country or even with the state. The only representative of government was a meteorologist of the Weather Bureau who took wind readings. It was these that had persuaded Wilbur that Kitty Hawk was the place for him. It was the sixth-windiest place in the United Sates, bereft of vegetation, offering low hills and sandy beaches several miles in length; and it was far from the public eye.

Wilbur was disingenuous in writing to his father that the problem of flight had "not been pursued by a multitude of investigators." Flight had been a Western obsession since the Renaissance. At the end of the eighteenth century the Montgolfier brothers had achieved aerostation, ascent by balloon, made lighter-than-air in their case by lighting fires under an open-mouthed envelope. In the nineteenth century the application of gases to aerostation had made balloons a common sight and their employment of practical use; Custer, as we have seen, had ascended in such a balloon to survey Confederate lines near Yorktown in 1862. Aerostation, however, did not satisfy man, since balloons had to be tethered if they were not to be playthings of the winds. What Wright wanted was to fly as the birds did, from point to point of choice, always under control and from a source of energy independent of the earth. The dirigible, a balloon with an engine and control surfaces, was half an answer; but it was large, clumsy, and fragile. It was not birdlike. In the last decades of the nineteenth century a "multitude of investigators" were indeed experimenting in the problem of birdlike flight. Some thought the solution would be found in imitating a bird's soaring capacity by building aerofoil gliders. Some thought it would be solved by applying brute mechanical power to a lifting surface. Some thought catapulting would allow an aerofoil with an on-board power source to proceed into controllable flight. All persisted with their experiments and all were disappointed; some were killed; none could demonstrate a machine which could do what a bird could do, which was, under its own power, to rise from the earth, sustain level and controlled flight, and land at a point not lower than that from which it had taken off. These were the criteria of true flight; they were those Wilbur Wright had taken as his challenge and believed he could meet.

It was an odd ambition for a small-town bicycle manufacturer from the Midwest. Wilbur and his brother, Orville, were American nobodies, of the sort who have so often surprised humanity; Dayton, Ohio, their home town, would still be a dull little place if it were not now the site of the greatest aeronautical museum on earth. Yet in the 1890s it was also a city typical of the United States during its surge to world industrial dominance: eighty thousand people, a thousand factories manufacturing farm implements, castings, railroad cars, cash registers—and bicycles. The Wright brothers' factory was small-time, scarcely more than a handwork shop. Because they made almost everything themselves, however, the Wrights were excellent practical engineers. They were also, like the Eisenhowers, members of a God-fearing family which venerated education and encouraged rigorous habits of mind. Bishop Wright, moreover, was a nicer man than the Eisenhower father, perhaps because he found advancement through his church—an offshoot of the Eisenhowers' Mennonites—rather than consolation in it for worldly failure. He brought his children toys when he came back from episcopal trips; one was a version of the Leonardo da Vinci helicopter, four blades on a spindle, which had been a popular European plaything since the sixteenth century. It engaged the brothers' attention; as they grew up they began to read the popular scientific literature, then appearing in sheaves, about experiments in flight. Neither was to go to college. Their sister attended Oberlin, one of the classic Midwest liberal art schools, and there was talk of sending Orville to Yale, but nothing came of it. The boys had nothing better than a high-school education, of the sort Ike had had before he secured a nomination to West Point; Latin, algebra, botany. The Wrights moved about even more than the Eisenhowers, between Indiana and Ohio; there were twelve moves before the bishop came back to Dayton to settle for good. Brothers went to farm in Kansas and Iowa. It was a very American family history. Orville and Wilbur tried printing before they turned to bicycles. They were also fascinated by the automobile. The predominant interest, however, was in flight. They sent for papers from the

Smithsonian, reworked the calculations of European and American would-be aeronauts, identified the problems. They saw that the chief one was control: how to manage a machine which moved in three dimensions: pitch—longitudinally; roll—latitudinally; yaw—side to side. They also saw that a controllable machine would have to combine all these movements, to produce what would later be called bank, turn, climb, and dive. Some kites they built seemed to obey the necessary rules. By 1900 Wilbur was ready to try out a glider, tethered and unmanned at first, manned and free-flying later, which would be the test-bed for powered flight.

Wilbur took the components of their first glider by train from Dayton in September 1900. He detrained at Old Point Comfort, Cornwallis's naval base for the Yorktown campaign, McClellan's for the Peninsula—eerie how the crosscurrents of American history run together—found some long wooden spars unavailable at home, loaded all the parts on a cranky schooner, and got to Kitty Hawk on the Outer Banks, after much bailing and tacking, on the afternoon of 12 September. There was a wooden post office, there were kindly people, nothing else; reading about his arrival, I felt tremors of Lumber City fifty-seven years later. He made arrangements to board, boiled some potable water, got down to work. The postmistress's sewing machine was conscripted to sew wing panels from sateen fabric; Orville turned up after a fortnight with a tent. They began to fly the glider off a rope in Kitty Hawk's steady Atlantic winds.

The machine worked but not well enough. They went back to Dayton, made test devices out of bicycle parts, recalculated, worked out from first principles optimal ratios of wing camber, perfected what would become the crucial feature of the true aeroplane—the aileron, which in their elegant version, never bettered, took the form of warping at the wing tips—and, as a by-blow, designed and built a gasoline internal-combustion engine producing enough power to lift itself, a flying machine, and its pilot from the ground. On top of all these extraordinary achievements—imagine a meeting between Leonardo and the brothers Wright—they also conceived flight's breakthrough idea. Everyone before them had, in one way or another, been fettered by the belief that an aeroplane—the word had not yet been coined—must, like a ship, be inherently stable. A ship, if rudder and sails were set right, would point itself into the seas, righting itself whatever the force of wind and water playing on its surfaces, and so sail as long as it retained its buoyancy. The Wrights hit on an alternative conception, that of an inherently *unstable* craft which, by the pilot's constant correction or application of pitch, yaw, and roll, could be made either to maintain level flight or to dive, climb, bank, and turn. It was a conception of genius. On 17 December 1903, in their fourth year of experiment, the Wright brothers set up their latest machine upwind on a wooden launching rail underneath Big Kill Devil Hill outside Kitty Hawk. Orville took the controls and ran up the engine. Wilbur stood alongside to steady the wing tip. In a wind gusting to twenty-seven miles an hour, the areoplane was released from its checks, accelerated, rose from the ground, flew 120 feet, and made a controlled return to the surface of the sand dunes twelve seconds later at an equal height to that from which it had taken off. The Wright brothers had shown that man could fly like a bird.

They made three more flights that morning, taking turns; the fourth lasted fifty-nine seconds and covered 852 feet. Then a sudden gust of the Atlantic wind which had brought them to Kitty Hawk flipped a wing and turned the aircraft upside down. The engine was unseated, the elevator broken. The pieces were carefully packed up and taken back to Dayton. Orville telegraphed ahead: "Success four flights Thursday morning. . . . started from level with engine power alone. . . . home Christmas." They brought with them, beside the broken *Flyer,* the glass negative snapped by a local lifeboat man at the instant of take-off, today the most famous and frequently reproduced of all photographs. It is also one of the most beautiful, an ethereal composition of horizontals and verticals, black struts against white fabric, grey sand and pale Atlantic sky, Wilbur in dark clothes and cap frozen in mid-stride as he releases his hold on the wing tip, his gaze fixed on the figure of Orville prone between the faint blur of the propellers. Chanced upon uncaptioned, it would speak for itself as the image of a revolutionary event. There is an extraordinary tension between the logic of the machine and the apprehension of the man left behind on the ground, who seems to be willing the frail construction skyward by locked muscle and psychological force. It is one of those rare photographs which has claims to be a chance work of art, for it captures a sense of moment which would escape the imagination of all but the greatest painter.

The photograph and the *Flyer* have survived to come down to us despite accident. In 1913, a year after Wilbur's death, aged only forty-five, Dayton was swept by flood. It was a recurrent event. The city stands at the confluence of four tributaries of the Ohio, and the river system of America is far mightier than man. Fire followed flood, and the city fathers spoke of $100 million of damage. The old bicycle shop escaped destruction, but its contents were soused. Orville, who treasured the glass negative, rescued it from the attic; only the bottom left corner of the collodion had lifted. The *Flyer,* still crated after its return from Kitty Hawk, had been under twelve feet of water but was protected by a thick layer of mud. Sentimentally—the brothers had a habit of abandoning old models around the countryside when an improved version engaged their enthusiasm—Orville scraped the remnants clean and stored them elsewhere. They remained forgotten until 1916, when the Massachusetts Institute of Technology asked permission to exhibit the machine at the opening of a new building. Orville and an assistant reassembled the bits, which subsequently became a much-seen centrepiece of displays at New York and in Dayton itself, the last in 1925.

By then the *Flyer* was the focus of a bitter controversy. The "multitude of investigators" whose existence Wilbur had so blithely dismissed in 1900 had stood forth in armed ranks as soon as the Wrights had shown what they could do. Some who had failed to fly before 1903 claimed to have done so none the less; others who suddenly saw wealth and fame awaiting them if they imitated the Wrights' achievements plagiarised their designs. Glenn Curtiss, a competitor of the Wrights in the aeroplane business, not only plagiarised; he invoked claims that others than the Wrights, notably Samuel Pierpont Langley, later Secretary of the Smithsonian Institution in Washington, had designed the first practicable aeroplane. There was method in his mischief. If Langley had indeed forestalled the Wrights, their patents, which they defended vigorously in the courts, would be invalid and he, like the Wrights a successful bicycle and motor engineer, could build aircraft without paying royalties. He did so in any case; but he went further. Langley's experimental machine, the *Aerodrome,* had been lodged in the Smithsonian Museum. In 1914, with the connivance of Langley's successor, Curtiss took the *Aerodrome* out of the museum, altered it enough to make it fly briefly and shakily before witnesses, removed the alterations, put it back in the museum, and brazenly challenged Orville in the courts. Orville was outraged. He was now less interested in the money than in his and his brother's reputation before history.

The rescue of the *Flyer* from the flood proved to have been auspicious. It was physical proof of all the claims the Wrights had made. Famous though Orville was, however, he could not clinch his argument that the *Flyer* was a true aeroplane while the unaltered *Aerodrome* had never been one, because authority would not agree to a fair comparison. The prestige of the Smithsonian, a great national institution, was at stake. Langley's successor had not only colluded in falsehood; he compounded it by further falsehoods which became part of the official *Annual Report* of the Smithsonian Institution; that of 1915 stated that "Secretary Langley had succeeded in building the first aeroplane capable of sustained free flight with a man." The disputes over the rival claims, and the means of settling them, dragged on long after the patent and royalty cases had been resolved. The courts made Orville a very rich man; the Smithsonian left him embittered. In 1925 he decided to use his own prestige against it. The *Flyer*, he announced, would be sent abroad for exhibition in the Smithsonian's British equivalent, the Science Museum in London, and would not be returned until the Wright claims were conceded; if this did not happen before his death, the *Flyer* would be willed to the Science Museum in perpetuity.

It was an inspired stroke of propaganda, but it took time to make its effect. Flight was still mysterious in the 1920s; many pioneers had their fingers in the pie. There were so many curious old machines, so many ancient mariners of the air with tales to tell. Over the years, however, the indignity of the situation bore in. Americans began to feel that it was monstrous for the Wright machine to languish abroad. Scholars progressively demolished the claims of anyone but the Wrights to have flown first; foremost among them was the keeper of the Department of Air Transport at the Science Museum itself, Charles Gibbs-Smith. He, more than anyone, was the man who disposed case by case of the pretensions of all other early flyers. With the departure from the Smithsonian of the last of the old guard after the Second World War the way was opened for the *Flyer*'s return. It was brought back in 1948 and hung in the entrance hall in the place of honour previously allotted to *The Spirit of St. Louis,* the aeroplane in which Lindbergh had made the first solo Atlantic crossing. Lindbergh announced he was honoured that his machine had once occupied the position belonging by rights to the *Flyer.* At its ceremonial unveiling the band of the United States Air Force, the independent air arm created the previous year, played "The Star-Spangled Banner" in front of the flag flown over Fort McHenry under British attack in 1814, which had inspired Francis Scott Key to write the words that became the national anthem. On the *Flyer* was affixed an inscription which proclaimed all the Wright brothers' achievements. It ended: "By Original Research the Wright Brothers Discovered the Principles of Human Flight. As Inventors, Builders and Flyers They Further Developed the Aeroplane, Taught Man to Fly, and Opened the Era of Aviation." Justice had been done. The date was 17 December, the time ten thirty-five, forty-five years to the minute since Orville had launched the *Flyer* into an Atlantic gale at Kitty Hawk. He had lived not quite long enough by a few months to witness his and Wilbur's apotheosis.

The *Flyer* hangs there to this day. Nine million visitors walk underneath it every year. I walked underneath it a year or two ago, on my way to give a lecture in the aeronautical collection, and stopped to salute an old friend. For I remembered it well from schoolboy visits to the Science Museum in dreary post-war London. There it had a place of honour too; but it seemed odd, even to a twelve-year-old, that it should be where it was. The aeroplane was so quintessentially *American*. The British built beautiful aircraft, the Spitfire, the Mosquito; we were even taught to believe, falsely, that the British had invented the jet aeroplane. Flight and fibbing seemed fated to go hand in hand. We were not taught, however, that anyone but the Wrights had flown first, and we had seen with our own eyes throughout the war years the skies filled with American aircraft. Mustangs there were, and Lightnings, that alluring and futuristic twin-boomed single-seater, and sturdy Liberators and tub-nosed Thunderbolts and workaday Dakotas and light bombers we called Bostons and Marylands, and, special in a way on which we could not quite put a finger, Flying Fortresses, which the Americans called the B-17. The B-17, of course, was special for reasons not frequently mentioned after the war, when the occupiers of Germany and the administrators of Marshall Aid were struggling to keep the survivors of defeat from starvation. The B-17 had been a principal instrument of the strategic bombing campaign which had reduced Berlin and the Ruhr to rubble. That slim, elegant, gleaming, high-finned creation, a model of which I had treasured from early in the war years, had been a cause of terror and certainly of death also to thousands of Germans of my own age in the years when I had flicked the model's tin propellers and imitated the sound of its four engines in front of the nursery fire. Those were not things to be mentioned in time of peace. They were not things to remember. Remember the omnipresence of American air power I did none the less. There was a weight and presence and self-confidence to American aircraft that seemed natural and appropriate. Long before I knew about the quarrel of Orville Wright with the Smithsonian, I accepted the aeroplane, just as I accepted the cinema, as something at which Americans were best.

They were best at it, of course, because America needed the aeroplane and the aeroplane was made for America. There is, in a poetically truthful sense, nothing accidental about the nationality of the Wrights. In Europe, aviation, before the Wrights, was a hobby, and it remained so even after Kitty Hawk. For the Wrights it was a deadly serious business. They were not interested in demonstrating that man could hop into the air. They wanted a machine that could cover real distance and perform useful tasks. In the aeroplane's potentiality to defeat distance, the enemy of American collective life, they glimpsed the means of transforming existence in the continent. Even after Kitty Hawk, therefore, they shunned stunting for publicity. They went back to Dayton, borrowed a ninety-acre field, the Huffman Prairie, from a well-wisher, and settled down to improve the *Flyer* and perfect their flying skills. When they were ready they decided to show the world what they could do. The place they chose was Le Mans in France, for the excellent reason that, while the American government shortsightedly refused to discuss business terms with them, the French government took the idea of the aeroplane seriously. The Wrights, canny businessmen, correctly perceived that until a passenger aircraft became a commercial viability, only government money could sustain their enterprise.

Nevertheless, before coming to France in 1908 the Wrights had made the first passenger-carrying flights in history, back in the obscurity of the Outer Banks, Mr. C. W. Furnas of Dayton sitting on the leading edge of *Flyer No. 3*'s lower wing beside each of the brothers in turn. On 8 August, Wilbur took the controls of a new *Flyer* at the Le Mans racecourse before an audience of European aviators. Some of them had flown after a fashion in cranks of their own design; Léon Delagrange had actually managed to keep airborne, on 22 June, for sixteen minutes. When Wilbur took off they did not know what to expect. Attempts to build versions of the *Flyer* in Europe from inexact descriptions had failed; reports of the Wrights' achievements in America were unverified. Wilbur therefore departed into the blue. Only two minutes later, during which he had banked, turned, and completed four perfect

circuits of the track, many of the watchers were speechless. Delagrange, when he found words, blurted out, "We are beaten. We
don't exist."

Over the next five months, Wilbur made longer and longer, more
and more complex flights, turning figures of eight, climbing, diving,
and gliding with the engine switched off, all under perfect control. On
31 December he stayed in the air for two hours twenty minutes and
covered a distance of seventy-seven miles. Major Baden-Powell, a
British War Office observer, gave as his judgement: "that Wilbur
Wright is in possession of a power which controls the fate of nations is
beyond dispute."

Neither of the Wrights wanted that. Though they sought government money, and accepted that their aircraft would initially be used for
military observation, they had a vague, idealistic feeling, beyond their
hard-headed determination to be rewarded for their discoveries, that
the aeroplane might be a means of bringing people together rather than
setting them at each other's throats. During the First World War,
Orville told reporters that he and his brother had never had any regret
about their invention of the aeroplane because they believed that it
would end warfare. On his seventy-fourth birthday in August 1945,
thirteen days after the destruction of Hiroshima, he said: "I once
thought the aeroplane would end wars. Now I wonder if the aeroplane
and the atomic bomb can do it." This wistful retrospection harked
back to their high-minded, Brethren in Christ upbringing in the innocent Ohio of the 1880s. The Wrights had been mighty fighters. Bishop
Milton was a valiant battler against error as he saw it, in his own
church, in the wicked world, and in public life; he opposed the influence of Masonic lodges and the power of the liquor trade. Orville and
Wilbur were teetotallers all their lives, non-smokers, notably pure in
speech and conduct, shy bachelors whose affections were given within
the family. They, too, battled for the rights that they were owed, but always with words and strict legality. They were the least rapacious of
industrialists who ever had the chance to make a fortune. They were
also among the most moral.

It was inevitable, however, that a practicable aeroplane, the
Wrights' bequest to the world, would be used for war-making purposes. Their competitor Glenn Curtiss dropped dummy bombs on to
the outline of a battleship in 1909; in 1911 the U.S. Army tested the
dropping of live bombs near San Francisco; in 1912 the recently

founded Royal Flying Corps conducted artillery-spotting tests on Salisbury Plain from a purpose-built military aircraft; in the same year a
short biplane took off from HMS *Hibernia* while under way. All, in
any case, had been anticipated: in 1849, during the first war for Italian
unity, the Austrians had launched explosive, pilotless Montgolfier balloons against Venice. Human ingenuity all too swiftly serves the devil.
Boys brought up in Bishop Milton Wright's household must have been
warned of that.

Yet the Wrights themselves never sought to exploit the military potentiality of their invention. That was left to others. During the winter
of 1910 the Wrights had taken their flying team away from the harsh
Ohio weather and established a base at Montgomery, Alabama. The
city stands in a level plain; even December days, though crisp, are calm
and sunny. During the First World War the old Wright aerodrome at
Montgomery became a military flying station, known as Maxwell
Field. In the years after the war the base languished as a backwater for
Air Corps observation squadrons. In 1927, however, it was chosen as
the new site for the Air Corps Tactical School, the training centre for
future commanders, and in 1930 a building programme was undertaken to provide teaching facilities and living quarters. Under the Roosevelt programme of economic revival during the Depression, more
money came Maxwell's way. By 1935 the station had become a handsome place, planted with shade trees standing between red pantiled,
Spanish-style buildings; the architecture was appropriate, for Hernando de Soto, the marauder after gold, had wintered at Montgomery
in 1540. The centrepoint of the station was the Tactical School itself, a
colonnaded, two-storey building near the old Wright flying field.

"That's where they worked it all out," an air force colonel said to
me as we circled the campus on a fall day in 1990. I had been summoned to address the Flag Officer course on the nature of leadership, a
wholly inappropriate commission, for all I know about leadership is
book learning. The visit was memorable none the less for meetings
with the recently sacked Air Force Chief of Staff, cast into darkness for
revealing that he planned to bomb Saddam Hussein in his bunker, and
with Newt Gingrich, who failed to convince me that he would one day
be Speaker of the House of Representatives.

"What do you mean," I said, "they worked it all out?"

He flapped a hand at the Tactical School. "Spaatz, Eaker, the
bomber barons. That's where they did all the thinking."

I peered at the building, which, with appropriate signs, might have been a minor Holiday Inn. There was not a uniform in sight, not even a military vehicle, only a few Chevrolets and Buicks parked in the fore-court behind mown grass and clipped bushes.

"What do you mean, all the thinking?" I repeated.

"Bombing," he said. "Pushing Germany over by the acre, burning Japan out. That's where they made the plans. Spaatz, Eaker, McNarney, Vandenberg, Stratemeyer, they were all here, captains, majors in the thirties. They worked out bombing from first principles. It shouldn't have been called the Tactical School. Strategic bombing was what came out of that little building. Firestorms, precision attack, victory through air power, you name it, they thought of it."

The day was sunny, the air still. Maxwell is a long way from anywhere.

"I'm going to Montgomery, Alabama," I had said to a Washington sophisticate.

"You get all the choice spots," he answered.

Peering again at the Tactical School, I reflected that he might not have been as smart as he thought.

I resolved then to come back. The chance did not offer until two years later, when I was invited to speak about how air power might alter the situation in Bosnia to an Air Force Chief of Staff's symposium. In the intervals of the meeting I dropped into the air force archives at the historical centre, ordered files, and consulted the base historian, Jerome Ennals. He confirmed all the colonel had told me. Maxwell had indeed been the old Wright winter field in 1910; he showed me where they flew. It had been the centre of Air Corps planning in the 1930s; he produced photographs which showed the hacienda building of the Tactical School under construction. It had been the place where the future lords of life and death, junior officers then in an under-funded and ill-equipped Air Corps, a mere appendage of the army, had argued and lectured and written their position papers in an aeronautical world of biplanes, pioneering postal flights, airship disasters, and stunt flying at state fairs. Air Corps officers wore riding breeches and took tea on pillared verandas. All that America knew of Montgomery was that it had been the first capital of the Confederacy. The idea, Jerome Ennals said, that an American bomber would bring wrath from heaven all over Europe and Asia was as near to fantasy in Roosevelt's Alabama as the thought that an American might one day stand on the moon.

The papers I pulled from the air force archives told another story. The first, oddly, from the Military Geography and Strategy Course of 1932, was a study of McClellan's operations in the Peninsula in 1862. The Peninsular campaign, the paper suggested, illuminated the difficulty of attacking the economic base of an enemy power. By 1936 the Tactical School had moved on to examining the modern city as a profitable target of air attack, against water supply, public utilities, transportation, and industry. The second course of 1936 used analysis of the economic structure of the United States itself as a guide to the destruction of what a later generation would call a "target-rich environment." It was all a bit theoretical. General Ira Eaker, reflecting in the record of an interview held in 1964, said as much. "You may have decided," he told the young officer questioning him, "that the Air Corps Tactical School told the active flying groups and commanders what to do. It was the other way around. We worked out what we thought was sound doctrine and they adopted it and codified it and put it into proper documentation." The general spoke true; the most useful military teaching comes from, not before, practice. The course of 1939, *Air Operations Against National Structures,* nevertheless contradicts him. Its subject matter is the theory of the destruction of the Japanese economy by bombing, and it tackles the matter under thirty-four headings, including aero-engine factories, coal liquefaction plants, hydroelectric facilities, mines, quarries, shipbuilding yards, and inter-island ferry terminals. The appendices to the study include detailed target maps, in which Nagasaki is identified as a key objective. *Air Operations Against National Structures* may have been drawn up as a teaching exercise. In practice it is a detailed war plan, on which the actual campaign of strategic bombing against Japan in 1945—which burnt out 60 per cent of the country's sixty largest cities before the atomic bombs had been dropped—could scarcely improve.

It is a shaking experience to hold in one's hand a sheaf of foolscap paper that spells out the future death of a society; Japanese imperial society died in 1945, and the instrument of its death was American air power. I fiddled about with the other papers the archivists found me. I kept on turning back to *Air Operations Against National Structures.* It was dated 11 April 1939; the impress of the typewriter keys was still sharp, the red and blue pencil markings fresh and bright on the target maps. A student or an instructor had taken a great deal of trouble with his presentation all those years ago in a Southern spring when the flowering trees were beginning to blossom along the neat concrete side-walks, over the pretty pantiled roofs of Maxwell. The Second World War had not started in Europe. The Pacific Fleet cruised the untroubled waters around Pearl Harbor. A few squadrons of ageing aircraft droned in practice flight from the old Wright flying ground. The last time a decisive act of war had touched Montgomery was in April 1861, when the orders to bombard Fort Sumter had gone down the telegraph wire from a building near Jefferson Davis's house. Forts again, I thought; forts always turn up at the beginning of American wars. It was not accidental that Fort McHenry's flag had been displayed behind the returned *Flyer*. It was, after all, the parent of the Flying Fortress. I wondered if the Tactical School archives had anything to say about that memorable aircraft.

I went back to the card index, made enquiries of the archivists. I knew a good deal about the Flying Fortress already, of course. It was the first successful four-engined bomber, and it had been built, offi-cially, to guard the United States against invasion. The United States Navy and the United States Army had an agreement; it was not one the army liked much, still less the Air Corps, which the army controlled, but it was policy and could be broken only at the cost of an inter-service quarrel. The navy and its aircraft carriers were responsible for the strategic, long-range defence of the American coastline. After 1938 the Air Corps was allowed to patrol only one hundred miles from the coast. The Flying Fortresses were literally that—airborne equivalents of Fort McHenry and Fortress Monroe—dedicated to preventing, with their bombs and machine guns, enemy warships and troopships from entering American harbours and estuaries, just as the great Federalist system of forts was dedicated to denying entrance with their cannon. Air power extended the range a little, that was all. The point was made in a test of 1937, before the hundred-mile limit had been imposed, when a flight of Fortresses intercepted the Italian liner *Rex* far out in the Atlantic. The *New York Herald Tribune* headline proclaimed: FLY-ING FORTS, 360 MILES OUT, SPOT ENEMY TROOPSHIP.

The Air Corps, however, had a different, secret idea, just as "Flying Fortress" had an alternative meaning: that of an aircraft capable of de-fending itself—it mounted thirteen machine guns—while dealing dis-abling blows against an enemy. The archivists produced for me a slim research pamphlet which revealed what the Air Corps had really been thinking while the navy was still trying to fetter it to coastal defence. It

was thinking of carrying war to the enemy. In the early 1930s it began
commissioning advanced bombers based on the designs of the new all-
metal, monoplane airliners which were revolutionising air travel within
the United States. They were quite unlike the clumsy tri-motors and giant biplanes which the European airline companies and air forces were
still operating. At the head of the field stood the Boeing 247, a sleek
twin-engined airliner with a range between airports of 750 miles,
enough to get from coast to coast in four hops. The 247 fathered the
Boeing 299 of 1935, its military equivalent. A year earlier the Air
Corps had issued the specification for its successor. Most of the con-
tractors tendering submitted designs for another twin-engined aircraft.
Boeing, though stuck away at Seattle in the extreme northwestern state
of Washington, was thinking further ahead. It proposed a four-engined
bomber, designated the YB-17, and, though given only a year to trans-
form a paper design into a working aircraft, had the prototype ready
within the time-limit.

It proved a sensation. With a top speed of 250 miles an hour and a
service ceiling of 30,000 feet, it could carry more than a ton of bombs
for over 2,000 miles, enough to cross the Atlantic. The advocates of
the doctrine of air attack against national economic structures as a
means of winning wars were exultant. Here was the machine which
would make their theories work; here was the instrument which those
teaching at the Tactical School at Maxwell needed to turn aspiration
into reality. Foremost among them was Colonel Henry "Hap" Arnold,
one of the most senior officers of the Air Corps bombardment branch.
Recalling the arrival of the first group of B-17s at Langley Field in Virginia in 1936, he wrote, "This was the first real American air power."
The new aircraft, he recognised, were not just aircraft for coastal defence, flying equivalents of the Federalist fortresses, but "for the first
time in history air power that you could put your hand on."

For a young country, the United States shows a strange dedication
to the apostolic succession in its public life. The defence of Fort
McHenry, built to resist the British at Baltimore, had, as noted earlier,
inspired "The Star-Spangled Banner." Its star-spangled banner was to
be displayed behind the first *Flyer* at its installation in the Smithsonian,
when the claims of the Wrights to have been the first men to fly were
endorsed by Federal authority for good. Among those present was Hap
Arnold, who had commanded the Army Air Forces (successor of the
Air Corps) during the Second World War, now first Chief of Staff of the

new independent United States Air Force. One of the earliest American pilots, he had been trained to fly at the Huffman Prairie in Dayton, Ohio, under the auspices of the Wright brothers. There is a certain inevitability in discovering that the official test flight of the B-17 ("sensational, record-breaking") was made from the Boeing works at Seattle to the Air Corps base at Wright Field, Dayton.

The Wright Field was the B-17's first destination. Its destiny lay elsewhere, above all in my own country. In Britain's time of desperation, when it alone among European nations continued to defy Hitler, though its cities burned and its women and childen died under the Luftwaffe's attack, President Roosevelt authorised the transfer of some Flying Fortresses to the Royal Air Force so that it could sustain its retaliation against the Reich; it was a model of one of these first fighting Fortresses with which I had played in the nursery of the country house to which my family had been evacuated from the Blitz on London during the winter of 1940. The terms of the deal were cash-and-carry; Britain liquidated most of its Victorian wealth to buy weapons while Roosevelt awaited the *casus belli* to bring the United States to Britain's aid. The occasion of war came in an unanticipated fashion; it was not Pearl Harbor but Hitler's quixotic decision to open hostilities against America four days later which provided this. Token forces were sent at once but it would be more than a year before the great build-up of American ground forces in Britain would begin. In the meantime the U.S. Army Air Force began to mobilise its squadrons for transfer to England. They were the first effective anti-Hitler units that could be deployed to the fighting front. It took seven months to complete preparations, but on 1 July 1942 the first Flying Fortress—a model B-17 E, serial number 41-9085—to cross the Atlantic as part of the Eighth Air Force, USAAF, landed at Prestwick in Scotland. It was to be followed during the course of the Second World War by another 6,500.

The arrival of the Flying Fortresses in Britain required the building of a small United States overseas. Admiral Byrd's base at the South Pole had been called "Little America." Soon bases many times the size of Admiral Byrd's outpost were springing up all over the flat farmland of East Anglia, from which the bombing routes towards Germany are shortest. There were to be sixty-three bomber bases eventually, lying about five miles apart in a crescent west, south, and east of the ancient university city of Cambridge, most of them alongside small villages whose names must have tripped haltingly at first off American tongues:

Chipping Ongar, Great Saling, Grafton Underwood, Little Staughton, Steeple Morden, High Roding, Earls Colne, Thorpe Abbots, Snetterton Heath, Old Buckenham, Deopham Green, Horsham St. Faith. Many were places in which little had happened since the Norman Conquest. Almost overnight each acquired a Little America of Quonset huts, control tower, PX, and a population of Americans which grew as fast as the bases could be finished. The standard strength at a bomber base was around 3,000, though some of the headquaters had many more During 1943 the Eighth Air Force deployed about 150,000 airmen to East Anglia, a sizeable proportion of the 1.7 million Americans who were to find themselves in Britain at the height of the build-up before D-Day.

Fewest among them, perhaps only one in twenty, were the aircrew, who flew the Fortresses to Germany and often did not come back. The Army Air Forces lost 52,173 aircrew in combat in the Second World War, four-fifths of them in Europe and the majority of these from the Eighth Air Force bomber crews who flew from Britain. Each crew had an obligation to fly twenty-five missions before earning a rest from operations. There was, roughly, an even chance of surviving the course; put the other way about, there was an even chance of not. The odds were worsened, however, because some individuals were lost to a crew by death in action. In a big and robust aircraft like the B-17, with two pilots, navigator, and seven gunners, it was not uncommon for antiaircraft or fighter fire to hit one or more of the crew without disabling the machine; a damaged aircraft might fly home with dead or wounded men aboard, some so severely wounded that they would succumb after it had made a safe landing. An analysis of the fate of 2,051 aircrew who set out on their series of twenty-five missions over Germany revealed that 1,195 were killed or missing in action, over 200 died of wounds, and only 599 survived to the end—about one in four of those who had begun.

Bomber Command, the Royal Air Force's equivalent to the Eighth Air Force, suffered similar casualties. Over 55,000 aircrew were lost in its bombing campaign against Germany. The human cost of what between them they did to Germany scarcely bears contemplation. Some 600,000 German civilians were killed by Allied bombing, almost all in 1942–44, and of those about 120,000 were children and nearly 400,000 women. They died in a series of raids which progressively destroyed urban Germany from its western border inwards—first the cities of the Ruhr, then those of the North Sea and Baltic coasts, then those of the interior, culminating in the destruction of the eastern city of Dresden in February 1945. The RAF bombed by night, from 1942 onwards according to a doctrine of "area" bombing which eschewed precision and simply sought to burn German cities to the ground. The U.S. Army Air Force clung longer to the idea of precision attack on "National Structures," first studied in the paper of 1939 I had found in the archive at Montgomery, Alabama, but it, too, was eventually drawn into the campaign of indiscriminate destruction. The madness which seized Europe in 1940–42, the madness of nihilism, ultimately seized the U.S. Army Air Force also, and at the end of the war it bombed and bombed and bombed as if bombing were simply an industrial process, a form of work, the human activity at which America excels above all other nations.

It was an extraordinary culmination to the history of Europe's and America's joint involvement in the business of warfare which is the substance of this book, an involvement with which my own life has been intertwined for nearly forty years. At the outset of that history, it was Europeans who fought each other in North America for possession of the continent, French against English, British against French. Then, when the issue seemed settled, it was immediately reopened by Americans settling to fight Europeans over who should be master. The defeat of the British appeared to determine that, as the Founding Fathers of the Republic wished, there should be no more war in America. Americans judged otherwise, and, in the Civil War, fought each other over the issue of whether there should be one America or two. The one America of 1865 decided that it had one more war to fight, a war with the native Americans who obstructed its passage to the Pacific coast and settlement of the Great Plains, a war that native Americans were foredoomed to lose but protracted none the less to the last decade of the nineteenth century. The defeat of native America appeared to close the last act, pacifying the continent for good. Thereafter honest friendship, as the Founding Fathers had willed, should have ensured its isolation from the world outside in perpetuity. Honesty in friendship negated that hope. In 1917 it drew the United States into the First World War. In 1941 it drew the United States into the Second. By a strange and unanticipated circularity, Americans came from 1942 onwards to be fighting in Europe over who should be master in that continent, on the side of the French and British, who had once contested ownership of theirs, from bases in the United Kingdom, to which nearly two hundred years earlier they had expelled their colonial rulers.

It was the beginning of an American military involvement in Europe, decisive in its effect, that persists to this day. Fifty years after the closing of the strategic bombing campaign, some of the Eighth Air Force's bases in East Anglia remain in American hands. Closer to home, on the outskirts of my village in the West Country, traces of wartime Little America linger. Older residents still speak of "the airfield" where a base depot of the Eighth Air Force was opened in July 1943; the control tower, now a private house, and parts of the airstrip remain. A little further away there is a more poignant reminder, a memorial tablet to a B-17 crew who did not go home. "This tablet," the inscription reads, "was erected by the people of Wincanton in honour of United States airmen who lost their lives when their Flying Fortress 'Old Faithful' crashed in flames on Snag Farm near this spot when returning disabled from an operational mission on June 25th, 1944." A list of names follows which is a short biographical history of European emigration to the United States, from England, Ireland, Scotland, Greece, perhaps Scandinavia and the Jewish diaspora, and ironically from Germany as well: 2nd Lt. Peter Mikonis, Margate City, New Jersey; 2nd Lt. Frank Pepper, Jr., Berkeley, California; 2nd Lt. Joseph Sullivan, Belmont, Massachusetts; 2nd Lt. Will Stevens, Smithfield, North Carolina; S/Sgt. Roy Anderson, Sacramento, California; S/Sgt. Douglas Deurmyer, Topeka, Kansas; Sgt. Ralph Stein, Savannah, Georgia; Sgt. Richard Mehlberg, Milwaukee, Wisconsin; Sgt. Dan McDowell, Omaha, Nebraska. How far they had come to die, those young men, from places which reverberate with the echo of battles long ago—Topeka and Nebraska in Indian territory, Belmont and Smithfield in the campaign theatre of the American Revolution, Savannah from the Civil War.

There are other traces of the connection between this tiny place, with its two hundred people, and the other England across the ocean. A daughter of the house in which I live, the village manor house, married a young architect who worked on the famous mansion of the Brown family on Benefit Street in Providence, Rhode Island; a farm at the bottom of the village is Berkeley Farm, once the property of the great Berkeley family who founded the Berkeley Plantation on the banks of the James River outside Richmond, Virginia, family seat of a signatory of the Declaration of Independence and of a President of the

United States. The Berkeleys and America belong together from the beginnings. My family does not. I am, I believe, the first member to have visited North America; but now, too, I belong in a way to it also. I have an American son-in-law, four American grandchildren. The tides which carried the Berkeleys across the Atlantic from the Old World have brought my descendants from the New World back again. Benjamin, my solemn, six-year-old grandson, a citizen of London, tells me he is "half-English, half-American." There seems nothing wrong with that.

Yet, even after forty years, after fifty transatlantic crossings, after uncountable transcontinental journeys, the sense of the American mystery remains strong with me. Canada I think I begin to understand, a bit of the European world implanted south of the icecap, alien in geography, familiar in custom and culture. The United States continues to elude me. If I understand it at all, it is through the strange profession that has shaped my life, the study of war. War is repugnant to the people of the United States; yet it is war that has made their nation and it is through their power to wage war that they dominate the world. Americans are proficient at war in the same way that they are proficient at work. It is a task, sometimes a duty. Americans have worked at war since the seventeenth century, to protect themselves from the Indians, to win their independence from George III, to make themselves one country, to win the whole of their continent, to extinguish autocracy and dictatorship in the world outside. It is not their favoured form of work. Left to themselves, Americans build, cultivate, bridge, dam, canalise, invent, teach, manufacture, think, write, lock themselves in struggle with the eternal challenges that man has chosen to confront, and with an intensity not known elsewhere on the globe. Bidden to make war their work, Americans shoulder the burden with intimidating purpose. There is, I have said, an American mystery, the nature of which I only begin to perceive. If I were obliged to define it, I would say it is the ethos—masculine, pervasive, unrelenting—of work as an end in itself. War is a form of work, and America makes war, however reluctantly, however unwillingly, in a particularly workmanlike way. I do not love war; but I love America.

Index

Abd-el Krim, 313
Abenaki Indians, 103, 114
Abercromby, James, 114–16
Abilene, Kans., 265–6
Acadia (Nova Scotia), 82, 100, 103–7, 109, 111, 113, 118, 121, 124, 200
Adowa, 313
Aerodome, 320, 321
Afghanistan, 52, 294, 310
Africa, 60, 67, 76, 133, 179, 180, 190, 191, 239, 271; imperialism, 30, 60–1, 283, 284, 285, 311, 313; slavery, 77, 98
Afrikaners, 67, 68
Air Operations Against National Structures, 327
air travel, 3–6, 10–12, 34–5, 63, 65, 145; *see also* flight, powered
Albany (Fort Orange), 99, 101, 102, 106, 168, 169
Albemarle Sound, 208, 315
Alcazar, 139
Alexandria, Va., 15, 109, 181, 198, 220
Algeria, 284, 285, 294, 298
Algonquin Indians, 98, 99, 103, 273
America, 5; cities, 15–16, 36; climate, 34, 257, 268–9; friendship, 12–15,

31–2; geography, 8–9, 15, 63, 89–93, 113, 138, 140, 173–4, 193, 197–213, 257–8, 260; landscape, 7–11, 17, 76, 251; literature, 19–21, 33; of 1957, 33–42; of 1977, 43–51; post–World War II, 27–8, 30, 32; twentieth-century, 3–22, 26–59, 315
American Civil War, *see* Civil War (1861–5)
American Fur Company, 260
American Revolution, *see* War of Independence (1776–81)
Amherst, Jeffrey, 118–19, 121
Anaconda Plan, 198–202, 207, 209, 212
André, John, 172
Annapolis, 180, 184, 219, 245; Naval Academy, 49, 141, 142
Anual, 313
Apache Indians, 254, 259, 277, 278, 283–4, 310, 311
apartheid, 30, 39–40
Appalachian Mountains, 63, 77, 88, 91, 92, 96, 102, 110, 135, 137, 145, 153, 161, 174, 175, 181, 199, 201, 203, 211, 215, 264
Appomattox, 181, 297
Arapaho Indians, 276–8